THE ARDEN SHAKESPEARE
GENERAL EDITOR: RICHARD PROUDFOOT

OTHELLO

THE ARDEN SHAKESPEARE

All's Well That Ends Well: edited by G. K. Hunter
Antony and Cleopatra: edited by M. R. Ridley
As You Like It: edited by Agnes Latham
The Comedy of Errors: edited by R. A. Foakes
Coriolanus: edited by Philip Brockbank
Cymbeline: edited by J. M. Nosworthy
Hamlet: edited by Harold Jenkins
Julius Caesar: edited by T. S. Dorsch
King Henry IV, Parts 1 & 2: edited by A. R. Humphreys
King Henry V: edited by John H. Walter
King Henry VI, Parts 1, 2 & 3: edited by A. S. Cairncross
King Henry VIII: edited by R. A. Foakes
King John: edited by E. A. Honigmann
King Lear: edited by Kenneth Muir
King Richard II: edited by Peter Ure
King Richard III: edited by Antony Hammond
Love's Labour's Lost: edited by Richard David
Macbeth: edited by Kenneth Muir
Measure for Measure: edited by J. W. Lever
The Merchant of Venice: edited by John Russell Brown
The Merry Wives of Windsor: edited by H. J. Oliver
A Midsummer Night's Dream: edited by Harold F. Brooks
Much Ado About Nothing: edited by A. R. Humphreys
Othello: edited by M. R. Ridley
Pericles: edited by F. D. Hoeniger
The Poems: edited by F. T. Prince
Romeo and Juliet: edited by Brian Gibbons
The Taming of the Shrew: edited by Brian Morris
The Tempest: edited by Frank Kermode
Timon of Athens: edited by H. J. Oliver
Titus Andronicus: edited by J. C. Maxwell
Troilus and Cressida: edited by K. J. Palmer
Twelfth Night: edited by J. M. Lothian and T. W. Craik
The Two Gentlemen of Verona: edited by Clifford Leech
The Winter's Tale: edited by J. H. P. Pafford

THE ARDEN EDITION OF THE
WORKS OF WILLIAM SHAKESPEARE

OTHELLO

Edited by
M. R. RIDLEY

ROUTLEDGE

LONDON and NEW YORK

The general editors of the Arden Shakespeare have been
W. J. Craig (1899–1906), R. H. Case (1909–44),
Una Ellis-Fermor (1946–58), Harold F. Brooks (1952–82),
Harold Jenkins (1958–82) and Brian Morris (1975–82)

Present general editor: Richard Proudfoot

This edition of *Othello*, by M. R. Ridley,
first published in 1958 by
Methuen & Co. Ltd.
Reprinted 1959
Reprinted with minor corrections 1962
Reprinted three times
Reprinted 1974

First published as a University Paperback 1965
Reprinted fifteen times
Reprinted 1987

Reprinted in 1989, 1990 by
Routledge
11 New Fetter Lane, London EC4P 4EE
29 West 35th Street, New York, NY 10001

Editorial matter © 1958 Methuen & Co. Ltd

ISBN (hardbound) 0 416 47440 3
ISBN (paperback) 0 415 02701 2

Printed in England by Clays Ltd, St Ives plc

CONTENTS

PREFACE

In editing this play afresh for the Arden edition, I have tried to keep certain limited aims in view: first, to help the reader to arrive at some reasonable conclusion as to what Shakespeare may be supposed to have written; second, to help him to appreciate Shakespeare's dramatic craftsmanship; and third, to help him to understand precisely what Shakespeare meant.

As a result, I have spent less time than is usual on, for example, the problem of the date of the play. The assignable limits are, by general consent, narrow, and to attempt with greater precision to determine the indeterminable seems to me of very little help in appreciating the play as great drama. Nor have I made any detailed comparison of the play with its presumed source; Cinthio's story is given in an appendix, so that any reader can make the comparison for himself.

On the other hand, in view of my first aim, I have spent a good deal of time, in the Introduction, on discussing the relation between the two main texts, not least because some points arise which are of importance for the study of other plays besides this. And in the notes (pursuing my second and third aims) I have included more than my predecessor did by way of comment on points of dramatic significance, but have greatly lightened them in another direction. The most useful help towards understanding Shakespeare's meaning is usually Shakespeare himself. When his use of a word or idiom is illustrated by other passages in his own work, I cannot see that much further light is shed by parallels adduced from the work of others. For the same reason, I have usually given the Shakespearean parallels in full, instead of giving only references, since the looking up of references is a toilsome business, which, in my experience, only the exceptionally industrious reader will undertake. There is, therefore, in the notes, deliberately, a marked lack of erudition. But I hope that this lack may make for clarity. And I hope also that the reader who takes the trouble to study the linguistic notes will agree that the trouble has been profitable, and will find that a careful study of Shakespeare's use of language in one play helps towards a proper understanding of his meaning in others.

Some readers, I know, and particularly those acquainted with Elizabethan idiom, will feel that there is a good deal of needless, and therefore vexatious, glossing. Johnson has some wise observations on this subject: "It is impossible for an expositor not to write too little for some, and too much for others. He can only judge what is necessary by his own experience; and how long soever he may deliberate, will at last explain many lines which the learned will think impossible to be mistaken, and omit many for which the ignorant will want his help. . . I have endeavoured to be neither superfluously copious, nor scrupulously reserved, and hope that I have made my author's meaning accessible to many who before were frighted from perusing him."

I find that many modern readers, far from "ignorant", and not at all "frighted", are yet, when reading fast or listening in the theatre, often apt to accept an Elizabethan word in its modern, and therefore apparently obvious, sense, and thereby miss the force or flavour which it had for the Elizabethans. Over-glossing is therefore, I think, preferable to under-glossing. Some words, even at the cost of seeming redundancy, I have glossed more than once, particularly those which are what one may call permanent traps, words which are almost invariably used in modern English in one sense, but were almost invariably in Elizabethan English used in another. For example, by "presently" Shakespeare meant "at once", and almost never meant anything else, whereas we mean "fairly soon", and unless we are permanently on guard we let a touch of "quite soon" colour the sense which we attach to Shakespeare's "presently"s. Sometimes this may matter little, sometimes it may weaken the whole force of a phrase, as when Desdemona says "Ay, but not yet to die" and Othello's reply is "Yes, presently".

I hope, at least, that there is little left unglossed which might cause a modern reader any difficulty, and no textual crux passed over in silence without at any rate some suggestions towards solution.

In the same way, a good deal of the textual section of the introduction will seem, to readers versed in textual criticism, a mere labouring of the elementary. But for other readers the study of the texts of *Othello* may well be their first—and I think uniquely illuminating, if arduous—experience of such problems, and some guidance about even the elementary may be not unwelcome.

This textual section (pp. xvi–xlv) is considerably longer than the corresponding section in most of the Arden volumes hitherto published. This I found almost impossible to avoid. When, for any play, we have only the Folio text, or when the Folio was clearly printed from a Quarto with little alteration, we have, in either case, only one text that matters, and any textual comment can be reduced to a minimum. But the textual problem which *Othello* presents is unhappily very intricate, and therefore the only alternatives seemed to be either to say very little about it or to say a good deal. Any middle road seemed to lead inevitably to the omission of essential data which the reader who is interested in the problem must have before him, if he is to have any basis for his own conclusions. But I have done my best to lighten this section by relegating to appendices a good deal of the more minute and detailed evidence, so that readers who are not interested in the problem need not burden themselves with the study of it. But for readers who are interested I ought to make it clear that much of the evidence so relegated is essential to the argument, and not a mere amplification of it.

For reasons explained in the relevant sections of the Introduction the text of the present edition is much nearer to that of the First Quarto than has lately been usual, and the apparatus criticus is much fuller than the limited and eclectic apparatus which seemed to me likely to be most helpful with *Antony and Cleopatra*. The problem of the relation to one another of the two main texts of *Othello*, and of either to Shakespeare's original, is a troublesome one, still *sub iudice*, and likely, I fancy, long to remain so. I have, as will appear, some clear, if heterodox, views of my own, but I have tried not unduly to obtrude them. I have done my best, within the limits of the space available, to put before the reader the data on which he can base his own judgement. For a balanced examination of this problem, unlike some others, specialized knowledge, bibliographical, palaeographical, or what not, is by no means essential, though it may often be helpful. Much more essential are a capacity for weighing evidence, a 'feel' for Shakespeare both as poet and as dramatist, and enough imagination to see the human and practical probabilities. Any intelligent reader, therefore, is as capable of arriving at a sane verdict as any editor. And, because of some peculiar features in the problem, it is more true of *Othello* than of almost any other of Shakespeare's plays that, in the end, every reader, every producer and actor, must make his own text.

But he cannot do this without adequate data. In preparing the apparatus criticus for *Antony and Cleopatra* in the present edition, since there is only one authoritative text for the play, I worked on a freely eclectic principle, thereby greatly lightening the apparatus, and, I hope, letting essential points stand out more clearly. But no such principle is properly applicable to *Othello*. Here we have to

deal with two main texts (as well as a third which, while in no sense
authoritative, is of considerable interest), and some of the evidence
on which we have to base conclusions is cumulative. There is for
example a class of variants, in themselves quite unimportant, since
they do not affect the sense, of the *I am—am I*, or *we have—have we*
type. If there were only a few of these, their importance would be
trifling, since they could be dismissed as no more than slips by compositors; but when they are numerous their mere number becomes
of possible importance, and they must be recorded. So must
printers' errors, however obvious, such as *hor* for *nor* or *Fuen* for
Euen or *apines* for *paines*, since the reader may wish to come to some
conclusion about the comparative degree of mechanical accuracy
shown by different compositors.[1] Again, the Second Quarto, apart
from its intrinsic interest as the first piece of Shakespearean editing
where we can completely check the editor's operations (since we
have both his material and his results, as we have not with F), provides, for reasons, and within limits, discussed in Appendix G,
a useful check. And its agreements and disagreements with the two
main texts must therefore be recorded.

On the other hand I have almost uniformly neglected the readings of the Third Quarto (a thoroughly debased text) and of Folios
later than the First. None of these latter has any sort of authority,
and when one of them makes an acceptable emendation it can be
treated as on a par with those of any later editor. For the same
reason I have dispensed altogether with the symbol "Ff". At best it
is apt to be misleading, since different editors use it to mean different things. Furness, through whose Variorum edition many of us,
I suppose, make our first acquaintance with the study of variants,
uses it, since he is reproducing the F1 text, to mean an agreement of
the Second, Third, and Fourth Folios; most other editors use it to
mean an agreement of all four. But what is much more seriously
misleading, to a reader not versed in textual criticism, is that the
symbol is apt to suggest that an agreement of all four has, in some
ill-defined way, an authority superior to that of F1 alone. Further,
I have been eclectic in recording suggestions of later editors, readings which have often commended themselves to no one but the
original proposer, and which throw no light on the relation between the two main texts. Pope, for example, in his desire to regu-
larize metre, often made quite unwarranted emendations, such as,
at I. i. 39 and 54, *If* for *Whether* and *folks* for *fellows*, against an
agreement of Q1 and F. A few of these emendations are worth recording, as illustrating the freedom which some eighteenth-century

1. See Appendix H.

editors permitted themselves, and the self-confidence with which
some, like Warburton, exercised the freedom; but to record them
all would only, I think, distract attention from things which matter
much more.

Attention should be drawn to one or two minor points:

(a) I have used "not in" instead of the more usual "omitted
by". The latter is a question-begging term, since it implies that
compositor or transcriber, whether by accident, or by design, or in
obedience to what he took to be directions in his copy, left out
something that was in front of him. But it *may* have been a later
addition, and not in his copy at all. It is true that we can often
guess, occasionally with something near to certainty, that the
"omission" was in fact an omission, however caused; but all we
know is that the word, phrase, or passage is "not in" one or other of
the texts.

(b) When (usually with stage-directions) a lemma is immediately followed by an editor's name and by nothing else, this indicates
that the word or phrase was *added by* the editor named, and that
there is nothing in Q or F to correspond to it.

(c) In preparing the apparatus for a text in modernized spelling
one is faced by a recurrent difficulty. For example, at II. i. 15, F
reads *euer-fixed*, and both Quartos *euer-fired*, while the modern text
reads *ever-fixed*. The full correct entry in the apparatus is of course
ever-fixed] *euer-fixed* F; *euer-fired* Qq. But the only point of the entry
is to show that the text adopts F's reading and to draw attention to
the *x–r* variant. It is natural, therefore, to save space, not to enter
the F reading in full, but to print "*ever-fixed*] F". So far, so good.
But if one then goes on "*euer-fired* Qq" it looks as though one were
drawing attention to a variant spelling (*ever* in F and *euer* in Qq),
which in fact does not exist, and which, even if it did, would be of
no importance. It seems reasonable in such cases to give the variant
reading in modern spelling, and not obscure the real point. But I
do not pretend to be at all happy about the uneasy compromise
which I have here and there adopted. Happily the number of
entries where it is called for is comparatively small.

Notes. Illustrative quotations in the notes are given in modernized spelling, unless the original spelling seems of some significance.
If Shakespeare's spelling is modernized in the text, it must clearly
be modernized in the notes, and to give quotations from other
authors in the original spelling would suggest that they were more
antiquated spellers than Shakespeare.

When a quotation follows immediately on a gloss, the usage is
being directly illustrated; when it is preceded by "cf." the impli-

cation is that a less close resemblance, sometimes even a contrast, may be found illuminating.

My thanks are due to the General Editor, and to Dr H. F. Brooks, whose unfailing patience is all the more thank-worthy because he regards my textual views with the sternly benevolent horror of an inquisitor labouring over an honest heretic whose textual soul he would have saved if he could.

M. R. R.

Note: The New Cambridge edition of the play has appeared when this volume is so far advanced through proof that any detailed comment is precluded. I wish that I could have made such comment on the emendations, one or two of which seem to me brilliant (like "tine" for "time"), others either needless or unwarrantable. But on the handling of the general problem I should in any case have had little more to say, since the section on "The Copy" is almost wholly a restatement, in compressed form and sometimes even more dogmatic tone, of Dr A. Walker's views, as expressed in "Textual Problems of the First Folio", which I had already examined at some length in the textual section of my introduction and in appendices.

ABBREVIATIONS

To conform with the practice of all but the first two or three volumes of the new Arden edition, the abbreviations of the titles of Shakespeare's plays and poems are those used in Onions' *Shakespeare Glossary*. References to passages in plays other than *Othello* are to the single volume Oxford edition (Craig).

The following list contains, besides a few other abbreviations, the titles of works referred to of authors who in introduction or notes are cited by name only. It does not include a list of editors of Shakespeare; when these are cited the reference is to their editions. Nor does it include authors' names when the titles of the relevant works are given in footnotes.

Abbott	*A Shakespearian Grammar*, E. A. Abbott, 1869.
Booth	*Prompt-Book of Othello*, Edwin Booth, 1878.
Bradley	*Shakespearean Tragedy*, A. C. Bradley, 1904.
Cotgrave	*French-English Dictionary*, R. Cotgrave, 1611.
edd.	editors.
edn	edition.
Ellacombe	*Plant-Lore and Garden-Craft of Shakespeare*, H. N. Ellacombe, 1878.
Granville Barker	*Prefaces to Shakespeare*, 4th series, H. Granville Barker, 1945.
Mason	*Comments, etc.* M. Mason, 1785.
M.L.R.	*Modern Language Review.*
O.E.D.	*Oxford English Dictionary.*
Onions	*A Shakespeare Glossary*, C. T. Onions, 1911.
Preston (Miss)	*Studies in Shakespeare*, Mary Preston, 1869.
Rymer	*A Short View of Tragedy*, Thomas Rymer, 1693.
Schmidt	*Shakespeare-Lexicon*, A. Schmidt, 1874–5.
Swinburne	*A Study of Shakespeare*, A. C. Swinburne, 1880.
Tannenbaum	*Shakespeare Forgeries in the Revels Accounts*, S. A. Tannenbaum, 1928.

INTRODUCTION

1. DATE OF THE PLAY

About this there has been much controversy, marshalled, down to 1886, in Furness's Variorum edition, pp. 344–57. Later developments are carefully examined by Chambers in *The Elizabethan Stage*, IV. 136–9, and in *William Shakespeare*, II. 330–1. The most significant comment is Malone's. In 1790 he placed the play, though with hesitation, in 1611; before the end of his life he records a change of mind: "but I now know from indisputable evidence that this was not the case", and "we know it [*Othello*] was acted in 1604". From an editor as careful as Malone, "indisputable" and "know" are strong words, but unhappily he did not record *what* his evidence was. It is generally agreed that it was probably an entry in the "Revels' Accounts", and the main issue in the controversy has been whether the entry is genuine or a forgery. The forgery view was at one time popular, but lately, in spite of a characteristic explosion from S. A. Tannenbaum, opinion has swung the other way, and Malone's redating can be reasonably accepted, particularly as it is much more congruous than 1611 both with mechanical tests of versification and with the play's general temper. Any ordinary reader will share Malone's uneasiness at a dating which puts *Othello* in the same period of Shakespeare's life as *The Winter's Tale* and *The Tempest*.

2. SOURCES

The main source is clearly the seventh story in the third decade of the *Hecatommithi* of Giraldi Cinthio, published in Venice in 1566. No English translation is known before 1753. A French translation was published in Paris in 1584. Whether Shakespeare knew enough Italian to read the story in the original, or enough French to read it in French, we have no means of knowing. Just possibly there was a contemporary English translation or adaptation which has disappeared. There are a few verbal parallels which may be taken to suggest an acquaintance with the original, but I do not think that they are very significant; and there is at least one verbal

point which tells in the other direction.[1] But the debt to Cinthio for
the general lines of the plot, and for some of the details, is plain.
A translation of the relevant part of Cinthio's story is given in
Appendix I, where attention is also drawn to resemblances and
divergences.

3. THE TEXTUAL PROBLEM

There are three printed texts of the play which have to be
examined, two of them being of primary importance, and the third
deserving, I think, closer attention than it often receives.

1. The First Quarto (Q1), printed in 1622, nearly twenty years
after the probable date of the writing and first playing of the play.

2. The First Folio (F), printed in 1623, either from an independent
MS. or, if we accept a recent theory, from an amended copy
of Q1.

3. The Second Quarto (Q2), printed in 1630, and I think demonstrably
printed from a copy of Q1 which had been corrected
as the result of a careful collation with F.

Notes: (i) The Third Quarto is a reprint of Q2, the later
Folios are reprints of F, and none of them therefore is of any importance
for the determination of the text, or of any interest
except as illustrating the blunders of compositors and the
vagaries of emenders.

(ii) Q1 in one point, that of date, is an oddity, since all the
other Quartos are much nearer in date to the writing of the
plays. The oddity is of some importance in two directions: (a)
the shortness of the interval between the publication of Q1 and
the printing of F may affect one's judgement of the probability
that F was set from a corrected copy of Q1; (b) the length of the
interval between first performance and publication makes it
possible (though not, I think, for reasons given elsewhere, very
likely) that the transcript (if any) which served as copy for Q1
was made after the play had been on the boards for a considerable
time, and therefore increases the possibility of a particular
type of error in that transcript.

(iii) The discussion of Q2 may be, for the moment, deferred.
Since it is the result of a conflation of two already printed texts,
and there is nothing to suggest that the conflator had access to
any independent MS., it has no primary importance. It is, I
think, often useful as a check, and it has an intrinsic interest as an
early example of editorial methods.[2]

(iv) The extant copies of Q1 represent two different 'states' of
the printed text, one after and one before press-correction. These

1. See p. 241, n. 2.   2. See Appendix G.

variants are interesting examples of a process even more strikingly exemplified in the copies of Q1 of *King Lear*, but since they have little bearing on the problem of the relation of Q1 and F, I have recorded only a few of them in the apparatus.[1] (See an article on the Second Quarto by C. K. Hinman in *J. Q. Adams Memorial Studies*, pp. 373–89.)

We have, therefore, to make up our minds on one of two points, either (a) which of the two main texts is to be adopted as the "copy-text" for a modern edition—which text, that is, we may suppose represents either what Shakespeare first wrote, or, if we assume that he revised the play, his final intentions, or, possibly, (b) whether we are driven to the depressing conclusion that for this play there can be no copy-text.

Fourteen of Shakespeare's plays had appeared as 'good' quartos before they appeared in the Folio. For the remainder the Folio is our only authoritative text. And so long as Heminge and Condell's "divers stolen and surreptitious copies" was mistakenly supposed to include all quartos, 'good' and 'bad' together, the Folio was paramount for those fourteen plays also. It is true that Malone was too acute a scholar not to see the difficulties involved, and to rate most of the quartos high, though he still regarded them all as "surreptitious". But it is only in the last half-century, and mainly by the work of Pollard and McKerrow, that the clear-cut distinction between 'good' and 'bad' quartos has been drawn, and the status of the good quartos demonstrated.

None the less, and in spite of the existence of a quarto which no critic, so far as I know, is prepared to regard as 'bad', it has been the common practice of editors to accept the Folio as the copy-text for *Othello*, occasionally modified, at the editor's discretion, from Q1. This acceptance may or may not be justified, but the reasons ordinarily adduced in support of it need to be scrutinized (not least because the same or similar reasons are sometimes adduced in connection with other plays), and I doubt whether they will stand up to close scrutiny.

The reasons fall into two main categories, which may be labelled "completeness" and "preferability". Hart, the original editor of the play in the Arden edition, will serve well enough as an example of the line of argument. He says (p. xii of the Introduction): "The superiority of the Folio is easily proved. In the first place it contains about 160 lines, undoubtedly genuine, omitted in the First Quarto. Again, there are very many errors or misprints in the First Quarto which are correctly rendered by the Folio. There are,

1. E.g. "since" and "saunce" in I. iii. 64.

indeed, a certain number of important exceptions, where the read-ings of the 1622 Quarto are better than the Folio." (And Dr Alice Walker, writing fifty years after Hart, says much the same: "The Folio copy was purged, at any rate in intention, of quarto errors, and was augmented by a number of passages omitted in the acting version in order to shorten the play for presentation. The general superiority of the Folio text has never been seriously in question.")

Now here, surely, there is a good deal of loose expression and even looser thinking. The fact that F contains about 160 lines which are not in Q1 does not, *ipso facto*, make it a "better" text; it makes it (granted that we accept the lines as genuine) a more *com-plete* text, which is quite another matter. (Much of the trouble lies in the use of the word "better", which so often, in the absence of any original MS. with which we can compare the printed text, means no more than "what I prefer".) Take a more modern example. Sup-pose that we had before us the following two printed versions of the third stanza of Keats' *To Autumn*:

(a)   Where are the songs of Spring? Ay, where are they?
        Think not of them, thou hast thy music too,—
    While barred clouds bloom the soft-dying day,
        And touch the stubble-plains with rosy hue;
    Then in a wailful choir the small gnats mourn
        Among the river sallows, borne aloft
          Or sinking as the light wind lives or dies;
    And full-grown lambs loud bleat from hilly bourn;
        The red-breast whistles from a garden-croft,
         And gathering swallows twitter in the skies.

(b)   Where are the songs of Spring? Ay, where are they?
        Think nought of them: thou hast thy music too.
    While barring clouds bloom the soft-dying day,
        And touch the stubble-plains with rosy hue.
    Then in a wailing choir the small gnats mourn
        Among the river sallows, borne aloft
          Or sinking as the slight wind lifts or dies;
    And full-grown lambs loud bleat from hilly bourne;
        Hedge-crickets sing; and now with tremble soft
        The red-breast whistles from a garden croft,
         And gather'd swallows twitter in the skies.

Now here we can check the two versions by Keats' own MS. in his letter to Woodhouse. Version (a), apart from the introduction of a few hyphens, one or two modifications of spelling and one or two of punctuation, and one real variant (*or* for *and* in line 7) exactly reproduces Keats' autograph, except for the omission of the extra line which was Keats' crowning technical achievement in the working out of his stanza for the Odes. Version (b) includes the missing line, but departs from the MS. in seven places. Yet none of the incorrect readings is in itself impossible, and indeed I fancy that some editors, if they had the two versions before them, but no MS., would argue for at least two of them as "preferable" to those of version (a). But would anyone, with the MS. before him, seriously argue that (b) is, in any proper sense of the word, the "better" text? It is more complete, and no sane editor, even lacking the MS., but observing the stanza form of the other two stanzas, would hesitate to reinstate the missing line. But it would be a very rash one who would take the presence of the extra line as evidence of the superiority of variant readings.

A somewhat similar confusion of thought underlies "many errors or misprints in the first Quarto . . . are correctly rendered by the Folio". The use of "correctly" is dangerously loose. Strictly it should not be used except when there is a MS. to refer to. It is true that with misprints, particularly those which have produced a *vox nihili*, one may often reasonably accept a correction as "correct", though even here one needs to be extremely cautious.[1] But "errors" is a very different matter. As between two variants, both of which make quite tolerable sense, the acceptance of one as "correct" and

1. Caution is needed because on occasion what looks like an obvious correction may, far from restoring the original reading, merely bury it deeper from sight. Take a hypothetical example: we have two texts, B and C, of an Elizabethan play. We have reason to suppose that B was printed not from the original (O) but from an earlier printed edition (A) of which no copies are extant. There is some doubt whether C was printed from O or A, but in any case it often corrects obvious misprints of B. B reads "that salbe Ethiop queene"; C reads "sable" for "salbe". Few editors would hesitate a moment before taking "salbe" to be a mere transposition error, and accepting C's reading as a certain correction. But the history of the reading may have been quite different. Suppose that O read "fabld" (i.e. "fabl'd"); the compositor of A, making one of the commonest errors with Elizabethan secretary hand, set the word as "fable"; the B compositor did indeed transpose, but he also made another error—also an easy one in setting from *print*—taking *f* as *s*, and so setting "salbe". Now, so long as this mysterious word was there to challenge attention, with nothing to replace it, there was some hope that some editor would see that "fabl'd", though due to a complicated process, was at least a possible alternative to an obvious "sable"; but when another early text reads "sable", it is almost certain to be accepted without scrutiny; it makes good sense, and it also makes the recovery of the true reading very improbable. There is perhaps an instance of the same thing in *Hamlet*, where at I. iv. 71 Q2 reads "bettles o'er his base", but F's "beetles" has been universally accepted, largely because the verb in that sense is familiar to us. But when one observes that (a) the familiarity depends solely on its use in the very passage under discussion (see *O.E.D.*) and (b) Q1 reads "beckles", one begins to wonder whether the acceptance has not been unduly facile.

the dismissal of the other as "error" depends either on the personal judgement of the editor,[1] or on an antecedent assumption that one of the two texts is "superior" to the other. And unless this assumption rests on foundations quite other than those of readings, it is clear that the argument is rapidly becoming circular. ("Many of F's readings are better than Q1's; therefore F is the superior text; therefore F's readings are for the most part to be accepted." No editor, of course, puts his findings so baldly, but that is what they often amount to.)

The ambiguity of the words "better" or "more correct" is increased by uncertainty about the criterion which is being applied. Suppose a piece of work, say an Elizabethan play, of 3,000 lines. It runs through five editions, A–E. A is printed from the original MS. —call this O—each of its successors from its predecessor, without reference to O. O is none too legible, and compositor A makes on an average one blunder in every 10 lines; compositors B, C, and D, working from print, average one blunder in every 30 lines. By the time, then, that we get to edition D, we have probably about 550 divergences from the original. (The figure will not be the full 600, since successive compositors will sometimes make a new blunder of an old one, so that there have been two blunders but only one divergence, and will sometimes by accident revert to an original reading—e.g. O *might*, A *night*, B *nigh*, C *night*, D *might*, where there have been four errors in the sense of divergence from copy, but no error at all in the sense of divergence from O.) But compositor E (since he is a hypothetical figure we can allow him an inhuman degree of accuracy) makes no blunders at all, and edition E therefore is a precisely faithful reproduction of D. Now, judged by the criterion of careful workmanship, compositor E is immeasurably "superior to", "better than", "more correct than" any of his predecessors, but the *text* which he has produced is, judged by the criterion of nearness to O, about 80 per cent "worse than" or "inferior to" A.

Now modify this hypothetical case so that it comes into closer relation to the problem before us. There is in existence a transcript (T) of O. It is unusually accurate, with an average of one error to 50 lines; and it is very legible. It is to be used as copy for an edition X. But before it is sent to the printer it is subjected to an editorial process, conducted by an editor who has a high regard for the

---

1. This "personal judgement" may be a mere matter of preference, but it may also be more firmly founded on an estimate, derived from experience, of the probabilities of particular kinds of corruption, or on an adherence (sometimes I think a too ready adherence) to the *difficilior lectio* principle.

author, and who thinks it not merely permissible, but incumbent on him, to tidy up awkwardnesses of scansion or phrasing, and in particular to replace by equivalents of his own such words or phrases as he considers too colloquial or too 'provincial' to be consistent with the author's repute. Suppose that he makes one such 'improvement' every 100 lines. The edited T is now handed to compositor Y, who, in view of the legibility of it, may be credited with the same degree of accuracy as B, C, and D, setting from print. Edition X, then, will include slightly fewer than 190 divergences from O. Now, is A or X the "better" text? Or, in more precise language, which of the two ought we to adopt as the basis for a modern edition? On the merely numerical count the answer is obvious. X, with its maximum of 190 divergencies, is considerably superior to A with its 300. But that is an over-simplification of the problem, because the divergences are of two quite different types. *All* those of A are blunders by an honest compositor doing his not very skilful best to reproduce a difficult MS. And the *majority* in X are the same. But there remains in X a residue of readings which have no typographical relation to O at all. The important point is this, that with a compositor's blunder one can, with anything from near certainty (as with *apines–paines*) to strong probability (as with *might–night*), recover the original, whereas with the editorial alteration the original, unless we can apply an independent check, is lost beyond recovery; we cannot, by any exercise of ingenuity, deduce it from what is before us, and indeed for the most part we are not even tempted to try to deduce it, since the reading often looks above suspicion. There is a very clear instance in a line so often quoted that one almost hesitates to quote it again. In *1 H 4*, v. iii. 11, Q1 reads "I was not borne a yeelder, thou proud Scot". This was correctly reproduced in the next three quartos, but Q5 went wrong and produced "I was not borne to yeeld, thou proud Scot". Whoever prepared the copy for F by correcting a copy of Q5, seeing that the line would not scan, changed it to "I was not borne to yeeld, thou haughty Scot". If all the quartos had disappeared, that line would not have been for a moment suspect, and yet it is almost certainly not what Shakespeare wrote. Again, though the line "But that the earth and the cold hand of death" might have seemed a trifle awkward, no editor would have had the temerity to emend it. Yet it is highly probable that Shakespeare wrote "But that the earthy and cold hand of death" (Q1), from which Q2, followed by Qq3–5, produced the halting line "But that the earth and cold hand of death", which was regularized for F by the easy insertion of a "the".

Having thus to some extent, I hope, cleared the ground by a general consideration of the issues involved, I propose to state, first briefly and then in more detail, the observable differences between the Q1 and F texts of *Othello*, making, at this stage, as little comment as may be on the conclusions which may be drawn from the differences.

1. *Lines present in one only of the texts.* F contains some 160 lines, including some passages of considerable length, which are not present in Q1. Q1 contains a few brief passages not present in F.

2. *Oaths.* The considerable number of oaths in Q1 is reduced and modified in F, apparently according to a rough sliding scale, so that mild expletives in Q1 disappear altogether, while more vigorous ones appear in a milder form (e.g. "Away!" for "Zounds!").

3. *Stage-directions.* The stage-directions of Q1 are noticeably more numerous and fuller than those of F, particularly with regard to 'business'.

4. *Variants.* There is a large number of variants, of very different types, both in words and in punctuation.

(One should perhaps add, as a possible fifth, that the compositor of F is sometimes assumed to have been a more careful workman than the compositor of Q1, but since I hope to show that this was not so, it is hardly an "observable difference".)[1]

To take these points in more detail:

1. In the heading to this paragraph above I avoided the word "omission", which is an uncritically question-begging term. The passages may have been insertions. The problem here is whether the absence in Q1 of lines present in F is due to carelessness of compositor or transcriber, or to dramatic cutting, or to the fact that the lines were never before compositor or transcriber, but were later additions. And to what can we attribute the absence from F of a few words and phrases which appear in Q1?

Both the "Q only" and the "F only" passages are given, with comments, in Appendix A. I will confine myself here to some general observations about them.

(i) The "Q only" passages are not, I think, of crucial importance. Some of them might have been omitted from F by carelessness, even if they were in the copy from which F was set. It may be significant that five of the nine are incomplete lines, suggesting perhaps that whoever prepared the copy for F disliked metrical irregularities, but, if this was so, regularity was sometimes secured at the price of an awkwardness in sense.

(ii) With the longer "F only" passages (those over three lines)

1. See Appendix H.

the problem itself (though not necessarily therefore its solution) is simple enough—which of them are likely to have been cuts and which additions? In other words, does Q1 represent the original text after it had been cut for presentation on the stage or the original text as Shakespeare handed it to his company and before he made additions to it? (I say "he made" since all but perhaps one of the passages are beyond the editorial latitude which Heminge and Condell seem to have allowed themselves, and probably also beyond their competence.) I think that with only one of these passages is absence from Q1 likely to have been due to a compositor's blunder, that of the rest, all but four are are almost certain cuts, and that those four are probable cuts but possible additions. My conclusion therefore is that the original probably contained both the "Q only" and these longer "F only" passages. But I realize that it may very reasonably be argued that one or two of the latter passages are more probably additions than cuts; that if we accept these as additions we ought to be ready to accept more; and that then we are well on the road to admitting the possibility that Shakespeare revised the whole text in minor points as well.

(iii) And in considering this possibility the shorter "F only" passages become of great importance. Few of them are probable cuts; a high proportion are at least possible additions. And the longer I study the texts of this play the stronger grows my impression that additions and alterations were at some stage made, whoever made them. These shorter passages, then, merit careful examination.

But the appearance of passages in one only of the two texts is of less importance than may at first appear as evidence towards determining which text, if either, should be adopted as copy-text—so long as we steer clear of the fallacious equation "More complete = better"—for this reason: with a few minor exceptions (all among the shorter passages) which may conceivably be regarded as editorial interpolations, all the passages are generally accepted as being Shakespeare's, so that even those editors (the great majority) who base their texts on F include the "Q only" passages. We have therefore to turn to other evidence.

And here it will, I think, make things clearer for the reader if I try to define what precisely the problem is. It is a matter of trying to determine, in the light of the available internal evidence, what are the probable links in transmission between Shakespeare's original MS. and the printed texts Q1 and F, and, further, what kinds of corruption or alteration may be reasonably inferred or imagined at various points in the transmission.

All we *know*, for certain, is that there must have been an original

MS. which has disappeared, and that two printed texts are extant. All that lies between is matter for conjecture. It is highly probable that as soon as Shakespeare handed over his MS. (call it O) to his company, a transcript was made of it (call this T1), to serve, amongst other things, as the prompt-book, while O was kept for reference. But this is no more than a probability, since there is some evidence that with some plays O was used as the prompt-book, and a transcript made only when O showed signs of wear, and also that with some plays O, and not a transcript, was sent to the printer. Now both the printed texts might be set from O, or both from T1, or one from O and the other from T1. Further, there might be a second transcript, made because it was not thought well to let either O or T1 out of the playhouse, and this second transcript might be made either from T1 (if T1 existed) or direct from O, independently of T1 (call these respectively T2 and TO). That, granted that we want to avoid Johnson's pessimistic error of multiplying transcripts *praeter necessitatem*, exhausts the possibilities, unless—and a very important "unless"—we admit the possibility of (*a*) corrections or additions at some stage, made either by Shakespeare himself or by someone preparing the copy for the printer, and (*b*) blunders in transcription of a different kind from those made by compositors. If we admit that possibility, the permutations are bewilderingly increased.

Examination of the texts rapidly makes it clear that we can discard at once at least one of the hypothetical possibilities. Q1 and F were not both set from a single MS., since there is a number of variants which cannot be accounted for by the different blunders of two different compositors, or different transcribers, working from the same original. We have then, for *either* text (X) the possibilities O–X, O–T1–X, O–TO–X, O–T1–T2–X, and of those possibilities we have to select *two*. We have further to admit the possibility that any transcript may embody not only ordinary corruptions of the text but also the results of an editorial process, and to bear in mind that corruptions will vary not only in degree, but—more important—in kind, both with the competence of the transcriber and his relation to the theatre, and, with one type of transcriber, with the length of time that has elapsed between the first performance of the play and the making of the transcript.

A word, therefore, about transcripts. It is not, I think, always kept clearly enough in mind that there are two quite different types of possible transcript. The one is the work of a professional scrivener. He is required to make as accurate a reproduction as he can of a MS. of which he knows nothing. His task therefore is the same as that of a compositor, and his errors will be of the same kind as the compositor's, though he is free from such liability to error as is caused by the mechanics of the printing-house (e.g. 'foul case', or letters pulled out of a badly locked forme in the course of printing and wrongly replaced). But the transcriber may be, and it is generally agreed that he sometimes was, the 'book-keeper', and if he was also the prompter a quite different type of transcript is liable to appear. If he makes his transcript soon after the MS. arrives in the theatre and before the play has gone into production, he is liable to make the same kind of errors as the professional scrivener, his liability being somewhat increased by the fact that he is not a professional, but somewhat decreased by the fact that he is a man of the theatre and probably familiar with the playwright's handwriting. (And even at this stage he is likely to make additions to the stage-directions to serve his own later purposes as prompter.) But if the transcript is made after the play has gone through rehearsal, and been several times produced, a different, and much more serious, type of error may appear.

In a hard-worked repertory company—and that is what, however high the standard of acting, Shakespeare's company was—which has to act different plays in rapid succession, very few actors, however good studies they are, learn their lines precisely as the author wrote them. I once watched through rehearsal a good repertory company at work on *The Winter's Tale*. The actor playing Leontes was an old and experienced Shakespearean actor. He departed from his text in something like a hundred places. But, because he had Shakespeare in his blood, what he substituted always scanned, always made the required sense, and was usually thoroughly Shakespearean. Now, no producer, when a scene is going well, wants to interrupt its flow by correcting verbal minutiae. But when an actor has delivered a line in his own way a dozen times, and is well into his part, it is a desperate business to get him to alter it. He will do his best, but in the excitement of performance he will probably slip back, and a large number of these errors will maintain themselves on the stage. And it is almost certain that many of them will also appear in a transcript if this is later made by the prompter, because he will write down not what is in front of his eye in the text, but what his ear is used to on the stage.[1]

1. A small specific instance is perhaps worth giving. An accomplished amateur actress, who in her young days had played an admirable Rosalind, was asked, twenty years later, to help some young players who were preparing a performance of *As You Like It* by reading the part of Rosalind against them. Not trusting her memory, she was using a printed text. But when she came to the

This type of error is well-recognized in, e.g., *Richard III*, where there is a large number of verbal variants, which are 'unimportant' in the sense that either reading gives the required meaning, between the Q and F texts—such pairs as *slew–killed, throw–hurl, dread–fear*, and so on—which can hardly be accounted for by a compositor's carelessness, but which are very natural 'actor's variants'. And this type of error, so prevalent in *Richard III*, may well be present, though less conspicuously, in other plays.

To return now to the consideration of observable differences between the texts.

2. *Oaths*. The evidence of presence or absence of oaths was at one time thought reliable for dating a text, in view of the famous Act of 1606 to "restrain abuses of players". But it has more lately been demonstrated that the use of this evidence had little to commend it but convenience. The Act aimed at controlling what might be said on the stage, not what might be printed; and it is observable that the later, post-1606 quartos cheerfully retained the oaths of the pre-1606 editions. Readers, it appears, might read what they liked, so long as their ears were unsullied in the theatre. "One does not see, then," as Chambers pertinently observes, "why the publishers of the First Folio should have gone to the pains of expurgation." Perhaps the most one can say is that drastic expurgation suggests a relation to a prompt-book, either made, or emended, after 1606, rather than to a pre-1606 original.

3. *Stage-directions*. Here the difference between Q1 and F is most striking. F's stage-directions are very thin, quite inadequate for a stage performance, but even more inadequate as a help to a reader trying to visualize the action. A complete list is given in Appendix B. (Greg's list, by the way, in *The Shakespeare First Folio*, pp. 359–60, is not quite complete, since he does not think worth notice some dozen places where one or other text (usually F) omits a necessary exit or entrance which is given by the other.) But some of the more salient examples may be mentioned here. None of the following appears in F: in his night-gown (I. i. 159); set at a table with lights (I. iii. 1); Exit two or three (I. iii. 120); a shot (II. i. 55); Trumpets within (II. i. 177); they kiss (II. i. 198); Help, help, within (II. iii.

---

line (I. iii. 11) "No, some of it is for my child's father", her memory went back over the twenty years to the 'politer' edition which she had then used, and without hesitation she said "No, some of it is for my father's child". And if any reader doubts the likelihood of this type of error, let him get a friend to write out any famous passage of Shakespeare, say fifteen lines or so of "To be or not to be", deliberately introducing half a dozen verbal variants, and then let him try to copy this MS. version. He is remarkably accurate if he does not slip over one or two of the errors, writing down what he *knows* is right, not what he *sees*.

136); they fight (II. iii. 147); A bell rung (II. iii. 151); he kneels (III. iii. 457); Iago kneels (III. iii. 469); A Trumpet (IV. i. 208); with a light (v. i. 45); with a light (v. ii. 1); He kisses her (v. ii. 15); she dies (v. ii. 126); Othello falls on the bed (v. ii. 199); The Moor runs at Iago. Iago kills his wife (v. ii. 236); she dies (v. ii. 252); in a chair (v. ii. 283); He stabs himself (v. ii. 357). The only contrary example, I think, is at the opening of v. ii, where F, though it does not give Othello a light, has "and Desdemona in her bed", which is absent from Q1.

It is clear, then, that Q1 is pretty fully, and F hardly at all, 'stage-directed' for 'business' in performance. But one has to be cautious in drawing conclusions from the fact. On the face of it, it looks as though a text with full stage-directions is likely to be in close relation to the original, since the author, if anyone, would know what business he wanted and would indicate it. But this is not necessarily so. The author, provided that he knew that he was going to be intimately concerned with the production of his play, might well be light on stage-directions in his MS. What one can, I think, say is that an adequately stage-directed text is probably in close relation to the *prompt-book*, since the prompter, if the directions are not there already, will write them in as delivered by word of mouth of the author-producer or add them, if he needs them, on his own account. And, working further along these lines, it might be argued that F is in closer relation than Q1 to an inadequately stage-directed original, by-passing the prompt-book.

Prompter's directions are often, though by no means always, imperatival (e.g. "kiss", or "Ring bell", rather than "they kiss" or "A bell rung"); on the other hand, as Greg points out, "permissive" directions are almost certainly the author's, like "Exit two or three" (I. iii. 120), since the prompter must know whether he is operating with two supers or three, whereas the author can safely leave the determination of the point to rehearsal.

But the discrepancy in stage-directions in Q1 and F, though slender evidence in helping to determine the comparative authority of the two texts, is, I think, almost decisive in the consideration, to which I shall come later, of Dr Alice Walker's recent theory about the copy prepared for the F text of *Othello*.

4. *Variants*

(i) There is a large number of spelling variants; Q1 frequently, for example, prints *ha* and *em* for *have* and *them*. Greg thinks that this points to a late Jacobean transcript.[1]

1. *The Shakespeare First Folio* (Oxford, 1955), p. 357.

(ii) There is a considerable number of pairs of variants in which one or other is almost certainly due to an error at some stage in transmission from a common original: e.g. *Dawes–Doves*, of which either makes sense. Such of these as seem significant are discussed in the notes.

(iii) There is a smaller, more puzzling, and much more important class of variants which are hardly referable to a common original: e.g., "the utmost pleasure of my lord" (Q1, I. iii. 251)— "the very quality of my lord" (F); "active instruments" (Q1, I. iii. 270)—"offic'd instrument" (F); "And swiftly come to Desdemona's arms" (Q1, II. i. 80)—"Make love's quick pants in Desdemona's arms" (F); and, perhaps most striking of all, the famous "essential vesture of creation" passage (II. i. 63–5). Some of these may be examples of the 'actor's errors' previously mentioned. It is, of course, not an impossible, though I think an improbable, supposition that Shakespeare revised the whole of his original. But it is quite possible that some of these variants are the result not of actors' *errors* but of actors' requests or of alterations made by Shakespeare in the course of rehearsal. It is in the last degree unlikely that, after any play (in any period) has taken shape in rehearsal, what the actors deliver on the first night will be identical with what the author first wrote. The changes may be made over his dead body, or, if he is a man of the theatre, at his own instance or with his willing co-operation; but they will be made. Now it is reasonably certain that Shakespeare, as a member of the company, was closely connected with the production of his own plays. If then an actor came to him and said, "Look here, I find this line very difficult to get over," or "I can't feel that that's right for the state of mind I'm supposed to be in, so may I say it *this* way, or will you give me something else?", the odds are that, unless the suggestion neutralized something which he had intended, Shakespeare would accede to the request. Further, even with a playwright so practical and experienced as Shakespeare, a play on the boards is a different thing from a play written, and he may often have felt during rehearsal that an alteration of a few words here, a deletion or addition there, would be effective. And he may well have simply said to the prompter, "Oh, give him what he wants," or "Write in this line"; and if the prompter was working from a transcript the alteration would never appear in the original at all.

This suggestion, I know, does little more than complicate the issue, since we have no way that I can see of determining, or even reasonably guessing, at what link in transmission the alterations were made. But it is perhaps indirectly useful, as helping to keep our

imaginations alive. When one is occupied with the sometimes dry
bones of textual theory, it is of real importance that we should be
imaginatively alive to practice, to what does in fact happen, and
presumably always has happened, in the theatre.

I should like to draw particular attention to two variants of this
type, closely adjacent and perhaps significant. At II. i. 63 Cassio
is describing Desdemona. In Q1 he says:

> One that excells the blasoning pens,
> And in the essentiall vesture of creation,
> Does beare all excellency.

and at line 79 he prays Jove to swell Othello's sail

> That he may blesse this Bay with his tall shippe,
> And swiftly come to Desdemona's armes.

In F the passages run thus:

> One that excels the quirkes of Blazoning pens,
> And in th'essentiall Vesture of creation,
> Do's tyre the Ingeniuer.

> That he may blesse this Bay with his tall Ship,
> Make loues quicke pants in Desdemonaes Armes . . .

Now surely no transcriber or compositor, however careless, could
produce the readings of either text from an original which was
intended to produce those of the other, unless indeed he found his
copy so completely illegible that he was driven to mere botching.
Are Q1's readings then an actor's errors, and F's those of the
original? The first possibly, since "tire the ingeniuer" (even assuming that *ingeniuer* = *ingenieur* = *ingener*) is not an easy phrase. But I do
not find the explanation at all convincing for the second. "Make
love's quick pants" is both straightforward and vivid, and why
should any actor slip up over it in this way? He might substitute,
say, "soft" for "quick" or even "Take love's swift joys" or the like
for the whole phrase, but he would not be likely to arrive at the Q1
version, which would probably seem to him pallid. But it will be
noticed that of the two F versions, the one is more 'conceited', and
the other more highly coloured, than Q1's, and that as a result both
are more in key with Cassio's high-flown utterance hereabouts,
with his unsurfeited hopes and ensteeped (or enscerped) traitors. I
do not think that the second F passage is very happily in character
for Cassio—certainly not for the Cassio whom two scenes later we
are going to watch so easily parrying Iago's probing attack—but
none the less I should guess that both the F versions are changes

made by Shakespeare himself. Before l. 43 of this scene, though we have heard something of Cassio from the prejudiced Iago, his appearance has been brief and his speeches limited to thirteen lines, all but two of which were no more than a second-in-command's report. It is therefore important to get him established as soon as possible as a recognizable man, as well as officer. And the F versions may be two firm strokes to that end.[1] I fancy that the same may be true of the First Senator's interruptive line at I. iii. 36, which not only stresses his fussy self-importance but also desirably breaks up a tiresome recitation from the messenger.

(iv) *Variants probably due to an editorial process*

It is generally thought that Heminge and Condell, or someone working under their instructions, in preparing the copy for the First Folio, made changes from the original, which they regarded as improvements but for which there was probably no Shakespearean warrant. They were not hampered by modern notions of scholarship, and would, we may suppose, have warmly sympathized with the attitude (though probably not with many of the detailed manifestations of that attitude) of some eighteenth-century editors which we deplore. They conceived it to be their business to present to their contemporaries and to posterity the work of their beloved and admired fellow in the 'best' shape that they could manage. If, therefore, Shakespeare had written what they considered he should not have written, they thought it laudable, and not, as we think it, reprehensible, to put him right. The process is ordinarily known as "sophistication", and though that is not, I think, a wholly satisfactory label, since it unduly narrows the field of operations, if it is taken to include specific "regularization" it serves well enough.

That is the hypothesis, and it is, I think, firmly based. The most familiar examples of supporting evidence are probably three in *King Lear*, where at III. vii. 58 and 63, v. iii. 157 Q reads *rash* (verb), *dern*, and *stople*, while F reads *stick*, *stern*, and *stop*, in each instance replacing the out-of-the-way or colloquial word by the more ordinary and 'correct' one. As to "regularization", the third instance from *King Lear* provides an example, since from Q's metrical line "Or with this paper will I stople it" the substitution of *stop* produced an unmetrical one, which was regularized, not very elegantly, by the addition of "Hold, sir!" at the end of the line. The two examples already given from *1 Henry IV* are of regularization by F, and the first is an interesting one, since it indicates that

1. Cf. also II. iii. 271–3, and comment on the passage in Appendix A.

sophistication was not the monopoly of F. It looks as though some-one, either compositor or preparer of copy for Q1, had been offended by "a yeelder", and, regardless of metre, emended to "to yeeld". But in the great majority of generally accepted instances of sophistication the sophisticator is F. And one must notice that the moment that the presence of sophistication is accepted at all there is no logical reason for limiting its frequency. Not only may it be held accountable for other, less obvious, variants, but it may be confidently suspected in plays for which we have only the Folio text.

In *Othello* there are at least three instances which I should regard as certain examples of sophistication: I. iii. 350, *acerb* (Q1)—*bitter* (F); v. ii. 318, *in the nick* (Q1)—*in the interim* (F); v. ii. 364, *lodging* (Q1)—*loading* (F). In the first, F substitutes an ordinary for an unusual word—how unusual is clear from the fact that *O.E.D.*, missing this occurrence in Q1, gives 1657 as the earliest date for the appearance of "acerb". In the second F gets rid of a colloquialism at the cost of a hypermetrical line. In the third a vivid country-man's word is ousted by a conventional one (see note *ad loc.*). There are other places where I think one can probably detect the hand of the sophisticator. Some are mere regularizations of metre, often not very skilful, as with v. i. 86, *To bear a part in this* (Q1)—*To be a party inthis injury* (F); IV. iii. 21, *Prithee unpin me—have grace and favour in them* (Q1), reduced by F to the regulation ten syllables, but to ten syllables which cannot be read as a line.

But others are of more interest, e.g. IV. ii. 111, *The smallest opinion on my greatest abuse* (Q1)—*The small'st opinion on my least misuse* (F), where an apparent regularization misses the point; Desdemona is saying that even her *greatest* fault is so trivial that it cannot merit the least adverse criticism. And v. ii. 320, *How came you, Cassio, by a handkerchief That was my wife's?* (Q1)—*How came you, Cassio, by that handkerchief That was my wife's?* (F). At first sight, and in view of the importance of the handkerchief in the plot, and the fact that it has been discussed a hundred lines earlier, "That" seems the natural reading. But is it? Cassio has been carried in too late to hear the discussion, and, so far as Othello knows, to him the handkerchief is just "a" handkerchief; and Othello therefore words his question rightly. It is true, however, that Othello is hardly in a state of mind to question with the cool logic of a cross-examining counsel.

5. *Variants in punctuation* The questions of punctuation in general, and of these variants in particular, are discussed in Appendix C.

There, then, are the types of corruption or alteration, ranging from the certain through the probable to the possible: blunders due to mere carelessness of compositor or transcriber (certain), or to well-meaning but unsuccessful attempts by either to make sense of illegible copy (highly probable); errors due to reliance on memory (probable, but, with our data, never provable; it is almost solely a transcriber's, not a compositor's, type of error, and its first begetter is usually an actor); changes made by the author himself (no doubt quite possible; one's estimate of likelihood depends largely on one's estimate of the author's temperament—was he the sort of man deliberately to revise his own work?); would-be improvements made by others than the author (almost certain). Since, further, there were almost certainly two chains of transmission and in both of them quite probably, in one almost certainly, a transcript intervened between original MS. and print, the complications are evidently considerable, and the reader whose patience has endured thus far may well ask whether there is any real chance of establishing an "authoritative" text for *Othello*, or indeed for any play of Shakespeare's.

For some of the plays, perhaps about half of the total, the answer is a slightly qualified "yes". For those plays for which our only text is that of F, and for those others which F reprinted with a minimum of alteration from a quarto, the text of F or of the first good quarto is at least the only text we have. But for *Othello*, as for some others, the only honest answer, I think, is an unqualified "no". All that the most patient and skilful investigation can hope to achieve is the demonstration that among various possibilities some are more likely than others. The plain truth is that today, now that certain main principles, largely through the work of Pollard, McKerrow, and Greg, have been generally accepted, a good deal of Shakespearean textual criticism is an elaborate game, entertaining to the players, entertaining also to such spectators as enjoy a display of technical expertise and of the perpetration of fouls which may escape the attention of the referee, but not very profitable to either, resulting in the end, as it is often bound to result, in a pointless draw.

Before I go on to examine the latest theory about *Othello*, I should like to draw attention to a parallel from later literature which, apart from being amusing in itself, throws, I think, a good deal of light on this problem of the difficulty, with some pieces of work, of establishing an authoritative text. Almost all modern readers know Keats' *The Eve of Saint Agnes* solely from the printed text of the 1820 volume, and do not realize that that text represents neither Keats' first nor his second thoughts. I think it is safe to say that no reader has ever read the poem as Keats left it in February 1819, since that version has, so far as I know, never been printed *in extenso* at all, and that few readers have ever read his revised version, since that, I believe, has been printed only once. And the reasons for the 1820 text being what it is are precisely relevant to our problem.

Keats wrote the poem in January 1819. Of that version, except for the first seven stanzas, which are missing, we have the holograph (call this K). Owing to a great deal of correction, deletion, and interlineation, it is often not very easy to decipher. Of this version Woodhouse made a very careful transcript (W1). In the late summer of 1819 Keats revised the poem, making some minor verbal and some more substantial alterations, including, I think, at least one stanza which, owing to Woodhouse's objections, has disappeared altogether. For this revision we have no holograph, but Woodhouse noted the revisions in a second transcript (W2). And for the revised version we have also a complete transcript made by George Keats in January 1820 (GK).[1]

Now here we have, it is clear, a fairly close parallel to what one may reasonably suppose lies behind our texts of *Othello*—an original MS., not very easily decipherable, a transcript of that, a revision, and two transcripts embodying the results of the revision. But much the most significant point is contained in a comment of Woodhouse's: "This copy [W2] was taken from Keats' original MS. He afterwards altered it for publication, and added some stanzas and omitted others. His alterations are noticed here. The Published copy differs from both in a few particulars. *Keats left it to his Publishers to adopt which they pleased, and to revise the whole.*" One could hardly wish for a clearer description of what we have seen reason to suppose were the operations of Heminge and Condell.

W1 is as nearly impeccable a transcript as one can hope to find, made by a man who was both very conscientious and also intimately familiar with the author's handwriting. There are one or two of the inevitable and unimportant verbal variants of the *thine* for *thy* type; where Keats had erased a word but made no substitution, Woodhouse often, to complete the line, reinstated the deleted word; where the holograph was desperate he very properly simply left a gap. There is only one major discrepancy, but it is a very interesting one. In the third line of stanza XXIX Keats first wrote "A Table light, and stilly threw thereon"; he then at once

1. For details, and discussion of one or two disputable points, I must refer the reader to my *Keats' Craftsmanship* (Oxford, 1933), pp. 97–101, note H on pp. 303–4, and, for the full text of GK, pp. 180–90.

altered this to "A Table, and with anguish spread thereon"; but, since he was interlineating his corrections, when he got to *anguish* he was in trouble with the upstanding *ll* of *stilly* and so wrote what looked like two words, *an guish*. Woodhouse read the second part of the word, very naturally, as *quick*, but then, valour for once triumphing over discretion, he transcribed *an* as *care*. Now, if the holograph had been lost and W1 had served as copy for the printer, the reading *and with care quick* would have maintained itself. And this is the sort of thing that has probably happened in Shakespearean texts oftener than we suspect.

There are some interesting parallels to the expurgations of F. At the end of stanza xvi Keats wrote *O Christ I deem*, and he never wrote anything else, since this is the reading of GK. But even as early as W1 Woodhouse pencilled in *Away!*, and in the 1820 text we have *Go! Go!*. But some even more interesting things happen at the opening of the next stanza, where Keats' Porphyro swears *by the great St Paul* in K and continues so to swear in GK. But in W1 a new figure comes on to the scene, and makes various pencilled suggestions, *by the Saints I swear*, and some consequential alterations for the sake of rhyme.[1] There is no reason to suppose that these alterations had any authority, but they appear in the 1820 text, though with modifications.

As to differences in substance, W1 gives a whole stanza between what are now iii and iv. It was no doubt one of the original stanzas which are missing from the beginning of the holograph. Keats later cancelled it, probably wisely. But, more important, when he was revising, Keats evidently wrote in the new stanza[2] which appears in GK between what are now vi and vii, but which does not appear in the 1820 text. The omission was caused, I suppose, by an access of delicacy on the part of the same board of censors which, interpreting Keats' permission with considerable latitude, refused to pass his revised version of stanzas xxxv and xxxvi. But the omission was unfortunate, since the stanza or something like it is badly needed to prepare for the otherwise unexpected cates and dainties, and even more the lute, of stanza xx. Finally, Keats changed the last three and a half lines of the poem so as "to leave on the reader a sense of pettish disgust" (Woodhouse), but his alteration was neglected.

In the upshot the 1820 text is something of a jumble, and by modern standards a deplorable text. Sometimes it agrees with K, W1, and W2 against GK (as with *midnight clarion* in xxix against *braying clarion*), sometimes it agrees with GK against the other three

1. See *Keats' Craftsmanship*, p. 133.   2. *Ib.* pp. 117, 119–20.

(as with *dying* for *faintest* in XXIX, or *dishes* for *salvers* in XXXI), some-times it has a reading peculiar to itself, as with *regardless eyes* in VIII where K and all three transcripts have *uneager eyes* (this might have been a last-minute correction of Keats' own), and sometimes it has readings for which the responsibility seems to rest with the pen-cilling improver in WI (as with the opening of XVII) or with the censors (as with *Go! go!* for *O Christ* in XVI).

It will be noticed that if a text had been printed straight from WI we should have had, apart from one bad transcriber's error, and no doubt a certain number of compositor's blunders, a reliable text of the poem as Keats left it in February 1819; and that if a text had been printed straight from GK we should have had something at least very close to Keats' revised version, since, though there are in that transcript three easily corrected errors, and there may be more—we have no holograph to check by—none the less it is the work of a man with no aim but to make an accurate copy of his brother's work. But the text with which since 1820 readers have been "abused" is neither one thing nor the other. When Keats' second thoughts commended themselves to his publishers we are allowed to have them; when they did not, they were suppressed. There are, further, three phrases certainly, possibly more, which are not Keats' own at any stage of composition or revision, but merely unwarranted, if laudably intentioned, alterations.

In brief, and to anticipate, I feel that the 1820 text presents a probably close parallel to the F text of *Othello*, and that the hypo-thetical text printed from WI would present a parallel to Q1.

But that is no more than a guess. Suppose for a moment that the original and all three transcripts of *The Eve of St Agnes* had dis-appeared and that we had nothing to examine but two printed texts, the 1820 and the hypothetical one printed from WI. Should we not be liable to base erroneous conclusions on a very sandy foundation?

The latest theory about the F text of *Othello* is that of Dr Alice Walker. She stated it first in a paper in *Shakespeare Survey* (1952). A study of that paper is well worth while, if only as an exercise in examining the relation between evidence and conclusions. But since it was, I think, unwarily vulnerable, and Dr Walker has more lately stated her case in less vulnerable form in the relevant chapter of her latest book,[1] we can confine our attention to the latter.

The theory is that F was set not from MS., as has hitherto been generally supposed, but from a corrected copy of Q1. The theory has certain obvious attractions, since it was normal practice for F to

1. *Textual Problems of the First Folio* (C.U.P., 1953).

be set from a good quarto where one was available, and the theory brings *Othello* into line with other plays. There are also certain obvious difficulties, amongst others the limited time that elapsed between the printing of Q1 and that of F, and the amount of correction that would be needed to convert Q1 into copy for F, resulting in rather messy copy. There is, however, some evidence that Jaggard's compositors preferred printed copy, even if heavily corrected, to MS. And in general Dr Walker marshals a good deal of persuasive evidence for her theory. I do not propose, for a reason which will appear later, to spend much time in a detailed examination of it. For that the reader may be referred to an admirably cool survey of it by Greg.[1] And in Appendix D, I draw attention to one rock on which the theory seems in danger of foundering.[2]

However, the theory, *per se*, seems of little importance for the determination of the text of *Othello*. The assumed corrections in a printed copy of Q1 did not fall like manna from heaven; they came from some human source, presumably a manuscript source, though a few of them might conceivably have come by word of mouth from Heminge and Condell, or even, at some stage, from Shakespeare himself. What concerns us, then, is the degree of authority which it seems proper to attribute to this source or these sources as compared with that attributable to Q1. And in this connection a considerable section of Dr Walker's chapter, though it has nothing essentially to do with her main theory, becomes of real importance, since she is too considerable a critic for her opinions to be dismissed, however far one thinks they are mistaken.

She starts with the assumption that F is the superior text, and devotes a good deal of space to depreciating Q1, which she finds frequently debased, and debased as a rule by the operation of "memorial contamination". "Vulgarization," she says, "is persistent throughout the quarto." One of the examples adduced in support of this thesis may be examined here; others are examined, with comment, in Appendix D.

At III. iii. 158, after Iago has spent some twenty lines over a refusal, which could have been delivered in one, to let Othello know his thoughts, Othello, in Q1, explodes with "Zouns!" In F he inquires "What dost thou mean?" Dr Walker, having begged the question by saying that Q1 "substitutes" its reading for F's, assures us that F's reading "is dramatically right. Restraint is the dominant trait in Othello's character". Is it? It is a strongly marked trait, but the control is particularly apt to break when he cannot

1. *The Shakespeare First Folio* (Oxford, 1955), pp. 362–70.
2. And see also Appendix C, pp. 216–17.

get a straight answer—a point which Dr Walker seems to miss. "Zouns!", Dr Walker feels, "vulgarizes Shakespeare's Othello". It is possible to feel that F's reading saves Othello from "vulgarization" (if any) at the cost of making him merely silly. It is perfectly obvious what Iago means, namely, in one word, "Shan't!" (though no doubt dressed up in circumlocutory innuendo, with the infuriating implication "but if I would . . ."). Dr Walker continues "The Folio reading, I have no doubt, is Shakespeare's and the quarto's no more than an insensitive effort to remedy by a commonplace expedient what the memory had failed to hold." Would it not be a singularly sieve-like memory that "failed to hold" so straightforward a phrase as "What do you mean?"?

If Dr Walker's examples are the most damaging evidence that can be aimed against Q1, I do not feel that the damage is extensive, and at least two of the shots seem to do more execution by recoil than by propulsion. But this is no more than a difference of opinion, and Dr Walker almost disarms criticism by a sentence in the opening paragraph of her "Conclusion", of which the honesty is as admirable as, in this kind of criticism, it is rare: "My conclusions represent, of course, rationalizations of my own objections to readings such as 'vaunt-couriers of oak-cleaving thunderbolts' or 'go to thy bed and warm thee' in *Lear*, and what is distasteful to one editor may not be equally so to another." None the less, I think that her procedure needs to be challenged. If, whenever a reading is "distasteful", a critic is entitled to summon the currently fashionable factotum djinn "Memorial Contamination" to remove the offending phrase, criticism seems to be out of control and drifting.[1] And I think that Dr Walker is sometimes ready to adopt a method too often observable in modern textual criticism, whereby a hypothesis, at first advanced to explain a particular problem, is later assumed as an axiom of general application.[2]

But I hope it will not be thought, because I have been necessarily concerned with Dr Walker's work on *Othello*, where I think she is at her least happy, that I am blind to the great value of her work in general. Even when she provokes disagreement, it is that best kind of fertile disagreement which compels one to examine one's premises, and may lead to a new line of approach. In particular her

1. Even so, it seems to me uncritical to limit the possibilities of memorial contamination to the unlucky Q1; why should not the process have been operative also in preparing the copy for F?

2. For example (not from Dr Walker) marginal corrections in the MS. are suggested, very properly, as a reasonable explanation of some particular bit of mislineation. But a few pages later we are apt to find mislineation offered as a *proof* of marginal corrections.

work suggests that with some plays a prudent eclecticism between texts is not only permissible to an editor, but obligatory. (I should like to draw especial attention to her chapter on *King Lear*.)

By way of summing up, I will give various views on the texts of *Othello*.

Walker. "We must deduce that both *Othello* texts were marred by negligence in printing, that the manuscript from which the quarto was printed was legibly and possibly professionally written, and that it was marred by memorial errors. . . . What I suppose is that a book-keeper, instructed to make a transcript of the prompt-book, relied so far as he could on what he recollected, or thought he recollected, of the matter and consequently introduced into his work not only some corruptions which had established themselves on the stage . . . but also some nonce readings of his own. . . When the Folio copy for *Othello* was prepared, the quarto was collated with an authoritative manuscript. . . Possibly the manuscript used for collation was fair copy. It is difficult to determine whether the fair copy was autograph since the Folio *Othello* was clearly an edited text. . . There is much that links the Folio *Othello* with the Folio *2 Henry IV*. Both texts are marred by literary pomposity that is not Shakespearian. . . In the literary pretensions of the Folio *Othello* there is naturally some loss. Linguistically neither the quarto nor the Folio gives any impression of immediacy to what Shakespeare wrote. The editorial interference (wherever it originated, whether in the collator's manuscript or with a later editorial hand) is seemingly less than in *2 Henry IV*, but the damage is the greater inasmuch as the Folio text of *Othello* is the authoritative text and must also serve as copy-text."

For the moment I will only comment that I do not feel that the superior "authoritativeness" of the MS. that lies behind F is adequately established.

Chambers. "Q and F are both good and fairly well-printed texts; and they clearly rest substantially upon the same original. . . . The purely verbal variants are very numerous. The great majority are due to different readings of the same word in the original, and generally, but by no means always, F has the better. But sometimes the divergence is greater than mere misreading will explain. There are some 'equivalents' probably due to subconscious substitution. There are some traces of sophistication by the F editor. But I think there must be perversion in Q. There are a good many passages in which more than one word is varied, and here Q often seems to have attempted an emendation of language or metre, or of a phrase found unintelligible, or to have started (iii. 4. 74–5; v. 1. 86) with a misreading and altered the context to suit it. These features suggest a transcriber rather than a printer, and the relation becomes intelligible if we regard F as printed from the original and Q from a not very faithful transcript, without a few passages cut in representation. It must have been an early transcript, in view of the profanities. Whether it was made for stage purposes or for a private collector one can hardly say. The F stage-directions seem to have been altered from those in Q, which are normal. . . The Q stage-directions may well be the author's, but the transcriber might have added some marginal notes for action, not in F."

Greg. [It is impossible in the space at my disposal to do any kind of justice to Greg's analysis of the problem, and his comments on Walker and Chambers. In no piece of his work are his scrupulous attention to detail, his fairness, and his refusal to burke one or other of conflicting pieces of evidence, more clearly and more salutarily displayed. I must content myself with his summary conclusions.] "When all is said it has to be admitted that the evidence for the textual history of *Othello* remains contradictory and ambiguous. In the present state of our knowledge perhaps the following outline seems the most likely. Somewhere about 1620, probably, a transcript was made from the foul papers[1] by a scribe of rather careless habits. He found a good deal of difficulty in interpreting the author's intention in a rather heavily corrected manuscript, and was not always happy in his selection of alternative possibilities. That he had some familiarity with the play on the stage is possible, but uncertain. He was occasionally high-handed and indulged in a certain amount of editing[2] in a literary rather than a theatrical direction. From this transcript Walkley printed his edition early in 1622. . . The text of *Othello* was printed in the Folio about August or September 1623, but the copy had doubtless been prepared some while before. The editors decided to use Q to print from, but they seem to have mistrusted the text—which would be natural if it had been printed from a private transcript not made under their own supervision—for they insisted on its being first collated with the prompt-book. This had, of course, been prepared many years before, presumably by the book-keeper of the time, whom we may assume to have been more successful than the later transcriber in interpreting the author's intention, and who may even

1. For the reader unversed in the vocabulary of textual criticism it should perhaps be explained that "foul papers" means simply the author's original MS. This may have been to any degree heavily corrected, interlineated, and illegible, or it may have been near to a fair copy, but the word "foul" is not, in this context, necessarily pejorative. There is an admirable exposition of the nature of foul papers in Greg's *The Shakespeare First Folio*, p. 106 onwards.

2. See Appendix E.

have had his assistance in the task. The collation generally resulted, therefore, in a considerable improvement of the text, but at the same time in some not very fortunate reduction of the stage-directions. There was a little superficial editing, as generally in the Folio."

It will perhaps be as well, even at the cost of some recapitulation, to preface a consideration of Greg's view by a statement, with a few comments, of the Q1 transcript problem as I see it. The crucial questions about the making of this assumed transcript seem to be (a) When? (b) By whom? (c) From what?

(a) It looks on the face of it as though two transcripts, both made from the foul papers, but one a number of years later than the other, should differ only in proportion to the accuracy of the transcribers, should be, in fact, for practical purposes contemporaneous, so that the actual date of the later transcript matters very little. But that holds only if the later transcriber was a professional scrivener with no more than a slight acquaintance with the play on the boards. If he was the book-keeper, the date matters a great deal; and indeed, if it could be proved both that he was the book-keeper and that he made the transcript long after the play was first produced, anyone who, like myself, is prepared to argue in favour of Q1, would find his arguments falling about his ears. Problem (a) therefore is closely linked with (b). For reasons given below I think that the probabilities are rather against the book-keeper, who would not, I think, even in an early transcript, have allowed indeterminate 'authorial' stage-directions to stand.

(c) From what? It is, I think, very nearly demonstrable that the assumed transcript, whoever made it, and whenever, was made either direct from the foul papers or from another early transcript (e.g. the first prompt-book), made before any modifications had crept in. I cannot see how any transcriber, whether book-keeper or scrivener, faced with "bitter", "foaming", and "loading" (to take only three examples of F readings) could have produced "acerb", "banning", and "lodging". But this does not, of course, put the book-keeper-transcriber out of court, since he might have retained some original readings while betrayed by his memory into modifying others. And I think that the retention of the authorial stage-directions is decisive in favour of the foul papers, and not the first prompt-book, as the source of the transcript.

To come now to Greg's views. It will be noticed that on his hypothesis *both* the assumed transcripts (i.e. that for the private collector and the first prompt-book) derive immediately from the foul papers, and that their comparative degree of authority depends solely on the comparative accuracy of the transcribers. Further, memorial contamination is excluded from the F transcript, since the first prompt-book must have been made before the play went into rehearsal. I think that there must have been some further stage in transmission to account for those verbal variants which can hardly be attributed to mere misreading of a common original by either transcriber. Further, I do not feel happy with the view that a prompt-book lies immediately behind F, in view of the stage-directions, which seem most inconveniently light for stage use, nor with the view that the assumed prompt-book was the first, or at least a very early, one, as "many years before" and "the book-keeper of the time" seem to imply, in view of the divergences. The idea that the Q1 transcript was direct from the foul papers (while highly attractive to anyone who, like myself, has a belief in Q1) presents its own difficulty, that, namely, of the cuts, since these would more probably be made in the prompt-book than in the foul papers. And Greg himself does not, I think, feel very happy about this. He says "A cut text more usually goes back to prompt-copy, but the cuts (except the Willow Song) may have been marked in the foul papers, and if we believe Moseley, it was customary to observe them in private transcripts." "May have been marked" no doubt, but why should they have been? And Moseley's remark, which Greg has quoted earlier, in fact provides no evidence at all on the particular point at issue. He says "When these Comedies and Tragedies [Beaumont and Fletcher's] were presented on the Stage, the Actours omitted some Scenes and Passages (with the Author's consent) as occasion led them; and when private friends desir'd a Copy, they then (and justly too) transcribed what they Acted." But this does not even suggest that they transcribed from foul papers, instead of, more naturally, from the prompt-book which offered precisely "what they Acted". A further question suggests itself: why did Heminge and Condell, when they wanted to correct Q1 by a more authoritative MS., not direct a collation with what, *prima facie*, was the most authoritative of all, the foul papers themselves?[1] Was it perhaps that they regarded the prompt-book as yet more authoritative, representing the play in the shape which it had by then taken, so that, with the cuts reinstated, and after being subjected to their own editing (which I fancy was neither so "super-

1. It is tempting here to add "particularly since they had anyhow to consult the foul papers for the recovery of the cuts". But this argument does not hold water. Theatrical cuts are probably not made till rehearsal shows their desirability; the first prompt-book, therefore, will represent the play in its entirety; the cuts will be indicated as rehearsal proceeds, but the passages will still be there, and recoverable.

ficial" nor so "little" as Greg thinks), it would provide the ideal
text? One last query: why was the assumed Q1 transcript made
from the foul papers? It must, I think, have been made for a private
collector (like those mentioned by Moseley), since there seems
no good reason why the theatre should want a second transcript
besides the prompt-book, and if so, why not transcribe the prompt-
book, which was probably more legible than the foul papers and
would give the private collector what he probably wanted (again
see Moseley), the play as acted. There is, however, one piece of
evidence which tells in favour of the foul papers. It would even seem
possible that Q1 was printed direct from the foul papers, with no
intervening transcript, were it not for the inherent improbability
that Heminge and Condell would hand over the foul papers for the
convenience of a publisher who was going to anticipate their own
edition, whereas Walkley might easily have come by a private
transcript.

In spite of all these doubts and queries, I feel that Greg's theory
probably comes nearer than the others to the truth, though I
should like to suggest one or two modifications in it. The only
serious difficulties in supposing that Q1 derives through a transcript from foul papers have been mentioned, and though I do not
think that Greg wholly solves them, there is, pointing the other way,
one clear piece of evidence. There are in Q1 two stage directions,
at I. iii. 120 and 170, "Exit two or three" and "and the rest", which
cannot, I think, be anything but authorial. Two stage-directions
may seem slender evidence, but I think that though slender it is
unbreakable and decisive; no prompter could let anything so imprecise stand in his prompt-book, even if it ever got there. I should
prefer an earlier date for the transcript than Greg assigns to it,
mainly on grounds of probability. The private collector would be
more likely to want his transcript while the play was new. The evidence for a late date is orthographical, and not I think conclusive—
I should echo Fredson Bowers' query[1] whether the spellings may
not as well be compositorial as transcriptorial. One may relevantly
ask a further question. If the transcriber was the book-keeper, why
should he, when asked to make a transcript, go to the trouble of
unearthing the foul papers, when he had ready at hand the prompt-
book that he was familiar with?

On the prompt-book source for F, Greg is, I think, less secure
because he perhaps over-simplifies the problem. The original
prompt-book, made from the foul papers as soon as they were
handed in, was most unlikely to differ from any other early tran-

1. Greg, *op. cit.*, p. 357, n. 6

script (whether by professional scrivener or by book-keeper), except for a certain number of verbal variants, where one or other transcriber had succeeded in decipherment where the other had failed (or both failed but with different results), and for such alterations in stage-directions as the prompter foresaw were going to be necessary for his purpose. There had as yet—a crucial point—been no time for the memorial contamination which arises from familiarity with the play on the stage. If this original prompt-book was anywhere near to Q1 (and though I admit that the "if" is a large one, I hope I have said enough to show that the supposition is at least tenable) to turn it into copy which would produce F, even apart from final editorial alterations, a good deal must have happened to it. I am inclined to assume a second transcript, made from the original prompt-book, and made either to serve as a fresh prompt-book because the old one was messy or was getting worn out, or perhaps, more probably, requested by Heminge and Condell so that they could have a clean copy on which to conduct their final editorial process. Now this second transcript would inevitably embody the divergencies from Q1, whether additions or alterations made by Shakespeare himself, to colour a colourless part, or actors' requests which he accepted; there would also, if the second transcript was made by the prompter, be almost certainly some memorial contamination (which now becomes transferred from Q1 to F). When Heminge and Condell had finished with it, this second transcript would provide exactly the sort of "composite" text with which I think F presents us. This, of course, is no more than an embroidery, perhaps a fanciful one, on Greg's theory, which I believe to be right. It also leaves untouched the problem of the F stage-directions, for which I can offer no solution.

In conclusion, then, I think that in Q1, amplified by the reinstatement of the cuts, we have as near an approximation as we are likely to get to the play as Shakespeare first wrote it, with nothing between us and him but the blunders of honest but not always skilful transcriber and compositor. On the other hand, I think that in F we have probably a good deal of Shakespeare's second thoughts, but also, almost certainly, a good deal of divergence from the original for which he was not responsible. And with each individual instance of divergence we are left to guess-work selection of the source, Shakespeare, the actors, memorial contamination, editorial sophistication. We are, in fact, I think, if I may revert for a moment to my earlier parallel, much in the position we should be in with *The Eve of St Agnes* if we had never seen the holograph or any of the three transcripts, and had nothing but two texts, one printed from Woodhouse's first transcript, and that of 1820.

And even if we could, by some touchstone more reliable than personal taste, determine which, if any, of F's divergences from Q1 are Shakespeare's own, should we feel bound to admit them to our text? Second thoughts are not always improvements, least of all when they are the outcome of a sudden mood or of a secondary design. Keats' revised conclusion to *St Agnes* is quite out of key, and, even though he intended the discord, most readers will acquiesce in the publishers' decision to retain the original ending; and it is very doubtful whether the 1850 version of *The Prelude* is artistically an "improvement" on that of 1805. At any rate it is surely wiser to read the earlier version first and then study the alterations of the later, than to reverse the process, as most readers do (and till thirty years ago all but a very few readers were compelled to do), and accept 1850 as the only text that matters, with occasional reference to 1805.[1]

I think that F is sometimes an 'improvement' on Q1, sometimes very much the reverse. I am not at all maintaining that F may not be a 'better' (in a loose sense) text, even in places a more Shakespearean text. But I *am* maintaining that, since the judgement of 'improvements' is a matter of purely personal opinion, and we have no means at all of deciding where the improvements came from, with F we do not know where we are, whereas with Q1 we do. And that, therefore, it is much more helpful to the reader to give him Q1, cured of obvious errors, and let him make up his own mind which of the divergences of F he will admit to the final text that he makes for himself.

In this edition, therefore, the text is a great deal nearer to Q1 than has of late been customary.[2] I have no doubt that I am, like Dr Walker, rationalizing personal preferences. But I have done my best honestly to draw attention to divergences, with some com-

---

1. de Selincourt's analysis of the various MSS. in his great edition of *The Prelude* is full of interest and instruction for textual students in other fields.

2. I say "of late" because both Johnson and Malone adhered more closely to Q1 than most of their successors. To take only two examples, both at I. i. 10 read "Oft capp'd" (Q1) rather than "Off-capp'd" (F), and Malone makes the interesting comment "This [the F] reading I once thought to be the true one. But a more intimate knowledge of the quarto copies has convinced me that they ought not without very strong reason to be departed from"; and at II. i. 65 both read "Does bear all excellency", though Johnson, quoting the F reading in a note, makes the even more interesting comment "This is the best reading, and that which the author substituted in his revisal"—making it plain that he took a "revisal" to be established fact.

ments which, even if subconsciously biased, may help any reader towards his own considered judgement.

4. THE PLAY AND THE CHARACTERS

Bradley thought *King Lear* Shakespeare's greatest work but not his best play, and most readers will concur in the judgement. *Othello*, to most readers, is not his greatest work, but is his best play, in the narrow sense of 'theatre' probably much his best. It has neither the variety nor the depth of *Hamlet*, none of the overwhelming power of *Lear*, none of that 'atmosphere' which in *Macbeth* keeps us awfully hovering on the confines of a world outside that of our normal experience, none of the sweep and exultant power of *Antony and Cleopatra*; nor has it that range in time which marks all the other four. But its grip upon the emotions of the audience is more relentless and sustained than that of the others. The plot is completely simple, with no sub-plot and no distractions; the number of characters presented is small; above all, from the moment of the landing in Cyprus the action moves fast, and the tension steadily mounts, with hardly an instant's relaxation, till the moment at which Othello kills himself; finally, the play is the nearest approach which Shakespeare made to a 'domestic' tragedy.

To take these points in order:

1. The plot is simple. A man, disappointed of promotion which he thought he had a right to expect, determines on revenge, and in part secures it. Or, in expanded form: An ensign, expecting promotion to a vacant lieutenancy, is exasperated when his general appoints another man over his head. He determines to revenge himself on the general and secure the dismissal of his rival. By a series of adroit moves he persuades the general of the adultery of the general's wife with the lieutenant. As a result the general kills first his wife and then himself, but the ensign fails in the second part of his design, since the plot is disclosed, the lieutenant receives yet further promotion, and he himself faces trial and torture. Nothing could be simpler, and when a story is that of a 'plot' in the sense of a scheme, proceeding by a series of linked moves towards a designed end, it provides ready-made a 'plot' in the dramatic sense. And when the scheme is largely concerned with one of the strongest and most distressing of human emotions, the plot is likely to be a 'powerful' one. It will be observed that none of the other three 'great' tragedies has much of a plot in this sense, and that *Antony and Cleopatra* has even less. *Hamlet* has the makings of a first-rate plot, an encounter à outrance between two mighty opposites, in

which we should watch move and counter-move with excitement, a plot in which the devising and execution of the play-scene would be a well-forged link. But as it is, owing to Hamlet's state of mind, the moves are all on one side, and the play-scene leads to nothing in action, only to intellectual confirmation. In *King Lear* the two sub-plots have a firm structure, with development and resolution, but the main action is not properly a plot at all, merely the progress, through madness to recovered sanity and a new sense of reality, of the great central figure. In *Macbeth* the only thing that can be called a plot is the murder of Duncan, and this comes so early, is so suddenly devised and hurriedly executed, that it does not seriously engage our interest and serves mainly as a starting point for the main action, which is concerned with the deterioration and steady progress to downfall of the two main figures. *Antony and Cleopatra* is deliberately episodic. In all four plays what grips our interest is, I think, the *characters*; we are not asking "what will the next move be?", "will he see the danger before it is too late?", but rather "what kind of people are these?", "what kind of people are they going to be by the end of the play?"; and the *events* are not a skilfully wrought concatenation, but are linked, if at all, by mere succession in time. In none of them is there that implication followed by explication which Aristotle thought one of the features of great tragedy, and of which, incidentally, Shakespeare was himself a master in another kind of play. *The Merchant of Venice*, *Much Ado*, and *Measure for Measure* have all theatrically effective plots. But Shakespeare used this form only once in high tragedy, and this is where *Othello* differs in structure and in effect from the others. This is not to say that *Othello* is either 'better' or 'worse' than the others; but it belongs to a different order of play, that order of which, ever since it was written, *Oedipus Tyrannus* has been justly held the great exemplar.

2. *Number of characters.* If we make a merely numerical count of those characters who in ordinary editions appear 'above the line' —i.e. excluding such people as Lords, Attendants, Murderers, "other apparitions", and so on, the result is interesting, though somewhat misleading: *Hamlet* 25, *King Lear* 20, *Macbeth* 24, *Antony and Cleopatra* 33, *Othello* 13. The count is misleading because a number of the minor, though named, characters do little more than "fill up the cry", even though, by mere weight of numbers and by producing often a well-filled stage, they do produce an appreciable effect. If however we confine ourselves to those characters who are either 'main' or who interest us enough to distract our attention, even for short periods, from the main figures, we get a different, but

still striking count. The selection must be arbitrary and largely personal, but my own count would be: *Hamlet* 12, *King Lear* 11, *Macbeth* 9, *Antony and Cleopatra* 11, *Othello* 7.

3. *Rapidity of action.* If we may regard Act I as being structurally in the nature of a prologue, *Othello* comes much nearer than any of Shakespeare's other great plays except *The Tempest* to observing the unities. The action in Cyprus occupies something a little less than thirty-six hours (see p. lxviii), and since some eight of those hours are compressed into one scene (II. iii) the audience's impression is of even shorter time. Now the 'rules' of the unities, codified by precisians from what Aristotle did not say but what they wanted him to have said, have provoked a deal of discussion, most of it I think much too categorical and one-sided. To the critics who believe in them they have been the law and the prophets; any play, if is it to be worth the name, must observe them. To others—notably to Johnson enjoying himself in running counter to generally accepted opinion—they are contrary to common sense, of negligible importance, and so not worth bothering about. Dryden, the craftsman, characteristically talks sense, and amusing sense, about them. The truth surely is, as so often with aesthetic questions which generate a great deal of heat, that "it all depends". If you want to produce a particular effect, you observe them; if you want to produce a different effect, you may wisely neglect them (the story of Antony and Cleopatra, for example, can hardly be handled in terms of the unities without losing its possibilities for grandeur, as Dryden found to his cost); and indeed there may be inherent in your plot the demand that you *must* neglect them (as in *Mary Rose* or *Milestones*).

But if the dramatist is aiming at intensity, he is almost certainly wise to adhere to the unity of time, since even a brief interval of imagined time allows the audience a respite for recuperation, and certainly wise to adhere to the unity of action, since a sub-plot provides the relief of temporary diversion of interest. And though the unity of place is probably less important, the adherence even to that helps, since it stimulates that natural, if irrationally claustrophobic, reaction of "we can't get out", which, at a lower level, the detective story writer exploits when he gets his characters snowed up for three days in a lonely shooting-lodge.

At all events, by whatever means, observance of the unities, short list of dramatis personae, almost complete absence of 'comic relief', and the very nature of the plot, Shakespeare achieves a tension far more tautly strained than that in any other of his plays.

4. *A domestic tragedy.* The figures are of lower rank, less removed

from ordinary life, than in the other tragedies. In those others we have a king, the ghost of another king, lately dead, a queen, and a prince; a king, three princesses, and two dukes; a king, soon murdered, a usurping king and queen, and two princes, one of whom succeeds to the crown; a queen and the two great rivals for the rulership of the world. In *Othello* the figure in the highest station is the "Duke" of Venice, who is no more than a figure-head, and apart from him we have a senator and his daughter, and three army officers, one of the highest rank. This, I think, makes more difference in impression than we always realize. It is no doubt true, as Johnson said, that Shakespeare, though he deals with kings and queens, thinks only on men; but, none the less, very high rank does, if only subconsciously, diminish our feeling of intimacy, lessens our feeling of "There, but for the grace of God . . .", and thereby makes the impact not less great but less stabbing. Further, in the other tragedies we are made aware that the fates of the characters, though they affect us by sympathy for them as individual men and women, affect also the destinies of kingdoms and peoples. It is noteworthy that all these other tragedies end with the re-establishment of ordered government, the note of "The king's government must be carried on." This is not true of *Othello*. It is no doubt an inconvenience for the Venetian state to be deprived of the services of its greatest general, but there is no more to it than that, and so we are left free to follow simply the disastrous fortunes of people like ourselves, and one of them caught in the cruel grip of an emotion to which we are all liable. There are few of us liable to be called upon to avenge the murder of a royal father, to be prompted by ambition to murder a king for his crown, to resign our crowns, or to waste outstanding talents and sacrifice the rule of half the world for love of a queen; but we are all liable to blinding jealousy. The effect of *Othello* upon us, though achieved with infinitely greater mastery and subtlety, is nearer, I think, than that of any other of Shakespeare's plays to the effect of Webster's two tragedies. Much in Shakespeare is clean outside Webster's range, but Webster can make us wince and shudder with a clean cut into the quick of emotion as Shakespeare seldom does or aims to do. In his other tragedies we are spectators; the spectacle may be in the highest degree terrifying, soul-searching, and in the end uplifting; but do we ever feel that we want to participate in it, to speak to the characters, to advise them or warn them? We watch the action; but in *Othello* we are involved in it.

There is an oddity about the opening of the play which is worth a moment's notice. In three of the other four tragedies hitherto mentioned, we are introduced to the main figure quite early, either by name and comment or by his own entrance, and, further, what comment is made creates expectations which are in accord with the impression produced by the character himself. We are introduced to Macbeth by name within thirty lines, and are given a very clear and even elaborate picture of the valiant and trusted general, though he does not himself enter till a hundred lines later. When he does, there is at least nothing in the impression he produces discordant with what has been said. In *King Lear* the king is mentioned, without comment, in the opening line, and enters himself, in full royalty, at the thirty-sixth. Antony's entrance is the earliest of all. We are given "our general" in the first line, followed by pictures of him both as he was and (rather distemperedly) as he is, and he enters, with Cleopatra, at the tenth line. Hamlet's entry is, for a deliberate purpose, much longer delayed. The first scene, of considerable length, is occupied with the creation of atmosphere, with exposition of the reasons for the post haste and romage, and with the appearance of a dead king's ghost. No mention is made of Hamlet till the end of the scene, but then specifically, by name, as the dead king's son, though no comment is made on him except that the ghost will speak to him. And Hamlet does not speak till sixty lines on in the next scene, where again he is introduced by name, and as the reigning king's cousin and son.

Now look at the difference in *Othello*. There come on to the stage two men, one a soldier, the other a young exquisite. They are discussing something which is vaguely alluded to as "this" and "such a matter" and is never further defined. They pass to the discussion of an equally indeterminate person alluded to as "he" and "him". We can infer (from "make me his lieutenant") that "he" is an officer of high rank, and we are told later that he is a "Moor". The soldier, who by now has a name, draws a singularly unflattering picture of him. He loves his own pride and purposes, he uses bombast circumstance, he stuffs his speech with epithets of war, he makes a thoroughly bad appointment out of favouritism, he is an old black ram and a Barbary horse, he is lascivious and an extravagant and wheeling stranger of here and everywhere (these last two items from Roderigo). All we have to set against this is an inference of our own that "he" is a man who knows his own mind, since he non-suits three great ones, and an admission by Iago that the state cannot with safety cast him, since they have no one else of "his fathom". It is true that Iago is clearly suffering from a rankling sense of injury, which is not calculated to make him fair, but the picture which we get, and not unjustifiably think we are intended to get, is surely that of an efficient, perhaps even great, but blustering and erratic, soldier of fortune, of no morals and unsound judgement. After 184 lines of these preliminaries "he" (he does not, by the way, get a name till well on in the third scene) at last enters; and the whole picture at once falls to pieces. The only bits of it that remain are his pride (I. ii. 18-24), though even that is of a different kind from that suggested by Iago, and his importance to the state (ll. 36-47). Otherwise he is quiet, laconic ("'Tis better as it is", "Not I, I must be found"), dignified, courteous, and controlled ("Keep up your bright swords, for the dew will rust 'em. Good signior, you shall more command with years Than with your weapons"). Now Shakespeare, being so assured and so skilful a craftsman, did not introduce his hero in this unusual way by accident;[1] he was aiming at something, and it is our business to find out, if we can, what this something was. I suggest that he achieved three things. First, and least important, he makes us distrust Iago even more than we should do in any case from his account of himself (I. i. 49-65). Second, I hope the parallel does not seem too far-fetched if I suggest that he is playing the same trick, or using the same device, though by very different, and subtler, technical means, as he used in the opening scene of *Hamlet*; he is, from the outset, creating suspense. When, in the audience, we are, perhaps rather irritatedly, asking ourselves "What is the unspecified 'this' and 'such a matter'? Who, and what like of a man, is the innominate 'he' that they are talking about?" we are not sitting in only half-attentive leisure, taking in a piece of necessary but unstimulating 'exposition'; we are being stimulated to a mood of uneasy expectation. Third, and I think the most important, we are forced, when "he" does enter, to make our own picture of "him" for ourselves by the mere fact that the picture which we may have been inclined to accept is so manifestly a caricature. And it will be noticed that Shakespeare, in the remainder of the first act, gives us every possible help in making the true picture, which is all the more indelible because it has had to be made after an erasure of presuppositions.

I think that what else I have to say about the play can be best said in the course of an examination of some of the characters.

Othello. It is perhaps as well to take first the question of Othello's colour, not only because it has been much disputed but because the picture we make as we read, or have presented to us upon the stage, of Othello's physical appearance is of real importance for the un-

1. One may notice that, pursuing the same tactics, he introduces his heroine in the same anonymous way, without even explaining how she comes into the picture (l. 74, "her father's house").

derstanding of the play. Much argument, and an even more plentiful lack of it, has been devoted to showing that Othello was not black, or alternatively that he was at least not what Coleridge calls a "veritable negro", but rather, like the Prince of Morocco in a Q stage-direction in *The Merchant of Venice*, a "tawny Moor"—Coleridge, rather surprisingly, admits the blackness but insists that he was a Moor in our sense of the word. The reductio ad absurdum of this line of criticism was achieved by a lady writing from Maryland, who said, "In studying the play of *Othello*, I have always *imagined* its hero *a white* man. It is true the dramatist paints him black, but this shade does not suit the man. It is a stage decoration, which *my taste* discards; a fault of colour from an artistic point of view. I have, therefore, as I have before stated in *my readings* of this play, dispensed with it. Shakespeare was too correct a delineator of human nature to have coloured Othello *black*, if he had personally acquainted himself with the idiosyncrasies of the African race.

"We may regard, then, the daub of black upon Othello's portrait as an *ebullition* of fancy, a *freak* of imagination,—the visionary conception of an ideal figure,—one of the few erroneous strokes of the great master's brush, the *single* blemish on a faultless work.

"Othello *was* a *white* man."[1]

Now a good deal of the trouble arises, I think, from a confusion of colour and contour. To a great many people the word "negro" suggests at once the picture of what they would call a "nigger", the woolly hair, thick lips, round skull, blunt features, and burnt-cork blackness of the traditional nigger minstrel. Their subconscious generalization is as silly as that implied in Miss Preston's "the African race" or Coleridge's "veritable negro". There are more races than one in Africa, and that a man is black in colour is no reason why he should, even to European eyes, look sub-human. One of the finest heads I have ever seen on any human being was that of a negro conductor on an American Pullman car. He had lips slightly thicker than an ordinary European's, and he had somewhat curly hair; for the rest he had a long head, a magnificent forehead, a keenly chiselled nose, rather sunken cheeks, and his expression was grave, dignified, and a trifle melancholy. He was coal-black, but he might have sat to a sculptor for a statue of Caesar, or, so far as appearance went, have played a superb Othello.

Now, for the moment leaving criticism on one side (though I shall return to Coleridge later), let us look for the available evidence in the only place where it is worth looking for it, not in the

1. Miss Preston (see Furness' Variorum edn, p. 395).

prejudices of critics but in Shakespeare himself. And, to begin with, let us glance at the other important "Moor" in Shakespeare, not often enough, I think, considered in this connection, probably because he comes in a play little liked and little read. Aaron in *Titus Andronicus* is regularly described as a "Moor". Here are the phrases which he himself uses to describe himself and his child: "My fleece of woolly hair" (II. iii. 34); "Aaron will have his soul black like his face" (III. i. 205); "Coal-black is better than another hue" (IV. ii. 100); "Look how the black slave smiles upon the father" (IV. ii. 121); "you thick-lipp'd slave" (IV. ii. 177). And the phrases used about him by other people, whatever allowance one makes for the prejudice of enemies, are confirmatory: "swarth Cimmerian", "her raven-coloured love", "a coal-black Moor". The only apparently dissonant word is Aaron's (reported) address to his child at v. i. 27 as "tawny" and since this is followed five lines later by "coal-black calf" it is perhaps a more significant pointer to the colour of the Prince of Morocco than to that of Aaron and his child. It is true that Shakespeare could use "black" by itself to mean "dark", brunette rather than blonde, usually in an uncomplimentary sense, but he could not, I think, so use such compounds as "coal-black" and "raven-coloured", and there is no getting round the fleece of woolly hair, so that these passages seem to put it beyond doubt that Shakespeare used, or could use, "Moor" to mean "blackamoor" (which is how Aaron's child is described in a stage-direction). Aaron then was "a veritable negro"; but he is a man of importance and he is the paramour of a white empress.

And now for Othello. Othello's comments on his own appearance are few: "I am black" (III. iii. 267); "begrim'd, and black As mine own face" (III. iii. 393); and the comments made by others on his colour are not frequent though they are all in a tale. "Thick-lips", "old black ram", "sooty bosom", "your son-in-law is far more fair than black". Now it may be observed that to give an insult any point and barb it must have some relation to the facts. A woman may call a pale-complexioned rival "pasty" or "whey-faced", but it would be silly to call her swarthy, just as it would be silly for Lysander to repulse Hermia as "Ethiop" and "tawny Tartar" unless she was dark, or for Helena to call her "little" and Lysander "minimus", "bead", and "acorn" if she had the stature of an Amazon. In the same way, "thicklips" would lose all its venom if it could not be recognizably applicable to Othello's mouth, if he had had the sort of mouth of, for example, Bellini's Doge, which one could derogatorily describe as "thin-lipped". And I think that the general impression of the phrases quoted is

that Othello was a negro. But the evidence is much slighter than
that for Aaron, and there are two words which point in the opposite
direction, "Barbary" and "Mauritania"; a "Barbary" horse is
what we should call an Arab, and Mauritania is the land of the
Moors. It is true that Iago's statement that Othello and Desdemona
are going into Mauritania is a lie, for the benefit of Roderigo, since
we know that Othello is being recalled to Venice, but it is unlike
Iago to tell stupid lies, and, unless he means not that Othello is
going home but merely that he is being transferred to another
appointment, he might just as well have said "Ethiopia".

So far, then, the evidence is somewhat indecisive. But there is
another aspect of the problem which has to be considered. What is
the general impression which the unprejudiced reader receives?
And here several of the critics who are seeking to show that Shakespeare cannot have meant Othello to be a negro seem to me to use
arguments which in fact strengthen the very assumption which
they are trying to destroy. Coleridge serves well as an example. He
says "It would be something monstrous to conceive this beautiful
Venetian girl falling in love with a veritable negro. It would argue
a disproportionateness, a want of balance, in Desdemona, which
Shakespeare does not appear to have in the least contemplated."
But that is precisely what, in the opinion of observers, it *does* argue,
and what, for the right appreciation of the two characters concerned, and of some of Iago's suggestions, it *should* argue. Roderigo
regards Desdemona's marriage as a gross revolt; Brabantio sees in
it a treason of the blood for which only her subjugation by charms
can account, and for which she will incur a general mock; nature,
he says, could not err so preposterously sans witchcraft; and Iago,
later, using almost Coleridge's words, says that one may smell
in such a marriage foul disproportion, thoughts unnatural. Even
Desdemona herself thinks that some explanation, if not defence, of
her conduct, of her "downright violence and scorn [or "storm"] of
fortunes", is appropriate, and says that she saw Othello's visage in
his mind. It is of the very essence of the play that Desdemona in
marrying Othello—a man to whom her 'natural' reaction should
(her father holds) have been fear, not delight—has done something peculiarly startling; and it would seem, therefore, that the
'disproportion', which only profound love can override, should,
from the purely dramatic point of view, be stressed, not minimized.
I feel, therefore, that Othello should be imagined in reading, and
presented on the stage, as coal-black, a negro, though not at all
necessarily of the particular negroid type which Coleridge presumably had in mind when he spoke of a "veritable" negro. But if it

is thought that such a presentation on the stage will, with a particular type of audience (one with a stronger sense of colour-bar than
we may suppose the Elizabethan audience to have had, say an
audience in the southern states of America), evoke a reaction of
disgust at Desdemona rather than one of startled sympathy and
admiration, then the presentation had better no doubt be modified,
since that reaction is certainly not what Shakespeare intended and
knew would be evoked in his own audience.

And now, what of the man himself, whatever his colour? In the
first place he is of high rank. There is no reason to distrust his own
statement of his royal descent. It is true that Coleridge asks whether
we can imagine Shakespeare so utterly ignorant as to make a barbarous negro plead royal birth—implying apparently that all
"negroes" are *ipso facto* "barbarous". But the modern reader, with
Toussaint L'Ouverture and John Laputa in mind, is not likely to
regard blackness of complexion, in fact or in fiction, as incom-
patible with high rank or blood royal. At all events he is the great
general of the Venetian state. He is "the noble Moor whom our full
senate Call all-in-all sufficient." Montano, a man "of most allowed
sufficiency" welcomes his appointment as a "worthy governor",
"For I have serv'd him, and the man commands Like a full
soldier". And it is to be noticed that no one, not even the distracted
Brabantio, suggests that Desdemona has lowered herself *socially* by
her marriage.

That he is dignified, and, normally, controlled, we can see for
ourselves in the earlier part of the play. We can see also that he is
profoundly in love with Desdemona, and our impression receives
confirmation from an unexpected quarter. Iago, though in the
same sentence he repeats that he cannot endure him, describes him
as of a constant, noble, loving nature, and his real prognosis for the
marriage—as distinct from the false one for Roderigo's benefit, and
apart from the poison he proposes to instil—is of the happiest:
"I dare think he'll prove to Desdemona A most dear husband."

But he has some vulnerable, and in certain circumstances very
dangerous, weaknesses. In the first place his intellectual power is
nowhere near on a par with his other qualities. "Whenever he
thinks he is a child" and not even a very intelligent child. It is
the fashion nowadays to discover 'themes' in Shakespeare's plays.
I believe that it is as a rule an unprofitable occupation, since I
think that Shakespeare's mind did not, as Ibsen's did, work along
those lines, and that therefore over-emphasis on a supposed theme
is liable to obscure things more important. But if I were challenged
to produce a 'theme' for *Othello* I should suggest "Reason versus

Instinct". Whenever Othello trusts his instinct he is almost invariably right ("If she be false, oh then Heaven mocks itself. I'll not
believe it"); whenever he thinks, or fancies himself to be thinking,
he is almost invariably and ruinously wrong.

His control, though strong, is far from unbreakable. He knows
this himself, as appears in the scene of the cashiering of Cassio, and
Iago not only knows it but knows also what is most certain to cause
the break. Othello is simple and straightforward himself, and he
demands simple straightforwardness in others, leading to perception of the truth, to certainty. He cannot endure to feel baffled, and,
when he does, passion not only assays to lead the way but succeeds.
He would always echo the cry of Ajax for light.

> Ζεῦ πάτερ, ἀλλὰ σὺ ῥῦσαι ὑπ' ἠέρος υἶας Ἀχαιῶν,
> ποίησον δ' αἴθρην, δὸς δ' ὀφθαλμοῖσιν ἰδέσθαι·
> ἐν δὲ φάει καὶ ὄλεσσον.

It is this that lies behind perhaps the most terrible of his lines, the
more terrible because it is so wholly in character, "Villain, be sure
thou prove my love a whore." Even that black certainty would be
better than doubt.

His "free and open nature" carries unsuspicious trust to the
frontiers of folly, and will, granted enough skill in the leader, "as
tenderly be led by the nose As asses are."

He is unduly sensitive and humble about his own deficiencies in
certain fields, particularly his own inexperience in the world of
society.

Finally, is he a jealous man? This may seem a surprising question
to ask about the hero of a play of which jealousy is the obvious
driving force, a man whose passionate sexual jealousy, once roused,
is insensately uncontrollable and brings catastrophe. But it is not
an absurd question, and the answer to it is of central importance to
the right understanding of the play. Shakespeare drew two pictures of "the jealous man", one in the near-tragic part of a tragi-
comedy, the other in a light comedy. Both Leontes and Ford,
surely, are utterly different from Othello. In both of them jealousy,
perhaps the ignoblest, as it is certainly one of the most ravaging, of
human emotions, is in grain. They are of those jealous souls of
whom Emilia speaks; who "are not ever jealous for the cause, But
jealous for they are jealous." They offer ever-renewed meat for the
green-eyed monster to mock and feed on, a sort of degraded Pro-
metheuses. Othello is no Leontes, no Ford; and one of the proofs of
this is that, if he were, the play would be far less moving than in fact
it is. To watch a jealous man wrung by the spasms of one of his re-

current seizures may provoke laughter of an acrid and ashamed kind, or it may be merely repellent. What we are watching in *Othello* is something different, a man of essential nobility debased by humiliating passion to a level not far above the animal, a level far lower than that to which any of Shakespeare's other heroes sink. The spectacle is pitiful, but because of the essential nobility which we never quite forget, and also because it is in part his good qualities which make possible the plot for his downfall, it is also tragic. And in the brief interval between his belated conviction of the truth and his death he recaptures all our earlier admiration and more than our earlier sympathy.

But even though he is not "a jealous man" it is idle to deny, as one or two critics have attempted to deny, that he is, for a considerable part of the play, dominated by jealousy. He is not only dominated but distorted by a barbaric crazed fury of physical jealousy, the jealousy that is the counterpart of lust, not that which is the counterpart of love. But part of the very power of jealousy over him is that it is to him an unfamiliar emotion which he has no notion how to handle. Loss of control in other spheres he has experienced, can foresee, and can guard against; but not in this sphere. Here, if control is once lost, it is lost beyond all recovery. What then is it that makes him such malleable material for Iago to work on? It is credulity, not innate jealousy. He thinks men honest that but seem to be so. When he describes himself at the end as one not easily jealous, but being wrought, perplex'd in the extreme, he is near the truth; had he said "not naturally" rather than "not easily" he would have hit the centre. Even as it is, a "wright" less horribly skilful than Iago would have had difficulty in rousing him to jealousy. And we should not allow ourselves to be trapped into thinking Othello's credulity merely silly, a view into which Stoll does his best to trap us. No doubt Emilia's strictures are a relief to our pent-up emotions, but if we really, and for more than a moment, agree that Othello is no more than a fool, a gull, and a dolt, much of our sympathy for him evaporates and the tragedy is enfeebled. Now Stoll makes a very remarkable judgement, which would, if it were not for evidence to the contrary, make one think that he had never read the play with any attention. He says this:[1] "Othello believes a person whom he does not love or really know and has no right reason to trust, to the point of disbelieving persons whom he loves and has every reason to trust." It would be hard to compress more mis-statement into thirty-four words. Othello "does not love" Iago. Verbally true, since Othello does not use the

1. *Art and Artifice in Shakespeare*, E. E. Stoll (C.U.P. 1934), p. 7.

word to Iago as he does to Cassio. But Othello is on intimate terms with him, can, in Iago's view, be brought to love him, and receives Iago's proffered love with acceptance bounteous. Othello "does not really know" Iago. I am not clear what the force of "really" is, unless it is to be a possible loophole; but he certainly knows Iago moderately well, since his eyes have seen the proof of him at Rhodes, at Cyprus, and on other grounds, Christian and heathen— Iago, that is, has served under Othello for a considerable period, and Othello "knows" him well enough to have summed him up as a man of honesty and trust to whose conveyance he is ready to assign his wife. (And Stoll at any rate cannot dismiss Iago's remark as fiction, since he advances as fact the doubtful thesis that any-thing said in soliloquy, or said by one character about another, is to be believed.) Othello "has no right reason to trust" Iago. Well, he has about as much, or as little, reason for trusting him as most of us have for trusting those of our friends whom we do trust, namely that he has never found cause for distrust; and he has had plenty of opportunity for testing Iago, as his subordinate, in conditions which are apt to reveal untrustworthiness. Even within the limits of the play it is Iago, as the loyal subordinate, who brings him news of the raised father and his friends; and Othello could cite everyone else's estimate of Iago to support his own. On the other side we are told that Othello "disbelieves persons whom he loves and has every reason to trust." Othello does love Cassio, and has, we may sup-pose, reason to trust him; but he never "disbelieves" him in any ordinary sense of the word, since—and it is a point of the utmost importance for the plot—he never gives him a chance of making a statement which could be either believed or disbelieved, till the very end, and then his answer is unhesitating, "I do believe it". But it is quite true that he is decoyed into suspecting Cassio. He does not love Emilia (except in Iago's sense if we believe Iago's sus-picion to be fact), and whether he has any right reason for trusting her we have no means of knowing; but he certainly disbelieves her (at the opening of the brothel scene), or, perhaps it would be truer to say, shuts his mind against believing her. He passionately loves Desdemona, and he both disbelieves her (over the handkerchief, and here justly) and suspects her. But to say that he has every reason to trust her is clean contrary to the presented facts. The actual wooing, after a number of visits of formal courtesy on Brabantio's invitation, is represented as a somewhat whirlwind affair, and after the marriage they have only a few hours together before they meet in Cyprus. He has had no chance to "know" her, "really" or otherwise, and therefore has no *reason* at all to trust her

—only instinct; and indeed his ignorance of her is precisely one of those chinks in his armour which Iago's poisoned stiletto so unerringly finds.

I have spent some time over Stoll's judgement, not for the sake of attacking him—I think many of his ideas mistaken, but many of them also, even if only by provoking reaction, illuminating—but because this is just one of those superficial judgements to which, or to something like which, we are apt to be led, not only with *Othello* but with other plays. And we are led into error not necessarily because we read superficially—we can read with real care and yet go wrong—but often because we do not allow for the fact that we know the characters so much better than they know each other. We know that Desdemona is true, and are exasperated with Othello for not being equally sure of it; we know that Iago is a villain (since we have had the advantage of hearing him think aloud) and consider Othello a blind gull to think him an honest man. But unless we keep this danger in mind, and continuously in mind, we seriously diminish for ourselves the greatness of the play, since a tragedy in which the main figure is, in plain terms, a credulous ass, is a bad tragedy, even though it may be raised by an effective plot to crudely effective melodrama, or to what Rymer called it, a "bloody farce".

The progress of Othello's downfall, and his slow rise, what one might call the graph of his emotions, is worth some attention, for there is a period in it which sometimes, I think, escapes notice; his recovery, both of his own self-control and of our sympathies, begins a good deal earlier than is often supposed.

For the first two acts and the first two scenes of the third, we see him as the great general, the trusted servant of the state, and, though less fully drawn, as the devoted lover and husband. Shakespeare, by every means in his power, stresses Othello's greatness as a public figure. This phase ends with a very brief scene (III. ii), which, like a number of others in Shakespeare, appears at first sight to have little purpose but on examination is seen to have much. No doubt one use of it is simply to assure us that Othello is out of the way while Cassio makes his plea to Desdemona. But there is more to it than that. For the last time we see Othello as the general. He is the military governor, making his report to the state, and then, without a care in the world, except some distress over Cassio's cashiering, pursuing his professional business, making an inspection of the fortifications of his command. And then within a hundred lines he is on the rack, later in the same scene his occupation's gone, and by the end of it he has determined on the deaths of both Cassio and

Desdemona, and Chaos is come again. But he still maintains some
sort of control. One or two of Iago's sudden touches on the levers
wring from him incoherent exclamations, but he can still try to
think, he can plan revenge, and he can still express himself in great
poetry. Then, after a brief interval (III. iv. 1–27), there comes a
short passage (ll. 28–95) which in a way epitomizes the progress
of the much longer preceding scene and carries it a little further.
He begins with at least enough control to dissemble; the mention
of Cassio reminds him of the handkerchief, but he can still express
himself in coherent poetry; but then the control begins to break and
in steadily less governable fury he can do little more than ejaculate
"The handkerchief" till he flings out with an oath. Then after
another short interval he reaches his nadir. With Iago's final
wrench on the levers, his brutally casual "With her, on her, what
you will," Othello lapses into almost incoherent ravings, hardly
any longer a human being, little better than a slavering mad dog.
But when he recovers from his fit there is surely a very marked
change. And it is this change that is not, I think, always observed,
partly because by no means all actors present it clearly. He watches
the Iago–Cassio interview comparatively coolly; he even draws
conclusions from it, hopelessly wrong though those conclusions are;
his first words after Cassio's exit are a practical question as to ways
and means; his heart is turned to stone; his control breaks for a
moment with "I will chop her into messes" but he quickly recovers
and comes to practical detail, first planning poison and then cool
enough to be pleased by the justice of Iago's alternative. The crisis
is over; he is now a far more menacing figure, but also a greater one.
The episode which follows, that in which he receives the letter from
Venice and strikes Desdemona is, I think, often misunderstood. In
it there are two Othellos, one the earlier, the servant of Venice who
accepted the senate's commission and now obeys its order for return, the other the (as he thinks) cuckolded husband. In his ex-
changes with Lodovico he is perfectly courteous, cool, and correct;
but Desdemona's unlucky remarks rouse him to fury. The two men
are vividly presented in his last four and a half lines, particularly
indeed in the last line of all:

> Sir, I obey the mandate,
> And will return to Venice. (*To D.*) Hence, avaunt!
> Cassio shall have my place. And, sir, tonight
> I do entreat that we may sup together;
> You are welcome, sir, to Cyprus. Goats and monkeys!

I do not think that the letter from Venice has anything whatever to do with his changes of mood. Critics often speak of it as containing Othello's "deposition". But why? It is true that Lodovico suggests that maybe the letter mov'd him; but the puzzled Lodovico is groping for some explanation of conduct which to him, naturally, is utterly inexplicable; and Desdemona, with her "If haply you my father do suspect . . .", is doing no more than pick up Lodovico's hint. And, as a matter of common sense, was not the senate likely to recall Othello and why should Othello be angry at the recall? Cassio is not being appointed over his head, he is being "deputed in his government" (though indeed why the government is not simply handed back to Montano does not appear). The last thing likely to content Othello would be the sinecure government of an island no longer menaced; and the senate, who made an emergency appointment to deal with a crisis, was little likely, when the crisis was over, to waste its ablest soldier in such a sinecure.

From this moment on until he sees the truth, Othello is completely master of himself. He is coldly determined on revenge, and, if revenge is a kind of wild justice, the element of justice, however distorted a justice, is more and more present to him. The 'brothel scene' is very horrible; but it is so horrible largely because it is not the outcome, as the striking of Desdemona was, of sudden passion; Othello is playing, with calculated brutality, a deliberate and ghastly travesty. We may hate him for it, but we no longer despise him. And from then on we do not even hate; we pity. And as pity grows, so also does respect. The Othello who sends his last message to the senate and dies upon a kiss is again the Othello who stood before the senate in Venice and greeted Desdemona in Cyprus.

Iago. Coleridge had, no doubt, many flashes of inspiration, but he did more to befog the right understanding of at least two of Shakespeare's greatest creations than a host of less gifted and more pedestrian critics who have been more wisely content to study what Shakespeare presented for their examination. Coleridge, with his famous "motive-hunting of a motiveless malignity" presents us with an inhuman abstraction; Shakespeare presents us with a figure far more human and therefore far more interesting. Iago is no doubt a villain; but he is a very human villain and very far from motiveless. He is a comparatively young and unqualifiedly ambitious professional soldier. War, as he says, is his "trade", his only trade, the only occupation in which he can look for advancement. He has been disappointed (in his view defrauded) of military promotion which he had every reason to expect, and, what is worse, the man who has been appointed is one of whose capacities as a

soldier he is contemptuous—his view of Cassio is the view tradi-
tionally held in all ages and armies by the 'practical' soldier, the
company officer and N.C.O., of the gilded and theoretic staff
officer. Any man in Iago's position would be riled, though, merci-
fully, few men would be prompted to plan such retaliation, and
even fewer have the skill to secure it. He has also another, though
from the point of view of his career irrelevant, motive; his suspicion
that Othello has cuckolded him is *not* a bit of momentary motive-
hunting; however ill-founded, it is, as a later remark of Emilia
shows, a genuine suspicion. And there is further, in Iago's temperament, a 'general' motive, quite apart from the immediate and
specific occasion. He has not, I think, an innate love of cruelty for
its own sake; the mere spectacle of suffering, caused by any agency
other than himself, would have, I fancy, little relish for him. But he
has a profound love of power, and there is no more certain proof of
one's power than the ability to hurt. He is like the child, pulling a
fly to pieces or tormenting his younger brother. It is not the pain
inflicted which delights him, but the fact that here is something or
someone on which he, otherwise harried and controlled by un-
reasonable adults, can exercise unfettered power. Further, Iago's
love of power is partly 'compensatory'. He despises most of the rest
of mankind; any man who does not keep his heart strictly attending
on himself, who allows anything but reason and self-interest to
guide his actions, is to Iago just a fool. Yet in this preposterous
world the men and women who have some instincts of generosity,
some regard for honesty and honour, somehow manage to be more
highly thought of than the self-seekingly reasonable Iago; they are
apt to have a daily beauty in their lives which (for Iago is honest
with himself) makes him ugly; they may even—most absurd of all
—be more successful. Can he be wrong? The idea is intolerable.
And when he can pull the puppets' strings, when he can make the
honest fools dance to his tune towards their own destruction, he can
for the time being reassure himself that he is right. He is the master
of destiny.

It is sometimes argued that Iago's revenge is so disproportionate
to the injury received that only an incarnate fiend could have conceived it. This is to misjudge and exaggerate both Iago's powers of
far-sighted planning and his "malignity". We suffer here from the
handicap already mentioned. We know so well the catastrophe in
which Iago's plot results that we are apt carelessly to assume that he
intended this result from the outset. He intended nothing of the
kind. He is not a long-term strategist, but a superbly skilful and
opportunist tactician. And the moment we realize this his progress

becomes immeasurably more exciting. His plot develops as it goes
along, and some moves in it, so far from being intended, are forced
on him. He has to evade dangers and turn fortuitous happenings to
account. It is worth while, therefore, to examine what he *did* intend.
He explains himself in his first soliloquy at the end of Act I. He
hates the Moor, for reasons already given. Further, "it is thought
abroad" that Othello has cuckolded him, and the repute of a
cuckold would be to Iago as bitter as the reality. The fact that
Othello holds him well, and has a free and open nature, will help;
so will the fact that Cassio's a proper man:

> let me see now,
> To get this place, and to make up my will,
> A double knavery . . . how, how ? . . . let me see,
> After some time, to abuse Othello's ear,
> That he is too familiar with his wife:

There is the rough draft of his scheme, still only in outline ("it is
engender'd"); he is in no hurry ("After some time") and the filling
in of the details must wait on fortune. By the time of his second
soliloquy, at the end of II. i, he has seen his chance to use Roderigo
in making probable the "displanting" of Cassio. But the actual
soliloquy does not carry things much further. He repeats his hatred
and suspicions of Othello, and adds Cassio to the list of suspects. He
adds a new possibility, of which we hear no more,[1] that of a revenge
in kind upon Othello, but then repeats his original design, of putting the Moor into a jealousy so strong that judgement cannot cure,
and practising upon his peace and quiet even to madness. But he
still has not got the detail worked out—"'Tis here, but yet confus'd". He has not yet perceived that he can use Cassio's projected
drunkenness and disgrace, which will, with luck, secure the one of
his two aims, as the starting point towards the other. That is a later
and brilliant inspiration, occurring to him at II. iii. 305, and
developed, this time in considered detail, in the soliloquy which
almost immediately follows. He is now on the full tide of delight in
evil creation, and he determines, in the last few lines of the act, on
the practical moves which will begin to transform the design into
working reality. But he has no quarrel with Desdemona. No doubt
she is also one of the honest fools, and if she is "enmesh'd" in the net
prepared for the other two, he will be quite content. But he has no
designs on her life, nor even, I think, on her happiness. The plot
will not work without her, and if, as a result, she suffers, that will
not, I think (in spite of Bradley), cause Iago a moment's discom-

1. It is perhaps a reminiscence of Cinthio.

fort. But her misery is a necessity, not an aim; and indeed, if he could have constructed his problem without this pivotal pawn, Iago's feeling for economical design would have been even better satisfied. But there comes a moment at which Desdemona's death, and also Cassio's, unexpectedly become imperative. "Unexpectedly" because Iago's prevision is restricted, and his reading of character, acute so far as it goes, is limited. It does not apparently occur to him to speculate what Othello's action is likely to be when he is moved "even to madness". He discovers this abruptly and alarmingly. Up to a point in his poisoning of Othello's mind he can, as no doubt he calculates, safely withdraw. Up to III. iii. 357 he has stated a few obvious facts (like "She did deceive her father, marrying you"), expressed some suspicions, and suggested a way of testing them. He can at any moment say in effect "My lord, I have done nothing but remind you of what you knew already, and suggest what my suspicious nature thought might be unhappily true. If you have proved my suspicions false, no one can be more delighted than I am." But from the moment at which Othello turns his fury upon Iago himself, probably takes him by the throat, and certainly delivers his threat

> Villain, be sure thou prove my love a whore,
> Be sure of it, give me the ocular proof,
> Or by the worth of man's eternal soul,
> Thou hadst been better have been born a dog,
> Than answer my wak'd wrath.

—from that moment he is in imminent danger. He is completely taken aback; he is indeed, I think, for the only time in the play, genuinely frightened, and it takes him a short time to recover his self-possession. When he does, he sees that now he must, to save himself, produce something much more specific, something that may serve as proof. So he gives the account of Cassio's talk in his sleep, and later the handkerchief. This restores the situation for the moment, but he has now committed himself; he can no longer retreat; he is in the open and exposed to attack. If Othello chooses to test him by a direct question to either Desdemona or Cassio his plot recoils on himself and he is ruined. There is nothing for it then but the deaths of both (he expresses this in so many words about Cassio: "the Moor May unfold me to him; there stand I in peril. No, he must die."), and he puts the pressure on as hard as he dares, though, finding that little is needed, and knowing that Othello is in a mood to react strongly against counsels of moderation, he ventures, with regard to Desdemona, the most daring of his finesses, "My friend is dead; 'tis done at your request: But let her live." And he triumphantly takes the trick.

The great 'temptation' scene is worth a word of comment, since in the rapid movement of the theatre it is easy to miss a good deal not only of the subtlety but also of the variety of Iago's attack unless we have studied it in the leisure of reading. His first reconnoitring approach (ll. 35–9, "I like not that" and "so guilty-like") misses fire because of Desdemona's directness, and at l. 94 he has to start again. He tries suggestion by inference ("no further harm", imply-ing that there is *some* harm) and then inflames Othello by refusing to be more explicit. He goes on (l. 140) to suggestion by hypothesis ("Utter my thoughts? Why, say they are vile and false"); he then momentarily withdraws (ll. 148–58) but returns to the attack with the explicit suggestion of jealousy. Othello's reaction to this en-ables him to consolidate the ground he has gained and to advance "with franker spirit" to detailed advice; and he here makes the most adroit of all his diabolically skilful moves, probing the weakest point in Othello's armour, his lack of social experience. "I know our country disposition well" (as you do not); "In Venice they do let God see the pranks . . ." By this he not only increases Othello's suspicions, but also does all he can to avert a direct chal-lenge from Othello to Desdemona. If to a Venetian lady of quality adultery is no more than a "prank", Othello dreads some such answer as "It is not so; but what an if it were?", or in other words "My dear Othello, why are you making such a pother about a trifle?" And he dare not risk that. Iago then attacks Othello's pos-sible sense of inferiority, or at any rate unsuitability, suggesting that Desdemona may have been only temporarily swept off her feet and may now "fall to match you with her country forms, And happily repent", and finally, the leperous distilment now safely poured into his victim's heart, he leaves it to corrode, with pre-tended counsels of moderation, "let me be thought too busy in my fears."

Iago is throughout aided by his reputation. It is a curious quirk in human nature that if a man is a bit of a cynic, bluntly outspoken, and preferably with a strong streak of vulgarity, he will be accepted as a rough diamond, a good-hearted, honest, dependable fellow. So with Iago. He is once described as "valiant" and once as "bold"; otherwise, with almost wearisome iteration, he is "honest Iago", and with cheerful irony he accepts the label for himself, "as honest as I am". To all appearance he is an example of one type of regi-mental sergeant-major, competent, bluff, assuming a crudely effec-tive bonhomie when it suits him, equally without subtlety or any fineness of instinct or perception, and ambitious for a commission.

Desdemona. She is often, perhaps usually, played as much less mature than I think Shakespeare intended her to be, as a sort of child-wife or second Ophelia. It is true that she has, in her first pleading for Cassio, a child's innocent, though in the circumstances fatal, persistence, calculated to exasperate a much more slow-tempered man than Othello. In just this way a child tries to pin down a treat. "Can we go to the zoo this afternoon?" "No, not this afternoon, dear, I'm busy." "Tomorrow morning, then?" "Well, we'll see, but I think not." "Tomorrow afternoon?" "No, dear, I've people coming in to tea." But there is much more to her than that. She has violated convention by her marriage, and knows it; she puts her case both to her father and to the senate simply indeed, but with strong sense, courage, and plain speaking; she is a soldier's wife, and fit to be so—even a man much more besotted with love than Othello could not have addressed Ophelia as "My fair warrior"; she can stand up to Othello, for the sake of what she thinks to be right, even when he is in a dangerous mood and few people would care to face him. It is true that she tells one lie, and it is less excusable than Ophelia's, since she is protecting herself whereas Ophelia is protecting her father. But there is one moment which always seems to me to put Desdemona's quality beyond doubt. After the brothel scene she is left "half asleep" and weeping, in the last extremity of bewildered distress. Yet, by Heaven knows what wrench of resolution, she pulls herself together for a formal banquet, at which she must entertain men who have seen her publicly struck, and, judging by the subsequent farewells, she acquits herself with at least decorum.

Cassio. He is somehow a rather indeterminate figure, and it is not altogether easy to see why this is so. It is not that he has little to say; he has a great deal more than, for example, Banquo, and slightly more than Enobarbus, but with these two every line tells, and they stand out firm and rounded, even though Banquo has only half a play in which to do it. The truth is, I think, that Cassio is primarily a 'pivotal' figure, of great importance to the movement of the plot, but not of much importance as a person, even as a commentator. Much the longest chance we have of observing him is when he is only half himself, either drunk or shocked out of drunkenness into bitter self-abasement. Otherwise his appearances, though frequent, are brief and sketchy, not giving him much chance to establish himself. Most important of all, we see oddly little of him with Othello—a brief interchange, purely on business, when he brings Othello the Senate's summons in I. ii; four and a half lines of his acceptance of Othello's order to set the guard, and Othello's good-night to him, at the opening of II. iii; two lines of question and answer later in the same scene and a line and a half of the actual cashiering; and, finally, the moving single line "Dear general, I did never give you cause", and five lines of question and answer about the handkerchief, in v. ii.

We know, with reasonable certainty, that he is a competent soldier, since not only does Othello appoint him his second-in-command, but the Venetian senate deputes him in Othello's government, over-riding Montano; he has seen service with Othello ("shar'd dangers with you") and is personally deeply attached to him, so that the "unkind breach" is a shattering blow ("the addition Whose want even kills me"). His feeling for Desdemona is clear—profound and loyal admiration, expressed in his description of her to the Cypriots in II. i, and directly to Desdemona herself in III. iii, "He's never anything but your true servant." One observes that in the early part of II. iii Iago again and again tries to get under his guard, and each time signally fails. He is not a strong character; he knows his failing, but allows Iago's plea of courtesy to the Cypriots to persuade him to his ruin. But he is most unmistakably a gentleman, against whom Iago makes, and knows he makes, a poor showing. There is throughout about him the "daily beauty" which Iago recognizes. He is wholly genuine, but he has a 'finish' which is apt to express itself on occasion in airs and graces.[1] It is one of the tests of a producer whether or not he can make Cassio tell; the effectiveness of the play is greatly enhanced if he can, but one has to admit, I think, that Shakespeare did not give him much help.

Roderigo. Poor gentleman—for he is a gentleman, though a "gulled gentleman"—he has a sad life in the play, bled white by Iago, disappointed of his hopes, making a botch of his attempted murder as he has of everything else, and coming to a miserable end by stabbing in the dark. He is a pathetic figure, a sort of Sir Andrew Aguecheek (and, one may guess, played by the same actor as Sir Andrew and Osric), with a few flashes of petulant spirit, but trying to swim in a sea much too rough for him. His main dramatic function seems to be to provide what little comic relief there is in the play (except for the rather distasteful passage between Iago and Desdemona), and to provide a medium between Iago and the audience and so avoid too much soliloquy. Apart from that he

1. I have suggested in introduction and notes that some of F's variants look a little like attempts to give more colour to the part by emphasizing this trait. See also Appendix A.

shares with Cassio the not very difficult task of throwing Iago's vulgarity into relief.

Emilia. She is one of those 'ordinary' people whom Shakespeare was fond of introducing, passing through the turmoil on an even keel, with reasonable perceptiveness and much common sense, acting as a foil to one or more of the leading characters, and acting also on occasion as chorus or commentator. Even though she hands the handkerchief to Iago, she is, in her way, loyal to Desdemona, though she has no understanding of her sensitiveness; she sees three-quarters of the truth earlier than anyone else, though it is not till the end that she identifies her "notorious villain" with her own husband; and in the last scene she says (like Paulina, though she is of far coarser grain) all the things which we have been longing to say. Her nearest relative in Shakespeare is perhaps Juliet's nurse. She has the same matter-of-fact materialism, and the sentiment of "Romeo's a dish-clout to him" might have been hers, though she would have phrased it more elegantly.[1] But also she can, under stress, rise to a region where the nurse could never follow her. In all the plays there is nothing more characteristic of Shakespeare than the way in which Desdemona's death kindles in her a bright flame of self-forgetful courage; it is not just that she faces the threats of both Othello and her husband, but rather that she neglects them, brushes them aside as irrelevant trivialities.

5. THE "DOUBLE TIME SCHEME"

The theory of the so-called "double time scheme" was first propounded by Wilson ("Christopher North") in three brilliant articles in *Blackwood's Magazine*,[2] and there has been a good deal of discussion of it, not always based on a clear understanding of the problem and the suggested solution. If the theory had ever meant that Shakespeare worked with, as it were, two clocks in front of him, one a 'short time' clock, A, and the other a 'long time' clock, B, and said every now and again "I have worked long enough by clock A and it is now time to write a passage by clock B," then the theory would have been, I think, clearly absurd. None but a very mechanical dramatist, and least of all Shakespeare, could work effectively in that fashion. But that there is an oddity about the duration of time represented and implied in *Othello* is not a matter of theory but of observable fact.

1. Indeed, if one could venture on a shifted speech-heading at IV. iii. 35 this is exactly what she does.

2. November 1849, April and May 1850.

The main action moves fast, with the exception of one interval which is irrelevant to its movement. The first act represents a period of time very little longer than that occupied on the stage. It will be noticed that scene ii can follow scene i with no supposed interval, that the first 56 lines of it serve to cover the interval during which Brabantio is seeking Othello, and that the movement of the whole party to the council chamber is covered by the 47 lines of discussion between the "Duke" and the senators. The only point at which the stage time is unduly brief is while Iago is going to the Sagittar and conducting Desdemona back again. But this is covered by the forty-odd lines of Othello's speech; and it is worth noticing, in passing, how skilfully it is covered. The speech lasts for no more than some two minutes; but it ranges widely both in time and in space, so that any normal audience, measuring it by impression and not by a stop-watch, feels that it has lasted longer than it has. The rapid movement of the first Act, seeing that it is separated from the second by a considerable interval, is important only thus far, that it sets the tempo for the rest of the play.

Between Acts I and II there is an interval of any length we choose; all we know about it from the text is that it is some days longer than the "sennight" of II. i. 77, though we can, if we care to, work out from a map how long it would take a sailing ship to complete a tempestuous voyage from Venice to Cyprus. But the supposed duration is quite unimportant because of the distribution of the main characters during the voyage, and as Shakespeare is at pains to stress this distribution we may reasonably assume that he made it deliberately. Othello sails in one ship, Cassio in a second, Desdemona, Iago, and Emilia in a third.

They meet again for the first time, and within half an hour of one another, in Cyprus. The represented time from then to the end of the play is some thirty-three hours. They land somewhere about four o'clock on Saturday (II. ii. 9–10, "this present hour of five"); the scene of the cashiering of Cassio begins just before ten o'clock (II. iii. 13) and lasts (with that compression of time at which the Elizabethan dramatists were so adept and which the Elizabethan audience evidently so readily accepted—cf. in particular the last scene of *Dr Faustus*) till early on Sunday morning (II. iii. 368, III. i. 32, and III. iii. 61). Cassio makes up his mind to petition Desdemona "betimes in the morning" (II. iii. 320). He does so, and there follows the long 'temptation' scene (III. iii). It is then just possible to assume some interval, but I think very awkward, since III. iv. 15, 16, 19, 30 seem to indicate continuity. Desdemona has become immediately aware of the loss of the handkerchief, and Othello's "O, hardness to dissemble" comes naturally only straight after the temptation scene.

Between Acts III and IV is the one place, so far as I can see, where an interval can be credibly inserted. I cannot find anything in the text which disproves the possibility, but I think that the 'feeling' both of the audience in the theatre and of the reader in the study is against it. When once Iago has Othello on the rack it would be undramatic to allow a respite. From the beginning of Act IV there is no possibility of an interval. The messengers from Venice arrive and are invited to supper "tonight" (IV. i. 257). This supper ends at the beginning of IV. iii. Later in the evening (between twelve and one—IV. ii. 236) Cassio is attacked and Roderigo killed, and very soon after this Othello kills Desdemona.

Now this rapid continuity of movement is not only, from the point of view of dramatic tension, desirable, but also, from the point of view of credibility, imperative. If Iago's plot does not work fast it will not work at all. If Othello meets Cassio and asks him the question which he asks too late, in the last scene, the plot will be blown sky high and the ingenious engineer hoist with his own petard. And Iago is acutely aware of this—"the Moor May unfold me to him; there stand I in peril" (v. i. 20). And not all Iago's adroitness can avert the likelihood of such a meeting for more than a short time: he is indeed only saved, by Othello's fit, at IV. i. 48, where Cassio enters and has to be got rid of.

But this rapidity of movement, from one point of view inevitable, from another point of view makes nonsense of the whole business. After the arrival in Cyprus there is no point of time at which the supposed adultery could have occurred; and even Othello's credulity cannot be supposed to accept blank impossibilities. Nor has there been any opportunity before the arrival, since Othello sails on the day after his marriage, and Shakespeare has been at pains to preclude the possibility of its occurrence during the voyage. (It should be observed that the whole of Iago's suggestions, and Othello's reactions to them, depend on the supposition of *adultery*, i.e. *after* marriage, and not of promiscuity or a liaison preceding it —cf. Iago's "In Venice they let God see the pranks They dare not show their *husbands*." Othello's poisoned fear is that he has been cuckolded, not that he has been merely anticipated.)

Something therefore had to be done, to make the whole progress of the plot credible. And Shakespeare does it by a number of indications of so-called "long time". Most of these indications (I hope) are pointed out in the notes, but the following list will serve for the moment to illustrate their nature: III. iii. 296, 313 (but might have been on voyage), 344–7, 419, III. iv. 97, 171, IV. i. 85, 132, 210–32 (a very clear instance, since the government of Venice can hardly be supposed to recall Othello till there has been time for the report of the Turkish disaster to reach them and for them to send the order for recall), 250, 273, IV. ii. 1–10, 23, V. ii. 213.

I cannot agree with the critics who hold that any examination of the double time scheme is an idle waste of time, on the grounds that no one in the theatre notices the discrepancies. In the first place any such examination of small points puts a keener edge on one's appreciation of the play as a whole; but apart from that it throws light on Shakespeare's astonishing skill and judgement as a practical craftsman. He knew to a fraction of an inch how far he could go in playing a trick on his audience, and the measure of his success is precisely the unawareness of the audience in the theatre that any trick is being played. What Shakespeare is doing is to present, before our eyes, an unbroken series of events happening in "short time", but to present them against a background, of events not presented but implied, which gives the needed impression of "long time".

OTHELLO

DRAMATIS PERSONÆ

OTHELLO, *a noble Moor in the service of the Venetian State.*
BRABANTIO, *a Senator of Venice and Desdemona's father.*
CASSIO, *Othello's Lieutenant.*
IAGO, *Othello's Ancient.*
RODERIGO, *a Venetian Gentleman.*
DUKE OF VENICE.
Other Senators.
MONTANO, *Othello's predecessor in the government of Cyprus.*
GRATIANO, *Brother of Brabantio.*
LODOVICO, *Kinsman of Brabantio.*
Clown, Servant to Othello.
DESDEMONA, *Brabantio's daughter and Othello's wife.*
EMILIA, *Iago's wife.*
BIANCA, *a Courtesan.*
*Sailor, Messenger, Herald, Officers, Gentlemen, Musicians, and
   Attendants.*

SCENE: Act I, *Venice*: Acts II-V, *Cyprus.*

Dramatis Personæ] There is no list in Qq; at the end of the play in F is the following: The Names of the Actors. Othello, *the Moore.* Brabantio, *Father to Desdemona.* Cassio, *an Honourable Lieutenant.* Iago, *a Villaine.* Rodorigo, *a gull'd Gentleman.* Duke *of Venice.* Senators. Montano, *Governour of Cyprus. Gentlemen of Cyprus.* Lodovico, *and* Gratiano, *two Noble Venetians.* Saylors. *Clowne.* Desdemona, *Wife to Othello.* Æmilia, *Wife to Iago.* Bianca, *a Curtezan.*

The list was elaborated, and its order changed, by later editors. I have retained some of the more detailed descriptions, but returned to F's order, which there seems no reason to desert. And I have retained F's description of Bianca, since the usual "*Mistress to Cassio*" implies a more permanent relationship than is anywhere implied in the text, except (possibly) in one disputed line.

OTHELLO

ACT I

SCENE I.—[*Venice. A Street.*]

Enter IAGO *and* RODERIGO.

Rod. Tush, never tell me, I take it much unkindly
  That thou, Iago, who hast had my purse,
  As if the strings were thine, shouldst know of this.
Iago. 'Sblood, but you will not hear me.
  If ever I did dream of such a matter,   5
  Abhor me.
Rod. Thou told'st me, thou didst hold him in thy hate.
Iago. Despise me if I do not: three great ones of the city,
  In personal suit to make me his lieutenant,
  Oft capp'd to him, and by the faith of man,   10

ACT I

Scene I

Act I. Scene I.]*Acts and Scenes are indicated throughout in F (except II. iii); Q1 indicates Act II, Scene 1, Act IV, Act V; Q2 indicates Acts from II onwards, and the first Scene only of each. There are no indications of locality in Qq or F.* S.D. Iago and Roderigo] *Qq;* Rodorigo, and Iago *F.* 1. Tush] *Qq; not in F.* 2. thou] *F, Q2;* you *Q1.* hast] *F, Q2;* has *Q1.* 4. 'Sblood] *Q1; not in F, Q2.* you will] *Q1;* you'l *F;* you'le *Q2; for lineation see App. F, p. 227.* 10. Oft capp'd] *Qq* (capt); Off-capt *F.*

1–81. The unusual technique employed by Shakespeare for this opening passage is commented on in the Introduction, pp. xlviii–l.

3. *this*] usually taken to mean Othello's marriage. If so, we have to supply for Roderigo "and not tell me about it". Even so, the sense does not dovetail particularly well with Roderigo's protest in l. 7, since Iago's personal attitude towards Othello is irrelevant to his marriage. It is at least

possible that it is idle to look for an exact interpretation of this. It is not uncommon in Shakespeare to have an entry of two or three characters covered by a few words of unrelated conversation e.g., in *R 2*, I. iv. 1, Richard's opening words are "We did observe" and he does not get to business till his immediately following address to Aumerle.

10. *Oft capp'd*] There is, in sense, nothing to choose between the Q and

3

I know my price, I am worth no worse a place.
But he, as loving his own pride and purposes,
Evades them, with a bombast circumstance,
Horribly stuff'd with epithets of war:
And in conclusion,   15
Nonsuits my mediators: for "Certes," says he,
"I have already chosen my officer,"
And what was he?
Forsooth, a great arithmetician,
One Michael Cassio, a Florentine,   20
A fellow almost damn'd in a fair wife,
That never set a squadron in the field,

[15. And in conclusion,] *Q1; not in F, Q2.*   17. chosen] *Q1; chose F, Q2.*

F readings, since *cap* formerly meant (and with schoolboys still means) to take the cap off. In *Cor.*, II. i. 77, "You are ambitious for poor knaves' caps and legs", "legs" (=bows) makes it clear that "caps" means the removal of the cap as a sign of respect. And cf. I. ii. 23 below, "unbonneted".

13. *bombast*] cotton material used as lining or stuffing, and so metaphorically "padding"; "We have receiv'd your letters, . . . rated them At courtship, pleasant jest, and courtesy, As bombast and as lining to the time" (*LLL.*, v. ii. 785).

circumstance] circumlocution, cf. "without more circumstance at all, I hold it fit that we shake hands and part" (*Ham.*, I. v. 127).

14. *epithets*] used by Shakespeare in our sense, but also as simply "phrases", as in *Ado*, v. ii. 69, "'Suffer love', a good epithet!"

16. *Nonsuits*] usually, as a legal term, of throwing up a case; but here it clearly means "refuses".

19. *arithmetician*] a sneer, parallel to the "bookish theoric" of l. 24; "a villain, that fights by the book of arithmetic" (*Rom.*, III. i. 107).

21. *A fellow . . . wife.*] Johnson commented "This is one of the passages which must for the present be resigned to corruption and obscurity"; and I do not know that there is much more to be said, though attempted explanations are innumerable. There is an Italian proverb which looks as though it should be helpful, *l'hai tolta bella? tuo danno*, i.e. "You have married a fair wife? You are damned." Iago's remark might be taken as an allusion to this if we discovered later that Cassio was within measurable distance of marrying Bianca. But he is not, and at the moment has not even met her. But I think it very likely that Granville Barker had the real explanation. He points out that in Cinthio Cassio has a wife (who does the "taking out" of the work in the handkerchief). And then "Shakespeare when he wrote the line, meant to follow the story in this respect. Later, for good reasons, he changed his mind and gave Bianca to Cassio for a mistress instead, omitting, however, to alter the text of this first scene." It is possible, however, as Dr Brooks suggests to me, that we should not look for too specific an application of a general sneer at Cassio as a ladies' man, a carpet knight, who is at any moment liable to be entangled in disastrous matrimony.

22. *squadron*] a body of troops, not necessarily of cavalry; "Set we our squadrons on yond side o' the hill" (*Ant.*, III. viii. 7).

Nor the devision of a battle knows,
More than a spinster, unless the bookish theoric,
Wherein the toged consuls can propose   25
As masterly as he: mere prattle without practice
Is all his soldiership: but he, sir, had the election,
And I, of whom his eyes had seen the proof,
At Rhodes, at Cyprus, and on other grounds,
Christian and heathen, must be lee'd, and
       calm'd,   30
By debitor and creditor, this counter-caster:
He, in good time, must his lieutenant be,

23. devision] *Q1,F;* division *Q2.*   25. toged] *Q1;* tongued *F, Q2.*   29. Cyprus
F2; Cipres Qq; Ciprus *F.*   other] *Qq;* others *F.*   30. Christian] *Q1;*
Christen'd *F;* Christn'd *Q2.*   be lee'd] *Malone;* be led *Q1;* be be-leed *F, Q2.*
31. creditor, this counter-caster:] *Qq* (Creditor, this Counter-caster); Creditor.
This Counter-caster, *F.*

23. *devision*] The spellings "devision" and "division" were often confused, but I think it is wiser to retain
here the spelling of both Q and F,
since it keeps us, probably rightly,
nearer to "devise" than to "divide".

24. *spinster*] not necessarily femin-
ne; "The spinsters, carders, fullers,
weavers" (*H 8,* I. ii. 33).

bookish] commonly glossed as "eru-
dite"; but surely it has a derogatory
connotation of *mere* book-learning;
"Whose bookish rule hath pull'd
fair England down" (*2 H 6,* I. i.
260).

theoric] "the art and practic part of
life Must be the mistress to this
theoric" (*H 5,* I. i. 51). The word
seems to have been introduced by
Gabriel Harvey, and was ridiculed by
Jonson.

25. *toged*] wearing a toga, which was
at Rome the characteristic dress of
senators and others of high rank, and
specifically the dress of peace (cf.
"cedant arma togae"). This form is
not elsewhere found, but cf. "Why in
this woolvish toge should I stand here"
(*Cor.,* II. iii. 122), where *toge* is the
universally accepted emendation of
F's *tongue.*

F's *tongued* is not wholly impossible

("all words and no deeds"), but almost
all edd., even the most determined
supporters of F, here accept Q1.

consuls] councillors, with no suggestion of the leadership in war which
the Latin word implies.

propose] set out, more definite than
our "put forward for discussion";
"Give but that portion which yourself
propos'd" (*Lr.,* I. i. 245).

30. *lee'd*] F's *be-lee'd* has been accepted by almost all edd. except Malone;
but if *calm'd* = "becalm'd" there
seems no reason why *lee'd* cannot =
"belee'd"; cf. "Like to a ship, that,
having scap'd a tempest, Is straight-
way calm'd, and boarded with a
pirate" (*2 H 6,* IV. ix. 32). (*Be*)*lee'd*
presumably means (of a sailing ship)
under the lee of an adversary, which
thus takes the wind out of her sails
and renders her helpless.

31. *debitor and creditor*] an account
book or a man who keeps an account
book; cf. "O the charity of a penny
cord! It sums up thousands in a trice;
you have no true debitor and creditor
but it" (*Cym.,* v. iv. 171).

counter-caster] strictly one who counts
with the assistance of counters or an
abacus, but here much the same as the
arithmetician of l. 19.

And I, God bless the mark, his worship's ancient.

Rod. By heaven I rather would have been his hangman.

Iago. But there's no remedy, 'tis the curse of service,   35
Preferment goes by letter and affection,
Not by the old gradation, where each second
Stood heir to the first: now sir, be judge yourself,
Whether I in any just term am affin'd
To love the Moor.

Rod.   I would not follow him then.   40

Iago. O, sir, content you.
I follow him to serve my turn upon him:
We cannot be all masters, nor all masters
Cannot be truly follow'd. You shall mark

---

33. I, . . . ancient] *Q1* (Worships Ancient) ; I (blesse the marke) his Mooreships Autient *F*; I Sir (blesse the marke) his Mooreships Ancient *Q2*.   35. But] *Qq*; Why, *F*.   37. Not by the] *Qq*; And not by *F*.   39. affin'd] *F, Q2*; assign'd *Q1*.   43. be all] *Q1*; all be *F, Q2*.

33. *God bless the mark*] The phrase, like "(God) save the mark!", was a common interjection, with the flavour of our "Heaven help us!", but its origin is obscure.

Q2, following F in excising the oath, takes the trouble to cure the metre.

ancient] a corruption of "ensign", properly the colour-bearer, though we hear nothing of Iago in that capacity. Our "colour-sergeant" or perhaps "regimental sergeant-major" would be an approximation. But Shakespeare's use of military ranks is both limited and loose. He might have said with Falstaff "My whole charge consists of ancients, corporals, lieutenants, gentlemen of companies". He has two well-known ancients and two equally well-known corporals; a memorable sergeant (bleeding), and several "lieutenants", whose military rank is variable. Peto, for example, as second-in-command to a captain, is presumably of lower rank than Cassio, who is second-in-command to a general. The proper technical description of Cassio would have been "Sergeant-major-general". Iago is Othello's third-in-command (who thinks he ought to have been second), but his status in the play, apart from the setting of the watch, seems rather that of Othello's A.D.C.

35. *there's no remedy*] a common colloquialism, like our "It's just one of those things", but usually in Shakespeare with the implication "there's no way out"; "You must send her your page; no remedy" (*Wiv.*, II. ii. 127).

36. *letter*] sc. of introduction or recommendation; "The duke hath offered him letters of commendations to the king" (*All's W.*, IV. iii. 91), "you shall have letters from me to some friends that will Sweep your way for you" (*Ant.*, III. ix. 15).

affection] less warm than our sense and nearer to "inclination"; "I have not known when his affections sway'd More than his reason" (*Cæs.*, II. i. 20).

37. *gradation*] seniority.

39. *affin'd*] bound, attached (to); cf. II. iii. 209 below, and "the bold and coward, the wise and fool, . . . seem all affin'd and kin" (*Troil.*, I. iii. 23).

Many a duteous and knee-crooking knave,   45
That, doting on his own obsequious bondage,
Wears out his time much like his master's ass,
For nought but provender, and when he's old, cashier'd,
Whip me such honest knaves: others there are,
Who, trimm'd in forms, and visages of duty,   50
Keep yet their hearts attending on themselves,
And throwing but shows of service on their lords,
Do well thrive by 'em, and when they have lin'd
    their coats,
Do themselves homage, those fellows have some soul,
And such a one do I profess myself, . . . for sir,   55
It is as sure as you are Roderigo,
Were I the Moor, I would not be Iago:
In following him, I follow but myself.
Heaven is my judge, not I for love and duty,
But seeming so, for my peculiar end.   60
For when my outward action does demonstrate
The native act, and figure of my heart,

48. nought] *F, Q2* (naught *F*); noughe *Q1*.   54. those] *Qq* (Those); These *F*.
For lineation see App. F, p. 229.   61. does] *Q1*; doth *F, Q2*.

45. *knee-crooking*] bowing, "making a leg"; "crook the pregnant hinges of the knee, Where thrift may follow fawning" (*Ham.*, III. ii. 66).

49. *Whip me*] here apparently just contemptuous, "A fig for . . ."; sometimes (with *me* as direct object) an interjection, "On my life"; "Nay, whip me, then" (*3 H 6*, III. ii. 28).

50. *visages*] almost = visors = masks.

53. *lin'd*] often with implication of strengthening, backing; "We will not line his thin bestained cloak With our pure honours" (*John*, IV. iii. 24), "hath sent for you To line his enterprise" (*1 H 4*, II. iii. 87).

57. *Were I . . . Iago*] This is not, I think, such plain sailing as the silence of most commentators suggests. To say "If I were the master, I would not be the man" sounds an oddly feeble remark from Iago. But it may be noticed that Shakespeare seems to

have deliberately given Iago a trick of speech by which he makes remarks which appear at first hearing well-turned and significant, and on examination turn out to mean very little. Cf. "Men should be what they seem, Or those that be not, would they might seem none" (III. iii. 130), "He's that he is; I may not breathe my censure, What he might be, if, as he might, he is not, I would to Heaven he were!" (IV. i. 267).

60. *peculiar*] particular, private; "groping for trouts in a peculiar river" (*Meas.*, I. ii. 96), "those unproper beds which they dare swear peculiar" (IV. i. 68 below).

62. *native*] innate; "And chase the native beauty from his cheek" (*John*, III. iv. 83), "In his true, native, and most proper shape" (*2 H 4*, IV. i. 37).

figure] "as a form of wax Resolveth from his figure 'gainst the fire" (*John*, V. iv. 24).

In complement extern, 'tis not long after,
But I will wear my heart upon my sleeve,
For doves to peck at: I am not what I am.   65

Rod. What a full fortune does the thicklips owe,
If he can carry 't thus!

Iago.   Call up her father,
Rouse him, make after him, poison his delight,
Proclaim him in the street, incense her kinsmen,
And though he in a fertile climate dwell,   70
Plague him with flies: though that his joy be joy,
Yet throw such changes of vexation on 't,
As it may lose some colour.

Rod. Here is her father's house, I'll call aloud.

Iago. Do, with like timorous accent, and dire yell,   75
As when, by night and negligence, the fire
Is spied in populous cities.

Rod. What ho! Brabantio, Signior Brabantio, ho!

Iago. Awake! what ho, Brabantio! thieves, thieves, thieves!

---

65. doves] *Q1* (Doues), *Malone;* Dawes *F, Q2.* 66. full] *Qq;* fall *F.* thicklips] *Qq;* Thicks-lips *F.* 67. carry't] *F, Q2;* carry'et *Q1.* 69. street, incense] *Qq;* Streets. Incense *F.* 72. changes] *Qq;* chances *F.* on't] *F;* out *Qq.* 77. spied] *Qq, F;* spred *Warburton.* 79. thieves] *three times in Qq, twice in F.*

63. *complement*] external show; there was no distinction recognized between this spelling and *compliment;* "not only in the simple office of love, but in all the accoutrement, complement and ceremony of it" (*Wiv.,* IV. ii. 4).

'tis] present, as often, for future; cf. III. iii. 92 below, "Chaos is come again."

65. *doves*] Most editors take F's *daws* but there is a relevant passage in *Euphues,* "I am more willing that a Raven should peck out mine eyes, than a Turtle peck at them." There is perhaps an additional touch of contempt in the idea of making one's heart vulnerable to so mild a creature as a dove. The alteration to "daws", as accepted peckers, would be natural enough, but *dawes* and *doues* would be easily confused.

66. *full*] swelling; cf. "the full-fortuned Caesar" (*Ant.,* IV. xiii. 24).

owe] own, as often; cf. III. iii. 338 below.

67. *carry't*] carry it off, "get away with it"; "Shall the elephant Ajax carry it thus?" (*Troil.,* II. iii. 2), "Do the boys carry it away?" (*Ham.,* II. ii. 385).

70. *though*] usually explained as = since, with III. iii. 149 below quoted in support. The evidence for this sense of "though" seems to me very slender, and it does not well fit the context here, where Iago appears to mean that Othello's *seeming* prosperity must be injured; in the next line there can be no question that *though* has its ordinary modern meaning.

73. *As it may*] that may cause it to.

75. *timorous*] The word, like several others in Elizabethan idiom (e.g. "fearful"), can be either active or passive; here, "terrifying".

76–7.] i.e., the fire, *caused by* negligence at night, is spied.

Look to your house, your daughter, and your bags.   80
Thieves, thieves!

BRABANTIO *at a window.*

Bra. What is the reason of this terrible summons?
    What is the matter there?
Rod. Signior, is all your family within?
Iago. Are all doors lock'd?
Bra.   Why, wherefore ask you this?   85
Iago. Zounds, sir, you are robb'd, for shame put on your
        gown,
    Your heart is bust, you have lost half your soul;
    Even now, very now, an old black ram
    Is tupping your white ewe; arise, arise,
    Awake the snorting citizens with the bell,   90
    Or else the devil will make a grandsire of you,
    Arise I say.
Bra.   What, have you lost your wits?
Rod. Most reverend signior, do you know my voice?
Bra. Not I, what are you?
Rod. My name is Roderigo.
Bra.   The worse welcome;   95
    I have charg'd thee, not to haunt about my doors;
    In honest plainness thou hast heard me say
    My daughter is not for thee; and now in madness,
    Being full of supper, and distempering draughts,
    Upon malicious bravery, dost thou come   100

80. your daughter] *F, Q2;* you daughter *Q1.* 81. S.D.] *Qq; not in F.* 82. Bra.]
Qq (Brab. Q1); Bra. Aboue F.   85. all] *Q1;* your *F, Q2.*   doors lock'd]
Doores lock'd *F;* doores lockt *Q2;* doore lockts *Q1.*   86. Zounds, sir, you are]
Q1; Sir, y'are *F;* Sir you are *Q2.* 88. now, very now] *Qq;* now, now, very
now *F.*   95. worse] *Qq;* worsser *F.*   100. bravery] *Qq;* knauerie *F.*

83. *What is the matter?*] not "What's
wrong?", but "What is your business?"

90. *snorting*] snoring.

97-8.] These lines are the first clear
indication that Roderigo aspires to
Desdemona.

99. *distempering*] exciting (not so
strong as "making drunk"); cf. "dis-
tempered.—With drink, sir?—No,

my lord, rather with choler" (*Ham.,*
III. ii. 317).

100. *bravery*] F's *knavery* is slightly
redundant after *malicious,* nor is it
wholly applicable. Brabantio is com-
plaining of Roderigo's vociferous intrusion; "the bravery of his [Laertes']
grief did put me Into a towering
passion" (*Ham.,* v. ii. 79); and cf. v. ii.
327 below.

> To start my quiet?

Rod. Sir, sir, sir,—

Bra.   But thou must needs be sure
> My spirit and my place have in them power,
> To make this bitter to thee.

Rod.   Patience, good sir.

Bra. What, tell'st thou me of robbing? this is Venice,   105
> My house is not a grange.

Rod.   Most grave Brabantio,
> In simple and pure soul I come to you.

Iago. Zounds, sir, you are one of those that will not serve
> God, if the devil bid you. Because we come to do
> you service, you think we are ruffians, you'll have   110
> your daughter cover'd with a Barbary horse; you'll
> have your nephews neigh to you; you'll have
> coursers for cousins, and gennets for germans.

Bra. What profane wretch art thou?

Iago. I am one, sir, that come to tell you, your daughter,   115
> and the Moor, are now making the beast with two
> backs.

Bra. Thou art a villain.

Iago.   You are a senator.

Bra. This thou shalt answer, I know thee, Roderigo.

Rod. Sir, I will answer anything. But I beseech you,   120
> If 't be your pleasure, and most wise consent,

101. quiet?] *Qq*; quiet. *F.*   103. spirit . . . them] *Qq*; spirits . . . their *F.*
105. What, tell'st] *Qq*; What tell'st *F.*   107. soul I] *Qq*; soul, I *F.*   108.
Zounds, sir,] Zouns sir, *Q1*; Sir: *F*; Sir, *Q2*.   110. service, you] *Qq*; service,
and you *F.*   112. neigh to you;] *Q2*; ney to you; *Q1*; neigh to you, *F.*
113. gennets for germans] Iennits for *Iermans Q1*; Gennets for Germaines *F;*
Gennets for *Germans Q2.*   115. come] *Qq*; comes *F.*   116. are now] *Qq*;
are *F.*   121–37. If't be . . . yourself] *F, Q2*; *not in Q1.*

101. *start*] startle; "You boggle
shrewdly, every feather starts you"
(*All's W.*, v. iii. 234).

106. *grange*] an isolated house, often
a farm; cf. *Meas.*, III. i. 279.

111. *Barbary*] Arab (a barb "was
strictly an Arab horse though the
meaning was extended").

112. *nephews*] Shakespeare normally
uses the word in the modern sense, but
here he clearly intends the original

sense of "nepotes" = "grandsons".

113. *germans*] blood relations; "wert
thou a leopard, thou wert german to
the lion" (*Tim.*, IV. iii. 344).

114. *profane*] foul-mouthed (not
necessarily with any implication of
"blasphemous"), cf. II. i. 163 below.

116–17. *the beast with two backs*] Cf.
Rabelais, "la beste a deux dos".

121. *wise*] not "prudent" but "fully
aware". When Beatrice in *Ado* says

(As partly I find it is) that your fair daughter,
At this odd-even and dull watch o' the night,
Transported with no worse nor better guard,
But with a knave of common hire, a gondolier,   125
To the gross clasps of a lascivious Moor:
If this be known to you, and your allowance,
We then have done you bold and saucy wrongs.
But if you know not this, my manners tell me,
We have your wrong rebuke. Do not believe   130
That from the sense of all civility,
I thus would play and trifle with your reverence.
Your daughter (if you have not given her leave,
I say again), hath made a gross revolt,
Tying her duty, beauty, wit, and fortunes,   135
In an extravagant and wheeling stranger,
Of here, and every where: straight satisfy yourself.
If she be in her chamber, or your house,
Let loose on me the justice of the state
For this delusion.

---

123. odd-even] *Malone;* odde Euen *F;* od euen *Q2.*   133-4. (if . . . again)] *Q2;*
(if . . . leaue) I say againe, *F.*   140. this delusion] *Q1;* thus deluding you *F, Q2.*

"Thou and I are too wise to woo peace-ably" (v. ii. 76) she does not mean that she and Benedick are too sensible, but that they are too knowledgeable. We retain this sense in colloquialisms, such as "Put me wise", "He's wise to that one."

123. *odd-even*] Cf. "What is the night?—Almost at odds with morning, which is which" (*Mac.*, III. iv. 126).

dull] lifeless; "dull, stale, tired bed" (*Lr.*, I. ii. 13).

125. *gondolier*] no accent on the last syllable; cf. *pioner* (III. iii. 352 below), *muleter* (*Ant.*, III. vii. 35).

127. *your allowance*] allowed by you, "I now grow fearful. . . That you protect this course, and put it on By your allowance" (*Lr.*, I. iv. 228).

128. *saucy*] insolent; stronger than our connotation of childish impertinence; "Am I not protector, saucy priest?" (*1 H 6*, III. i. 45).

129. *manners*] manual of etiquette;

"books for good manners" (*AYL.*, v. iv. 95).

131. *from*] away from, neglecting; "to be so odd and from all fashions As Beatrice is" (*Ado*, III. i. 72), " 'Twas from the canon" (*Cor.*, III. i. 89), "which I best thought it fit To answer from our home" (i.e. when we were elsewhere than at home; *Lr.*, II. i. 125).

135. *wit*] intellect; no sense of verbal cleverness; see note on II. i. 129 below.

136. *extravagant*] vagrant outside its due limits; "the extravagant and erring spirit hies To his confine" (*Ham.*, I. i. 154).

wheeling] moving circuitously (not merely "wandering", since there is probably a suggestion of the movement of planets, which, moving in fact orbitally, yet seem to "wander" among the fixed stars); "I was forc'd to wheel Three or four miles about" (*Cor.*, I. vi. 19).

Bra.   Strike on the tinder, ho!   140
    Give me a taper, call up all my people:
    This accident is not unlike my dream,
    Belief of it oppresses me already:
    Light I say, light!   [*Exit above.*
Iago.   Farewell, for I must leave you:
    It seems not meet, nor wholesome to my place,   145
    To be produc'd, as if I stay I shall,
    Against the Moor, for I do know the state,
    However this may gall him with some check,
    Cannot with safety cast him, for he's embark'd,
    With such loud reason, to the Cyprus wars,   150
    Which even now stands in act, that, for their souls,
    Another of his fathom they have not
    To lead their business, in which regard,
    Though I do hate him, as I do hell's pains,
    Yet, for necessity of present life,   155
    I must show out a flag, and sign of love,

---

144. *Exit above*] Exit *F; no* S.D. *Qq.*   145. place] *F, Q2;* pate *Q1.*   146. pro-
duc'd] *Qq;* producted *F.*   152. fathom] fathome *Qq;* Fadome *F.*   not] *Q1;*
none *F, Q2.*   154. hell's pains] hells paines *Qq;* hell apines *F.*

---

141. *taper*] candle (tapering in shape): more substantial than our taper, cf. *Cæs.*, II. i. 7, where Brutus asks for a taper to be lighted in his study, and *Cym.*, II. ii. 3–5, where Imogen has been reading for three hours by the light of a "taper".

148. *check*] reprimand; see note on IV. iii. 20 below.

149. *cast*] four times in this play in this sense of "discard" (see II. iii. 14, 265, v. ii. 328) and once in *Tw.N.*, "cast thy humble slough" (II. v. 163), but not elsewhere in Shakespeare in this sense without "away", "off", etc.

150. *With such loud reason*] In the opinion of all reasonable judges he is the obvious choice.

to the Cyprus wars] It would appear from this that Othello has already been appointed, and that therefore his summons to the meeting of the senate is only to give him instructions for

immediate departure. If this is so, and the present passage is not a slip on Shakespeare's part, the Duke's remarks at I. iii. 222–6 are not conferring the command, but merely giving reasons for a command already conferred.

151. *stands in act*] are in full progress.

152. *fathom*] usually glossed as "intellectual grasp"; it is true that the original meaning of "fathom" is "the embrace of two arms" from which comes the sense of a six-foot measure of length, and particularly that measure as one in sounding the depth of water. I think that it is this derivative sense which is operative here, and that the word means "depth", or as we should say, with a different figure, "calibre".

156. *flag*] used sometimes for "sign", as in *R 3*, IV. iv. 88, "a breath, a bubble, A sign of dignity, a garish flag"; here a misleading sign.

Which is indeed but sign. That you shall surely
    find him,
Lead to the Sagittar the raised search,
And there will I be with him. So farewell.   [*Exit.*

Enter BRABANTIO *in his night-gown, and Servants with torches.*

Bra. It is too true an evil, gone she is,   160
    And what's to come, of my despised time,
    Is nought but bitterness. Now Roderigo,
    Where didst thou see her? (O unhappy girl!)
    With the Moor, say'st thou? (Who would be a
        father?)   164
    How didst thou know 'twas she? (O thou deceivest me
    Past thought!) What said she to you? Get more tapers,

---

158. Sagittar] *Q1;* Sagitary *F;* Sagittary *Q2.*   159. S.D.] *Qq* (Barbantio
Q1); *Enter Brabantio, with Servants and Torches F.*   162. bitterness. Now] *F*
(bitternesse); bitternesse now *Qq.*   165. thou deceivest] *Q1;* she deceiues *F,*
Q2 (deceaues *F*).   166. more] *Qq;* moe *F.*

---

158. *Sagittar*] The difference of
readings is of small importance, except
in so far as F's *Sagitary,* with its suggestion of an official building, has perhaps helped to mislead commentators.
Knight, for example, says that it was
"the residence at the Arsenal of the
commanding officers of the navy and
army of the republic". For this statement there seems to be no authority;
but in any case this identification
makes nonsense of two later passages.
At I. ii. 49 Cassio asks "Ancient, what
makes he here?" which he could not
have done if Othello had just gone into
his ordinary place of residence. At
I. iii. 121 Othello says "Ancient, conduct them, you best know the place";
no one in the service of the state could
have required guidance to so important a building as the Arsenal. Miss
V. M. Jeffery, in *MLR* for January
1932, advanced the view that the word
was Shakespeare's equivalent for the
Frezzaria, the street of the arrow-
makers. But the trouble with that
prima facie attractive explanation is
that the locality which Iago is thereby

made to indicate is not specific
enough. An informer does not say
"Bring half a dozen constables to
Park Lane and I'll give you your
man." I think that the old explanation, which Knight rejected in favour
of his Arsenal, is probably the right
one, namely that "the Sagittar" was
either the name of an inn, like "the
Elephant" in *Tw.N.,* III. iii. 39, or "the
Centaur" (who is the same as the
zodiacal Sagittarius) in *Err.* passim,
or possibly the name of a private house,
like "the Phoenix" in *Err.,* I. ii. 88–9
and II. ii. 10–11. It is perhaps just
in favour of the inn that Othello
in speaking to Iago uses the same
word as Bardolph in replying to
the Prince's "Where sups he?" in
2 H 4 II. ii. 161, "At the old place, my
lord".

165. *thou deceivest*] One may suppose
either that the Q1 compositor carried
on *thou* from earlier in the line and then
changed the verb to correspond, or
that F disliked the rather awkward, but
not unnatural, direct address to the
absent Desdemona.

Raise all my kindred, are they married, think you?

Rod. Truly I think they are.

Bra. O heaven, how got she out? O treason of the blood!
Fathers from hence, trust not your daughters' minds 170
By what you see them act, is there not charms,
By which the property of youth and maidhood
May be abus'd? Have you not read, Roderigo,
Of some such thing?

Rod. I have, sir.   175

Bra. Call up my brother: O that you had had her!
Some one way, some another; do you know
Where we may apprehend her, and the Moor?

Rod. I think I can discover him, if you please
To get good guard, and go along with me.   180

Bra. Pray lead me on, at every house I'll call,
I may command at most: get weapons, ho!
And raise some special officers of night:
On, good Roderigo, I'll deserve your pains.   [*Exeunt.*

170. Fathers from hence,] *Qq;* Fathers, from hence *F.*   172. maidhood] *F;*
manhood *Qq.*   174. thing?] *F;* thing. *Qq.*   175. I have, sir] *Q1;* Yes sir:
I have indeed *F, Q2.*   176. that] *Q1;* would *F, Q2.*   177. you] *F, Q2;* yon
Q1.   181. Pray lead me on] *Q1;* Pray you lead on *F, Q2.*   183. night] *Q1;*
might *F, Q2.*   184. I'll] *Qq* (Ile)*;* I will *F.*

167. *Raise*] Early printings of the
Oxford edition read *Rise*, an example
of how even the most carefully corrected and printed modern text may
go wrong, since the reading has no
authority and is just a blunder.

172. *property*] normal nature; "Sweet
love, I see, changing his property,
Turns to the sourest and most deadly
hate" (*R 2*, III. ii. 135).

maidhood] Q1's *manhood* is not impossible, taking *youth and manhood* as =
"young human beings (of either sex)",
but *maidhood* is no doubt more pointed,
and graphically the confusion with *n*
of an *i* followed by a cramped *d* is more
probable than might appear.

175.] F completes Brabantio's half
line; but it is hard to see why a compositor, if faced with F's reading, left
out two words of it and changed the
order of the others.

179. *discover*] uncover (not just
"find"); "It were good that Benedick
knew of it by some other, if she will not
discover it" (*Ado*, II. iii. 172), "I can
discover all The unlucky manage of
this fatal brawl" (*Rom.*, III. i. 148),
"you, that have so traitorously discovered the secrets of your army"
(*All's W.*, IV. iii. 342).

183. *officers of night*] Q1 is almost certainly right, and has been almost
universally accepted. Lewkenor, in his
translation (1599) of Contareno's
Venice, has a considerable paragraph
explaining the duties of the "officers of
the night". Furness defends F, not very
convincingly, on the grounds that
these officers were part of the ordinary
police machinery, and in no sense
"special".

184. *I'll deserve*] i.e. my gratitude will
be worthy of, and so = I'll requite.

SCENE II.—[*Before the Sagittar.*]

Enter OTHELLO, IAGO, *and attendants with torches.*

Iago. Though in the trade of war I have slain men,
　　　Yet do I hold it very stuff of conscience
　　　To do no contriv'd murder; I lack iniquity
　　　Sometimes to do me service: nine or ten times
　　　I had thought to have yerk'd him here, under the ribs. 5
Oth. 'Tis better as it is.
Iago.　　　　　　　　Nay, but he prated,
　　　And spoke such scurvy and provoking terms
　　　Against your honour,
　　　That with the little godliness I have,
　　　I did full hard forbear him: but I pray, sir,   10
　　　Are you fast married? For be sure of this,
　　　That the magnifico is much belov'd,
　　　And hath in his effect a voice potential
　　　As double as the duke's; he will divorce you,
　　　Or put upon you what restraint, and grievance,   15
　　　That law (with all his might to enforce it on)
　　　Will give him cable.

Scene II

S.D. *and attendants*] *Qq; Attendants F.*   2. stuff of] stuft of *Q1*; stuffe o'th' *F, Q2.*
4. Sometimes] *Qq;* Sometime *F.*   5. to have yerk'd] t'haue yerk'd *F;* to haue
ierk'd *Qq.*   10. pray] *Qq;* pray you *F.*   11. For be sure] *Qq;* Be assur'd *F.*
15. and] *Qq;* or *F.*   16. That] *Q1;* The *F, Q2.*   17. Will] *F;* Weele *Qq.*

12. *magnifico*] apparently first introduced by Gabriel Harvey, as a general
term; but it began as a specific title—
"The chief men of Venice are by a
peculiar name called *Magnifici*, i.e.
Magnificoes" (Tollet quoting Min-
sheu).

13–14. *hath ... duke's*] Shakespeare's
meaning seems clear enough, in spite
of a cloud of comment. He must, I
think, have supposed (erroneously)
that the "duke" had a casting vote, and
so, on an equal division, two votes; and
Iago says that Brabantio is so well
beloved that he can, in practice, get
his own way as effectively as if he also
had two votes.

15. *grievance*] not "what makes one
feel aggrieved", but "what causes pain
or annoyance"; "I'll know his [the
melancholy Romeo's] grievance"
(*Rom.*, I. i. 162).

17. *cable*] not elsewhere in Shakespeare in this metaphorical sense of
"scope", though Iago uses it in a different metaphorical sense at I. iii. 338.
It is odd that Iago, who, so far as we
know, is purely an infantry soldier,
should show a taste for nautical metaphor (*lee'd and calm'd, fathom, cable*).
But it is true, as Dr Brooks points out to
me, that a soldier in the service of
Venice might well be used to amphi-
bious warfare, in a day when ships

Oth.   Let him do his spite;
My services, which I have done the signiory,
Shall out-tongue his complaints; 'tis yet to know—
Which, when I know that boasting is an honour,   20
I shall provulgate—I fetch my life and being
From men of royal siege, and my demerits
May speak unbonneted to as proud a fortune
As this that I have reach'd; for know, Iago,
But that I love the gentle Desdemona,   25
I would not my unhoused free condition

20. Which . . . know] *F, Q2; not in Q1.*   21. provulgate] *Q1;* promulgate *F, Q2.*
22. siege] *F* (Seige); height *Qq.*   23. to as] *Q1, F;* as *Q2.*

were not only troop carriers, but formed, as soon as they grappled, a platform on which something like a land battle could be conducted.

18. *signiory*] the whole Venetian oligarchy, consisting, according to a traveller of 1581, of about 300, of whom some forty formed an inner council.

21. *provulgate*] On the *difficilior lectio* principle Q1 carries it away, since *O.E.D.* does not even recognize the word, whereas *promulgate* had been in use from 1530. Further, *promulgate* has a certain connotation of publication by official authority which is not particularly appropriate to Othello's hypothetical action as a private individual in presenting the common people (*vulgus*) with the facts. The substitution of the ordinary word for the unusual is a common error. But supporters of F will rightly point out that to misread *m* as *u* is no more than a normal minim error.

22. *siege*] lit. seat, as in *Meas.*, IV. ii. 101, "upon the very siege of justice, Lord Angelo hath profess'd the contrary"; and thence "rank", "rating", as in *Ham.*, IV. vii. 73, "your sum of parts Did not together pluck such envy from him As did that one, and that, in my regard, Of the unworthiest siege".

It is possible to defend the *height* of Qq, since Shakespeare does elsewhere use the word to mean specifically high *rank*, and not merely metaphorical elevation (cf. *R 2*, I. i. 189, *R 3*, I. iii. 83) but it is a somewhat colourless word, and the confusion of the words, especially with the F spelling *seige*, is not unnatural, whether with the long lower-case or the upper-case *s*.

demerits] merits; "if things go well, Opinion, that so sticks on Marcius, shall Of his demerits rob Cominius" (*Cor.*, I. i. 276).

23 *unbonneted*] This must, in the context, mean "*without* taking the bonnet off", i.e. "on equal terms"; but the word does not occur elsewhere in Shakespeare and the only occurrence of "bonnet" as verb is indecisive. In *Cor.*, II. ii. 29, we have "those who, having been supple and courteous to the people, bonneted, without any further deed to have them at all into their estimation and report", of which the natural interpretation is that after being supple and courteous they put their bonnets on and walked off; but it can be taken to mean that they showed themselves supple and courteous, and then, as an additional mark of courtesy, took their bonnets off, but did no more. The point is of some importance in its connection with "off-capp'd" or "oft capp'd" at I. i. 10 above.

26. *unhoused*] unconfined—the opposite of "cabined" as in "cabin'd, cribb'd, confin'd".

Put into circumscription and confine
For the sea's worth. But look what lights come
　　yonder.

Iago.　These are the raised father and his friends,
You were best go in.

Oth.　　　　　　　Not I, I must be found: 　　30
My parts, my title, and my perfect soul,
Shall manifest me rightly: is it they?

Iago.　By Janus I think no.

Enter CASSIO, *with Officers, and torches.*

Oth.　The servants of the duke, and my lieutenant.
The goodness of the night upon you, friends! 　　35
What is the news?

Cas.　　　　　　The duke does greet you, general,
And he requires your haste post-haste appearance,
Even on the instant.

Oth.　　　　　　What's the matter, think you?

Cas.　Something from Cyprus, as I may divine;
It is a business of some heat, the galleys 　　40
Have sent a dozen sequent messengers
This very night, at one another's heels:
And many of the consuls, rais'd and met,
Are at the duke's already; you have been hotly call'd for,
When, being not at your lodging to be found, 　　45

28. yonder.] *Q1*; yond? *F*; yonder? *Q2*.　　29. These] *Qq*; Those *F*.　　32. me rightly] *Q1, F*; my right by *Q2*.　　is it they?] *F, Q2*; it is they. *Q1*.　　33. S.D.] *Enter* Cassio *with lights, and torches Qq (after* worth, *l. 28*); *Enter Cassio, with Torches F (after* yonder, *l. 28*).　　34. duke, and my lieutenant.] *Q1* (Duke ... Leiutenant); Duke, and my Leiutenant, *Q2*; Dukes? / And my Lieutenant? *F*.　　35. you, friends!] you (Friends) *F*; you (friends,) *Q2*; your friends, *Q1*.　　38. Even] *Qq* (Euen); Enen *F*.　　What's] *Qq*; What is *F*.　　41. sequent] *F, Q2*; frequent *Q1*.　　42. at one] *Q1, F*; one at *Q2*.

28. *sea's worth*] The sea was regarded as a treasure-house, whether of sunken treasures or (particularly) of pearls; "rich . . . as is the ooze and bottom of the sea With sunken wrack and sumless treasuries" (*H 5*, I. ii. 163).

31. *perfect*] (confident in being) fully prepared; "when you have A business for yourself, pray heaven you then Be perfect" (*Meas.*, v. i. 80).

33. *Janus*] the two-faced god.

38. *matter*] business.

41. *sequent*] Why should the hypothetical corrector of Q1 go out of his way to change a printed *sequent* to a weakly redundant "frequent"? But "frequent" would be an easy misreading of a written *sequent* with long *s*.

43. *consuls*] as at I. i. 25 above.

The senate sent about three several quests
To search you out.

Oth.   'Tis well I am found by you:
I will but spend a word here in the house,
And go with you.   [*Exit.*

Cas.   Ancient, what makes he here?

Iago. Faith, he to-night hath boarded a land carrack: 50
If it prove lawful prize, he's made for ever.

Cas. I do not understand.

Iago.   He's married.

Cas.   To who?

Enter OTHELLO.

Iago. Marry to ... Come, captain, will you go?

Oth.   Ha' with you.

Cas. Here comes another troop to seek for you.

Enter BRABANTIO, RODERIGO, *and others with lights and weapons.*

Iago. It is Brabantio, general, be advis'd,   55
He comes to bad intent.

Oth.   Holla, stand there!

Rod. Signior, it is the Moor.

Bra.   Down with him, thief!
                              [*They draw on both sides.*

Iago. You, Roderigo, come sir, I am for you.

46. sent] *Qq*; hath sent *F*.   about] *F*; aboue *Qq*.   48. I will but] *F, Q2*; Ile
Q1 (*for lineation see App. F, p. 229*).   49. *Exit*] *Rowe*.   50. carrack] Carrick *Q1*;
Carract *F*; Carriact *Q2*.   51. he's made] hee's made *Qq*; he' made *F*.
52. To who?] *Q1, F*; To whom. *Q2*.   S.D.] *Capell* (*Re-enter*).   53. Ha' with
you] *Q2*; Ha, with who? *Q1*; Haue with you. *F*.   54. comes another] *Qq*;
come sanother *F*.   S.D.] *Qq* (*after* To who? (whom.), *l. 52*; *Enter Brabantio,
Rodorigo with Officers, and Torches F* (*after* for you, *l. 54*).   57. S.D.] *Rowe*.
58. come] *Qq*; Cme *F*.

46. *about*] all round the city; Q's
"aboue" seems impossibly feeble.

50. *carrack*] a Spanish and Portuguese treasure ship.

52.] It is, as Theobald pointed out,
odd that Cassio, who had been (see
III. iii. 71–4 and 95–7 below) in
Othello's confidence in his wooing,
should here be puzzled. Perhaps, as
Blackstone suggested, it is an assumed
puzzlement, to avoid betraying the

confidence. Booth took this view:
"Feign much surprise, but do it carefully."

who] This nominative for accusative
is comparatively common in Shakespeare, particularly with the interro-
gative pronoun, but see *she* at IV. ii. 3
below.

58.] Iago singles out Roderigo; he
will not have his source of supply cut
off in a casual brawl if he can avoid it.

Oth. Keep up your bright swords, for the dew will
           rust 'em;
           Good signior, you shall more command with years   60
           Than with your weapons.
Bra. O thou foul thief, where has thou stow'd my
           daughter?
           Damn'd as thou art, thou hast enchanted her,
           For I'll refer me to all things of sense,
           (If she in chains of magic were not bound)   65
           Whether a maid, so tender, fair, and happy,
           So opposite to marriage, that she shunn'd
           The wealthy curled darlings of our nation,
           Would ever have (to incur a general mock)
           Run from her guardage to the sooty bosom   70
           Of such a thing as thou? to fear, not to delight.
           Judge me the world, if 'tis not gross in sense,
           That thou has practis'd on her with foul charms,
           Abus'd her delicate youth, with drugs or minerals,
           That weakens motion: I'll have 't disputed on;   75
           'Tis probable, and palpable to thinking.
           I therefore apprehend and do attach thee,
           For an abuser of the world, a practiser

59–61. Keep . . . weapons] *Qq; as prose F.*   63. Damn'd] *F;* Dambd *Qq.*
64. things] *F, Q2;* thing *Q1.*   65. (If . . . bound)] *F, Q2; not in Q1.*   68. darl-
ings] *Qq;* Deareling *F.*   71. thou?] *Qq;* thou: *F.*   72–7. Judge . . . thee] *F,
Q2; not in Q1.*   78. For] *F, Q2;* Such *Q1.*

64. *refer me*] submit my case to; "I do
refer me to the oracle" (*Wint.*, III. ii.
116).
   all things of sense] anyone of normal
perception; see note on III. iii. 344
below.
   70. *her guardage*] (my) guardianship
over her.
   71. *fear*] frighten (trans., as often in
Shakespeare); "How I may be cen-
sured, . . . fears me to think of" (*Lr.*,
III. v. 3).
   72. *gross in sense*] obvious to perception; "now to all sense 'tis gross You
love my son" (*All's W.*, I. iii. 180),
"With character too gross is writ"
(*Meas.*, I. ii. 165).
   74. *minerals*] properly a mineral (as

distinct from vegetable) drug, and
with a stronger implication of "poisonous"; cf. II. i. 292 below, and *Cym.*,
v. v. 49, "She did confess she had For
you a mortal mineral".
   75. *weakens motion*] This evidently
means "acts as a narcotic on normal
reactions". *Motion* in Shakespeare
often means "emotion" or "impulse"
(e.g. "Between the acting of a dreadful
thing And the first motion, all the
interim is . . ." (*Cæs.*, II. i. 63)), but the
only precise parallel that I can find for
the use here, and an interesting parallel, is the suggested reading in *Lr.*, I.
iv. 250, "his motion weakens, his dis-
cernings Are lethargied", where F's
notion produces a certain redundancy.

Of arts inhibited, and out of warrant;
Lay hold upon him, if he do resist,   80
Subdue him at his peril.

Oth.   Hold your hands,
Both you of my inclining and the rest:
Were it my cue to fight, I should have known it,
Without a prompter; where will you that I go,
And answer this your charge?

Bra.   To prison, till fit time   85
Of law, and course of direct session,
Call thee to answer.

Oth.   What if I do obey?
How may the duke be therewith satisfied,
Whose messengers are here about my side,
Upon some present business of the state,   90
To bear me to him?

Off.   'Tis true, most worthy signior,
The duke's in council, and your noble self,
I am sure is sent for.

Bra.   How? the duke in council?
In this time of the night? Bring him away;
Mine's not an idle cause, the duke himself,   95
Or any of my brothers of the state,
Cannot but feel this wrong, as 'twere their own.
For if such actions may have passage free,
Bond-slaves, and pagans, shall our statesmen be. [*Exeunt.*

83. cue] *F, Q2* (Cue *F*)*;* Qu. *Q1.*   84. where] *Qq;* Whether *F.*   85. And]
Q1; To *F, Q2.*   87. if I do] *Qq;* if do *F.*   91. bear] *Qq;* bring *F.*

79. *inhibited*] prohibited; "the most
inhibited sin in the canon" (*All's W.,*
I. i. 160).

out of warrant] illegal; cf. "fetch of
warrant" (*Ham.,* II. i. 38).

82. *my inclining*] my party; more
specific than our use, cf. *Ant.,* IV. vi. 13,
"there did persuade Great Herod to
incline himself to Caesar, And leave

his master Antony", where "incline
to" means "go over to"

86. *course of direct session*] normal
process of law; *direct* in Shakespeare
usually means "straightforward", as
in "be even and direct with me"
(*Ham.,* II. ii. 304), "To be direct and
honest, is not safe" (III. iii. 384
below).

SCENE III.—[*A Council Chamber.*]

Enter Duke and Senators, set at a table with lights and Attendants.

Duke.　There is no composition in these news,
　　　That gives them credit.
First Sen.　　　　　　　　　Indeed they are disproportion'd;
　　　My letters say, a hundred and seven galleys.
Duke.　And mine a hundred and forty.
Sec. Sen.　　　　　　　　　And mine two hundred:
　　　But though they jump not on a just account,　　　5
　　　(As in these cases, where they aim reports,
　　　'Tis oft with difference,) yet do they all confirm
　　　A Turkish fleet, and bearing up to Cyprus.
Duke.　Nay, it is possible enough to judgement:
　　　I do not so secure me to the error,　　　　　10
　　　But the main articles I do approve
　　　In fearful sense.
Sailor. [*Within*]　　　What ho! what ho! what ho!
Off.　A messenger from the galleys.

Enter Sailor.

Duke.　　　　　　　　　Now, the business?

Scene III

S.D.] *Qq; Enter Duke, Senators, and Officers F.*　1. There is] *Qq;* There's *F.*
these] *Qq;* this *F.*　4. and forty] *Qq;* fortie *F.*　6. they aim] *Q2* (ayme)*;*
they aym'd *Q1;* the ayme *F.*　10. to] *Qq;* in *F.*　11. articles] *Q1* (Articles)*;*
Article *F, Q2.*　12–13. S.D. *and speech-headings*] *see note below.*　13. galleys]
Gallies *F;* Galleys *Q2;* Galley *Q1.*　Now,] *Qq;* Now? What's *F.*

1. *composition*] consistency; usually of
a formal agreement, as in "Mad
world! mad kings! mad composition!"
(*John,* II. i. 561].

　5. *jump*] coincide; "Both our inven-
tions meet and jump in one" (*Shr.,* I. i.
194); and cf. the adverbial use of
jump, as at II. iii. 376 below.

　just] exact; "just pound" (*Mer.V.,*
IV. i. 328).

　6. *aim reports*] make approximate or
conjectural reports; cf. "What you
would work me to I have some aim"
(*Cæs.,* I. ii. 162).

10. *secure me to the error*] rely upon the
inconsistency (sc. so as to discredit the
whole).

　11. *main articles I do approve*] I accept
as true the main items (i.e. the Turkish
fleet and its destination); "Hast thou,
spirit, Perform'd to point the tempest
that I bade thee?—To every article"
(*Tp.,* I. ii. 193).

　12–13.] This is *F*'s arrangement,
and quite clear. The sailor shouts
"within" and is then introduced by the
officer. In Q "one within" shouts and
the sailor then introduces himself.

Sail. The Turkish preparation makes for Rhodes,
    So was I bid report here, to the state,   15
    By Signior Angelo.
Duke. How say you by this change?
First Sen.   This cannot be
    By no assay of reason . . . 'tis a pageant,
    To keep us in false gaze: when we consider
    The importancy of Cyprus to the Turk;   20
    And let ourselves again but understand,
    That as it more concerns the Turk than Rhodes,
    So may he with more facile question bear it,
    For that it stands not in such warlike brace,
    But altogether lacks the abilities   25
    That Rhodes is dress'd in. If we make thought of this,
    We must not think the Turk is so unskilful

16. By . . . Angelo] *F, Q2; not in Q1.*
Q1.   25. But] *F;* Who *Q2.*

24–30. For . . . profitless] *F, Q2; not in*

16. *Signior Angelo*] And who is he?
And why, whoever he is, is his name
mentioned? He does not appear in
Q1, whether through mere carelessness on the part of compositor (or possible transcriber), or by deliberate
omission to avoid an incomplete line
and an otherwise unknown person. He
is clearly not an early variant for
Montano—Shakespeare having not
yet made up his mind what the
Governor of Cyprus was to be called—
since the message is from ships at sea
who have been watching the enemy
fleet. Angelo is therefore presumably
the commander of the galleys. But his
introduction by name seems almost as
irrelevant as that of Luccicos later, and
rather suggests some hitherto undis-
covered source for this part of the
scene.

17. *by*] about; "virtuous In anything that I do know by her" (*Ado*,
v. i. 316).

18. *assay of reason*] test of common-
sense.

pageant] show; a pageant was properly the wheeled vehicle or platform
on which an episode in a miracle play
was staged, and so came to be used for

the episode itself, first in a miracle
play, later in any play; "some delightful ostentation, or show, or pageant, or
antick, or firework" (*LLL.*, v. i. 120).

19. *false gaze*] I think a specific metaphor from hunting, cf. "gaze-hound",
one which hunts by sight.

23. *with more facile question bear it*]
carry it (in the military sense of "win
it") with less arduous fighting; that is
clearly the meaning, but *question* is not
elsewhere used in Shakespeare in that
sense. However, "debate" is fairly
common for "fight" (e.g. "debate
with angry swords" (*Lucr.*, 1421), and
"question" can mean "debate", as in
Wiv., iii. i. 78.

24. *brace*] state of defence; so Johnson, most commentators, and Onions,
but it is not very easy to see how the
meaning is arrived at. "Brace" (verb)
can mean to "tighten" or "tighten up"
in readiness for something, so that the
noun might come to mean "in a state
of taut readiness". But Halliwell
appositely pointed out that the verb
was also used to mean "defy". The
obvious fact that *brace* can mean a
particular piece of armour is not
helpful.

To leave that latest, which concerns him first,
Neglecting an attempt of ease, and gain,
To wake and wage a danger profitless.   30
Duke. Nay, in all confidence, he's not for Rhodes.
Off. Here is more news.

Enter a Messenger.

Mess. The Ottomites, reverend and gracious,
Steering with due course, toward the isle of Rhodes,
Have there injointed with an after fleet—   35
First Sen. Ay, so I thought; how many, as you guess?
Mess. Of thirty sail, and now they do re-stem
Their backward course, bearing with frank appearance
Their purposes towards Cyprus: Signior Montano,
Your trusty and most valiant servitor,   40
With his free duty recommends you thus,
And prays you to believe him.
Duke. 'Tis certain then for Cyprus;
Marcus Luccicos is not here in town?

31. Nay,] *F, Q2;* And *Q1.*   32. S.D.] *F; Enter a 2. Messenger Qq.*   35. injointed] *Q1* (inioynted) *; inioynted them F, Q2.*   36–7. *First Sen.* Ay, . . . guess? *Mess.*] *F, Q2; not in Q1.*   37. re-stem] *F;* resterine *Q1;* resterne *Q2.*   39. towards] *Qq* (towarcs *Q2*) *;* toward *F.*   44. here in town?] here in Towne? *Q1;* he in towne? *F, Q2* (Towne *F*).

30. *wage*] risk; that is evidently the meaning, but the parallels adduced are not satisfactory, since in them either the word is used in the common sense of "wage battle", or it means to lay a wager, the object being the stake laid. But one can hardly "wage" a "danger" in either sense. The argument is that the Turks would not be likely to accept long odds against success. The nearest parallel I can find is that in *1 H 4,* IV. iv. 19, "I fear the power of Percy is too weak To wage an instant trial with the king", but even there "wage" can mean simply "engage in".

36.] The First Senator's interruptive line (and if this line, then perhaps also ll. 24–30) looks very much like an addition by Shakespeare, giving more individuality to the speaker, who

emerges as an officious, opinionated old gentleman, rather like Polonius.

37. *re-stem*] No doubt "restemme" could easily be misread as "resterine" and if there was such a word one would be content. But it is worth observing that the editor of Q2 was clearly not happy with the supposition that the Q1 compositor had produced a *vox nihili* out of a straightforward "re-stemme".

41. *free duty*] unqualified expressions of respect; "I salute you.—My duty to you both . . . Great kings" (*H 5,* v. ii. 22).

recommends] informs. Montano concludes his message in formal style.

44. *Marcus Luccicos*] He is even more mysterious than Signior Angelo. Othello's appointment and his departure are matters of urgency, and he is

First Sen. He's now in Florence.   45
Duke. Write from us, wish him post post-haste, dispatch.
First Sen. Here comes Brabantio and the valiant Moor.

Enter BRABANTIO, OTHELLO, CASSIO, IAGO, RODERIGO, *and*
Officers.

Duke. Valiant Othello, we must straight employ you,
          Against the general enemy Ottoman;
          [*To Brabantio*] I did not see you; welcome, gentle
              signior,   50
          We lack'd your counsel and your help to-night.
Bra. So did I yours: good your grace, pardon me,
          Neither my place, nor aught I heard of business,
          Hath rais'd me from my bed, nor doth the general care
          Take any hold of me, for my particular grief   55
          Is of so flood-gate and o'erbearing nature,
          That it engluts and swallows other sorrows,
          And it is still itself.
Duke.   Why, what's the matter?
Bra. My daughter, O my daughter!
All.   Dead?
Bra.   Ay, to me:
          She is abus'd, stol'n from me and corrupted,   60

46. us, wish him post] *Q1;* vs, / To him, Post *F;* vs to him post *Q2.*   47. S.D.]
F; Enter Brabantio, Othello, Roderigo, Iago, Cassio, Desdemona, *and Officers Qq.*
51. lack'd] lack't *F;* lacke *Q1;* lackt *Q2.*   53. nor] *Qq;* hor *F.*   55. any hold
of] *Q1;* hold on *F;* hold of *Q2.*   grief] *F, Q2;* griefes *Q1.*   57. and] *Qq;* snd
F.   59. *All*] *Qq;* Sen *F.*

going to be on the high seas long before
Luccicos can arrive, with whatever
"dispatch" he comes.

54, 55.] Two suspiciously hypermetrical lines. The first line, except for
F's semi-colon for comma, is identical
in Q1 and F. In the second it is not
easy to see why the Q1 compositor
should have gone out of his way to
insert a non-existent *any,* and F was
probably tidying the metre by omission. Various cures have been proposed, none convincing; Johnson, for
example, suggested the omission of
care, Steevens that of *Hath* and the *my*
before *bed.* I rather suspect that there

was some re-writing, and that Shakespeare's deletions and corrections were
not understood. To add yet another
conjecture, perhaps he intended the
lines to stand as *Hath rais'd me from my*
bed, nor generall care Tane [i.e. *Ta'en*]
hold on me... The substitution of *ane* for
an imperfectly deleted *ake* might
account for the *any.*

56. *flood-gate*] sluice-gate, which,
when opened, allows the full head of
water to pour through; "the flood-
gates of her eyes" (*1 H 4,* II. iv. 440);
and hence simply "torrent"; "Of her
gored wound . . . He . . . did the flood-
gate stop" (*F.Q.,* II. i. 43).

By spells and medicines, bought of mountebanks,
For nature so preposterously to err,
(Being not deficient, blind, or lame of sense,)
Sans witchcraft could not.

Duke. Whoe'er he be, that in this foul proceeding   65
Hath thus beguil'd your daughter of herself,
And you of her, the bloody book of law
You shall yourself read, in the bitter letter,
After its own sense, though our proper son
Stood in your action.

Bra.   Humbly I thank your grace;   70
Here is the man, this Moor, whom now it seems
Your special mandate, for the state-affairs,
Hath hither brought.

All.   We are very sorry for 't.

Duke. [*To Othello*] What in your own part can you say to
    this?

Bra. Nothing, but this is so.   75

Oth. Most potent, grave, and reverend signiors,
My very noble and approv'd good masters:
That I have ta'en away this old man's daughter,
It is most true: true, I have married her,
The very head and front of my offending   80
Hath this extent, no more. Rude am I in my speech,

---

63. (Being . . . sense,)] *F, Q2; not in Q1.*   64. Sans] *F, Q2;* Saunce *Q1 (one British Museum copy* Since). 69. its] *Qq;* your *F.* sense, though] *Q1* (tho); sense: yes, though *F;* sense, yea tho *Q2.*   74. your] *Qq;* yonr *F.*   77. masters:] maisters: *Q1;* Masters; *F;* Masters: *Q2.*

---

61. *mountebanks*] charlatans; "I bought an unction of a mountebank" (*Ham.*, IV. vii. 141).

62. *preposterously*] as usual in Shakespeare, in the loose general sense of "absurdly".

63. *sense*] here of physical, rather than mental, perception.

64. *Sans*] common Elizabethan for "without" ("Sans teeth, . . ." (*AYL.*, II. vii. 166)); the spelling "sance" or, as here in Q1, "saunce", indicates the Anglicized pronunciation.

69. *its*] F's *your*, though superficially effective, and acclaimed by Dyce as "manifestly the true reading", does not stand up to closer inspection. The Doge of Venice, a state which (as Shakespeare very well knew and in *Mer.V.* showed that he knew) prided itself on impartial justice, would hardly encourage even a "senator" to suppose that he can interpret the law as he likes. What he says is that Brabantio will have the strictest justice whoever the man against whom his action lies.

proper] own; "your own proper wisdom" (*All's W.*, IV. ii. 49); cf. IV. i. 68 below and note.

And little blest with the set phrase of peace,
For since these arms of mine had seven years' pith,
Till now some nine moons wasted, they have us'd
Their dearest action in the tented field,   85
And little of this great world can I speak,
More than pertains to feats of broil, and battle,
And therefore little shall I grace my cause,
In speaking for myself: yet, (by your gracious patience)
I will a round unvarnish'd tale deliver,   90
Of my whole course of love, what drugs, what charms,
What conjuration, and what mighty magic,
(For such proceedings am I charged withal)
I won his daughter.

Bra.   A maiden never bold of spirit,

82. set] *Qq;* soft *F and most edd.*   87. feats of broil] feate of broyle *Q1;* Feats of
Broiles *F;* feates of broyles *Q2.*   90. will] *Q1, F;* would *Q2.*   unvarnish'd]
vnuarnish'd *Q1;* vn-varnish'd u *F;* vnrauish'd *Q2.*   93. proceedings am I]
Qq; proceeding I am *F.*   94–5. bold of spirit, / So] *Q1;* bold: / Of spirit so *F;*
bold, / Of spirit so *Q2.*

82. *set*] *soft,* as is often the way of F
variants, looks at first sight the more
apt, as stressing the contrast between
peace and war. But this is not Othello's
point. He is a soldier; his speech will
therefore be "rude", "unvarnish'd"
and not "grac'd" with well-turned
conventional phrases; cf. "good set
terms" (*AYL.*, ii. vii. 17), "these set
kind of fools" (*Tw.N.*, i. v. 94).

83. *pith*] strength; "grandsires,
babies, and old women, Either past or
not arriv'd to pith and puissance"
(*H 5*, iii. Chor. 20).

85. *dearest*] See note on l. 259 below.

90. *round*] blunt; "Your reproof is
something too round" (*H 5*, iv. i.
219).

94–6. *A maiden . . . her self*] The first
problem in these lines is the lineation
and punctuation. Q1 reads *A maiden
neuer bold of spirit, / So still and quiet, that
her motion / Blusht at her selfe:*; F reads
*A Maiden, neuer bold: / Of Spirit so still,
and quiet, that her Motion / Blush'd at her
selfe,*; Q2, adopting F's lineation, but
retaining Q1's punctuation with the

transposition of a comma, reads
*A maiden neuer bold, / Of spirit so still and
quiet, that her motion/Blusht at her selfe:*. It
will be observed (*a*) that Q1's l. 95,
with trisyllabic *motion*, is a normal
light-running line, whereas F produces a tolerable l. 94 out of Othello's
last four words and Brabantio's first
four at the cost of an awkwardly congested l. 95; and (*b*) that there seems
no reason why the Q1 compositor, if he
found *Of spirit* at the beginning of l. 95,
should take it up to the end of the preceding line, and even less reason if he
found *bold* followed by a heavy mark of
punctuation and *spirit* by no mark of
punctuation at all. It is, I think, a
reasonable inference that Q1 probably represents the punctuation, and
possibly also the lineation, of the
original.

The second problem is the meaning
of *her motion blush'd at her self*. *Motion* is
usually explained as "natural impul-
ses" or "movement of the soul", and
her self taken as = "itself". This second
usage is common enough, but not,
I think, in this context, natural, since

So still and quiet, that her motion   95
Blush'd at her self: and she, in spite of nature,
Of years, of country, credit, everything,
To fall in love with what she fear'd to look on?
It is a judgment maim'd, and most imperfect,
That will confess perfection so would err   100
Against all rules of nature, and must be driven
To find out practices of cunning hell,
Why this should be; I therefore vouch again,
That with some mixtures powerful o'er the blood,
Or with some dram conjur'd to this effect,   105
He wrought upon her.
Duke.   To vouch this is no proof,
Without more certain and more overt test;
These are thin habits, and poor likelihoods
Of modern seemings, you prefer against him.
First Sen. But, Othello, speak,   110
Did you by indirect and forced courses

98. on?] *Qq;* on; *F.*   99. maim'd] *Qq* (maimd); main'd *F.*   100. would]
Qq; could *F.*   106. wrought] *Qq;* wtought *F.*   *Duke*] *Qq (Du); not in F.*
vouch] *F, Q2;* youth *Q1.*   107. certain] *Qq;* wider *F.*   overt test;] *Qq*
(ouert); ouer Test *F.*   108. These are] *Qq;* Then these *F.*   109. seemings,
you] *Qq;* seeming, do *F.*

the immediately preceding *her* leads
one to suppose (especially when *her*
and *self* are separate words) that the
'possessors' of the motion and the self
are the same person. In any case the
whole phrase is one of those, common
in Shakespeare, of which the meaning
has to be felt rather than arrived at by
analysis, since how can a "motion",
however interpreted, blush at either
itself or Desdemona? But I think
that the straightforward meaning for
motion of *physical* movement has been
too readily abandoned. Does the
phrase amount to anything more
subtle than, in more modern terms,
"She couldn't even get up and cross
the room without blushing"?

102. *cunning*] with a stronger implication of knowledge and less of trivial
trickery than in our use; see note on
III. iii. 50 below.

105. *conjur'd*] made powerful by

spells; not elsewhere in this sense in
Shakespeare.

107. *test*] testimony. (It is odd that
so many editors, normally devoted to
F, here readily desert it for Q1. Testimony which came from more witnesses and covered more points might
well be described as *wider.*)

108. *thin habits*] "your accusation
has a shabbily threadbare dress"; cf.
"the tune of the time and outward
habit of encounter" (*Ham.*, v. ii. 198)
and III. iii. 437 below.

poor likelihoods] shaky grounds for
inference; "These likelihoods confirm
her flight" (*Gent.*, v. ii. 43).

109. *modern*] commonplace; "wise
saws and modern instances" (*AYL.*,
II. vii. 156), "to make modern and
familiar, things supernatural and
causeless" (*All's W.*, II. iii. 2).

111. *forced*] This seems to have the
unusual meaning of "tortuous", and

Subdue and poison this young maid's affections?
Or came it by request, and such fair question,
As soul to soul affordeth?

Oth.   I do beseech you,
Send for the lady to the Sagittar,   115
And let her speak of me before her father;
If you do find me foul in her report,
The trust, the office, I do hold of you,
Not only take away, but let your sentence
Even fall upon my life.

Duke.   Fetch Desdemona hither.   120
                [Two or three attendants move towards the door.

Oth. [*to Iago*] Ancient, conduct them, you best know the
        place: [*Exeunt Attendants and Iago.*
And till she come, as faithful as to heaven
I do confess the vices of my blood,
So justly to your grave ears I'll present
How I did thrive in this fair lady's love,   125
And she in mine.

Duke. Say it, Othello.

Oth. Her father lov'd me, oft invited me,
Still question'd me the story of my life,
From year to year; the battles, sieges, fortunes,   130
That I have pass'd:
I ran it through, even from my boyish days,
To the very moment that he bade me tell it.
Wherein I spake of most disastrous chances,

115. Sagittar] *Q1*; Sagitary *F*; Sagittary *Q2*.   118. The . . . you] *F, Q2; not in
Q1*.   120. S.D. *Two or three . . . door*] *Exit two or three Q1; Exeunt two or three Q2;
no S.D. in F.*   121. S.D.] *Capell.*   122. till] *Qq*; tell *F.*   faithful] *Q1*; truely *F,
Q2*.   123. I . . . blood] *F, Q2; not in Q1*.   130. battles] battailes *Qq*; Bataile *F.*
fortunes] *Qq*; Fortune *F.*   134. spake] *Qq*; spoke *F.*

the nearest Shakespearean parallel is
that in *Ham.,* v. ii. 397, "deaths put on
by cunning and forc'd cause". Or is it
no more than a "passive for active",
and so = "forcible"?

115. *Sagittar*] See note on I. i. 158
above.

120, 121. S.Ds.] The two S.Ds. I
hope represent what is needed. F has
no S.D., Q1 only "Exit two or three"

after *hither.* Othello's direction to Iago
must precede the actual disappearance
of the attendants.

123.] One must, I suppose, attribute
the absence of the line from Q1 to
mere blunder, but it is an odd one,
particularly when taken with the
variant *faithfull* for *truely,* since *as
faithfull* less imperatively demands the
missing line than *as truly.*

Of moving accidents by flood and field;   135
Of hair-breadth scapes i' th' imminent deadly breach;
Of being taken by the insolent foe;
And sold to slavery, and my redemption thence,
And with it all my travel's history;
Wherein of antres vast, and deserts idle,   140
Rough quarries, rocks and hills, whose heads touch
    heaven,
It was my hint to speak, such was the process:
And of the Cannibals, that each other eat;
The Anthropophagi, and men whose heads
Do grow beneath their shoulders: this to hear   145
Would Desdemona seriously incline;
But still the house-affairs would draw her thence,
And ever as she could with haste dispatch,
She'ld come again, and with a greedy ear
Devour up my discourse; which I observing,   150
Took once a pliant hour, and found good means
To draw from her a prayer of earnest heart,

135. accidents by] *F;* accident of *Q₁;* accidents, by *Q₂.*   138. slavery, and] *Q₁;* slauery. Of *F;* slauery; of *Q₂.*   139. with it all] *Q₁;* portance in *F, Q₂.* travel's] trauells *Qq;* Trauellours *F.*   140. antres] Antrees *Q₁;* Antars *F, Q₂.* 141. rocks and hills] *Qq;* Rocks, Hills *F.*   heads] *Qq;* head *F.*   142. hint] *F, Q₂;* hent *Q₁.*   the] *Q₁;* my *F, Q₂.*   143. other] *Qq;* others *F.*   144. Anthropophagi] *Anthropophagie Qq; Antropophague F.*   145. Do grow] *Qq;* Grew *F.*   this] *Q₁;* These things *F;* these *Q₂.*   147. thence] *Qq;* hence *F.* 148. And] *Q₁;* Which *F, Q₂.*

139.] This line is an illuminating example of editorial operations, since the acceptance of F's *portance* is almost as unanimous as the rejection of F's *Trauellours.* But if one, why not the other? Judged by 'preferability'— that dangerous criterion—*portance* is no doubt a good mouth-filling phrase, by the side of which *with it all* seems anaemic. But is it not also seriously out of character? Othello is the last man to expatiate on his own creditable behaviour under stress, and *portance* has inescapably the connotation of "how a man carries himself" and not merely "what happens to him". Further, *with it all* marks a transition; so far Othello had related his adventures in war;

then, along with those, he went on to relate the scenes and people he had met with on his travels.

140. *antres*] caves; *O.E.D.* records no example before this passage, or till 1818 (in *Endymion*) after it.

idle] usually glossed as "serving no useful purpose", "sterile", but I think Shakespeare used it to convey the *emptiness* of the desert; cf. "idle times" (*2 H 4,* II. ii. 14), "idle hours" (*R 2,* III. iv. 66).

143-5. *Cannibals . . . shoulders*] Such travellers' tales were current, and it seems as idle as the deserts to try to determine whether Shakespeare was primarily indebted to Mandeville or Raleigh or Holland's Pliny.

That I would all my pilgrimage dilate,
Whereof by parcel she had something heard,
But not intentively: I did consent,   155
And often did beguile her of her tears,
When I did speak of some distressed stroke
That my youth suffer'd: my story being done,
She gave me for my pains a world of sighs;
She swore i' faith 'twas strange, 'twas passing
    strange;   160
'Twas pitiful, 'twas wondrous pitiful;
She wish'd she had not heard it, yet she wish'd
That heaven had made her such a man: she thank'd me,
And bade me, if I had a friend that lov'd her,

---

154. parcel] parcell *Q1;* parcels *F;* parcells *Q2.*   155. intentively] *Qq;*
instinctively *F.*   157. distressed] *Q1;* distressefull *F;* distresfull *Q2.*   159.
sighs] *Qq;* kisses *F.*   160-1. strange, 'twas passing strange; 'Twas pitiful,
'twas] *Qq;* strange: 'twas passing strange, 'Twas pittifull: 'twas *F.*

153. *dilate*] narrate at length; "Do
me the favour to dilate at full What
hath befall'n of them and thee till
now" (*Err.*, I. i. 122).

154. *parcel*] detail; usually plural, as
"the parcels and particulars of our
grief" (*2 H 4*, IV. ii. 36).

155. *intentively*] The usual meaning
was "attentively". But there is no
reason to suppose that Desdemona did
not listen to the "parcels" with the
most flattering attention, and the
word must here mean "continuously",
"at a stretch".

156. *beguile*] The word in Shakespeare normally means either "while
away", as in *All's W.*, IV. i. 25, "to
beguile two hours in a sleep", or
"trick", as in *Shr.*, III. i. 36, "that we
might beguile the old pantaloon", or
"trick someone *out of* something", as in
Troil., IV. iv. 33, "injury of chance . . .
rudely beguiles our lips Of all rejoin-
dure" and *1 H 4*, III. i. 186, "leaves
behind a stain Upon the beauty of all
parts besides, Beguiling them of com-
mendation"; the meaning required
here seems to be "coax tears from her"
to which the nearest parallel, and not
a very satisfactory one, is *Wiv.*, IV. v.

37, "the very same man that beguiled
Master Slender of his chain cozened
him of it".

159. *sighs*] *kisses* is as difficult to
account for as to accept, and the
motion of F's Desdemona would surely
have blushed at herself. The word can
hardly have been a misreading of
sighs, however ill-written, yet it is
hard to imagine anyone making the
alteration deliberately. Perhaps the
compositor had recently been setting a passage in which "world of
kisses" occurred, and it stuck in his
mind.

163. *made her*] Is *her* accusative or
dative? The supporters of either view
are apt to regard those of the other as
obtuse. The straightforward accusative seems to me certainly right. With
the dative the wish not only is unexpectedly 'forward', but also makes
the following "hint" quite needless;
and further, the use of the word *made*
gives the wish an arrogance which is
still more out of character, since
heaven is then thought of not as just
bringing such a man across her path,
but as manufacturing such a man for
her alone.

I should but teach him how to tell my story,   165
And that would woo her. Upon this hint I spake:
She lov'd me for the dangers I had pass'd,
And I lov'd her that she did pity them.
This only is the witchcraft I have us'd:
Here comes the lady, let her witness it.   170

Enter DESDEMONA, IAGO, *Attendants.*

Duke. I think this tale would win my daughter too, . . .
Good Brabantio,
Take up this mangled matter at the best;
Men do their broken weapons rather use,
Than their bare hands.
Bra.   I pray you hear her speak.   175
If she confess that she was half the wooer,
Destruction light on me, if my bad blame
Light on the man! Come hither, gentle mistress:
Do you perceive in all this noble company,
Where most you owe obedience?
Des.   My noble father,   180
I do perceive here a divided duty:
To you I am bound for life and education,
My life and education both do learn me
How to respect you, you are lord of all my duty,   184
I am hitherto your daughter: but here's my husband:
And so much duty as my mother show'd
To you, preferring you before her father,

---

166. hint] *F;* heate *Qq.*   170. S.D.] *F; Enter* Desdemona, Iago, *and the rest Qq.*
177. light on me] *Qq* (lite *Q1*); on my head *F.*   184. lord of all my] *Q1* (Lord);
the Lord of *F, Q2.*

177. *light on me*] The repeated *light on* is effective, but may none the less be an effective blunder; F's *on my head* may be the original, or a correction by someone who thought the repetition too mechanical.

184. *lord of all my duty*] F's *the Lord of duty* looks like an attempt to avoid the apparent difficulty of *all*, and Q2 evidently felt the same difficulty. But the attempt is not a very successful one, and the difficulty more apparent than real. What Desdemona is trying to say is quite clear, even if she does not say it very clearly, granted that we take "duty" to mean "what is due", and not "obedience". The key word is *divided*, in l. 181. She owes, and always has owed, to Brabantio all that is due from daughter to father; but "all that is *due*" is no longer, as hitherto it has been, "all she has to give" since now she has a duty also to her husband.

So much I challenge, that I may profess,
Due to the Moor my lord.
Bra.   God bu'y, I ha' done:
Please it your grace, on to the state-affairs;   190
I had rather to adopt a child than get it;
Come hither, Moor:
I here do give thee that, with all my heart,
Which, but thou hast already, with all my heart
I would keep from thee. For your sake (jewel)   195
I am glad at soul I have no other child,
For thy escape would teach me tyranny,
To hang clogs on 'em; I have done, my lord.
Duke. Let me speak like yourself, and lay a sentence,
Which as a grise or step may help these lovers   200
Into your favour.
When remedies are past, the griefs are ended,
By seeing the worst, which late on hopes depended.
To mourn a mischief that is past and gone,
Is the next way to draw more mischief on.   205
What cannot be preserv'd when fortune takes,
Patience her injury a mockery makes.

---

189. God bu'y, I ha' done] *Qq;* God be with you: I haue done *F.*   194. Which
. . . heart] *F, Q2; not in Q1.*   198. 'em] *Qq;* them *F.*   201. Into your favour]
Qq; not in F.   205. more] *Qq;* new *F.*   206. preserv'd] *Qq* (preseru'd)*; *pre-
sern'd *F.*

189. *God bu'y*] one of the ordinary
abbreviations of "God be with
you".

194.] The passage is in fact more
logical in Q1, without this line,
since then Brabantio says bluntly that
he gives (sc. reluctantly) to Othello
what with all his heart he would keep
from him, while F makes him say that
he is giving with all his heart, which is
not true. But the verbal play is undeniably Shakespearean and the
omission, if it is an error, a very easy
one, the compositor taking off for
l. 195 from the second *heart.*

195. *For your sake*] on your account
(not "for your benefit").

199. *like yourself*] Does the Doge
mean "in your well-known sententious

vein" or "with the paternal kindliness
that you would yourself show if you
were in a better mood"?

sentence] Latin "sententia", a gnomic
saying.

200. *grise*] step; "every grize of fortune Is smooth'd by that below"
(*Tim.*, IV. iii. 16).

201. *Into your favour*] F, wanting
these words, does not explain how the
"grise" is to be helpful; it need not be
so *per se,* and indeed may be the
reverse, as in *Mac.,* I. iv. 48, "that is a
step On which I must fall down, or else
o'er-leap".

203. *which*] The antecedent is *griefs.*

207. *Patience . . . makes*] Patient endurance enables one to shrug one's
shoulders at an irrevocable loss.

The robb'd that smiles, steals something from the thief,
He robs himself, that spends a bootless grief.

Bra. So let the Turk of Cyprus us beguile,   210
We lose it not so long as we can smile;
He bears the sentence well, that nothing bears
But the free comfort which from thence he hears:
But he bears both the sentence and the sorrow,
That, to pay grief, must of poor patience borrow.   215
These sentences to sugar, or to gall,
Being strong on both sides, are equivocal:
But words are words; I never yet did hear
That the bruis'd heart was pierced through the ear:
Beseech you now, to the affairs of the state.   220

Duke. The Turk with most mighty preparation makes
for Cyprus: Othello, the fortitude of the place is
best known to you, and though we have there a
substitute of most allowed sufficiency, yet opinion,
a sovereign mistress of effects, throws a more safer   225
voice on you: you must therefore be content to
slubber the gloss of your new fortunes, with this
more stubborn and boisterous expedition.

---

210. So let] *Qq, F;* So, let *Theobald.*   219. ear] *Qq;* eares *F.*   220. Beseech
you now, to] *Qq;* I humbly beseech you proceed to *F.*   of the state] *Qq;* of
State *F.*   221. most] *Qq;* a most *F.*   225. sovereign] *Qq* (soueraigne) *;* more
soueraigne *F.*   227. gloss] glosse *Qq, F;* grosse *F2.*

---

209. *bootless*] unavailing; "Doth not
Brutus bootless kneel?" (*Cæs.*, III. i.
75).

216. *gall*] bitterness; "You have the
honey still, but these the gall" (*Troil.*,
II. ii. 144).

219. *bruis'd . . . ear*] Brabantio must,
apparently, mean that the *bruis'd*
heart is not to be lanced—and so
relieved—through the ear. Other passages in Shakespeare are not helpful.
Ears are often pierced by words, as in
LLL., v. ii. 761, "Honest plain words
best pierce the ear of grief", but the
only cure suggested for an inward
bruise is parmaceti, in *1 H 4*, I. iii. 58,
while there is an odd passage in *H 5*,
III. vi. 132, "we thought not good to
bruise an injury till it were full ripe",

where lancing would seem a more
appropriate treatment for a "ripe"
injury than bruising.

222. *fortitude*] strength; a most
unusual use, of an inanimate object
and of a purely physical quality.

223–6. *though we have . . . on you*]
Montano is admitted to be thoroughly
competent, but general opinion,
which finally determines what ought
to be done, will feel safer with you in
command.

227. *slubber*] smear over; "tickle our
noses with spear-grass to make them
bleed, and then to beslubber our gar-
ments with it" (*1 H 4*, II. iv. 343).

228. *stubborn*] rough; often without
our implication of obstinacy; "I fear
these stubborn lines lack power to

Oth. The tyrant custom, most grave senators,
Hath made the flinty and steel couch of war   230
My thrice-driven bed of down: I do agnize
A natural and prompt alacrity
I find in hardness, and would undertake
This present wars against the Ottomites.
Most humbly therefore, bending to your state,   235
I crave fit disposition for my wife,
Due reference of place, and exhibition,
With such accommodation and besort
As levels with her breeding.

Duke.   If you please,
Be 't at her father's.

Bra.   I'll not have it so.   240

Oth. Nor I.

Des.   Nor I, I would not there reside,

229. grave] *F, Q2;* great *Q1.*   230. couch] *Pope;* Cooch *Qq;* Coach *F.*
232. alacrity] *Qq;* Alacartie *F.*   233. would] *Q1;* do(e) *F, Q2.*   234. wars]
warres *Q1;* Warres *F;* warre *Q2.*   237. reference] *F, Q2;* reuerence *Q1;* preference *Johnson conj.*   239–40. If . . . father's] *Qq (as one line);* Why at her
Fathers? *F.*   240. I'll] *Qq (Ile);* I will *F.*   241. Nor I, I would not] *Qq;* Nor
would I *F.*

move" (*LLL.,* IV. iii. 55). Cf. "trans-
late the stubbornness of fortune Into
so quiet and so sweet a style" (*AYL.,*
II. i. 19).

boisterous] The word in Shakespeare has a more pronounced connotation of harshness and violence, and
less of crude high spirits, than with us;
"A sceptre snatch'd with an unruly
hand Must be as boisterously maintain'd as gain'd" (*John,* III. iv. 135).

expedition] more often in Shakespeare in the sense simply of "speed"
than in that of a military enterprise;
"if thou linger . . . Longer than swiftest
expedition Will give thee time to
leave" (*Gent.,* III. i. 163).

231. *thrice-driven*] softest possible; a
current of air drifted the finer and
lighter feathers away from the coarser
and heavier.

agnize] recognize in myself; "Happy
is that man . . . that . . agniseth his
faults" (Wootton, 1576).

236–8. *disposition . . . besort*] a slightly

suspicious passage; *disposition* is not
used elsewhere in Shakespeare except
for "mental or emotional make-up or
mood", though no doubt it can well be
taken as the noun of "dispose" as used
in *Meas.,* II. ii. 16, "Dispose of her To
some more fitter place"; *reference* does
not occur in any sense suitable to this
context; *besort* occurs only as verb =
"befit"; *accommodation* does not occur
in any sense that is helpful; indeed the
only straightforward word is *exhibition*
= "maintenance" as in *Lr.,* I. ii. 24,
"subscrib'd his power! Confin'd to
exhibition". And the passage seems
overloaded with words expressing
"suitability"—*fit, due, besort, levels,* and
perhaps *accommodation.*

I suspect that there has been some
confusion, resulting in redundancy,
and, in particular, that *besort* was intended as a verb, in some such phrase
as "As may besort her breeding"
which was intended to replace or be
replaced by "As levels with . . ."

> To put my father in impatient thoughts,
> By being in his eye: most gracious duke,
> To my unfolding lend a gracious ear,
> And let me find a charter in your voice,   245
> And if my simpleness . . .
>
> *Duke.* What would you . . . speak.
> *Des.* That I did love the Moor, to live with him,
> My downright violence, and scorn of fortunes,
> May trumpet to the world: my heart's subdued   250
> Even to the utmost pleasure of my lord:
> I saw Othello's visage in his mind,

243. gracious] *Qq;* Grcaious *F.*   244. a gracious] *Qq;* your prosperous *F;*
your gracious *Pope, Theobald.*   246–7. And if . . . speak] *Q1;* T'assist my
simplenesse. *Duke.* What would you Desdemona? *F, Q2* (*Q2 with dash after*
simplenesse.).   248. did] *Qq; not in F.*   249. scorn] *Q1* (scorne)*;* storme
F, Q2.   251. Even] *F, Q2* (Euen)*;* Fuen *Q1.*   utmost pleasure] *Q1;* very
quality *F, Q2* (qualitie) *Q2*).

245. *charter*] strictly "a right formally granted", but often little more
than "permission"; cf. "my mother,
Who has a charter to extol her blood"
(*Cor.*, i. ix. 13).

246.] Desdemona's hesitation is
both natural and effective, while F's
reading looks like a sophisticating
completion of syntax. On the other
hand it is true that interruption of
speeches in Shakespeare is not as a rule
due to mere hesitation, but either to
death (as with the last broken utterances of Hotspur and Cleopatra,
which are completed by Prince Hal
and Charmian) or to deliberate action
by the interlocutor (as Macmorris
breaks in on Fluellen in a temper, and
Cressida teases Pandarus by interrupting him).

249. *scorn*] The Q1 and F readings
are graphically almost indifferent,
since the *c : t* confusion is common and
a minim error even commoner, so that
either word might easily be read as the
other.

251. *utmost pleasure*] Q1's reading is
quite straightforward, and if it stood
alone would arouse no suspicion; *very
quality* looks like an alteration by some
one who wanted to lead up to and
emphasize the point of the next line.
But this is, I think, to misunderstand
the gist of Desdemona's argument, in
which the mention of Othello's visage
is merely parenthetic. She is saying
"My love for Othello makes me want
to live with him; I do not want to be a
grass widow, but to live with him in
full marital intercourse; and since he
is a soldier and now ordered on foreign
service, I can do that only by going to
the wars with him." Desdemona, like
all Shakespeare's best women, is outspoken, and part of the trouble here is
caused by the commentators who
boggle at allowing her to mean what
she says, prefer *very quality* as more
'maidenly' and want, needlessly and
even insultingly, to preserve Desdemona's 'delicacy' by reading "rights"
for *rites* six lines below. But *utmost pleasure* surely includes, though it is not
limited by, what Othello later calls
"the profit". It may be noticed that
Othello himself has so far not even
hinted that Desdemona may come
with him, with whatever alacrity he
welcomes the suggestion when she
makes it. See Introduction, p. lxv.

And to his honours, and his valiant parts
Did I my soul and fortunes consecrate:
So that, dear lords, if I be left behind,   255
A moth of peace, and he go to the war,
The rites for which I love him are bereft me,
And I a heavy interim shall support,
By his dear absence; let me go with him.

Oth. Your voices, Lords: beseech you, let her will   260
Have a free way; I therefore beg it not
To please the palate of my appetite,
Nor to comply with heat, the young affects

---

257. which] *Qq*; why *F*.   260–1. Your voices ... way; I] *Q1* (way, I) *;* Let her have your voice. / Vouch with me Heaven / *F;* Your voyces ... will / Have ... way: / Vouch with me heauen, I *Q2*.

---

256. *moth*] This seems to mean "an unprofitable idler", as we should say "drone" and much as Volumnia uses the word in *Cor.*, I. iii. 93, "all the yarn she [Penelope] spun . . . did but fill Ithaca full of moths". Other uses in Shakespeare are not illuminating, and there seems to be no implication of the moth as a destroyer (as in "moth and rust do corrupt"); but it is perhaps just worth noticing that in one passage *peace* is connected with the other of these two corrupting agencies, "This peace is nothing but to rust iron" (*Cor.*, IV. v. 235).

257. *rites*] Cf. "Lovers can see to do their amorous rites By their own beauties" (*Rom.*, III. ii. 8). A. Walker says "The 'rites' of modern editions (based on the ambiguous spelling 'rites' of the early texts and interpreted as 'love's rites') is a misunderstanding of Desdemona almost as bad as the quarto's 'utmost pleasure'." I suggest that to retain "rites" is to "misunderstand" a Desdemona of Dr Walker's creation, not of Shakespeare's. And "ambiguous spelling" is, I think, definitely misleading. It seems to imply that the spellings 'rite' and 'right' were more or less indifferent, so that wherever the one occurs we can, if we choose, read the other. To substantiate Dr Walker's view we need to

find instances where the context clearly demands 'rights' but the texts give us 'rites'. Such instances are hard to find. On checking some 50 occurrences of the two words (38 of 'rights' and 15 of 'rites') in places where the demands of the context are fairly decisive, I found in the early texts a handsome tally of 'rights' for 'rites' (10), as, for example, "we have perform'd Our Roman rightes" (*Tit.*, I. i. 142), and (surprisingly) "Lovers can see to do their amorous rights" (*Rom.*, III. ii. 8) but only a single instance of 'rites' for 'rights', at *Ham.*, v. ii. 403, "I have some rites of memory in this kingdom".

We are, I think, justified, not so much in "basing" a reading "on an ambiguous spelling", as in, more simply, accepting a concurrence of Q1 and F.

259. *dear*] a good example of the Elizabethan use of this word, which it is often easy to miss: it is applicable to anything or anyone which touches one closely, not at all necessarily pleasurably; "Which art my near'st and dearest enemy" (*1 H 4*, III. ii. 123), "And strain what other means is left to us In our dear peril" (*Tim.*, v. i. 232).

263–4. *Nor to comply . . . satisfaction*] one of the most famous cruxes in Shakespeare. The texts give no clue,

In my defunct, and proper satisfaction,
But to be free and bounteous of her mind;   265
And heaven defend your good souls that you think
I will your serious and great business scant,
For she is with me; . . . no, when light-wing'd toys,
And feather'd Cupid, foils with wanton dullness
My speculative and active instruments,   270
That my disports corrupt and taint my business,

265. of her] *Q1*; to her *F, Q2*.   267. great] *F*; good *Qq*.   268. For] *Qq*;
When *F*.   268-9. toys, And] *Qq* (toyes); Toyes Of *F*.   269. Cupid, foils]
Cupid foyles *Qq; Cupid*, seele *F*.   269-70. dullness My] *F* (dulnesse); dulnesse,
My *Qq*.   270. active instruments] *Qq*; offic'd Instrument *F*.

since, apart from two insignificant
spelling variants, and the absence in F
of the comma after *heat*, Q1 and F are
identical. I will make only one or two
comments. (a) The usual meaning of
defunct is simply "dead"; (b) *affects* can
be either noun or verb, so that the
young affects will mean either "the passions of the young", in apposition to
heat, though with an awkward plural,
or "(which) affects the young", with
the frequent Elizabethan omission o.
the relative; (c) if we retain *my*, then
we must, I think, either emend *defunct*
or assume that Shakespeare was for
once using it in some such sense as
"normal", "part of a natural function", a sense which it bears nowhere
else whether in Shakespeare or any
other writer (but see II. iii. 339 below);
(d) if for *my* we read *me*, which is the
commonest emendation, then *the
young affects in me defunct* can be an
absolute construction, to which the
objection is not syntactical awkwardness but improbability in sense, unless
Othello means that he is too mature
for the *uncontrolled* passions of youth;
(e) I think that by *proper satisfaction*
Othello implies that the desire for
satisfaction is a legitimate one, even
though he will not allow it to dominate
him. It may be noticed that in l. 271 he
does not say that the *disports* will not
exist, only that they will not interfere
with his military competence.

    But, after all the discussion,

Othello's meaning is moderately
clear. He is too mature to be subju-
gated by physical desire, and, though
the satisfaction of that is proper, he
wants also the marriage of true minds.

    269-70. *foils . . . instruments*] On the
meaning of the passage and the operations of earlier editors, Knight (1841)
makes these just comments: "The
modern editors have made up a text
between the Qto and Ff. They reject
the *foils* of the Qto, and adopt the
'seel' of the Ff, while they substitute
the *active* of the Qto for the 'offic'd' of
the Ff. [Knight might have added the
further permutation introduced by the
arbitrary selection of *instruments* or
'instrument'.] Having accomplished
this hocus-pocus, they tell us that
speculative instruments are the eyes,
and active instruments the hands and
feet; that to 'seel' is to close the eyelids
of a bird, which applies very properly
to the speculative instruments, but
that *foils* better suits the active. It is
their own work they are quarrelling
with, and not that of the author.
Either reading is good if they had let
it alone. The speculative and *active
instruments*, which are *foiled*, are the
thoughts and the senses; the speculative and *offic'd instrument*, which is
seeled, is the whole man in meditation
and in action." (Knight would perhaps have made things even clearer if
he had included limbs as well as
senses under "active instruments".)

     Let housewives make a skillet of my helm,
     And all indign and base adversities
     Make head against my reputation!
Duke. Be it, as you shall privately determine,   275
     Either for stay or going, the affairs cry haste,
     And speed must answer; you must hence tonight.
Des. Tonight, my Lord?
Duke.   This night.
Oth.   With all my heart.
Duke. At ten i' the morning here we'll meet again.
     Othello, leave some officer behind,   280
     And he shall our commission bring to you,
     With such things else of quality or respect
     As doth concern you.
Oth.   Please your grace, my ancient,
     A man he is of honesty and trust,
     To his conveyance I assign my wife,   285

---

274. reputation] *Qq;* Estimation *F.* 276. stay] *Qq;* her stay *F, Q2.* 277–8. answer; you . . . This night] answer, you . . . This night *Qq* (answere *Q2*)*;* answer it. / *Sen.* You must away to night *F.* 279. ten] *Q1;* nine *F, Q2.* 282. With] *Qq;* And *F.*   or] *Q1;* and *F, Q2.* 283. concern] *Q1;* import *F, Q2.*   Please] *Qq;* So please *F.*

---

272. *skillet*] saucepan. (A Mr Fairholt, writing to Halliwell, recorded the dredging from the Thames of a sixteenth-century morion fitted with hook and chain for use as a campkettle.)

273. *indign*] shameful (L. indignus).

274. *Make head against*] bring a body of troops against; "Three times hath Henry Bolingbroke made head Against my power" (*1 H 4*, III. i. 65). The picture is of a concerted, not a sporadic, assault.

277–9. *you must . . . ten*] In F, for the sake of getting rid, for whatever reason, of Desdemona's remark, the First Senator is introduced again, and this time he is inappropriately officious, since so imperative a command to a highly placed servant of the state could surely come only from the Doge himself. Perhaps it was felt that after her previous speech Desdemona was unlikely to express dismay at the suddenness of the departure. Both this change and that at l. 246 seem to present a more mature Desdemona. The variant "nine" for *ten* seems without cause.

282. *quality or respect*] Both words are probably being used in the sense of "rank", "position"; (Henry to the French herald) "What is thy name? I know thy quality" (*H 5*, III. vi. 149), (the herald to the incognito Edgar) "What are you? Your name? Your quality?" (*Lr.*, v. iii. 121), " 'tis worse than murder To do upon respect such violent outrage" (*Lr.*, II. iv. 23). But the line seems somewhat redundant, since Othello's status is presumably going to be made explicit in the "commission".

284. *honesty*] the first of the many times in the play that this quality is attributed to Iago.

With what else needful your good grace shall think
To be sent after me.
Duke.   Let it be so.
Good night to every one; and, noble signior,
If virtue no delighted beauty lack,
Your son-in-law is far more fair than black.   290
First Sen. Adieu, brave Moor, use Desdemona well.
Bra. Look to her, Moor, have a quick eye to see:
She has deceiv'd her father, may do thee.
                    [*Exeunt Duke, Senators, Officers, &c.*
Oth. My life upon her faith: honest Iago,
My Desdemona must I leave to thee;   295
I prithee, let thy wife attend on her,
And bring her after in the best advantage;
Come, Desdemona, I have but an hour
Of love, of worldly matters, and direction,
To spend with thee; we must obey the time.   300
                    [*Exeunt Othello and Desdemona.*

Rod. Iago!
Iago. What sayest thou, noble heart?
Rod. What will I do, thinkest thou?
Iago. Why, go to bed and sleep.
Rod. I will incontinently drown myself.   305
Iago. Well, if thou doest, I shall never love thee after it.
Why, thou silly gentleman?
Rod. It is silliness to live, when to live is a torment; and

292. have a quick eye] *Q1*; if thou hast eyes *F, Q2, and most edd.*   293. may do]
Q1; and may *F, Q2.*   297. her] *Qq;* them *F.*   299. worldly matters] *Qq;*
wordly matter *F.*   300. the] *Qq;* the the *F.*   S.D.] *Exit* Moore *and* Desde-
mona *Qq; Exit F.*   306. Well, if] *Qq;* If *F.*   after it] *Qq;* after *F.*   307.
Why, ... gentleman?] Why, ... Gentleman. *Q1;* Why ... Gentleman? *F;* Why
... Gentleman. *Q2.*   308. a torment] *Qq;* torment *F.*

289. *delighted*] delightful (endowed
with delight); "to make my gift, The
more delay'd, delighted" (*Cym.,* v. iv.
101).
293. *may do thee*] Q1 is slightly more
colloquial, and perhaps therefore
more telling, than F.
294.] There is irony in the juxta-
position of Othello's unquestioning
trust in Desdemona's faith and his

equally unquestioning conviction of
Iago's honesty.
297. *in the best advantage*] as opportunity best serves; "The next advantage Will we take throughly" (*Tp.,*
III. iii. 13).
305. *incontinently*] forthwith; more
often the adjective is used adverbially,
as in IV. iii. 12 below, "He says he will
return incontinent".

then we have a prescription to die, when death is
our physician.   310

Iago. O villainous! I ha' look'd upon the world for four
times seven years, and since I could distinguish
between a benefit and an injury, I never found a
man that knew how to love himself: ere I would
say I would drown myself, for the love of a guinea-   315
hen, I would change my humanity with a baboon.

Rod. What should I do? I confess it is my shame to be
so fond, but it is not in my virtue to amend it.

Iago. Virtue? a fig! 'tis in ourselves, that we are thus,
or thus: our bodies are gardens, to the which our   320
wills are gardeners, so that if we will plant nettles,
or sow lettuce, set hyssop, and weed up thyme;
supply it with one gender of herbs, or distract it
with many; either to have it sterile with idleness,
or manur'd with industry, why, the power, and   325

---

309. we have] *Qq;* haue we *F.*   311. O villainous!] *F, Q2; not in Q1.*
313. between] *Qq;* betwixt *F.*   313–14. a man] *Qq;* man *F.*   320. gardens]
Qq; our Gardens *F.*   322. hyssop] Isop *Qq;* Hisope *F.*

---

309. *prescription*] doctor's orders (in
general, not the specific directions for
compounding a medicine); cf. (in
reply to a passage of advice) "I am
thankful to you, and I'll go along By
your prescription" (*H 8,* I. i. 150).

311–12.] Shakespeare is as precise
about Iago's age as he is about Hamlet's, and Juliet's, and Leontes', who,
by the way, is a good deal younger
than he is usually played (*Wint.,* I. ii.
155).

315–16. *guinea-hen*] There seems
very slender evidence for Steevens's
gloss "anciently the cant term for a
prostitute". I doubt whether Iago
means more than something generally
derogatory, a "skirt", a "bit of fluff".
His opinion of all women is low, and
Desdemona is a woman, but even he
would hardly call her a prostitute.

318. *fond*] infatuated; but Shakespeare uses the word also in the
modern sense, without the notion of
foolish affection, as in "Are you so fond

of your young prince as we Do seem to
be of ours?" (*Wint.,* I. ii. 164).

319. *a fig*] a type of valuelessness,
like "a pin", "a straw"; cf. "a fig for
Peter" (*2 H 6,* II. iii. 68).

322–4. *set hyssop . . . with many*] It is
doubtful whether Iago is choosing his
examples with any horticultural particularity, but Ellacombe drew attention to a passage in Lyly where
"Hisoppe" and "Time" are mentioned as "aiders the one to the growth of
the other; the one being dry, the other
moist". And Hart points out that the
herbalists drew the same distinction
between the nettle (hot and dry, under
Mars) and the lettuce (cold and
moist). *Set* = plant, *gender* = kind (as
in "general gender" (*Ham.,* IV. vii. 18)
though Shakespeare normally uses it of
difference of sex), and *supply* = satisfy,
thus making an adequate contrast to
distract (cf. "And did supply thee at thy
garden-house In her imagin'd person" (*Meas.,* v. i. 206)).

corrigible authority of this, lies in our wills. If the
balance of our lives had not one scale of reason, to
poise another of sensuality, the blood and baseness
of our natures would conduct us to most preposterous conclusions. But we have reason to cool our   330
raging motions, our carnal stings, our unbitted
lusts; whereof I take this, that you call love, to be a
sect, or scion.

Rod. It cannot be.

Iago. It is merely a lust of the blood, and a permission   335
of the will. Come, be a man; drown thyself? drown
cats and blind puppies: I profess me thy friend,
and I confess me knit to thy deserving, with cables
of perdurable toughness; I could never better stead

327. balance] *Qq* (ballance); braine *F.*   331. our unbitted] *Qq*; or unbitted *F.*
333. sect] *Qq, F*; set *Johnson.*   scion] *Steevens (1793)*; syen *Qq*; Seyen *F.*
337. profess] *Qq*; haue profest *F.*

326. *corrigible*] in the active sense,
"able to correct or control"; only once
elsewhere in Shakespeare, and there in
the passive sense, "bending down His
corrigible neck" (*Ant.,* iv. xii. 73).

327. *balance*] F's *braine*, though an
improbable misreading of *balance*, is a
quite possible misreading of *beame*,
which some edd. read; but most, even
of those who in general prefer F, are
content to adopt Q1's reading. It may
be noticed that where Shakespeare
elsewhere uses *balance* he is talking of
the whole apparatus, when he uses
beam, of *part of* the apparatus; "you
weigh this well; therefore still bear the
balance" (*2 H 4,* v. ii. 102), "Commit
my cause in balance to be weighed"
(*Tit.,* i. i. 55), "We, poising us in her
defective scale, Shall weigh thee to the
beam" (*All's W.,* ii. iii. 161), "poise
the cause in justice' equal scales,
Whose beam stands sure" (*2 H 6,* ii. i.
202), "till our scale turn the beam"
(*Ham.,* iv. v. 156). But it is true that of
two transcribers, both faced with an
illegible *beame*, one might misread it as
braine, and the other give it up and
write *balance* as giving the general
sense needed.

328. *blood and baseness*] baser passions; for *blood* = passion cf. *Ham.,* iii.
ii. 74, "Whose blood and judgement
are so well commingled".

331. *motions . . . stings*] impulses . . .
compelling desires; *sting,* even when
unqualified, often implies specifically
sexual desire; "The wanton stings and
motions of the sense" (*Meas.,* i. iv. 59),
"As sensual as the brutish sting itself"
(*AYL.,* ii. vii. 66).

333. *sect*] cutting; but the word does
not appear elsewhere in this sense, and
this may be a misreading of "sett",
which would be more appropriate to
the context, since "set" means a shoot
(as does "scion"), coming out of the
main plant, which is Iago's picture
rather than a "cutting" in the gar-
dener's sense to be removed and
planted elsewhere.

339. *perdurable*] everlasting; "O
perdurable shame!" (*H 5,* iv. v. 7),
where the phrase picks up "everlasting
shame" from three lines earlier and is
picked up by "eternal shame" three
lines later).

stead] help; "it nothing steads us
To chide him from our eaves" (*All's
W.,* iii. vii. 41).

thee than now. Put money in thy purse; follow   340
these wars, defeat thy favour with an usurp'd
beard; I say, put money in thy purse. It cannot be
that Desdemona should long continue her love
unto the Moor, . . . put money in thy purse, . . . nor
he to her; it was a violent commencement, and   345
thou shalt see an answerable sequestration: put but
money in thy purse. . . These Moors are change-
able in their wills: . . . fill thy purse with money.
The food that to him now is as luscious as locusts,
shall be to him shortly as acerb as the coloquintida.   350
When she is sated with his body, she will find the

341. these] *Qq;* thou the *F.*   342-3. be that . . . should long] be, that . . .
should long *Qq;* be long that . . . should *F.*   344. unto] *Qq;* to *F.*   345. he to
her] *Q1;* he his to her *F, Q2.*   commencement] *Qq;* Commencement in her
F.   350. acerb as the] *Q1;* bitter as *F, Q2.*   350-1. coloquintida. When] *Q1;*
Coloquintida. She must change for youth: when *F;* Coloquintida: She must
change for youth; when *Q2.*

341. *defeat*] change for the worse
(just possibly with a play on "overcome"); "She was defeated and dis-
figured by the great abstinences which
she made" (Caxton).

favour] appearance; see note on
III. iv. 122 below.

usurp'd] adopted as disguise; "this
my masculine usurp'd attire" (*Tw.N.*,
v. i. 260), and cf. "the boy will well
usurp the grace, Voice, gait, and
action of a gentlewoman" (*Shr.*, Ind.
I. 131), "painting, and usurping hair,
Should ravish doters with a false
aspect" (*LLL.*, IV. iii. 259).

346. *sequestration*] here apparently
simply "cessation"; elsewhere in
Shakespeare with the sense of "con-
finement" or "retirement from": (the
imprisoned Mortimer) "This loathsome sequestration have I had" (*1 H 6*,
II. v. 25), "never noted in him any
study, Any retirement, any sequestration From open haunts and popu-
larity" (*H 5*, I. i. 57); and cf. "this hand
of yours requires A sequester from
liberty" (III. iv. 35 below).

349. *locusts*] This clearly means
something that was sweet and a delicacy. Of the many passages cited in

the attempt to define it more precisely,
and adjudicate between carob and
honeysuckle, the most significant is
that from Gerarde's *Herball* (1597):
"The carob groweth in Apulia . . . and
other countries eastward, where the
cods are so full of sweet juice that it is
used to preserve ginger. . . Moreover
both young and old feed thereon with
pleasure. This is of some called St.
John's bread, and thought to be that
which is translated *locusts*."

350. *acerb*] It is reasonable to suppose that Shakespeare wrote *acerb* and
not "bitter" since no actor, compositor, or editor would be likely to substitute the rare word for the common.
O.E.D. does not recognize the word
till 1657. An editorial comment is here
worth citing as a warning: "Not by
any means so good as the simple
'bitter'." "Bitter" was therefore read,
as being "better". "Shakespeare
seems to give Iago these more outré
expressions in soliloquy or in talk with
Roderigo—does not this help to mark
that his bluff plainness is assumed, not
native to him?" (Dr Brooks.)

coloquintida] the bitter-apple or colo-
cynth, yielding a purgative.

error of her choice; she must have change, she
must. Therefore put money in thy purse: if thou
wilt needs damn thyself, do it a more delicate way
than drowning; make all the money thou canst. If   355
sanctimony, and a frail vow, betwixt an erring barbarian, and a super-subtle Venetian, be not too hard
for my wits, and all the tribe of hell, thou shalt enjoy
her; therefore make money, . . . a pox o' drowning,
'tis clean out of the way: seek thou rather to be   360
hang'd in compassing thy joy, than to be drown'd,
and go without her.

Rod. Wilt thou be fast to my hopes?

Iago. Thou art sure of me . . . go, make money . . . I have
told thee often, and I tell thee again, and again, I   365
hate the Moor; my cause is hearted, thine has no
less reason, let us be communicative in our revenge
against him: if thou canst cuckold him, thou doest
thyself a pleasure, and me a sport. There are many
events in the womb of time, which will be delivered.   370
Traverse, go, provide thy money, we will have more
of this to-morrow; adieu.

---

352. error] *Qq;* errors *F.*   352–3. she . . . she must] *Qq; not in F.*   357. a
super-subtle] *Qq* (super subtle *Q1);* super-subtle *F.*   359. o'drowning] a
drowning *Qq;* of drowning thy selfe *F.*   363. hopes?] *Q1;* hopes, if I depend
on the issue? *F, Q2.*   365. tell] *Qq;* re-tell *F.*   367. communicative] *Q1;*
coniunctiue *F, Q2.*   369. and me] *Q1;* me *F, Q2.*

356. *sanctimony*] I think here near to
"ritual"; "the rites are solemnised
with greatest sanctimony" (Purchas).

erring] errant, vagabond; cf. "extravagant and wheeling" at I. i. 136
above.

357. *super-subtle*] "Super" is a fa-
vourite Elizabethan intensive prefix;
"subtle" had often. as here, the meaning of "refined", "delicate" (and so
likely to find a "barbarian" repellently
crude), with no overtones of trickery or
hair-splitting; "subtle, tender, and
delicate temperance" (*Tp.,* II. i. 42),
"some joy too fine, Too subtle,
potent" (*Troil.,* III. ii. 22).

360. *out of the way*] off the track; cf.
"God amend us, God amend! we are

much out o' the way" (*LLL.,* IV. iii.
76).

366. *hearted*] full of vigour; "I will
be treble-sinew'd, hearted, breath'd"
(*Ant.,* III. xi. 177).

367. *communicative*] It may be regarded as for or against the Q1 reading that
Shakespeare uses "conjunctive" once
elsewhere (*Ham.,* IV. vii. 14, "She's so
conjunctive to my heart and soul")
and *communicative* nowhere else. The
words are nearly synonymous but not
quite, since *communicative* has a touch of
"keeping each other informed".

371. *Traverse*] If this could mean
simply "quick march!", all would be
simple, and thus Onions takes it, "to
march, esp. backwards and forwards";

Rod. Where shall we meet i' the morning?

Iago. At my lodging.

Rod. I'll be with thee betimes.   375

Iago. Go to, farewell:... do you hear, Roderigo?

Rod. What say you?

Iago. No more of drowning, do you hear?

Rod. I am chang'd.

Iago. Go to; farewell! put money enough in your purse.   380

[*Exit Roderigo.*

Thus do I ever make my fool my purse:

377–80. *Rod.* What say you?... in your purse] *Q1; Rod.* Ile sell all my Land *F; Rod.* What say you?) | *Iag.* No more of drowning, doe you heare? | *Rod.* I am chang'd, Ile goe sell all my land. *Q2.*

but though no doubt the word can mean that, the other Shakespearean instances do not seem to exemplify this meaning. In *Wiv.*, II. iii. 24 we have "To see thee fight, to see thee foin, to see thee traverse; to see thee here, to see thee there; to see thee pass thy punto, thy stock . . ." where it clearly does not mean anything so deliberate as marching, but either a fencer's rapid shift of ground, or some movement of the foil; in *2 H 4*, at III. ii. 292, Falstaff says "Put me a caliver into Wart's hands, Bardolph" and Bardolph then begins to drill him, with "Hold, Wart, traverse; thus, thus, thus" (or in Q's, and perhaps the drill-sergeant's, pronunciation, "thas, thas, thas"), and it is natural to suppose that "traverse" is an arms-drill order, like "Slope arms" or, more closely to the root meaning, "Port arms"; but it may there mean no more than "March". But there can be no doubt that the word can be used in connection with weapons. At the end of *Tim.* Alcibiades arrives "with his powers" before the walls of Athens; he says that they have "wander'd with travers'd arms". Onions glosses the word here as "(of the arms) folded", but that, surely, is impossible; the picture of Alcibiades and his troops wandering about with arms (of the body) "in this sad knot" is ridiculous, and the

phrase must, I think, mean "with arms (weapons) in a posture for carrying, not for discharging bullets", a posture which might be, with us, the slope, the trail, or the port, of which the last is the least convenient but also the nearest to the "across" meaning of *traverse*. Perhaps traversing arms was the normal preliminary to moving off. (It may be noted that the "port" was a recognized position; in *Paradise Lost*, iv. 980 the whole point of the simile of the corn bent by the wind is the slanting position of the "ported" spears.)

376–80. *Go to . . . your purse*] The text here given is that of Q1. F has a much abbreviated version, consisting of "*Iago* Go to, farewell. Do you heare *Rodorigo? Rod.* Ile sell all my Land. *Exit.*" The movement of the dialogue is a good deal more natural in Q1, but the repetition of *purse*, first at the end of Iago's farewell and again at once at the end of the first line of his soliloquy, is perhaps awkward. "I'll sell all my land" is an effective remark, but even more effective if prefaced by *I am chang'd*. It is not easy to explain why F, in adding one remark, omitted three speeches, the last of which led up to it, or why the Q1 compositor omitted the same remark if it was before him. Q2 combines the two texts (adding a "go" before "sell") and has been followed by most editors.

For I mine own gain'd knowledge should profane,
If I would time expend with such a snipe,
But for my sport and profit: I hate the Moor,
And it is thought abroad, that 'twixt my sheets　　　385
He's done my office; I know not if 't be true . . .
Yet I, for mere suspicion in that kind,
Will do, as if for surety: he holds me well,
The better shall my purpose work on him.
Cassio's a proper man, let me see now,　　　　　390
To get this place, and to make up my will,
A double knavery . . . how, how? . . . let me see,
After some time, to abuse Othello's ear,
That he is too familiar with his wife:
He has a person and a smooth dispose,　　　　　395
To be suspected, fram'd to make women false:
The Moor a free and open nature too,

383. a snipe] *Qq; Snpe F.*　　386. He's] Ha's *Qq*; She ha's *F.*　　387. Yet] *Qq;* But *F.*　　391. this] *Qq;* his *F.*　　make] *Q1;* plume *F, Q2.*　　392. A] *Qq;* In *F.*　　let me] *Qq;* Let's *F.*　　393. ear] *Qq;* eares *F.*　　395. has] *Qq;* hath *F.*　　397. a free] *Q1;* is of a free, *F, Q2* (free *Q2*).　　nature too] *Q1;* nature *F, Q2* (Nature *F*).

383. *snipe*] a contemptuous term for a dupe, perhaps as being even more contemptible than the usual "woodcock".

384–402.] It is important for the proper understanding of Iago to notice the very gradual stages by which his plot takes shape, how far, at each stage, he intends it to go, and what motives, at each stage, he alleges. In this, his first, soliloquy, he is concentrating primarily upon supplanting Cassio; revenge on Othello is so far only secondary; and he sums up the qualities in both Cassio and Othello which will help him. He sees also that the readiest means of discrediting Cassio is to rouse Othello's suspicions of his relations with Desdemona. But, so far, the plot is no more than "engendered".

388. *as if for surety*] as though it were a proved fact.

390. *proper*] handsome, but I think almost always with the additional sense of "complete", "A1" in other ways than looks; cf. *Tp.,* II. ii. 64, "as proper a man as ever went on four legs cannot make him give ground".

391. *make up*] As between this and F's *plume up* other passages in Shakespeare are not helpful, since he nowhere uses *plume* as a verb, and the three occurrences of *plumed* are straightforwardly concrete; but "plume-pluck'd Richard" (*R 2,* IV. i. 108) would support "plumed up" = "in full feather". For *make up* = "complete" see *O.E.D. s.v.* 96.

395. *dispose*] seems here to mean "manner", "bearing"; in *Troil.,* II. iii. 176, "carries on the stream of his dispose", it means "settled temper", almost "determined attitude".

397. *The Moor a free . . . too*] The staccato apposition is not unnatural in Iago's itemization of the pawns in his game; nor is the colloquially appended *too* F's reading may be the true one, but looks suspiciously like a smoothing.

That thinks men honest that but seems to be so:
And will as tenderly be led by the nose . . .
As asses are.   400
I ha't, it is engender'd; Hell and night
Must bring this monstrous birth to the world's light.

[*Exit.*

398. seems] *Qq;* seeme *F.*   401. ha't] *Qq;* haue't *F.*   402. S.D.] *Qq; not in F.*

399. *led by the nose*] Cf. Florio,   "Menar per il naso", "To lead by the
Worlde of Wordes (1598), translating   nose, to make a fool of".

ACT II

SCENE I.—[*A Sea-port in Cyprus. An open place near the Quay.*]

Enter MONTANO, *with two other Gentlemen.*

Mon. What from the cape can you discern at sea?
First Gent. Nothing at all, it is a high-wrought flood,
    I cannot 'twixt the heaven and the main
    Descry a sail.
Mon. Methinks the wind does speak aloud at land,   5
    A fuller blast ne'er shook our battlements:
    If it ha' ruffian'd so upon the sea,
    What ribs of oak, when the huge mountains melt,
    Can hold the mortise? . . . What shall we hear of this?
Sec. Gent. A segregation of the Turkish fleet: 10
    For do but stand upon the banning shore,
    The chiding billow seems to pelt the clouds,
    The wind-shak'd surge, with high and monstrous main,

ACT II

Scene 1

S.D.] *Enter* Montanio, *Gouernor of Cypres, with two other Gentlemen Qq* (*Cyprus Q2*); *Enter Montano, and two Gentlemen F.*   3. heaven] *F, Q2;* hauen *Q1, Malone.*   5. does speak] *Qq* (speake); hath spoke *F.*   8. the huge mountains melt] the huge mountaine meslt *Q1;* Mountaines melt on them *F;* mountaine melt on them *Q2.*   9. mortise] morties *Qq, F.*   11. banning] *Q1;* Foaming *F, Q2* (foaming *Q2*).   12. chiding] *Qq;* chidden *F.*   billow] *Q1, F;* billowes *Q2.*   13. main] mayne *Qq;* Maine *F;* mane *Knight.*

10. *segregation*] dispersal; a very uncommon use.

11. *banning*] F's "foaming" is a facile variant; *banning,* because of the absence of an object, is difficult, but not impossible. The shore is forbidding the encroachment of the waves, as it "spurns back the ocean's roaring tides" in *John,* II. i. 24, and "beats back the envious siege Of watery Neptune" in *R 2,* II. i. 62; and cf. "As doth a rock against the chiding flood" (*H 8,* III. ii.

198), and "the sea That chides the banks . . ." (*1 H 4,* III. i. 44).

13. *main*] It was only by a kind of compression or ellipse that the word came to be used as in "the Spanish main"; it meant properly the main body of something, such as waters, as in "as doth an inland brook Into the main of waters" (*Mer. V.,* v. i. 96), or troops, as in "We must with all our main of power stand fast" (*Troil.,* II. iii. 276).

Seems to cast water on the burning bear,
And quench the guards of the ever-fixed pole;   15
I never did like molestation view
On the enchafed flood.

Mon.   If that the Turkish fleet
Be not enshelter'd, and embay'd, they are drown'd,
It is impossible they bear it out.

Enter a third Gentleman.

Third Gent. News, lords, your wars are done: 20
The desperate tempest hath so bang'd the Turk,
That their designment halts: another ship, of Venice,
Hath seen a grievous wrack and sufferance
On most part of the fleet.

Mon. How, is this true?

Third Gent.   The ship is here put in,   25
A Veronesa; Michael Cassio,

15. fixed] *F; fired Qq.*   19. they] *Q1; to F, Q2.*   S.D.] *Qq; Enter a Gentleman F.*
20. lords] *Q1, Steevens, Malone; Lads Q2 and most edd.; Laddes F.*   your] *Qq;*
our *F.*   21. Turk] *Qq; Turkes F.*   22. another] *Another Q1; A Noble F, Q2.*
24. the] *Q1; their F, Q2.*   25-6. in, A Veronesa; Michael] in: A Veronessa,
Michael Qq; in: A *Verennessa, Michael F.*

14. *bear*] probably the Little Bear, since the *guards* are the two stars in that constellation next in brightness to the Pole Star. They are frequently mentioned, along with the Pole Star, as guides to navigation.

22. *designment*] plan; "served his designments In mine own person" (*Cor.*, v. v. 35).

halts] is crippled (rather than "is at a stand", a sense which the verb does not apparently bear till later).

another ship] F's "a Noble ship" looks like an attempt to get over the difficulty of the Gentleman talking of another ship of Venice when so far there has not been even one. If we retain Q1 we must punctuate so that *of Venice* is a parenthesis. It will be noticed that in both texts the words *of Venice* are hypermetrical, and that the plain "a ship of Venice" would be more satisfactory than either.

23. *sufferance*] damage; an uncommon extension of the meaning "suffering".

26. *Veronesa*] Why, having given the ship as a Venetian, suddenly attribute her to another, and an inland, city? Or ought we to take the word as an error for Veronese, a description of Cassio? But in any case, in the excitement of the moment, is the Gentleman likely to have troubled about the provenance of either the ship or of Cassio? I think that Elze was almost certainly on the right tack in suggesting that under F's "Verennessa" is hidden a *type* of ship. He points out that there was an Italian nautical term "verrinare" meaning "to cut through" (the water), so that a noun derived from this verb would be what the French call a "perceflot"—and both would be exact equivalents, as Furness says, of our "cutter".

    Lieutenant to the warlike Moor Othello,
    Is come ashore: the Moor himself at sea,
    And is in full commission here for Cyprus.
Mon. I am glad on 't, 'tis a worthy governor.   30
Third Gent. But this same Cassio, though he speak of comfort,
    Touching the Turkish loss, yet he looks sadly,
    And prays the Moor be safe, for they were parted,
    With foul and violent tempest.
Mon.   Pray heaven he be:
    For I have serv'd him, and the man commands   35
    Like a full soldier: let's to the seaside, ho!
    As well to see the vessel that's come in,
    As to throw out our eyes for brave Othello,
    Even till we make the main and the aerial blue
    An indistinct regard.
Third Gent.   Come, let's do so,   40
    For every minute is expectancy
    Of more arrivance.

Enter CASSIO.

Cas. Thanks to the valiant of this worthy isle,
    That so approve the Moor, and let the heavens
    Give him defence against their elements,   45

28. ashore] *Q1;* a shore *Q2;* on Shore *F.*   himself] *Qq, F;* himself's *most edd.*
33. prays] prayes *Qq;* praye *F.*   34. heaven] *Qq;* Heauens *F.*   39–40. Even
. . . regard] *F, Q2; not in Q1.*   39. the aerial] *Pope;* th' Eriall *F;* th' Ayre all
Q2.   42. arrivance] *Qq;* Arrivancie *F.*   43. Thanks to the] *Qq;* Thankes
you, the *F.*   this worthy] *Q1;* the warlike *F;* this *Q2.*   44. Moor, and let]
Qq; Moore: Oh let *F.*   45. their] *Qq;* the *F.*

32. *sadly*] gravely; "sad" is often
contrasted with "merry", but even
then rather in the sense of "serious"
than in that of "gloomy", as it often
also is when standing alone; "a serious
brow, Sad, high and working" (*H 8*,
Prol. 2), "sad brow and true maid"
(*AYL.*, III. iii. 228), "sadly tell me
who" (*Rom.*, I. i. 207).

39–40. *Even till . . . regard*] till our
strained eyes cannot distinguish sea
from sky at the horizon. *Q2*'s reading
looks more of an oddity than it is;
I fancy that the corrector, having to
insert the line and a half in his copy of

Q1, and not being satisfied with the
spelling "Eriall", wrote "Ayreall",
which was then spaced by the compositor.

43. *worthy*] This may be a repetition
error from Montano's *worthy* in l. 30,
but to have both *valiant* and "warlike"
is perhaps redundant.

45. *elements*] powers of air and water
(i.e. winds and waves); (Boatswain
speaking) "if you can command these
elements to silence" (*Tp.*, I. i. 24), "I
tax not you, you elements, with unkindness" (*Lr.*, III. ii. 16); see note on
II. iii. 333 below.

For I have lost him on a dangerous sea.

Mon. Is he well shipp'd?

Cas. His bark is stoutly timber'd, and his pilot
        Of very expert and approv'd allowance,
        Therefore my hopes, not surfeited to death,   50
        Stand in bold cure.

> [*Within:* "A sail, a sail, a sail!"

Enter a messenger.

Cas. What noise?

Mess. The town is empty, on the brow o' the sea
        Stand ranks of people, and they cry "A sail!"   54

Cas. My hopes do shape him for the governor.   [*A shot.*

Sec. Gent. They do discharge the shot of courtesy,
        Our friend at least.

Cas.   I pray you sir go forth,
        And give us truth, who 'tis that is arriv'd.

Sec. Gent. I shall.   [*Exit.*

Mon. But, good lieutenant, is your general wiv'd?   60

Cas. Most fortunately, he hath achiev'd a maid

---

48. pilot] Pilate *Q1;* Pylot *F;* Pilote *Q2.*   50. hopes, not . . . death,] hope's
(not . . . death) *F, Q2;* hope's not . . . death *Q1.*   51. S.D.] *see note.*   53.
Mess] *Qq;* Gent *F.*   54. Stand] *F;* otand *Q1;* Stands *Q2.*   55. governor] *F;*
guernement *Q1;* gouernement *Q2.*   55. S.D.] *Qq (after* least, *l. 57); not in F.*
56. the] *Qq;* their *F.*   57. friend] *Qq;* Friends *F.*

---

49. *of very expert . . . allowance*] admitted on good evidence to be expert;
"give him allowance as the worthier
man" (*Troil.,* I. iii. 377).

50–1. *my hopes . . . cure*] Cassio is
throwing off a conceit, a verbal bubble
that disappears if one examines it too
closely, as many commentators, from
Johnson downwards, have done.
Cassio means, I take it," my hopes are
reasonably temperate and so healthily
strong"; one may push the thought a
little further by saying "if they were
unreasonably excessive they would be
liable to a deathly shock of disappoint-
ment". Both Q1 and F read *hope's,* an
instance which Dr Walker might well
have used to support her theory.

cure] almost = "state of health"; if

the hopes were ailing one could gloss
by "curability", as in "This rest might
yet have balm'd thy broken sinews,
Which . . . Stand in hard cure" (*Lr.,*
III. vi. 108).

51–9.] The distribution of speeches
and the S.D.s are those of Q1, except
that Q1 attributes "A sail . . ." to the
Messenger after his entrance. F has no
S.D.s except *Exit,* making "Within" a
speaker, and making an unnumbered
"Gent" serve for both Messenger and
Second Gentleman.

53. *brow*] more, I think, than merely
"edge" (Hart); Shakespeare does not
often use the word metaphorically, but
when he does it is in the sense of something "standing up above": and cf.
IV. i. 132 below.

That paragons description, and wild fame:
One that excels the quirks of blazoning pens,
And in the essential vesture of creation
Does bear all excellency: ...

Enter Second Gentleman.

Now, who has put in?   65
Sec. Gent. 'Tis one Iago, ancient to the general.

63. quirks of] *F, Q2; not in Q1.*   64. the essential] *Qq;* th' essential *F.*
65. bear all excellency:] *Q1, Pope, Steevens, Malone;* tyre the Ingeniuer. *F and
(with various spellings) most edd.;* beare an excellency: *Q2, Rowe.* . . . Now,] *Qq;*
How now? *F.*   S.D.] *Enter 2. Gentleman Qq (after* put in); *Enter Gentleman F
(after* Ingeniuer).

62. *paragons*] here seems necessarily to mean "surpasses"; in *Ant.*, I. v. 71, it means "compare", "If thou with Caesar paragon again My man of men", while in "before the primest creature That's paragon'd o' the world" (*H 8*, II. iv. 227) it seems to mean "counted the non-pareil", a use similar to that of the noun in Hamlet's "the paragon of animals" (II. ii. 327).

63. *quirks*] extravagant conceits; no real parallel in Shakespeare, but cf. "I may chance have some odd quirks and remnants of wit broken on me" (*Ado*, II. iii. 255).

blazoning] Though properly a heraldic term, the word had come to mean simply "setting out the praises of" or even just "proclaim"; "thy skill be more To blazon it, then . . . Unfold the imagin'd happiness" (*Rom.*, II. vi. 25).

64–5. *And in . . . excellency*] The first line, in spite of the heavy weather which some of the earlier editors, notably Warburton, made of it, seems plain—"just as God made her". But the half line presents a real problem, since by no possibility could the same original lead to both readings. Q1 is plain and adequate, but perhaps a trifle colourless; its reading might possibly be a watering down of F's reading by someone who thought it too involv-

ed. On the other hand, if Q1 represents the original, then someone felt that it was not high-falutin enough for Cassio, and altered it; and the someone may have been Shakespeare, since this is an alteration far beyond the usual sophistications of F. (It is to be noted that "excellent" and "excellence" have often in Shakespeare a sense much stronger than ours, not just "very good" but "surpassing all rivals"; "Yet was Samson so tempted, and he had an excellent strength" (*LLL.*, I. ii. 182), "Excellent falsehood" (*Ant.*, I. i. 40).) One or two smaller points in the passage are worth comment: (*a*) Q1's omission of *quirks of* is probably just carelessness, but the lines will be rhythmical without the words if relineated (*pens, and in / The essential*); (*b*) F's *ingeniuer* need not give one pause, since it is merely a variant spelling of the common "ingener" (i.e. inventor); (*c*) Q2, by an alteration apparently deliberate (since *an* for *all* is not a natural error), makes Q1's phrase yet more colourless, but evidently did not approve of the high colour of F.

I have adhered to Q1 on principle, but with the feeling that this is one of the (I think very few) places where the F variant more probably than not is Shakespeare's own. (And see note on l. 80 below.)

Cas. He has had most favourable and happy speed:
      Tempests themselves, high seas, and howling winds,
      The gutter'd rocks, and congregated sands,
      Traitors ensteep'd, to clog the guiltless keel,   70
      As having sense of beauty, do omit
      Their common natures, letting go safely by
      The divine Desdemona.
Mon.   What is she?
Cas. She that I spoke of, our great captain's captain,
      Left in the conduct of the bold Iago;   75
      Whose footing here anticipates our thoughts
      A se'nnight's speed... Great Jove, Othello guard,
      And swell his sail with thine own powerful breath,
      That he may bless this bay with his tall ship,
      And swiftly come to Desdemona's arms,   80

                Enter DESDEMONA, IAGO, EMILIA, *and* RODERIGO.

      Give renew'd fire to our extinct spirits,
      And bring all Cyprus comfort, ...

                                             O, behold,

67. *Cas*] *Cassio F; not in Qq.*   He has] *Qq;* Ha's *F.*   68. high] *F, Q2;* by *Q1.*
70. ensteep'd,] *F, Q2;* enscerped; *Q1;* enscarp'd *Grant White.*   clog] *Qq;* en-
clogge *F.*   72. common] *Qq;* mortall *F.*   74. spoke of, our] *Q1;* spake of,
our *Q2;* spake of: / Our *F.*   80. And swiftly come to] *Qq;* Make loues quicke
pants in *F.*   S.D.] *Qq* (Emillia *Q1;* Emilla *Q2*); *Enter Desdemona, Iago, Rodo-*
rigo, and Æmilia F (after l. 81).   82. And ... comfort] *Qq; not in F.*

   67. *speed*] includes the idea of "fortune", as well as that of celerity; "conceit and fear Of the queen's speed"
(*Wint.*, III. ii. 145).
   69–70. *gutter'd, ensteep'd*] *gutter'd* can
no doubt mean "channelled", but if so,
what is the point of it? A channelled
rock is no more dangerous than any
other. But a submerged rock is, and I
suspect that *gutter'd* and *ensteep'd* both
mean, in Cassio's high-flown diction,
no more than "under-water", though
ensteep'd may have a hint of "double-
dyed". One would feel happier if one
could find a meaning for Q1's *en-*
scerped, since though graphically the
misreading of *ensteep'd*, with the *c : t*
error, is moderately easy, *enscerped*
looks like a word which might as easily

have been misread or emended the
other way into the more ordinary
ensteep'd.
   72. *common*] If F's "mortal" is preferred, it still, I think, means the same,
as in "This is no mortal business" (*Tp.*,
I. ii. 403), and not "deadly".
   76. *footing*] landing; "Shall we, upon
the footing of our land, Send fair-play
orders?" (*John*, v. i. 66).
   80. *And swiftly come to*] F's variant
seems to me out of character or
Cassio and his usual attitude towards
Othello and Desdemona. It is noticeable that all the F variants hereabouts
in Cassio's part are in the direction of
colouring it up by verbal "quirks".
   82.] Almost all edd. concur in attributing F's omission to a blunder.

The riches of the ship is come ashore!
Ye men of Cyprus, let her have your knees:
Hail to thee, lady! and the grace of heaven,   85
Before, behind thee, and on every hand,
Enwheel thee round!

Des.   I thank you, valiant Cassio:
What tidings can you tell me of my lord?

Cas. He is not yet arriv'd, nor know I aught,
But that he's well, and will be shortly here.   90

Des. O, but I fear: ... how lost you company?
                    [*Within:* "A sail, a sail!"]

Cas. The great contention of the sea and skies
Parted our fellowship: but, hark! a sail.   [*A shot.*

Sec. Gent. They give their greeting to the citadel,
This likewise is a friend.

Cas.   So speaks this voice.   95
Good ancient, you are welcome, [*To Emilia*] welcome,
      mistress:
Let it not gall your patience, good Iago,
That I extend my manners; 'tis my breeding

83. ashore] *Q1;* on shore *F, Q2.*   84. Ye] *Qq;* You *F.*   88. tell me] *Qq;* tell
F.   92. the sea] *Qq;* Sea *F.*   93. *A shot*] Guns *Capell; no* S.D. *Qq, F.*
94. their] *Qq;* this *F.*   95. So ... voice] *Q1;* See for the Newes *F, Q2* (newes
Q2).   96. *To Emilia*] *Rowe.*

87.] This is the first time in the play
that Desdemona and Cassio have
spoken to one another, and Shakespeare is at pains to show her attitude.
She thanks Cassio with courtesy, but
his only importance to her at the
moment is that he may be able to give
her news of Othello.

95. *So speaks this voice*] Cassio's confirmation of the gentleman's remark is
natural enough, but F's reading, even
though it gives no exit for the gentleman, is perhaps preferable, as preparing for Desdemona's question and
Iago's answer in ll. 120, 121.

98. *extend*] stretch, give (sometimes
undue) scope to; "You do extend
These thoughts of horror further than
you shall Find cause in Caesar" (*Ant.,*
v. ii. 62).

manners] forms of politeness; "use

your manners discreetly in all kind of
companies" (*Shr.,* I. ii. 245). The
whole phrase seems to mean "stretch
my greeting to the permissible limits
of familiarity".

breeding] I suppose that Cassio
means "my training in the niceties of
etiquette", i.e. "I know exactly what's
what", with perhaps a slight implication that Iago does not, though such a
side-glance at Iago's social inferiority
is not characteristic of Cassio. "Breeding" is usually, in Shakespeare, "upbringing", often specifically "gentle"
upbringing, and sometimes almost
"social position"; "She had her breeding at my father's charge" (*All's W.,*
II. iii. 121), "And that tny tongue some
say of breeding breathes" (*Lr.,* v. iii.
145), "as levels with her breeding"
(I. iii. 239 above).

That gives me this bold show of courtesy.   [*Kissing her.*

Iago. Sir, would she give you so much of her lips   100
       As of her tongue she has bestow'd on me,
       You'ld have enough.

Des.   Alas! she has no speech.

Iago. I know, too much:
       I find it, I; for when I ha' list to sleep—
       Marry, before your ladyship, I grant,   105
       She puts her tongue a little in her heart,
       And chides with thinking.

Emil. You ha' little cause to say so.

Iago. Come on, come on, you are pictures out o' doors;

100. Sir] *F, Q2;* For *Q1.*   101. has bestow'd] *Qq;* oft bestowes *F.*   102.
You'ld] *Qq;* You would *F.*   103. I know] *Q1;* In faith *F, Q2.*   104. I find . . .
sleep—] I finde it, I; for when I ha list to sleepe, *Q1;* I finde it still, when I haue
leaue to sleepe. *F;* I find it still, for when I ha leaue to sleepe, *Q2.*   109–12.] *as
in Qq; as prose F.*   109. o' doors] adores *Q1;* of doore *F;* of dores *Q2.*

104. *list*] wish; the verb is much
commoner than the noun in this sense.

106–7. *puts . . . thinking*] holds her
tongue and thinks the more.

109–66.] This is to many readers,
and I think rightly, one of the most
unsatisfactory passages in Shakespeare. To begin with it is unnatural.
Desdemona's natural instinct must
surely be to go herself to the harbour,
instead of asking parenthetically
whether someone has gone. Then, it is
distasteful to watch her engaged in a
long piece of cheap backchat with
Iago, and so adept at it that one wonders how much time on the voyage
was spent in the same way. All we gain
from it is some further unneeded light
on Iago's vulgarity. It is true that it
leads up to ll. 163–77, which are
dramatically effective, but they could
have been introduced otherwise and
much more briefly. The fact that
Othello would then enter after too
short an interval would hardly
trouble an Elizabethan audience.
Perhaps the passage was just a sop to
the groundlings, for whom otherwise
—the clown being negligible—there is
little comic entertainment; this is just
the sort of interchange that might

occur between the great lady and the
professional jester. It is difficult not to
sympathize for once with Rymer, who,
for all his regrettably crude ebullience
of expression, does sometimes hit the
nail on the head. "Now follows a long
rabble of Jack-pudding farce [i.e.
stuffing, padding] between Jago and
Desdemona, that runs on with all the
little plays, jingle, and trash below the
patience of any Country Kitchenmaid
with her Sweetheart. The Venetian
Donna is hard put to't for pastime!
And this is all, when they are newly got
on shore, from a dismal Tempest, and
when every moment she might expect
to hear her Lord (as she calls him) that
she runs so mad after, is arrived or
lost."

Granville Barker, however, in a brilliant analysis of the passage says
"Shakespeare now stimulates suspense
by giving no less than a ninety-line
stretch of the scene to showing us
Desdemona's silent anxiety, which he
frames (for emphasis by contrast) in a
bout of artificially comic distraction."

109. *pictures*] Cf. "I have heard of
your paintings too, well enough; God
hath given you one face, and you make
yourselves another" (*Ham.,* III. i. 150).

Bells in your parlours; wild-cats in your kitchens;   110
Saints in your injuries; devils being offended;
Players in your housewifery; and housewives in your
    beds.

Des. O, fie upon thee, slanderer!

Iago. Nay, it is true, or else I am a Turk,
You rise to play, and go to bed to work.   115

Emil. You shall not write my praise.

Iago.   No, let me not.

Des. What wouldst thou write of me, if thou shouldst
    praise me?

Iago. O gentle lady, do not put me to 't,
For I am nothing, if not critical.

Des. Come on, assay . . . there's one gone to the harbour? 120

Iago. Ay, madam.

Des. I am not merry, but I do beguile
The thing I am, by seeming otherwise:

---

113. *Des.*] *F, Q2; not in Q1.*   117. wouldst thou] *Qq;* would'st *F.*   118. to 't]
Qq; too ‚t *F.*

---

110. *Bells*] Cf. "He hath a heart as
sound as a bell, and his tongue is the
clapper" (*Ado*, III. ii. 12).

wild-cats] I do not understand the
point of this gibe. Why should the
kitchen be a more inappropriate place
for a wild-cat than either parlour or
bed?

111. *Saints . . . injuries*] "When you
have a mind to do injuries, you put on
an air of sanctity" (Johnson).

112. *Players*] either "play-actors",
i.e. "deceivers", or perhaps more
probably "gamblers", i.e. "spend-
thrifts"; but it may mean no more than
"triflers", as three lines below.

housewifery] skilful housekeeping;
"Let housewifery appear" (*H 5*, II. iii.
66, Pistol to his wife, where his next
words, "keep close, I thee command"
suggest a pun on "keeping house", i.e.
not gadding).

housewives] perhaps only "wantons"
(see note on IV. i. 94 below); but the
antithesis in this line and again in
l. 115 suggests two other possibilities,
either that in bed women are unduly

economical of their favours or that it is
only in bed that women really give
their minds to business.

114. *Turk*] infidel; cf. "if I do not
love her, I am a Jew" (*Ado*, II. iii. 284);
in the phrase "turn Turk", as in *Ado*,
III. iv. 56, and *Ham.*, III. ii. 292, the
word had a strong and specific sense
of "renegade" from the traditional
"Islam or —" alternative offered to
prisoners.

119. *critical*] censorious; "satire
keen and critical" (*MND.*, v. i. 54),
"critic Timon" (*LLL.*, IV. iii. 170).

122. *beguile*] The meaning "disguise", as in "Tarquin . . . beguil'd
With outward honesty" (*Lucr.*, 1544),
makes *by seeming otherwise* awkwardly
redundant. I think that in Desdemona's thought *The thing I am* is
equated with "my non-merriness", so
that *beguile* has its much commoner
meaning of "divert attention from",
as in *Tit.*, IV. i. 35, "beguile thy sorrow", and the whole phrase means "I
distract my own attention from my
anxiety".

Come, how wouldst thou praise me?

Iago. I am about it, but indeed my invention   125
Comes from my pate as birdlime does from frieze,
It plucks out brain and all: but my Muse labours,
And thus she is deliver'd:
If she be fair and wise, fairness and wit;
The one's for use, the other using it.   130

Des. Well prais'd! How if she be black and witty?

Iago. If she be black, and thereto have a wit,
She'll find a white, that shall her blackness hit.

Des. Worse and worse.

Emil. How if fair and foolish?   135

Iago. She never yet was foolish, that was fair,
For even her folly help'd her, to an heir.

Des. These are old paradoxes, to make fools laugh i' the

125–8.] as *Qq; as prose* F.   127. brain] *Qq;* Braines F.   129, 130, 132, 133
136, 137, 141, 142, 148–58, and 160.] *Q1; in italic* F, *Q2.*   130. using] *Q1;*
useth F, *Q2.*   133. hit] *Q1;* fit F, *Q2.*   137. her, to an heir] her to an heire,
F, *Q2;* her, to a haire *Q1.*   138. old] *Qq;* old fond F.

126. *birdlime*] a viscous preparation spread on bushes to snare birds; "O limed soul, that struggling to be free Art more engaged" (*Ham.*, III. iii. 68), "The bird that hath been limed in a bush" (*3 H 6*, v. vi. 13).

frieze] coarse woollen material.

129, 131. *wit, witty*] "Wit" in Shakespeare commonly goes beyond cleverness in the use of words (though it sometimes includes that) and means "quickness of apprehension"; "The deep-revolving witty Buckingham" (*R 3*, IV. ii. 42), "She's making her ready: she'll come straight: you must be witty now" (*Troil.*, III. ii. 29, where Pandarus does not mean "you must be ready to entertain her with sparkling remarks" but "you must keep your head and be quick to answer her mood").

131. *black*] It was an Elizabethan convention to prefer blondes; the dark lady of the Sonnets is "a woman colour'd ill" (cxliv. 4), and cf. Berowne's unconventional praises of his dark love in *LLL.*, IV. iii. 247–77.

137. *folly*] a pun on the two senses, "foolishness" and "wantonness"; "He pieces out his wife's inclination; he gives her folly motion and advantage" (*Wiv.*, III. ii. 35), "She turn'd to folly, and she was a whore" (v. ii. 133 below and n.). As to the general argument of the line Halliwell appositely quotes "If one have so much knowledge as to measure a yard of cloth; number twenty pence rightly; name the days of the week; *or become the parent of a child*, he shall not be accounted an idiot by the laws of the realm".

138. *old*] perhaps just "hackneyed", as in "your fooling grows old, and people dislike it" (*Tw.N.*, I. v. 118), but possibly in the colloquially ironic sense of "fine", as in "here will be an old abusing of God's patience and the king's English" (*Wiv.*, I. iv. 5), "If a man were porter of hell-gate he should have old turning the key" (*Mac.*, II. iii. 1). If we admit F's *fond*, the first meaning is the more likely.

paradoxes] views contrary to received opinion (the original meaning, almost

alehouse; what miserable praise hast thou for her
that's foul and foolish?   140

Iago. There's none so foul, and foolish thereunto,
But does foul pranks, which fair and wise ones do.

Des. O heavy ignorance, that praises the worst best: but
what praise couldst thou bestow on a deserving
woman indeed? one that in the authority of her   145
merits did justly put on the vouch of very malice
itself?

Iago. She that was ever fair, and never proud,
Had tongue at will, and yet was never loud,
Never lack'd gold, and yet went never gay,   150
Fled from her wish, and yet said "Now I may;"
She that, being anger'd, her revenge being nigh,
Bade her wrong stay, and her displeasure fly;
She that in widsom never was so frail
To change the cod's head for the salmon's tail;   155

---

143. ignorance, that praises] *Qq*; ignorance: thou praisest *F*.   146. merits]
Qq; merit *F*.

= heresies); "this was sometime a
paradox, but now the time gives it
proof" (*Ham.*, III. i. 115).

142. *pranks*] can be used in our
general sense, though commonly with
stronger condemnation implied, as in
"thy audacious wickedness, Thy lewd,
pestiferous, and dissentious pranks"
(*1 H 6*, III. i. 14), but has often the
narrower connotation of infidelity or
promiscuity; "Husband, I'll dine
above with you to day, And shrive you
of a thousand idle pranks" (*Err.*, II. ii.
211), "they do let God see the pranks
They dare not show their husbands"
(III. iii. 206 below).

145.] whose merits are so outstanding that she can claim (?compel) the
witness to them of even malice itself;
for *vouch* = "testimony" cf. "To the
king I'll say't; and make my vouch as
strong As shore of rock" (*H 8*, I. i. 157).

153. *wrong stay*] sense of injury cease.

155. *change . . . tail*] The difficulties
over this line arise largely from an
ambiguity in the Elizabethan use of
"change", which can mean "accept in

exchange for"; hence the stupidity
may consist in giving away the salmon's tail for the cod's head, and not
vice versa. Then there is dispute over
the comparative value of cods' heads
and salmons' tails. White, e.g., glosses
the line by "to give up the best part of
a homely thing for the worst part of
something very fine", whereas Steevens says "to exchange a delicacy for
coarser fare". A quotation which
Steevens gives from Queen Eliza-
beth's Household Book shows that
salmons' tails were perquisites of the
Master Cooks, but does not show
whether or not they were valuable perquisites. Hart has a highly relevant
quotation from Holland's Pliny, "in
other fishes [i.e. other than the Tunny]
the taile-piece is in greatest request".
Lastly, there is almost certainly—particularly since Iago is the speaker—a
strong under-meaning of bawdry in
cod and *tail*. The detailed interpretation, therefore, is very much "to
taste", but the general sense is clear,
"to make a foolish exchange".

She that could think, and ne'er disclose her mind,
See suitors following, and not look behind;
She was a wight, if ever such wight were—

Des. To do what?

Iago. To suckle fools, and chronicle small beer.   160

Des. O most lame and impotent conclusion: do not learn
of him, Emilia, though he be thy husband; how say
you, Cassio, is he not a most profane and liberal
counsellor?

Cas. He speaks home, madam, you may relish him more 165
in the soldier than in the scholar.

Iago. [*Aside*] He takes her by the palm; ay, well said,
whisper: as little a web as this will ensnare as great
a fly as Cassio. Ay, smile upon her, do: I will catch
you in your own courtesies: you say true, 'tis so in- 170

157. See . . . behind] *F*, *Q2; not in Q1*.   158. such wight] *Qq;* such wightes *F.*
161–4.] *as verse Qq, lines ending* conclusion: / husband: / liberall /.   167. S.D.]
Rowe.   168. as little] *Q1;* With as little *F*, *Q2*.   this will] *Q1;* this, will I *F*, *Q2*.
169. fly] *F;* Flee *Q1;* Flie *Q2*.   169–70. will . . . courtesies] *Q1;* will giue thee
in thine owne Courtship *F;* will catch you in your own courtship *Q2*.

160. *small beer*] trivialities; properly
"a weak brew", as in "Doth it not
show vilely in me to desire small beer?
Why, a prince should not be so loosely
studied as to remember so weak a composition" (*2 H 4*, II. ii. 7).

163. *profane*] usually with an implication of "blasphemous" but here not
much more than "indelicately outspoken"; cf. I. i. 114 above.

liberal] from the common sense of
freely and easily open-handed comes
the sense of "*too* free and easy"
whether in speech or action; "That
liberal shepherds call a grosser name"
(*Ham.*, IV. vii. 171), and cf. the corresponding use of "liberty" as in
"liberty plucks justice by the nose"
(*Meas.*, I. iii. 29), "Lust and liberty
Creep in the minds and marrows of our
youth" (*Tim.*, IV. i. 25), and see III. iv.
34 below.

165. *speaks home*] *home* is used of a
sword-thrust which finds its mark and
goes deep; "a quick venew of wit!
snip, snap, quick and home" (*LLL.*,
v. i. 63), and then in more general

senses, such as "charge home" (*Cor.*,
I. iv. 38), "trusted home" (*Mac.*, I. iii.
120); for the use, as here, to describe
words that go home, cf. "Speak to me
home, mince not the general tongue"
(*Ant.*, I. ii. 114).

166. *in the*] in the character of.

167. *well said*] well done (as often,
approving action, not speech); "Well
said, i' faith, Wart" (*2 H 4*, III. ii. 298,
Wart not having opened his mouth),
"Now, masters, draw. (*They shoot*). O!
well said, Lucius!" (*Tit.*, IV. iii. 63),
and cf. v. i. 97 and n. below.

169. *catch*] F's "give" (i.e. gyve) is
quite possible, but I think a needless
and rather clumsy change of metaphor; Iago does not want to "fetter"
Cassio, but to catch him like a fly help-
lessly struggling in a spider's web.

170. *courtesies*] F's "courtship" can
no doubt mean just "courtliness" as
in "Trim gallants, full of courtship and
of state" (*LLL.*, v. ii. 364), but is it not
more pointed for Iago to repeat,
bitterly, Cassio's own word from "bold
show of courtesy"?

deed. If such tricks as these strip you out of your
lieutenantry, it had been better you had not kiss'd
your three fingers so oft, which now again you are
most apt to play the sir in: good, well kiss'd, an excellent courtesy; 'tis so indeed: yet again, your fin-   175
gers at your lips? would they were clyster-pipes for
your sake . . . [*Trumpets within.*] The Moor, I know
his trumpet.
Cas. 'Tis truly so.
Des. Let's meet him, and receive him.   180

Enter OTHELLO *and Attendants.*

Cas. Lo, where he comes!
Oth. O my fair warrior!
Des.   My dear Othello!
Oth. It gives me wonder great as my content
    To see you here before me: O my soul's joy,
    If after every tempest come such calmness,   185
    May the winds blow, till they have waken'd death,
    And let the labouring bark climb hills of seas,

172. kiss'd] *F*; rist *Qq*.   174. good] *Q1*; very good *F, Q2*.   an] *Q1*; and *F*
Q2.   176. at] *Qq*; to *F*.   177. S.D.] *Qq* (*after* trumpet); *not in F*.   180.
S.D.] *before l. 179 Qq; after l. 181 F*.   185. calmness] *Qq* (calmenesse)*;*
Calmes *F*.

172-3. *kiss'd your three fingers*] The
kissing of his hand was a quite normal
courteous gesture from gentleman to
lady; "To see him walk before a lady,
and to bear her fan! To see him kiss his
hand" (*LLL.*, IV. i. 148), "Why dost
thou smile so and kiss thy hand so oft?"
(*Tw.N.*, III. iv. 36).

174. *play the sir*] play the fine gallant;
a "sir", as a noun, not a vocative of
address, can be quite neutral, and =
"man", or be used with a note of
respect, as in "Sole sir o' the world"
(*Ant.*, v. ii. 119) or with a note of sar-
casm, as here, and in "To draw upon
an exile! O brave sir!" (*Cym.*, I. i. 166).

176. *clyster-pipes*] syringe for a
(vaginal) douche.

178. *trumpet*] trumpet-call; dis-
tinguished people had their own

recognizable calls, described in S.D.s
as "tuckets"; e.g. in *Lr.*, II. i. 80, where
the arrival of Cornwall is unlooked for,
"(*Tucket within*) Hark! the duke's
trumpets. I know not why he comes",
and, though the arrival is here
expected, "(*A tucket sounds*) Your husband is at hand; I hear his trumpet"
(*Mer.V.*, v. i. 121).

182. *warrior*] Othello welcomes Desdemona as his companion-in-arms;
there is no need to trouble with Ron-
sard and his "guerrières".

185. *calmness*] I see no reason to
desert *Q1*; F's "calms" is, both metrically and for the expected contrast,
more obvious, but the falling cadence
of the feminine ending, and the
abstract word, have their own effectiveness.

Olympus-high, and duck again as low
As hell's from heaven. If it were now to die,
'Twere now to be most happy, for I fear   190
My soul hath her content so absolute,
That not another comfort, like to this
Succeeds in unknown fate.

Des.   The heavens forbid
But that our loves and comforts should increase,   194
Even as our days do grow.

Oth.   Amen to that, sweet powers!
I cannot speak enough of this content,
It stops me here, it is too much of joy:
And this, and this, the greatest discord be   [*they kiss.*
That e'er our hearts shall make!

Iago.   [*Aside*] O, you are well tun'd now,
But I'll set down the pegs that make this music,   200
As honest as I am.

Oth.   Come, let us to the castle.
News, friends, our wars are done, the Turks are drown'd
How do our old acquaintance of the isle?
Honey, you shall be well desir'd in Cyprus;
I have found great love amongst them: O my sweet, 205
I prattle out of fashion, and I dote

193–5.] *as Qq; F lineates* forbid / Loues / encrease / grow. /   195. that, sweet
powers!] that, sweet Powers; *Q2;* that (sweet Powers) *F;* that sweete power, *Q1.*
198. discord] *Qq;* discords *F.*   S.D.] *Q1; Kisse Q2; no S.D. in F.*   199. S.D.]
Rowe.   202. friends] *Q1, F;* friend *Q2.*   203. do our] do's my *F, Q2* (dos
Q2).   the] *Q1;* this *F, Q2.*

200. *set down the pegs*] *pegs* are the
pins whereby the strings of a stringed
musical instrument are slackened or
tightened, and *set*, for what it is worth,
elsewhere means "to tune". The meaning of the whole phrase is clear, that
Iago will slacken the strings to produce
a discord or even no music at all, but
precisely why it means that remains
doubtful, since no one has found a
parallel, in Shakespeare or elsewhere,
for *set down pegs*.

201. *As honest as I am*] for all my
(supposed) honesty.

203. *old acquaintance*] This makes

even clearer than the Doge's and Montano's remarks that Othello has
served in Cyprus before.

204. *Honey*] not elsewhere in Shakespeare as vocative standing alone, but
common as adjective in address, as
"honey love" (*Shr.*, IV. iii. 52), "good
sweet honey lord" (*1 H 4*, I. ii. 178),
"sweet honey Greek" (*Troil.*, v. ii.
18), "honey nurse" (*Rom.*, II. v. 18).
America has retained it as plain
vocative.

206. *out of fashion*] irrelevantly,
when I ought to be thinking of other
things.

In mine own comforts: I prithee, good Iago,
Go to the bay, and disembark my coffers;
Bring thou the master to the citadel;
He is a good one, and his worthiness   210
Does challenge much respect: come, Desdemona,
Once more well met at Cyprus.

        [Exeunt all but Iago and Roderigo.

Iago. Do thou meet me presently at the harbour: come
hither. If thou be'st valiant—as, they say, base men
being in love have then a nobility in their natures 215
more than is native to them—list me; the lieutenant
to-night watches on the court of guard: first, I will
tell thee this, Desdemona is directly in love with him.

Rod. With him? why, 'tis not possible.

Iago. Lay thy finger thus, and let thy soul be instructed: 220

---

212. S.D.] *Exit Q1; Exeunt Q2; Exit Othello and Desdemona F.*   214. hither] *Qq;*
thither *F.*   217. will] *Qq;* must *F.*   218. thee this, Desdemona] *Q2;* thee
this: Desdemona, *F;* thee, this Desdemona *Q1, Theobald.*

208. *coffers*] usually "strong-boxes", for money or jewels, but here just "luggage".

211. *challenge much respect*] makes it incumbent on us to show him all the respect we can.

212. *well met*] a common form of greeting; cf. "Ill met by moonlight, proud Titania" (*MND.*, II. i. 60).

213. *presently*] one of the few places in Shakespeare where the word is used in something near its modern sense. It almost invariably means "at once", and is one of the words about which one needs to be perpetually on guard, since often the modern meaning makes a kind of sense but weaker sense than what Shakespeare intended; "Go hie thee presently post to the road" (*Err.*, III. ii. 153), "For the love of God, a surgeon! send one presently to Sir Toby" (*Tw.N.*, v. i. 176), "You must away to court sir, presently; A dozen captains stay at door for you" (*2 H 4*, II. iv. 406), "I'll call him presently, my noble lord" (*2 H 6*, III. ii. 18, which is not in evasion of, but in direct obedience to, the King's "Go, call our uncle to our presence *straight*"), "guilty creatures sitting at a play Have . . . Been struck so to the soul that presently They have proclaim'd their malefactions" (*Ham.*, II. ii. 626), "Go, tell the duke and's wife I'd speak with them, Now, presently" (*Lr.*, II. iv. 117), and, notably, in this play, "thou'rt on thy death-bed. *Des.* Ay, but not yet to die. *Oth.* Yes, presently" (v. ii. 53). It is perhaps a reflection on human nature that words of temporal immediacy seem to have a way of slipping—"anon" had gone down-hill even by Shakespeare's time (cf. the bewildered drawer in *1 H 4*, II. iv. 38–72), and suddenness of service is the last thing an impatient diner expects when he hears "subito". Part of the Elizabethan sense is retained in modern American "presently"="at the present time"—"he is presently ambassador in London".

217. *court of guard*] guard house; "If we be not reliev'd within the hour, We must return to the court of guard", "Let us bear him To the court of guard" (*Ant.*, IV. ix. 2, 32).

mark me, with what violence she first lov'd the Moor,
but for bragging, and telling her fantastical lies; and
will she love him still for prating? let not the discreet
heart think so. Her eye must be fed, and what delight
shall she have to look on the devil? When the blood 225
is made dull with the act of sport, there should be
again to inflame it, and give satiety a fresh appetite,
loveliness in favour, sympathy in years, manners and
beauties; all which the Moor is defective in: now, for
want of these requir'd conveniences, her delicate 230
tenderness will find itself abus'd, begin to heave the

222–3. and will she love] *Qq;* To love *F.*   223. the] *Qq;* thy *F.*   224. so] *Q1;* it
F, Q2.   227. again] againe *Q1;* a game *F, Q2.*   give satiety] giue saciety
Qq; to giue Satiety *F.*   227–8. appetite, loveliness] *Theobald;* appetite. Loue
lines *Q1;* appetite. Louelinesse *F;* appetite. Louelines *Q2.*

222. *but for*] only for, for nothing
more than; cf. "They are all but
stomachs and we all but food" (III. iv.
101 below).

226. *act of sport*] "sport" is common
Elizabethan, though not very common
in Shakespeare, for pleasure of coitus;
"let Kate be chaste, and Dian sport-
ful" (*Shr.*, II. i. 256), "there was good
sport at his making" (*Lr.*, I. i. 23), and
"Desires for sport and frailty" (IV. iii.
101 below); and for clearer examples
see Donne, e.g. "Only let me love
none, no, not the sport" (*Love's Usury*,
13), "as she [Nature] would man
should despise The sport" (*Farewell to
Love*, 26).

227–8. *again . . . favour*] I have
accepted the reading which almost all
edd. except Rowe and Pope have constructed from a conflation of Q1 and
F, but I think it is thoroughly suspect.
The relevant points are these: (*a*) Q1
reads *againe,* F *a game*; (*b*) both texts
have a full stop after *appetite* and follow
it with an upper-case *L*; (*c*) Q1 reads
Loue lines, F *Louelinesse*; (*d*) Q2 preferred F's *a game,* retained the full stop
of both the other texts, and equalized
Q1 with F by joining Q1's two words
into one, *Louelines.* To take these points
in order; (*a*) *againe* and *a game* are
graphically indifferent, since either

could be an easy misreading of the
other (*in* for *m,* minim error), but
againe is impossible with the full stop
after *appetite*; for *game* in a relevant
sense cf. "daughters of the game"
(*Troil.*, IV. v. 63), and, even more significant "I'll warrant her full of game"
(II. iii. 19 below); the difficulty is the
indefinite article, which demands
some meaning such as "relish" or
"piquancy" to whet the jaded appetite; (*b*) the full stop is obstinately
there; (*c*) if *Loue lines* stood in isolation,
though *Louelines* is an obvious correction, another would be equally obvious, namely *Loue liues,* which is only a
matter of a turned letter. I suggest
therefore as a possible reading which
merits consideration *a game to inflame it,
and give satiety a fresh appetite. Love lives
in favour. . .* It has the advantage of
retaining *game.* the implications of
which are typical of Iago.

228. *favour*] appearance; see note on
III. iv. 122 below.

230. *conveniences*] advantages, desir-
abilities, but with a strong under-
current of the other meaning, "apt-
nesses"; Iago sees, and later effectively
uses, the apparent *unsuitability* of the
match.

231. *abus'd*] cheated, almost "revolted".

gorge, disrelish and abhor the Moor, very nature
will instruct her to it, and compel her to some second
choice. Now, sir, this granted (as it is a most pregnant
and unforc'd position) who stands so eminently in 235
the degree of this fortune as Cassio does? a knave
very voluble, no farther conscionable than in putting
on the mere form of civil and humane seeming, for
the better compassing of his salt and hidden affections: a subtle slippery knave, a finder out of occa- 240
sions; that has an eye can stamp and counterfeit the
true advantages never present themselves. Besides,
the knave is handsome, young, and hath all those
requisites in him that folly and green minds look

233. to it] *Qq;* in it *F.*　　235. eminently] *Qq;* eminent *F.*　　238. humane
seeming] *F, Q2;* hand-seeming *Q1.*　　239. compassing] *Qq;* compasse *F.*
239–40. hidden affections] *Q1;* most hidden loose Affection? Why none, why
none *F;* most hidden loose affections *Q2.*　　240. subtle slippery] *Qq;* slipper,
and subtle *F.*　　240–1. a finder out of occasions] *Qq;* a finder of occasion *F.*
241. has] *Qq;* he's *F.*　　241–2. the true advantages] *Q1;* Aduantages, though
true Aduantage *F, Q2* (aduantages, tho ... aduantage *Q2*).　　242. themselves.]
Q1; it selfe. A diuelish knaue: *F;* it selfe. *Q2.*

232. *very nature*] natural instincts
themselves.

234. *pregnant*] often used in the sense
"obvious" or "natural" which seems
to have little to do with its ordinary
meaning; " 'Tis very pregnant, The
jewel that we find, we stoop and take
it" (*Meas.*, II. i. 23), "Were't not that
we stand up against them all, 'Twere
pregnant they should square between
themselves" (*Ant.*, II. i. 44).

235. *position*] hypothesis, something
"posited"; see note on III. iii. 238
below.

235–6. *in the degree of this fortune*] next
in the line of promotion.

237. *voluble*] possibly in our sense,
but more probably in the more
general sense of "facile" (*volubilis*,
running easily).

conscionable] not elsewhere in Shakespeare and not clear in meaning
here; it seems to mean "behaving
in a way that would give a clear conscience".

239. *salt*] lecherous, "hot"; "salt

imagination" (*Meas.*, v. i. 402), "salt
Cleopatra" (*Ant.*, II. i. 21), "As salt
as wolves, in pride" (III. iii. 410 below).

239–42.] As will be seen by reter-
ence to the apparatus criticus, F has
some additions, and irons out a syntactical awkwardness, though the
omission of the relative (after *advantages*) is not uncommon. It should be
noted that Q1's *the*, after *counterfeit*,
might easily be a misreading of *tho*, and
that the repeated *advantage(s)* might
cause a telescoping. On the other hand
the additions might easily be those of
an actor who felt that they "came
natural".

241. *stamp*] as in a mint, "do coin
heaven's image In stamps that are forbid" (*Meas.*, II. iv. 46).

244. *folly*] See note on l. 137 above,
and v. ii. 133 below.

green] unripe, inexperienced; "My
salad days, When I was green in judgement" (*Ant.*, I. v. 73), "a green girl"
(*Ham.*, I. iii. 101).

after; a pestilent complete knave, and the woman 245
has found him already.

Rod. I cannot believe that in her, she's full of most blest
condition.

Iago. Blest fig's-end! the wine she drinks is made of
grapes: if she had been blest, she would never have 250
lov'd the Moor. Didst thou not see her paddle with
the palm of his hand?

Rod. Yes, but that was but courtesy.

Iago. Lechery, by this hand: an index and prologue to the
history of lust and foul thoughts: they met so near 255
with their lips, that their breaths embrac'd together.
When these mutualities so marshal the way, hard at
hand comes the main exercise, the incorporate conclusion. But, sir, be you rul'd by me, I have brought
you from Venice: watch you to-night, for your com- 260
mand, I'll lay 't upon you, Cassio knows you not, I'll
not be far from you, do you find some occasion to
anger Cassio, either by speaking too loud, or tainting
his discipline, or from what other cause you please;
which the time shall more favourably minister.   265

Rod. Well.

Iago. Sir, he is rash, and very sudden in choler, and haply

246. has] *Qq;* hath *F.*   251. Moor] *Qq;* Moore; Bless'd pudding *F.*   252.
hand?] *Q1;* hand? Didst not marke that? *F, Q2* (did'st *Q2*).   253. Yes,] *Qq;*
Yes, that I did: *F.*   254. prologue] *Q1;* obscure prologue *F, Q2.*   256–7. together. When] *Q1;* together. Villanous thoughts *Rodorigo,* when *F;* together,
villanous thoughts, when *Q2.*   257. mutualities] *Qq;* mutabilities *F.*
hard] *F;* hand *Qq.*   258. comes] *Q1, F;* comes Roderigo, *Q2.*   main] *Q1;*
Master, and maine *F;* master and the maine *Q2.*   258–9. conclusion] *Qq;*
conclusion: Pish *F.*   260. for your] *Q1;* for the *F;* for *Q2.*   264. cause] *Q1;*
course *F, Q2.*

246. *found him*] has her eye on him
(the sense "find the weakness of" as in
All's W., v. ii. 46, "you were the first
that found me", and elsewhere, does
not suit the context here).

248. *condition*] disposition, character; "condition of a saint" (*Mer.V.,*
I. ii. 141).

249. *fig's-end*] as we should say "my
foot".

252–9.] more additions in F, all

quite effective, but none necessary.

251. *paddle*] Cf. "paddling palms
and pinching fingers" (*Wint.,* I. ii. 116).

254. *index*] table of contents (at the
beginning of a book, not, as with us,
at the end); "in such indexes, although
small pricks To their subsequent
volumes" (*Troil.,* I. iii. 343).

263. *tainting*] disparaging; cf. "To
taint that honour every good tongue
blesses" (*H 8,* III. i. 54).

SC. I]   OTHELLO   **65**

    with his truncheon may strike at you: provoke him
that he may, for even out of that will I cause these of
Cyprus to mutiny, whose qualification shall come 270
into no true trust again, but by the displanting of
Cassio. So shall you have a shorter journey to your
desires by the means I shall then have to prefer them,
and the impediment most profitably remov'd, without which there were no expectation of our pros- 275
perity.

Rod. I will do this, if I can bring it to any opportunity.

Iago. I warrant thee, meet me by and by at the citadel:
    I must fetch his necessaries ashore. . . Farewell.

Rod. Adieu.   [*Exit.* 280

Iago. That Cassio loves her, I do well believe it;

---

268. with his truncheon] *Qq* (Trunchen); *not in F.*   271. trust] *Q1*; taste *F*,
Q2.   again] *F* (againe); again't *Qq.*   275. which] *Qq*; the which *F*.
277. if I can] *Qq*; if you can *F*.

268. *truncheon*] a staff carried by military officers, but usually, it would seem, of higher rank than Cassio; the instances in Shakespeare are a marshal, Mars, and the elder Hamlet, though one use of the verb brings it as low as captains. There is no truncheon in F, perhaps because it was thought to be "counter-indicated" in the next scene, where Cassio makes for Montano with his sword; but he beats Roderigo, and unless he does it with the flat of his sword, the truncheon is appropriate enough.

270–1. *qualification . . . trust*] a highly compressed phrase; "qualify" can mean simply "appease", as in "Your discontenting father strive to qualify" (*Wint.*, IV. iii. 545), and so *qualification* can mean no more than "appeasement", but if we accept *taste* there is probably a touch of the meaning which appears in iii. 36 below, "dilution". The heady, fiery Cypriots will be "allayed" into temperate mildness by . . .

273. *prefer*] advance; "Have I not reason to prefer mine own?" (*Gent.*, II. iv. 157, where Valentine's rejoinder "And I will help thee to prefer her

too: She shall be dignified with this high honour" saves one from supposing that *prefer* means "like better".

277. *if I can . . .*] F reads "if you can"; the timorous "if I can manage it" is like Roderigo, and the F reading looks like an attempt to make *I warrant thee* less colloquial; with the Q1 reading it means "I'll go bail for you", or, in modern idiom, "Stout fellow!" or "Attaboy!"; with the F reading it means "I will guarantee you the opportunity". But it is true that it is in fact Iago who does "manage it".

281–307. In this second soliloquy the emphasis has changed. Iago is now plotting for revenge, and the motive advanced is no longer anger at missed promotion, but plain sexual jealousy. It will be observed that there is no suggestion of any animus against Desdemona, though no doubt if Othello's jealousy is to be roused she cannot escape being involved. Even yet Iago has not got his design worked out in any detail; it is still "confused". And the last line stresses Iago's opportunism; he knows that he can trust himself to take advantage of any opening that fortune offers him.

That she loves him, 'tis apt and of great credit:
The Moor, howbe't that I endure him not,
Is of a constant, noble, loving nature;
And I dare think, he'll prove to Desdemona   285
A most dear husband: now I do love her too,
Not out of absolute lust, (though peradventure
I stand accountant for as great a sin)
But partly led to diet my revenge,
For that I do suspect the lustful Moor   290
Hath leap'd into my seat, the thought whereof
Doth like a poisonous mineral gnaw my inwards,
And nothing can, nor shall content my soul,
Till I am even with him, wife, for wife:
Or failing so, yet that I put the Moor,   295
At least, into a jealousy so strong,
That judgement cannot cure; which thing to do,
If this poor trash of Venice, whom I trash

284. noble, loving] *Qq;* louing, Noble *F.*   289. led] *F;* lead *Qq.*   290. lustful] *Qq;* lustie *F.*   293. nor] *Qq;* or *F.*   294. even] *Q1;* eeuen'd *F;* euen'd *Q2.*   for wife] *Qq;* for wist *F.*   298. I trash] *Steevens;* I crush *Q1;* I trace *F,* *Q2.*

282. *apt . . . credit*] natural and wholly credible.

292. *poisonous mineral*] See note on I. ii. 74 above.

298. *trash*] hang weights on a hound to prevent him hunting too fast; "who t'advance, and who To trash for over-topping" (*Tp.*, I. ii. 80). The reading is Steevens's, and is generally adopted, even if only in despair. It is, graphically, an easy emendation of Q1's *crush*, less easy of F's and Q2's *trace*. The trouble is—apart from the fact that Iago is not normally addicted to puns—that the meaning produced does not seem appropriate to Iago's line of thought *at the moment*. It is true that as a rule Iago has to trash Roderigo, to slow down his impatient hunting of Desdemona; but here he is wanting to *incite* him, to "put him on", to the attack on Cassio. And it seems singularly clumsy to say "I usually trash him, but now I want to do the opposite"—why bother about the

trashing at all? Things are not made easier by the fact that *for* in the context can mean either "to promote" or "to prevent". Attempts to justify and retain *trace* seem to me hopeless. No parallel usage is adduced from Shakespeare, nor anything helpful from anywhere else. I have sometimes wondered whether a case cannot be made out for *crush*, in something like the sense of "crowding" a horse at a fence—which is just what Iago is trying to do—and the words occur together, in the sense of "force" in "The time misorder'd doth . . . Crowd us and crush us to this monstrous form" (*2 H 4,* IV. ii. 33), but the possible relevance of this passage is weakened by the other joint occurrence in "a man into whom nature hath so crowded humours that his valour is crushed into folly" (*Troil.,* I. ii. 22). And *O.E.D.* does not offer an example of the required sense. I have therefore, reluctantly and perhaps spiritlessly, adopted the usual reading.

For his quick hunting, stand the putting on,
I'll have our Michael Cassio on the hip,   300
Abuse him to the Moor, in the rank garb
(For I fear Cassio with my night-cap too)
Make the Moor thank me, love me, and reward me,
For making him egregiously an ass,
And practising upon his peace and quiet,   305
Even to madness: 'tis here, but yet confus'd;
Knavery's plain face is never seen, till us'd.   [*Exit.*

SCENE II.—[*The same.*]

Enter a Gentleman reading a proclamation.

It is Othello's pleasure; our noble and valiant gen-

300. our] *F, Q2;* out *Q1.*   301. rank] *Qq;* right *F.*   302. with] *Qq, F;* wore
Anon. MS. (Devonshire Q1).   night-cap] *Qq;* Night-Cape *F.*

Scene II

S.D.] *Q1; Enter Othello's, Herald with a Proclamation F; Enter Othello's Herauld,
reading a Proclamation Q2.*   1.] *no speech heading Qq;* Her. *F.*

299. *putting on*] inciting; "Say you
ne'er had done't . . . but by our putting
on" (*Cor.*, II. iii. 259), "you protect this
course, and put it on By your allowance" (*Lr.*, I. iv. 230).

300. *on the hip*] a wrestling term; in
the position from which I can give him
the decisive throw, e.g. a "cross-
buttock"; as we should say "just where
I want him"; "Now, infidel, I have
thee on the hip" (*Mer. V.*, IV. i. 335).

301. *Abuse*] slander.

rank garb] The immediately succeeding night-cap tempts one to misunderstand *garb*, which is never used
by Shakespeare of dress, but as =
"manner", "fashion", and usually
fashion of *speech*; "he could not speak
English in the native garb" (*H 5*, v. i.
80), "commanding peace Even with
the same austerity and garb As he con-
troll'd the war" (*Cor.*, IV. vii. 43).
Rank originally meant no more than
"luxuriant in growth", then "coarsely
over-luxuriant", then "unpleasantly

strong", especially in taste or smell,
and it took on frequently in Shakespeare, as I think certainly here, a
sexual undertone and became =
"hot"; "The even mead, that erst
brought sweetly forth The freckled
cowslip, burnet, and green clover,
Wanting the scythe, all uncorrected,
rank, Conceives by idleness, and nothing teems But hateful docks . . ."
(*H 5*, v. ii. 48), " 'tis an unweeded garden . . . ; things rank and gross in
nature Possess it merely" (*Ham.*, I. ii.
135), "as rank as a fox" (*Tw. N.*, v.
138), "my offence is rank, it smells to
heaven" (*Ham.*, III. iii. 36), "the ewes,
being rank, In end of autumn turned
to the rams" (*Mer. V.*, I. iii. 81), "Foh!
one may smell in such a will most rank,
Foul disproportion, thoughts unnatural" (III. iii. 236 below).

Scene II

1–11.] This scene, like others of the
same type in Shakespeare (cf. III. ii

eral, that upon certain tidings now arrived, import-
ing the mere perdition of the Turkish fleet; that
every man put himself into triumph: some to dance,
some make bonfires; each man to what sport and   5
revels his mind leads him; for besides these beneficial
news, it is the celebration of his nuptials. So much
was his pleasure should be proclaimed. All offices are
open, and there is full liberty, from this present hour
of five, till the bell hath told eleven. Heaven bless the   10
isle of Cyprus, and our noble general Othello!   [*Exit.*

3. mere] *F, Q2* (Meere); meete *Q1.*   3-4. that every] *Qq;* every *F.*   5.
make] *Qq;* to make *F.*   6. mind] *Q1;* addition *F;* addiction *Q2.*   7. nup-
tials] *Qq;* Nuptiall *F.*   9. liberty] *Qq;* libertie of Feasting *F.*   present] *Qq;*
presenr *F.*   10. Heaven bless] *Qq;* Blesse *F.*   11. S.D.] *F; not in Qq.*

below), is the equivalent of the
modern "the curtain will be lowered
to indicate the passage of four or five
hours", though Shakespeare uses it to
make the indications of time precise.

3. *mere*] The word in Shakespeare
more often than not = "absolute,
complete, pure" rather than our
modern depreciatory or corrective
"only"; "what discord follows; each
thing meets In mere oppugnancy"
(*Troil.*, I. iii. 110), "To thy further fear,
Nay, to thy mere confusion . . ." (*Cym.*,
IV. ii. 91), "*Sic.* This is clean kam. *Bru.*
Merely awry" (*Cor.*, III. i. 302, where
Brutus does not mean "Oh no, not so
bad as that, only a trifle askew" but
"Yes, indeed, absolutely so"), and cf.
"mere English"—when the Queen so
described herself the last thing she
meant was that she was "only English".

4. *triumph*] revelry—a more general
sense than ours; "I will wed thee in
another key, With pomp, with
triumph, and with revelling" (*MND.*,
I. i. 18), "O, thou art a perpetual
triumph, an everlasting bonfire-light"
(*1 H 4*, III. iii. 46).

6. *mind*] F reads "addition" and
heroic attempts have been made to
defend it, Furness's being the best,
since, admitting that "addition" in
Shakespeare normally means "title",
he cites the passage from *Troil.*, I. ii.
19, "This man hath robbed many
beasts of their additions: he is as
valiant as the lion, churlish as the
bear", and says that "addition" here
seems to stand for characteristic
quality or natural bent. But is it not
more probable that the word there
means "label", the lion being pro-
verbially valiant, the bear churlish,
and so on. "Addiction" is the obvious
emendation, made first by Q2, and
accepted by most edd. But what is the
matter with the straightforward *mind*?
Perhaps it was felt to be too straightforward for the rather pompous
gentleman; and it is worth noticing
that where "addiction" occurs again
in Shakespeare (*H 5*, I. i. 54) it is in the
mouth of the high-flown Canterbury.

8. *offices*] kitchens, butteries and the
like (cf. our "usual offices") "Sent
forth great largess to your offices"
(*Mac.*, II. i. 14).

SCENE III.—[*A Hall in the Castle.*]

Enter OTHELLO, CASSIO, *and* DESDEMONA.

Oth. Good Michael, look you to the guard to-night:
Let's teach ourselves the honourable stop,
Not to outsport discretion.

Cas. Iago hath directed what to do:
But notwithstanding with my personal eye   5
Will I look to it.

Oth.   Iago is most honest,
Michael, good night, to-morrow with your earliest,
Let me have speech with you; come, my dear love,
The purchase made, the fruits are to ensue,
The profit's yet to come 'twixt me and you.   10
Good night.   [*Exeunt Othello and Desdemona.*

Enter IAGO.

Cas. Welcome, Iago, we must to the watch.

Iago. Not this hour, lieutenant, 'tis not yet ten o' clock:
our general cast us thus early for the love of his Desdemona, who let us not therefore blame: he hath not   15
yet made wanton the night with her; and she is sport
for Jove.

Cas. She is a most exquisite lady.

Iago. And I'll warrant her full of game.

Cas. Indeed she is a most fresh and delicate creature.   20

Iago. What an eye she has! methinks it sounds a parley of
provocation.

Scene III

S.D.] *Qq; Enter Othello, Desdemona, Cassio, and Attendants F.*   2. the] *Q1;*
that *F, Q2.*   4. directed] *Q1;* direction *F, Q2.*   6. to it] *Qq;* to't *F.*   10.
The] *Q1;* That *F, Q2.*   'twixt] *Qq;* 'tweene *F.*   11. S.D.] *Qq; Exit F.*
13. o'clock] aclock *Qq;* o'th'clocke *F.*   21. of] *Qq;* to *F.*

13. *Not this hour*] not for an hour yet;
eleven has been announced as "closing
time".

14. *cast*] See note on I. i. 149 above.
16. *sport*] See note on II. i. 226 above.
19. *game*] in modern idiom "expert
love-play"; no exact parallel in
Shakespeare, but cf. "daughters of the

game" (*Troil.*, IV. v. 62), "Were you a
gamester at five or at seven?" (*Per.*,
IV. vi. 82, to Marina in the brothel).

21–2. *parley of provocation*] an odd
phrase, since a parley, or parle, was
almost always the prelude to an intended *cessation* of hostilities, not, like
the *alarm* of two lines below, a pre-

Cas. An inviting eye, and yet methinks right modest.

Iago. And when she speaks, 'tis an alarm to love.

Cas. It is indeed perfection.   25

Iago. Well, happiness to their sheets! . . . Come, lieutenant, I have a stoup of wine, and here without are a
   brace of Cyprus gallants, that would fain have a
   measure to the health of the black Othello.

Cas. Not to-night, good Iago; I have very poor and un-   30
   happy brains for drinking: I could well wish courtesy
   would invent some other custom of entertainment.

Iago. O, they are our friends, . . . but one cup: I'll drink
   for you.

Cas. I ha' drunk but one cup to-night, and that was   35
   craftily qualified too, and behold what innovation it
   makes here: I am unfortunate in the infirmity, and
   dare not task my weakness with any more.

Iago. What, man, 'tis a night of revels, the gallants desire
   it.   40

Cas. Where are they?

Iago. Here at the door, I pray you call them in.

Cas. I'll do't, but it dislikes me.   [*Exit.*

Iago. If I can fasten but one cup upon him,
   With that which he hath drunk to-night already,   45
   He'll be as full of quarrel and offence

---

24. 'tis an alarm to love.] *Qq;* Is it not an Alarum to Loue? *F.*   25. It is] *Q1;*
She is *F, Q2.*   29. the black] *Qq;* blacke *F.*   35. ha'] *Qq;* haue *F.*   37. un-
fortunate] *Qq;* infortunate *F.*

liminary to an encounter (of arms or
love).
   24. *alarm*] the "stand to" or the sig-
nal for onset; "as the sleeping soldiers
in the alarm . . . starts up" (*Ham.*, III.
iv. 119), "Sound, trumpets, alarum to
the combatants" (*2 H 6*, II. iii. 97).
   27. *stoup*] tankard of two quarts.
   36. *qualified*] not "laced" but
"diluted" (like Menenius' "allaying
Tiber"); usually in Shakespeare,
when used metaphorically, of heat, as
in "till some little time hath qualified
the heat of his displeasure" (*Lr.*, I. ii.
182).
   innovation] revolution (like Latin

res novae); "some fine colour that may
please the eye Of fickle changelings
and poor discontents, Which gape and
rub the elbow at the news Of hurly
burly innovation: And never yet did
insurrection want Such water-colours
to impaint his cause" (*1 H 4*, v. i. 75).
   37. *here*] pointing, presumably, to
his head.
   46. *offence*] presumably "readiness to
take offence", not, I think, to offer it;
" 'Tis wonderful What may be
wrought out of their discontent, Now
that their souls are topful of offence"
(*John*, III. iv. 178), "good uncle, banish
all offence" (*1 H 6*, v. v. 96).

As my young mistress' dog: . . . Now my sick fool
   Roderigo,
Whom love has turn'd almost the wrong side outward,
To Desdemona hath to-night carous'd
Potations pottle-deep, and he's to watch: 50
Three lads of Cyprus, noble swelling spirits,
That hold their honour in a wary distance,
The very elements of this warlike isle,
Have I to-night fluster'd with flowing cups,   54
And they watch too: now, 'mongst this flock of drunkards,

47. Now my] *Q1, F;* Noy mw *Q2.*   48. outward] *Qq;* out *F.*   51. lads] *Qq;*
else *F;* elks *Jackson conj.*   52. honour] *Qq;* Honours *F.*   55. they] *F;* the *Qq.*

47. *my young mistress' dog*] The silence
of most commentators ought to imply
that they see no need for comment;
but I do not see the point of the
phrase. The young mistress can hardly
be Desdemona, since Iago would not
admit the inferiority which the phrase
would imply; nor have we any reason
to suppose that Iago has a mistress in
the other sense, or that either she, if
she exists, or Desdemona, has a dog.
My, then, is presumably "generalizing", like "your" in "your philo-
sophy", and the phrase begins to have
a proverbial flavour. But why should
the dog of a young mistress, or the
young dog of a mistress, be noted for
quarrelsomeness? The only other possibility is, I fear, no more than a
laughable effort of despair, namely
that Mistress Dog is a title (as one
might have said in a beast-fable "Then
comes me in Master Lion"); but then
the title would almost certainly have
been Mistress Brach.

49. *carous'd*] A carouse is properly
not a drinking-bout, but a single
draught with "no heel-taps" (*gar aus*
= "all out"); "quaff carouses to our
mistress' health" (*Shr.,* I. ii. 280),
"The queen carouses to thy fortune,
Hamlet" (*Ham.,* v. ii. 303).

50. *pottle-deep*] to the bottom of the
(two quart) tankard.

51. *lads*] Delius ingeniously suggested that F's odd reading, *else,* was an

error (he would have been wise to add
"auditory") for "Ls", a common
abbreviation for "Lords". But one
may pursue the same line further by
assuming an original "Lds", expanded
to *lads* by Q1, misread as "les" and
transposed by F, and by pointing out
that the *Lords-Laddes* variant (the other
way round) occurs at II. i. 20 above.
But *else* is not impossible, with the
meaning not "three other Cypriots"
but "three others, and they Cypriots";
cf. "Bastards, and else" (*John,* II. i.
276).

swelling] arrogant, "throwing their
weight about"; "something showing a
more swelling port" (*Mer.V.,* I. i. 125),
"here he [Pistol] comes, swelling like
a turkey-cock" (*H 5,* v. i. 15).

52. *That hold . . . distance*] an awkward phrase, since the natural meaning is that they keep their honour at
arm's length, but I suppose the meaning is that they are on guard to keep
their honour out of reach of slur, and so
take ready offence.

53. *elements*] The word properly
meant "essential constituents", and
here it seems to mean "just the types
that make up this island"; see note on
l. 333 below.

55. *they watch*] F's reading is the
easier in run of thought, but it has
disadvantages: three Cypriots plus
Roderigo are hardly a "flock", and
Montano is of too high rank to be a

I am to put our Cassio in some action
That may offend the isle.

Enter MONTANO, CASSIO, *and others*.

               But here they come:
If consequence do but approve my dream,
My boat sails freely, both with wind and stream.
Cas. 'Fore God they have given me a rouse already.   60
Mon. Good faith, a little one, not past a pint,
    As I am a soldier.
Iago. Some wine, ho!
    [*Sings*]   *And let me the cannikin clink, clink,*
             And let me the cannikin clink, clink: 65
                A soldier's a man,
                A life's but a span,
             Why then let a soldier drink.
    Some wine, boys!
Cas. 'Fore God an excellent song.   70
Iago. I learn'd it in England, where indeed they are most

---

56. I am to put] *Qq;* Am I put to *F.*   57. S.D.] *Qq* (Montanio); *Enter Cassio,*
Montano, and Gentlemen F.   60. God] *Qq;* heauen *F.*   65. clink, clink] *Qq;*
clinke *F.*   66–7.] *as one line Qq, F.*   67. A life's] *Qq;* Oh, mans life's *F.*
70. God] *Q1;* Heauen *F, Q2.*

natural member of "the watch". But *they* in l. 57 makes it clear that Montano is one of the flustered lads or lords. And incidentally the fact that he is makes it the more tempting to try to educe "Lords" out of "else" in l. 51.

58. *consequence*] succeeding events; "Some consequence yet hanging in the stars Shall bitterly begin his fearful date" (*Rom.*, I. iv. 108).

approve] confirm; "He may approve our eyes" (*Ham.*, I. i. 29).

59. *stream*] current in the sea, as in "Gulf Stream"; "floating straight, obedient to the stream, Were carried towards Corinth" (*Err.*, I. i. 86).

60. *rouse*] draught.

67. *span*] Cf. *Ps.* xxxix. 6 (Prayer Book version) "thou hast made my days as it were a span long".

71–2. *England . . . in potting*] Hart

appositely quotes Nashe, *Pierce Penni-lesse* (ed. McKerrow, I. 209), "Superfluity in drink: a sin that ever since we have mixed ourselves with the Low Countries is counted honourable; but before we knew their lingring wars was held in the highest degree of hatred", and Steevens quotes Peacham, *Compleat Gentleman* (1622, p. 193) as saying, in a section called "Drinking the Plague of our English Gentry", that sixty years earlier it had been rare to see a drunken Englishman, "our nation carrying the name of the most sober and temperate of any other in the world", and, like Nashe, attributing the decline to Dutch customs brought back by soldiers returning from the "quarrel of the Netherlands". But Hart also points out that as early as 1530 Rabelais had felt justified in saying "drunk as an Englishman".

      potent in potting: your Dane, your German, and
      your swag-bellied Hollander,—drink, ho!—are
      nothing to your English.

Cas. Is your Englishman so expert in his drinking?   75

Iago. Why, he drinks you with facility your Dane dead
      drunk; he sweats not to overthrow your Almain; he
      gives your Hollander a vomit ere the next pottle can
      be fill'd.

Cas. To the health of our general!   80

Mon. I am for it, lieutenant, and I will do you justice.

Iago. O sweet England!

  [*Sings*]   *King Stephen was a worthy peer,*
            His breeches cost him but a crown;
         He held 'em sixpence all too dear,   85
            With that he call'd the tailor lown,
         He was a wight of high renown,
            And thou art but of low degree,
         'Tis pride that pulls the country down,
            Then take thine owd cloak about thee.   90
      Some wine, ho!

Cas. 'Fore God this is a more exquisite song than the
      other.

Iago. Will you hear't again?

Cas. No, for I hold him unworthy of his place, that does   95
      those things: well, God's above all, and there be
      souls that must be saved, and there be souls must not
      be saved.

---

75. Englishman] *Qq;* Englishmen *F.*   expert] *Q1;* exquisite *F, Q2.*   81. I
will] *Qq;* Ile *F.*   83. a] *Q1;* and-a *F;* and a *Q2.*   85. 'em] *Qq;* them *F.*
90. Then] *Qq;* And *F.*   thine] *Qq;* they *F.*   owd] *Q1;* awl'd *F;* auld *Q2.*
92. 'Fore God] *Q1;* Why *F;* Why, *Q2.*   95. him unworthy] *Qq;* him to be
unworthy *F.*   96. God's] *Q1;* heau'ns *F;* Heauen's *Q2.*   97. that must] *Qq;*
must *F.*   97–8. and . . . not be saved] *F; not in Qq.*

---

    73. *swag-bellied*] pendulous-bellied;
perhaps a reminiscence of Nashe's
description of the Danes as "bursten-
bellied sots" in his excoriation of their
intemperance (loc. cit.).

    77. *Almain*] German.

    81. *do you justice*] drink level with
you; cf. "you have done me right"
(*2 H 4*, v. iii. 74).

    86. *lown*] lout (variant of "loon").

    90. *owd*] F *awl'd*, Q2 *auld*. All three
bear out the statement of Hales and
Furnivall, in their edition of the
Percy MS, about one version of this
song, that the dialect clearly implies a
northern origin (Q1 would make it
northern English, the other two Scot-
tish).

Iago. It is true, good lieutenant.

Cas. For mine own part, no offence to the general, nor any 100
man of quality, I hope to be saved.

Iago. And so do I, lieutenant.

Cas. Ay, but by your leave, not before me; the lieutenant
is to be saved before the ancient. Let's ha' no more of
this, let's to our affairs: God forgive us our sins! 105
Gentlemen, let's look to our business. Do not think
gentlemen I am drunk, this is my ancient, this is my
right hand, and this is my left hand: I am not drunk
now, I can stand well enough, and speak well
enough.   110

All. Excellent well.

Cas. Very well then; you must not think, that I am drunk.

[Exit.

Mon. To the platform, masters. Come, let's set the watch.

Iago. You see this fellow that is gone before,
He is a soldier fit to stand by Cæsar,   115
And give direction: and do but see his vice,
'Tis to his virtue a just equinox,
The one as long as th' other: 'tis pity of him,
I fear the trust Othello put him in,
On some odd time of his infirmity,   120

---

102. I] *Qq;* I too *F.*   105. God forgive] *Q1;* Forgiue *F;* forgiue *Q2.*
108. left hand] *Qq;* left *F.*   109. speak] *Qq;* I speake *F.*   112. Very] *Q1;*
Why very *F, Q2.*   think] *Q1;* thinke then *F, Q2.*   113. the platform,
masters. Come] the plotforme masters. Come *Qq* (maisters *Q1*); th' Platforme
(Masters) come *F.*   119. put] *Qq;* puts *F.*

112.] Furness quotes an interesting
passage from Hawkins's *Life of Kean.*
"He was one night asked by a friend
when he studied? Indicating a man on
the other side of the room who was
very much intoxicated, but who was
labouring to keep up an appearance of
sobriety, he replied, 'I am studying
now. I wish some of my Cassios were
here. They might see that, instead of
rolling about in the ridiculous manner
they do, the great secret of delineating
intoxication is the endeavour to stand
straight when it is impossible to do
so.'"

113. *platform*] gun-platform in a
fort; cf. *Ham.,* I. ii. 251.
set the watch] mount the guard.
115. *stand by Caesar*] act as Caesar's
right-hand man; but a parallel passage at IV. i. 180 suggests that it may
be more hyperbolical and mean "treat
Caesar as his subordinate".
117. *'Tis . . . equinox*] counter-
balances his virtue as exactly as day
and night are equal at the equinox.
120. *odd*] casual, some (time) or
other (just the Scots "orra"); "Some
few odd lads that you remember not"
(*Tp.,* v. i. 255).

Will shake this island.

Mon.   But is he often thus?

Iago. 'Tis evermore the prologue to his sleep:
He'll watch the horologe a double set,
If drink rock not his cradle.

Mon.   'Twere well
The general were put in mind of it;   125
Perhaps he sees it not, or his good nature
Praises the virtues that appear in Cassio,
And looks not on his evils: is not this true?

Enter RODERIGO.

Iago. [*Aside to him*] How now, Roderigo,
I pray you, after the lieutenant, go.   [*Exit Roderigo.* 130

Mon. And 'tis great pity that the noble Moor
Should hazard such a place as his own second
With one of an ingraft infirmity:
It were an honest action to say so
To the Moor.

Iago.   Not I, for this fair island: 135
I do love Cassio well, and would do much
                    [*Cry within:* "Help! help!"]
To cure him of this evil:—but hark, what noise?

Enter CASSIO, *driving in* RODERIGO.

Cas. Zounds, you rogue, you rascal!

Mon. What's the matter, lieutenant?

122. the] *Qq;* his *F.*   124. 'Twere] *Qq;* It were *F.*   127. Praises] *Qq;* Prizes
F.   virtues] *Q1;* vertue *F, Q2.*   128. looks] *F, Q2* (lookes)*;* looke *Q1.*
128. S.D.] *F* (Rodorigo)*; after l. 129 Qq.*   129. *Aside to him] Capell.*   134–5.
It were . . . Moor] *as F; one line Qq.*   135. Not] *F, Q2;* Nor *Q1.*   136. S.D.]
Helpe, helpe, within Qq; not in F.   137. S.D.] *Enter, . . . , driving in Qq;*
Enter . . . pursuing F.   138. Zounds, you] *Q1;* You *F, Q2.*

123. *horologe . . . set*] twice round the
clock.

127. *Praises*] perhaps our sense but
more probably "appraises"; "Were
you sent hither to praise me?" (*Tw.N.,*
I. v. 270), "As you shall prove us,
praise us" (v. i. 66 below, in answer to
"are you of good or evil?").

132. *hazard . . . With*] take a chance
on . . . by giving the appointment to.

133. *ingraft*] ingrained; an incorrect
use, but cf. "the engrafted love he
bears to Caesar" (*Cæs.,* II. i. 184).

134.] When Iago is offered a task
which would be "honest", he declines
it.

Cas. A knave, teach me my duty! But I'll beat the knave 140
    into a wicker bottle.

Rod. Beat me?

Cas. Dost thou prate, rogue?   [*Striking Roderigo.*

Mon. Good lieutenant; pray sir, hold your hand.

Cas. Let me go, sir, or I'll knock you o'er the mazzard. 145

Mon. Come, come, you are drunk.

Cas. Drunk?   [*They fight.*

Iago. [*Aside to Roderigo*] Away I say, go out and cry a mutiny.
        [*Exit Roderigo.*

    Nay, good lieutenant: God's will, gentlemen,
    Help, ho!—Lieutenant:—sir,—Montano,—sir,— 150
    Help, masters, here's a goodly watch indeed,
        [*A bell rings.*

    Who's that that rings the bell?—Diablo . . . ho,
    The town will rise, God's will, lieutenant, hold,
    You will be sham'd for ever.

    Enter OTHELLO, *and Gentlemen with weapons.*

Oth. What is the matter here?

Mon.   Zounds, I bleed still, 155
    I am hurt, to the death.

---

140. But] *Qq; not in F.*   141. wicker bottle] *Qq;* Twiggen-Bottle *F.*   143.
S.D.] *Capell (Beats Rod).*   144. Good lieutenant; pray sir] *Qq;* Nay, good
Lieutenant: I pray you Sir *F.*   147. S.D.] *Qq; not in F.*   148. S.D.] *Aside
Capell; Exit Roderigo Q2; not in Q1, F.*   149. God's will] *Qq* (Godswill *Q1,*
Gods-will *Q2*)*;* Alas *F.*   150. Lieutenant:—sir,—Montano,—sir,— [*Capell and
most later edd.; *Leiutenant: Sir Montano, sir, *Q1;* Lieutenant. Sir Montano: *F;*
Leiutenant: Sir, Montanio, sir, *Q2.*   151. S.D.] *Q2; A bell rung Q1 (after
mutiny, l. 148); not in F.*   152. that that] *Qq;* that which *F.*   153. God's
will] *Q1;* fie, fie *F, Q2.*   hold] *Qq; not in F.*   154. You will be sham'd] *Qq;*
You'le be asham'd *F.*   155. Zounds] *Q1; not in F, Q2.*   156. hurt, to the
death.] *Q1* (death:)*;* hurt to th'death, He dies. *F;* hurt to the death. *he faints. Q2.*

---

141. *wicker*] cased in wicker-work
(like a Chianti flask); "twiggen"
means the same, and here it is F that
has the less usual word.

145. *mazzard*] head; "knocked
about the mazzard with a sexton's
spade" (*Ham.,* v. i. 95).

148. *mutiny*] riot (less specific than
our use); "You'll make a mutiny
among my guests!" (*Rom..* i. v. 84).

155.] F, omitting the initial oath,

completes the line with "He dies", to
which (even if we take it to be a S.D.
that strayed into the text) the objection is that Montano, though gravely
wounded, is far from dead, and thirty
lines later is capable, though with difficulty, of an eight-line speech. Q2,
seeing the difficulty, substituted a
S.D. "He faints", which at least makes
sense. Perhaps "He dies" was an inter-
jected comment from Iago, or some

Oth.   Hold, for your lives!
Iago.   Hold, hold,
    Lieutenant,—sir,—Montano,—gentlemen,—
    Have you forgot all place of sense, and duty?
    Hold, the general speaks to you; hold, hold, for shame!
Oth. Why, how now, ho! from whence arises this?   160
    Are we turn'd Turks, and to ourselves do that
    Which heaven has forbid the Ottomites?
    For Christian shame, put by this barbarous brawl;
    He that stirs next, to carve for his own rage,
    Holds his soul light, he dies upon his motion;   165
    Silence that dreadful bell, it frights the isle
    From her propriety: what's the matter, masters?
    Honest Iago, that looks dead with grieving,
    Speak, who began this? on thy love I charge thee.
Iago. I do not know, friends all but now, even now,   170
    In quarter, and in terms, like bride and groom,

156. Hold, hold] *Qq*; Hold hoa: *F*.   157. sir,—Montano] *most edd.*; sir Montanio *Qq*; Sir Montano *F*.   158. place of sense] *Qq*, *F* (sence *Qq*); sense of place *Hanmer and many edd.*   159. hold, hold] *Qq*; hold *F*.   160. arises] *Qq*; ariseth *F*.   162. has] *Qq*; hath *F*.   164. for] *F*, *Q2*; forth *Q1*.   167. what's] *Qq*; What is *F*.

other bystander(s). But some edd. (e.g. Steevens) take *He dies* to be a threatening ejaculation from Montano, the *He* being Cassio.

158. *place of sense*] Hanmer's emendation is attractive.

161–2. *turn'd Turks . . . Ottomites*] Turn Turk no doubt meant "turn renegade", as in "if you be not turn'd Turk" (*Ado*, III. iv. 56), and "if the rest of my fortunes turn Turk with me" (*Ham.*, III. ii. 292), but in spite of this and a complicated note that "Heaven forbade the Turks to destroy themselves by doing it for them in wrecking them", I think that Othello's meaning is quite straightforward, with "forbid" = "prevent"; "Are we, in destroying ourselves, going to do the Turks' job for them, now that Heaven has prevented them doing it for themselves?"

164. *carve . . . rage*] To carve for oneself had the idiomatic meaning of "choose for oneself", as in "He may

not, as unvalu'd persons do, Carve for himself" (*Ham.*, I. iii. 19, where Onions's gloss of "indulge himself" misses the essential point of the metaphor, which is the *choice* of the best cut), but I doubt whether more is here meant than "cut people up as his anger prompts".

165. *light*] of light weight (and so) of small value.

upon his motion] the instant he moves.

167. *propriety*] natural temper (of quiet decorum); "it is the baseness of thy fear That makes thee strangle thy propriety" (*Tw.N.*, v. i. 150).

171. *In quarter*] Hart explains as "on good terms" and Onions as "on terms" both quoting "So he would keep fair quarter with his bed" (*Err.*, II. i. 108). But I doubt, in view of other passages, whether the interpretation is justified even there. The most significant occurrence of the word seems to me that in *Ant.*, IV. iii. 21, where the soldiers on

Devesting them to bed, and then but now,
As if some planet had unwitted men,
Swords out, and tilting one at other's breast,
In opposition bloody. I cannot speak   175
Any beginning to this peevish odds;
And would in action glorious I had lost
These legs, that brought me to a part of it!
Oth. How came it, Michael, you were thus forgot?
Cas. I pray you pardon me, I cannot speak.   180
Oth. Worthy Montano, you were wont be civil,
The gravity and stillness of your youth
The world hath noted, and your name is great
In mouths of wisest censure: what's the matter,
That you unlace your reputation thus,   185
And spend your rich opinion, for the name
Of a night-brawler? Give me answer to 't.
Mon. Worthy Othello, I am hurt to danger,

172. to] *Qq*; for *F*.   174. breast] *Qq*; breastes *F*.   178. These] *Q1*; Those
F, Q2.   179. came . . . were] *Qq*; comes . . . are *F*.   181. be] *Qq*; to be *F*.
184. mouths] *F, Q2*; men *Q1*.   187. to't] *Qq*; to it *F*.

guard say they will "Follow the noise [the "music of hautboys under the stage"] so far as we have quarter", which clearly means "so far as our assigned limits permit"; in *John*, v. v. 20, we have, from Lewis, giving orders for the night bivouac, "keep good quarter and good care tonight", which can be loosely glossed as "keep good guard" but means, I think, strictly "let each man stick to his assigned position". And in the light of these passages I think that the line from *Err.* means "If only he would regard his (and my) bed as the limits beyond which he ought not to stray". If that is so, Iago here means that they were all quietly on duty.

172. *Devesting*] undressing.

173. *planet*] i.e. the malign influence of some planet, in accordance with astrological belief.

176. *peevish odds*] silly quarrel; often in Shakespeare just "trivial", without our note of childish sulks, as in *1 H 6*,

v. iii. 184, where Margaret, having said that she will send Henry a pure unspotted heart, is invited by Suffolk to send him a kiss, and replies "I will not so presume, To send such peevish tokens to a king".

182. *stillness*] sobriety.

184. *wisest censure*] most acute judgement; "go we to determine Who they shall be that straight shall post to Ludlow. Madam, and you my mother, will you go To give your censures in this business" (*R 3*, II. ii. 141).

185. *unlace*] probably not the simple "undo", i.e. "make slovenly", but the stronger hunting (and carving) term. There was, inherited from earlier days, a pleasant particularity about the operations conducted on a dead beast of chase; one "undid" a deer, but "unlaced" a boar, and also, oddly, a rabbit, for which Hart quotes from *Return from Parnassus*.

186. *your rich opinion*] high opinion people have of you.

Your officer Iago can inform you—
While I spare speech, which something now offends
      me—   190
Of all that I do know; nor know I aught
By me that's said or done amiss this night,
Unless self-charity be sometime a vice,
And to defend ourselves it be a sin
When violence assails us.

Oth.   Now by heaven   195
My blood begins my safer guides to rule,
And passion having my best judgement collied
Assays to lead the way. Zounds, if I stir,
Or do but lift this arm, the best of you
Shall sink in my rebuke: give me to know   200
How this foul rout began, who set it on,
And he that is approv'd in this offence,
Though he had twinn'd with me, both at a birth,
Shall lose me: what, in a town of war,
Yet wild, the people's hearts brim full of fear,   205
To manage private and domestic quarrels,
In night, and on the court and guard of safety?
'Tis monstrous. Iago, who began?

193. sometime] *Qq;* sometimes *F.*   197. collied] *F;* coold *Qq.*   198.
Zounds, if I] *Q1;* If I once *F;* If once I *Q2.*   206. quarrels,] *Qq;* Quarrell? *F.*
207. and guard of] *Qq, F;* of guard, and *Theobald and many edd.*   208. began]
Qq; began't *F.*

196.] The thing most apt to break
Othello's normal control is failure to
get a straight answer to a straight question. Iago knows this and later uses his
knowledge; cf. III. iii. 158 below.

197. *collied*] clouded; "Brief as the
lightning in the collied night" (*MND.*,
I. i. 145).

202. *approv'd*] proved (guilty); "Is
he not approved in the height a villain?" (*Ado*, IV. i. 306), "He be
approv'd in practice culpable" (*2 H 6*,
III. ii. 22).

204. *town of war*] garrison town; "To
line and new repair our towns of war
With men of courage and with means
defendant" (*H 5*, II. iv. 7).

206. *manage*] conduct; "The unlucky

manage of this fatal brawl" (*Rom.*, III.
i. 148). In Shakespeare's use of the
word there is usually implicit a touch of
the sense of manège (explicit in "Wanting the manage of unruly jades" (*R 2*,
III. iii. 179)), e.g., "You must take some
pains to work her to your manage"
(*Per.*, IV. vi. 68) and with one doubtful
exception he never uses the word in
our sense of "contrive", as in "I can
just manage to do it".

207. *court and guard of safety*] Theobald's emendation is very tempting,
like Hanmer's (also a transposition) in
l. 158, the only objection to it being
that *safety* is a rather weak general
word to stand on equal terms with
guard.

Mon. If partially affin'd, or leagu'd in office,
    Thou dost deliver more or less than truth,   210
    Thou art no soldier.

Iago.   Touch me not so near,
    I had rather ha' this tongue cut from my mouth,
    Than it should do offence to Michael Cassio:
    Yet I persuade myself, to speak the truth
    Shall nothing wrong him. Thus it is, general: 215
    Montano and myself being in speech,
    There comes a fellow, crying out for help,
    And Cassio following him with determin'd sword,
    To execute upon him: sir, this gentleman
    Steps in to Cassio, and entreats his pause;   220
    Myself the crying fellow did pursue,
    Lest by his clamour (as it so fell out)
    The town might fall in fright: he, swift of foot,
    Outran my purpose: and I return'd the rather,
    For that I heard the clink and fall of swords;   225
    And Cassio high in oaths, which till to-night
    I ne'er might see before: when I came back
    (For this was brief) I found them close together,

209. partially] *F;* partiality *Qq.*   leagu'd] *Pope, Steevens, etc.;* league *Qq, F.*
212. cut from] *F;* out from *Q1;* out of *Q2.*   215. Thus] *Qq;* This *F.*   222.
his clamour] *Qq;* hisc lamour *F.*   224. the] *Qq;* then *F.*   226. oaths] *Q1;*
oath *F, Q2.*   227. see] *Q1;* say *F, Q2.*

209.] To make a tolerable line from
either text some emendation is needed,
but with F it is no more than the very
common *e : d* change, so that it is
probably best to assume that Q1 blun-
dered over *partially* as well. But I feel
the whole passage a trifle suspect,
from the awkward run of the first line
and the awkward repetition of *Thou
dost—Thou art.* The natural run would
be "If partiality or league in office
Bids thee . . ." But any explanation
leading back to that is too complicated to stand up to examination.

    affin'd] bound by ties, whether of
blood or otherwise—here of partiality;
see I. i. 39 above.

    212. *cut*] Q1's *out* is probably a foul-
case error.

    218. *sword*] If this detail of Iago's

account is true—and in the presence of
other witnesses it is likely to be—it goes
far to settle the "truncheon" problem
above. But one should perhaps notice
that it is not *exactly* true; it presents a
Cassio more blood-thirsty and farther
from his victim than the Cassio we
have seen run across the stage *beating*
Roderigo; Iago's Cassio, if he had been
close enough to do that, would have
run him through, "executed upon
him". Further, Cassio's first reaction
to Montano's interposition had not
been sword-play but a threat to knock
him o'er the mazzard, an operation
more for truncheon than for sword.
So after all *truncheon* may perhaps
stand.

    219. *this gentleman*] Montano (not the
crying fellow).

At blow and thrust, even as again they were,
When you yourself did part them.   230
More of this matter can I not report,
But men are men, the best sometimes forget;
Though Cassio did some little wrong to him,
As men in rage strike those that wish them best,
Yet surely Cassio, I believe, receiv'd,   235
From him that fled, some strange indignity,
Which patience could not pass.
Oth.   I know, Iago,
Thy honesty and love doth mince this matter,
Making it light to Cassio: Cassio, I love thee,
But never more be officer of mine.   240

Enter DESDEMONA, *with others.*

Look if my gentle love be not rais'd up!
I'll make thee an example.
Des. What is the matter?
Oth. All's well now, sweeting; come away to bed:
Sir, for your hurts, myself will be your surgeon;   245
Lead him off.   [*Montano is led off.*
Iago, look with care about the town,
And silence those whom this vile brawl distracted.
Come, Desdemona: 'tis the soldiers' life,
To have their balmy slumbers wak'd with strife.   250
                          [*Exeunt all but Iago and Cassio.*

231. can I not] *Qq;* cannot I *F.*   240. S.D.] *Qq; Enter Desdemona attended. F.*
243. What is the matter?] *Q1;* What is the matter (Deere?) *F;* What's the
matter? *Q2.*   244–6.] *as three lines Qq, F* (sweeting: / hurts, / off: /).   244.
well now] *Qq;* well *F.*   250. S.D.] *Exit* Moore, Desdemona, *and Attendants Qq*
(*after l. 251*); *Exit F.*

237. *pass*] pass over.
238. *mince*] tone down; cf. "Speak to
me home, mince not the general
tongue" (*Ant.*, I. ii. 114).
239. *Cassio*] Hitherto Othello has
addressed Cassio as "Michael" (ll. 1
and 179).
241.] The line, I think, is parenthetic, not giving an additional reason for
the cashiering of Cassio, which is
coolly a matter of discipline.
246. *Lead him off*] Malone thought

these words were a S.D. that crept into
the text, like (possibly) *He dies*, at l.
155. White supported Malone by suggesting that while *off* is natural in
an imperatival S.D., Othello would
more naturally have said "Lead him
away".
249–50. *'tis . . . strife*] not just a
general reflection; he is saying in
effect, "You see, my dear, what you
have let yourself in for by being my
warrior".

Iago. What, are you hurt, lieutenant?

Cas. Ay, past all surgery.

Iago. Marry, God forbid!

Cas. Reputation, reputation, I ha' lost my reputation! I
    ha' lost the immortal part, sir, of myself, and what 255
    remains is bestial; my reputation, Iago, my repu-
    tation!

Iago. As I am an honest man, I thought you had receiv'd
    some bodily wound, there is more offence in that
    than in reputation: reputation is an idle and most 260
    false imposition, oft got without merit, and lost with-
    out deserving. You have lost no reputation at all,
    unless you repute yourself such a loser; what man,
    there are ways to recover the general again: you are
    but now cast in his mood, a punishment more in 265
    policy than in malice, even so, as one would beat his

---

253. God] *Q1*; Heauen *F*, *Q2*.   254. Reputation] *twice Qq; three times F.*
I ha'] *Q1*; oh I ha *Q2*; Oh I haue *F*.   255. part, sir,] *Qq*; part *F*.   258. thought]
Qq; had thought *F*.   259. offence] *Qq*; sence *F*.   264. are] *Qq*; are more *F*.

254-7.] Booth, whose comments,
like Granville Barker's, are always
illuminating because based on practical experience of the stage, says "In
Cassio's speech don't preach; be not
violent, avoid rant; yet be impas-
sioned,—feel thoroughly disgusted
with yourself, and you'll be natural.
Walk about, but don't stamp or 'saw
the air'" (*Prompt-Book of Othello*,
1878).

258-68.] Another good comment
from Booth: "Do not smile, or sneer,
or glower,—try to impress even *the
audience* with your sincerity. 'Tis better,
however, always to ignore the audience; if you can forget that you are a
'shew' you will be natural. The more
sincere your manner, the more devilish
your deceit. I think the 'light come-
dian' should play the villain's part, not
the 'heavy man'; I mean the Shakespearian villains. Iago should appear
to be what all but the audience believe
he is. Even when alone, there is little
need to remove the mask entirely.
Shakespeare spares you that trouble."

259. *offence*] hurt; cf. "which something now offends me" in l. 190
above, and "You have some sick
offence within your mind" (*Cæs.*, II. i.
268). F's "sense" is quite possible, if we
take the word to mean "percepti-
bility" rather than the usual Elizabethan "perception". Or even, as Dr
Brooks suggests, we can keep the usual
meaning, but make *that* refer not to the
wound but to the body which feels it.
But I suspect that *offence* was read as
two words and the *of* dropped.

261. *imposition*] something laid upon
one from without; "But if black
scandal or foul-fac'd reproach Attend
the sequel of your imposition" (*R 3*,
III. vii. 229, where the word means
"the burden of kingship which you are
laying upon me"), and cf. "the imposition clear'd Hereditary ours" (*Wint.*,
I. ii. 74), where it seems to mean "the
evils which high rank [or perhaps
original sin] brought upon us".

264. *recover*] sc. to friendship.

266. *malice*] often in Shakespeare =
simply "enmity", without the under-

offenceless dog, to affright an imperious lion: sue
to him again, and he's yours.

Cas. I will rather sue to be despis'd, than to deceive so
good a commander, with so light, so drunken, and 270
indiscreet an officer. Drunk? and speak parrot? and
squabble? swagger? swear? and discourse fustian
with one's own shadow? O thou invisible spirit of
wine, if thou hast no name to be known by, let us call
thee devil!   275

Iago. What was he, that you followed with your sword?
What had he done to you?

Cas. I know not.

Iago. Is 't possible?

Cas. I remember a mass of things, but nothing distinctly; 280
a quarrel, but nothing wherefore. O God, that men
should put an enemy in their mouths, to steal away
their brains; that we should with joy, revel, pleasure,
and applause, transform ourselves into beasts!

Iago. Why, but you are now well enough: how came you 285
thus recovered?

Cas. It hath pleas'd the devil drunkenness to give place to
the devil wrath; one unperfectness shows me another, to make me frankly despise myself.

---

267. to] *Qq;* ro *F.*   270. light] *Qq;* slight *F.*   and] *Qq;* and so *F.*   271–3.
Drunk? . . . shadow?] *F, Q2; not in Q1.*   281. O God,] *Q1;* Oh, *F;* O *Q2.*
283. revel, pleasure] *Qq;* pleasance, reuell *F.*

tone of spitefulness which it later
acquired; "Be friends awhile and both
conjointly bend Your sharpest deeds of
malice on this town" (*John*, II. i. 379).

266–7. *beat . . . lion*] Hart has the explanation, in Cotgrave, where, under
chien is "*Batre le chien devant le lion.* To
punish a mean man in the presence of,
and for an example to the mighty",
and again under *Batre*, with a varia-
tion "to the terror of a great one".

270. *light*] irresponsible; F's "slight"
means rather "feeble", "valueless";
"this is a slight unmeritable man"
(*Cæs.*, IV. i. 12).

271. *speak parrot*] Parallels are hard
to find, but I think it means "talk
without understanding what one is

saying" rather than "repeat oneself".
And I owe to Dr Brooks an interesting
parallel for this sense in Skelton's
Speke Parrot, ii. 10, "Peace, Parrot, ye
prate as ye were *ebrius*."

272. *fustian*] This word, which started as the generic name for coarse
cotton fabrics of the corduroy type,
came by transition through the meaning of "bombast" (see note on I. i. 13
above) to mean just "nonsense"; see
Cotgrave, defining *Barragouin* as "Ped-
lar's French, fustian language; any
rude gibble-gabble".

276. *sword*] This is explicit, and
Cassio accepts it; so the truncheon
fades again, unless we stress the following *nothing distinctly*.

Iago. Come, you are too severe a moraler; as the time, 290
the place, the condition of this country stands, I
could heartily wish this had not so befallen; but
since it is as it is, mend it, for your own good.

Cas. I will ask him for my place again, he shall tell me I
am a drunkard: had I as many mouths as Hydra, 295
such an answer would stop 'em all: to be now a sensible man, by and by a fool, and presently a beast!
Every unordinate cup is unbless'd, and the ingredience is a devil.

Iago. Come, come, good wine is a good familiar creature, 300
if it be well us'd; exclaim no more against it; and,
good lieutenant, I think you think I love you.

Cas. I have well approv'd it, sir, . . . I drunk!

Iago. You, or any man living, may be drunk at some
time: I'll tell you what you shall do. . . Our general's 305
wife is now the general; I may say so in this respect,
for that he has devoted and given up himself to the
contemplation, mark and denotement of her parts

291. place,] *Qq;* Place, & *F.*   292. not so] *Qq;* not *F.*   297-8. beast! Every]
Qq; Beast. Oh strange! Euery *F.*   298. unordinate] *Q1;* inordinate *F, Q2.*
298-9. ingredience] *Qq;* Ingredient *F.*   304-5. some time] *Q1;* a time man
F; some time man *Q2.*   305. I'll] *Qq;* I *F.*   308. mark and] *Qq;* marke:
and *F.*   denotement] *Q2;* deuotement *Q1, F.*

290. *moraler*] moralizer.

295. *Hydra*] the monstrous many-
headed snake of Greek mythology
which it was one of Heracles' labours
to destroy; as each head was cut off,
two more grew in its place; cf. the
exasperated Douglas's "Another king!
they grow like Hydra's heads" (*1 H 4,*
v. iv. 25).

296-7. *sensible*] usually closely connected with the senses as methods of
perception, meaning either "sensitive", as in "I would your cambric
were sensible as your finger" (*Cor.,* 1.
iii. 95), or "perceivable by the
senses", as in "Art thou not, fatal
vision, sensible To feeling as to
sight?" (*Mac.,* 11. i. 36); but sometimes
it drifts closer to our modern meaning
and = "in full possession of his faculties", as here and (with a pun) in

2 H 4, 1. ii. 222, "he gave it like a rude
prince, and you took it like a sensible
lord", or "The savage bull may; but if
ever the sensible Benedick bear it . . ."
(*Ado,* 1. i. 272).

298-9. *ingredience*] The word occurs
twice in *Macbeth,* "the ingredience of
our poison'd chalice" (1. vii. 11) and
"the ingredience of our cauldron"
(1v. i. 34), though most edd. needlessly
change the F word to "ingredients".

300. *familiar*] on the face of it, simply
"friendly" but Iago is, I think, pun-
ning on the sense of "familiar spirit",
with an emphasis on *good;* he half
admits that wine may be a devil, but
good wine well used is a *good* devil.

306. *in this respect*] if we look at the
fact that.

308. *denotement*] I think Q2 was
right in assuming a turned letter. Q1

and graces. Confess yourself freely to her, importune
her she'll help to put you in your place again: she is   310
so free, so kind, so apt, so blessed a disposition, that
she holds it a vice in her goodness not to do more than
she is requested. This brawl between you and her
husband, entreat her to splinter, and my fortunes

310. her she'll help] *Q1*; her helpe *F*; her, she'll helpe *Q2*.   310–11. is so] *Qq*;
is of so *F*.   311–12. that she] *Qq*; she *F*.   313. brawl] braule *Q1*; broken
ioynt *F*, *Q2*.

and F can be defended, but the repetition is awkward, and "devotement" in
the sense of "adoration of" is out of
tone with *contemplation* and *mark*. F's
punctuation seems impossible.

310.] The omission of "that" between *her* and *she'll* is quite normal,
though the absence of *she'll* in F, and
the presence of *of* no doubt make
things easier; Q2, retaining Q1's
words, made the neat simplification of
a comma after *her*.

312. *vice*] deliberately hyperbolical,
I think, but see note on III. iii. 382
below.

313. *brawl*] It is important, when
considering the readings here, to
recognize that *brawl* (noun) has not
necessarily in Shakespeare the implication of noise and confusion which
we attach to it; "he is a devil in private
brawl" (*Tw.N.*, III. iv. 261, where the
word clearly = quarrel or the resul-
tant duel), "a matter of brawl between
my uncle and one of the emperial's
men" (*Tit.*, IV. iii. 92, where again the
issue is clearly between two people
only). There is no need, therefore, to
abandon *brawl* on the ground that it
does not make sense. Next, it is clear
that the Q1 and F readings cannot
derive through a mere compositor's
error from a common original (unless
indeed we assume a *broken ioynt* so ill-
written that the compositor could read
nothing of it but the first two letters
and invented for the rest), and therefore that someone for some reason
made a deliberate alteration. I think
the alteration from *braule* to *broken
ioynt* is more likely than the reverse, for

the same reason which, I suppose, has
led all edd. to accept F's reading,
namely that it seems to make the passage easier and the picture clearer.
Even that it does only partially, since
a joint is not properly *broken* but dis-
located, and the immediately succeeding *crack* is not appropriate to a joint at
all, but to a limb (unless indeed we are
to desert the bodily metaphor altogether and take the joint to be one in a
piece of woodwork, and *splinter* to
mean "splice", rather than "apply
splints to"). But, even granted that F's
reading makes the passage easier, does
it make it more Shakespearean, or
even leave it equally so? I think not. It
is characteristic of Shakespeare's later
manner to leave his metaphors half
worked out, and invite the co-operation of the reader's or hearer's imagination to complete them. The most
famous example (if we trust F and do
not hurry down the primrose path of
explanatory emendation) is Macbeth's
"my way of life Is fall'n into the sere,
the yellow leaf", where Shakespeare
no doubt *meant* "May" or spring, but
deliberately did not *say* so; any more
than in *Hamlet* he says "to grunt and
sweat under a weary *load*" but "under
a weary *life*". I think that "broken
joint" is a clear example of F's simpli-
ficatory or sophisticating methods,
and to be regarded with the utmost
suspicion.

314. *splinter*] apply splints to; "The
broken rancour of your high-swoln
hearts, But lately splinter'd, knit, and
join'd together" (*R 3*, II. ii. 117) where
the metaphor is fully worked out.

against any lay worth naming, this crack of your love 315
shall grow stronger than 'twas before.

Cas. You advise me well.

Iago. I protest, in the sincerity of love and honest kindness.

Cas. I think it freely, and betimes in the morning will I 320
beseech the virtuous Desdemona, to undertake for
me; I am desperate of my fortunes, if they check me
here.

Iago. You are in the right. Good night, lieutenant, I must
to the watch.   325

Cas. Good night, honest Iago.   [*Exit.*

Iago. And what's he then, that says I play the villain,
When this advice is free I give, and honest,
Probal to thinking, and indeed the course
To win the Moor again? For 'tis most easy   330
The inclining Desdemona to subdue,
In any honest suit; she's fram'd as fruitful
As the free elements: and then for her

316. 'twas] *Qq*; it was *F.*   320. will I] *Qq*; I will *F.*   323. here] *Qq*; *not in F.*
326. S.D.] *Qq*; *Exit Cassio F.*

315. *lay*] wager; "*Clif.* My soul and
body on the action both! *York.* A
dreadful lay!" (*2 H 6*, v. ii. 26), "I will
have it no lay" (*Cym.*, I. iv. 164).

321. *undertake*] sc. my business; not
elsewhere in Shakespeare without an
object except in *Lr.*, IV. ii. 13, "that
dares not undertake".

327–53, 372–8.] The plot at last
takes specific shape, as Iago brilliantly
improvises. The drinking episode was
devised to put Cassio in some action
that might offend the isle—i.e. it was
aimed at discrediting Cassio *as a
soldier*, and was part therefore of the
'ousting-Cassio' part of Iago's design.
But Cassio's mood, refusing to appeal
to Othello direct (294–6), plays
straight into Iago's hands, and he
seizes his chance in a flash, advising an
appeal to Desdemona (305–16). In
this soliloquy for the first time he sees
his design no longer "confused" but a
complete linked chain, and we sense

not only his delight at the prospect of
revenge, but his sheer intellectual
pleasure in a subtle and finished piece
of black artistry.

328. *free*] either "generous", as in
"your free and noble nature" (III. iii.
203 below), or "innocent", as in
"Make mad the guilty and appal the
free" (*Ham.*, II. ii. 598) and "hold her
free" (III. iii. 259 below); or perhaps
both.

329. *Probal to*] sure to be approved
by.

332. *fruitful*] generous; "That
churchman bears a bounteous mind
indeed, A hand as fruitful as the land
that feeds us" (*H 8*, I. iii. 55).

333. *elements*] a word as hard to pin
down as Proteus; sometimes all four
(earth, air, fire, water) are alluded to,
"Does not our life consist of the four
elements?" (*Tw.N.*, II. iii. 10), sometimes particular ones are specified,
"the dull elements of earth and water"

To win the Moor, were 't to renounce his baptism,
All seals and symbols of redeemed sin,   335
His soul is so infetter'd to her love,
That she may make, unmake, do what she list,
Even as her appetite shall play the god
With his weak function. How am I then a villain,
To counsel Cassio to this parallel course,   340
Directly to his good? Divinity of hell!
When devils will their blackest sins put on,
They do suggest at first with heavenly shows,
As I do now: for while this honest fool
Plies Desdemona to repair his fortunes,   345
And she for him pleads strongly to the Moor,

334. were't] *Qq* (wer't); were *F*.   342. their] *Qq*; the *F*.   344. while] *Q1*; whiles *F*; whilst *Q2*.   345. fortunes] *Qq*; Fortune *F*.

(*H 5*, III. vii. 23), "I am fire and air; my other elements I give to baser life" (*Ant.*, v. ii. 291); *element*, in the singular, seems to mean the sky (or the sun), "The element itself, till seven years' heat, Shall not behold her face" (*Tw.N.*, I. i. 26), "the element shows to him as it doth to me" (*H 5*, IV. i. 108), and sometimes almost "the weather", "the complexion of the element In favour's like the work we have in hand" (*Cæs.*, I. iii. 128), "Contending with the fretful element" (*Lr.*, III. i. 4, where texts vary between singular and plural); then it comes to mean "temper", or "sphere of action", "you are idle shallow things: I am not of your element" (*Tw.N.*, III. iv. 138), "Down, thou climbing sorrow! Thy element's below" (*Lr.*, II. iv. 57), and the meanings of "sky" and sphere are interestingly combined, with a comment, by Feste "who you are and what you would are out of my welkin; I might say 'element', but the word is overworn" (*Tw.N.*, III. i. 65); and in II. iii. 53 above it means something near to "types" ("the very elements of this warlike isle"). In the present passage what is being stressed is the spontaneity, and effectiveness, in action of the elements, and the nearest parallel

in Shakespeare is perhaps Prospero's farewell to Ariel, when the spirit of the air is restored to his native freedom, "then to the elements Be free, and fare thou well!" (*Tp.*, v. i. 317).

338. *her appetite*] *her* is objective, not possessive—his desire for her.

339. *function*] Onions glosses as "activity or operation of intellectual or moral powers", but I think it means here "natural instincts"; and does it perhaps throw a glint of light on the vexed "defunct" in I. iii. 264 above?

340. *parallel*] perhaps no more than "in accord with his purpose", but I think there is a hint of the military technicality of "driving a parallel" in siege operations.

341. *Divinity of hell!*] "Evil, be thou my good".

342–3. *When devils . . . shows*] Cf. "Devils soonest tempt, resembling spirits of light" (*LLL.*, IV. iii. 257). (Hart.)

343. *suggest*] Besides its modern meaning (which will serve here) the word can in Shakespeare mean "seduce" or "tempt", "I give thee not this to suggest thee from thy master" (*All's W.*, IV. v. 47), "What Eve, what serpent, hath suggested thee To make . . . ?" (*R 2*, III. iv. 75).

I'll pour this pestilence into his ear,
That she repeals him for her body's lust;
And by how much she strives to do him good,
She shall undo her credit with the Moor;   350
So will I turn her virtue into pitch,
And out of her own goodness make the net
That shall enmesh 'em all.

Enter RODERIGO.

How now, Roderigo?
Rod. I do follow here in the chase, not like a hound that
hunts, but one that fills up the cry: my money is   355
almost spent, I ha' been to-night exceedingly well
cudgel'd: I think the issue will be, I shall have so
much experience for my pains, as that comes to, and
no money at all, and with that wit return to Venice.
Iago. How poor are they that ha' not patience!   360
What wound did ever heal, but by degrees?
Thou knowest we work by wit, and not by witch-
craft,
And wit depends on dilatory time.
Does't not go well? Cassio has beaten thee,
And thou, by that small hurt, hast cashier'd Cassio; 365
Though other things grow fair against the sun,

348. lust;] *Qq;* Lust' *F.*   349. him] *Qq;* hⁱm *F.*   353. enmesh] *Qq;* en-mash *F.*
'em] *Q1;* them *F, Q2.*   358-9. pains . . . Venice] *Q1;* paines; And so, with no
money at all, and a little more Wit, returne againe to Venice *F;* paines, and so
no mony at all, and with a little more wit returne to Venice *Q2.*   360. ha']
Q1; haue *F, Q2.*   364. has] *Qq;* hath *F.*

348. *repeals*] recalls, as in "repeal
thee home again" (*Gent.*, v. iv. 143).

351. *pitch*] perhaps only for the suggestion of blackness and foulness, but
I think also of a snaring substance,
like birdlime, and leading on to the
net.

355. *cry*] pack, as in "You common
cry of curs" and "You have made
Good work, you and your cry" (*Cor.*,
III. iii. 118 and IV. vi. 148); but here in
a more literal and limited sense, of the
hounds who merely give tongue as
they follow those who are really running the scent.

358-9.] F's version is no doubt the
neater and more finished, though one
is sorry to lose the petulant *as that comes
to.* Q2 (probably because the compositor misunderstood the place for the
insertion of *with*) produces an awkward conflation.

362. *wit*] See note on II. i. 129 above.

366-7. *Though other things . . . ripe*]
not very lucid, and none of the explanations that I have seen are, I think,
satisfactory, since they mostly neglect
or slur the antithesis which is clearly
marked by the *though.* The first problem is the meaning of *against*, and the

But fruits that blossom first, will first be ripe;
Content thyself awhile; by the mass 'tis morning;
Pleasure, and action, make the hours seem short:
Retire thee, go where thou art billeted,   370
Away I say, thou shalt know more hereafter:
Nay, get thee gone. [*Exit Rod.*] Some things are to
    be done,
My wife must move for Cassio to her mistress,
I'll set her on.
Myself awhile to draw the Moor apart,   375
And bring him jump when he may Cassio find,
Soliciting his wife: ay, that's the way,
Dull not device by coldness and delay.   [*Exit.*

367. But] *Q1;* Yet *F, Q2.*   368. by the mass] *Qq* (bi' the *Q1,* by 'th *Q2*);
Introth *F.*   372. S.D.] *F* (*Rodorigo*)*; not in Qq.*   Some] *Qq;* Two *F.*
374–5. I'll ... apart] *Qq; one line F.*   on. Myself a while] *Qq* (while,)*; on my
selfe, a while, F.*   378. S.D.] *F; Exeunt Qq.*

second that of the variant readings *but*
and *yet*; as to the second, if *but* is
adversative there is, as regards sense,
no superiority of one over the other,
and either could very naturally have
been substituted for the other.
against is usually taken as meaning
simply "in" or "facing". If *but* is
adversative it makes the *though* awkward (the natural lead-up would be
something like "Other things indeed
... sun, *But*") whereas Though ... *yet*
is normal. But this meaning of *against*
surely leaves a very feeble antithesis, if
an antithesis at all, since the sentence
is saying in effect, "Other things grow
fair in the sun, *and so do* fruits". I suggest that if we take *against* = "contrary to" and retain Q1's *but*, in the
sense of "only", we extract some sort
of antithetical sense. "Though other
things (than fruits) may prosper in
spite of the weather, it's only the first-
blossoming fruits that ripen first." I do
not pretend that this is satisfactory,
but even a forced point is perhaps
better than no point at all.
    368. *'tis morning*] a good example of
the Elizabethan courage in grasping
the nettle of discrepancy between

stage time and represented time. The
most famous example is the last
speech of Faustus in Marlowe's *Dr
Faustus*. The speech takes perhaps ten
minutes to deliver, and Marlowe goes
out of his way to stress the full hour
which it is supposed to occupy, not
only by marking its opening at 11
o'clock, but by having an actual bell
strike at the half hour. Here it is
stressed that the scene opens at 10 in
the evening, it lasts perhaps twenty
minutes, and in this line Shakespeare
deliberately stretches its duration till
dawn.
    376. *jump*] exactly on time; "jump
at this dead hour" (*Ham.,* I. i. 65),
"jump upon this bloody question"
(*Ham.,* v. ii. 389); the verb in Shakespeare has either a similar sense, "to
coincide", as in "till each circumstance Of place, time, fortune, do
cohere and jump" (*Tw.N.,* v. i. 261),
"it jumps with my humour" (*1 H 4,*
I. ii. 77), or else the quite different
sense of "to risk", "to take a chance
on", as in "We'd jump the life to
come" (*Mac.,* I. vii. 7), "jump the
after enquiry on your own peril"
(*Cym.,* v. iv. 187).

ACT III

SCENE I.—[*Before the Castle.*]

Enter CASSIO, *with Musicians and the Clown.*

Cas. Masters, play here, I will content your pains,
    Something that's brief, and bid "Good morrow,
      general."   [*They play.*
Clo. Why, masters, ha' your instruments been at Naples,
    that they speak i' the nose thus?
First Mus. How, sir, how?   5
Clo. Are these, I pray, call'd wind-instruments?
First Mus. Ay marry are they, sir.
Clo. O, thereby hangs a tail.
First Mus. Whereby hangs a tale, sir?

ACT III
Scene 1

S.D.] *Q1* (*Musitians*); *Enter Cassio, Musitians, and Clowne F; Enter* Cassio, *with Musitians Q2.*   2. S.D.] *They play, and enter the Clowne Q2; no* S.D. *Q1, F.* 3. ha'] *Qq;* haue *F.*   at] *Qq;* in *F.*   5. *Mus.*] *F; Boy Qq.*   6 pray, call'd] *Qq;* pray you *F.*   8–9. tail . . . tale] tayle . . . tayle *Qq;* tale . . . tale *F.*

3–4. *Naples . . . speak i' the nose*] "A reference, undoubtedly," says Hart, "to the venereal disease," but makes no attempt to explain the point, which is far from obvious. It is true that venereal disease was known as "the Neapolitan disease" and that jokes about it are in Elizabethan writers almost as tediously iterative as those about the cuckold's horns. But Shakespeare only once elsewhere connects Naples with it (in *Troil.*, II. iii. 20, "the Neapolitan bone-ache")—his use of Naples or Neapolitan is otherwise as a term of purely geographical or historical reference—and only once connects noses with it, in *Tim.*, IV. iii. 158, in the address to the whores, "down with the nose, Down with it flat; take the bridge quite away". But there is no obvious reason why "*speaking* in the nose" should be a symptom, even for purposes of a clown's joke. Shakespeare uses this phrase once elsewhere, but apparently as a quite straightforward description of the music of bagpipes, and with no double entendre, though a specifically diuretic effect is ascribed to it, "when the bagpipe sings i'the nose" (*Mer.V.*, IV. i. 49). However, there must be some point to the clown's remark, and it is pretty certainly a bawdy one, even if we have lost it.

8–10.] Shakespeare's bawdry is not always worth exposition, but the

Clo. Marry, sir, by many a wind-instrument that I know.   10
       But, masters, here's money for you, and the general
       so likes your music, that he desires you, of all loves, to
       make no more noise with it.

First Mus. Well sir, we will not.

Clo. If you have any music that may not be heard, to 't   15
       again, but, as they say, to hear music, the general
       does not greatly care.

First Mus. We ha' none such, sir.

Clo. Then put your pipes in your bag, for I'll away; go,
       vanish away!   [*Exeunt Musicians.*   20

Cas. Dost thou hear my honest friend?

Clo. No, I hear not your honest friend, I hear you.

Cas. Prithee keep up thy quillets, there's a poor piece of
       gold for thee: if the gentlewoman that attends the
       general's wife be stirring, tell her there's one Cassio   25
       entreats her a little favour of speech . . . wilt thou do
       this?

Clo. She is stirring, sir, if she will stir hither, I shall seem
       to notify unto her.

                          Enter IAGO.

Cas. Do, good my friend.   [*Exit Clown.*
                    In happy time, Iago.   30

12. of all loves] *Q1;* for loues sake *F, Q2.*   18. ha'] *Qq;* haue *F.*   19. put]
Qq; put up *F.*   for I'll away] *Qq, F* (Ile)*;* fore all, away *Anon. conj.* (*in
Jennens*)*;* and hye away *Hanmer.*   20. vanish away] *Q1;* vanish into ayre,
away *F, Q2* (aire *Q2*).   S.D.] *Exit Mu. F; not in Qq.*   21. hear my] *Qq;*
heare me, mine *F.*   25. general's wife] *Qq* (Cenerals *Q1*)*;* Generall *F.*
30. *Cas.* Do . . . friend.] *Qq; not in F.*   S.D.] *Q2; after l.* 29 *F; not in Q1.*

clown's remarks are otherwise so flat
that it is perhaps worth remarking that
tail is common Elizabethan (and later)
colloquial for "penis" (cf. Donne
" 'Tis but applying wormseed to the
tail") and that the wind-instrument is
the adjacent "wind-breaker".

   12. *of all loves*] "for any sake", a
common colloquial phrase. An illuminating example of the selective
method—-Hart adopts the Q1 reading
simply because he thinks it "more
expressive".

23. *quillets*] probably a corruption
of "quidlibet" and so a (lawyer's) verbal trick; ". . . the skull of a lawyer?
Where be his quiddities now, his
quillets . . . ?" (*Ham.*, v. i. 105).

   28-9. *seem to*] arrange to, be by way
of . . . ; "let the prologue seem to say"
(*MND.*, III. i. 18).

   30. *In happy time*] well met—of an
opportune meeting; "you are come to
me in happy time" (*Shr.*, Ind. i. 90),
"In happy time; *Enter a gentle Astringer.*
This man may help me . . ." (*All's W.*,

Iago. You ha' not been a-bed, then?

Cas. Why no, the day had broke before we parted:
     I ha' made bold, Iago,
     To send in to your wife, . . . my suit to her
     Is, that she will to virtuous Desdemona   35
     Procure me some access.

Iago.   I'll send her to you presently,
     And I'll devise a mean to draw the Moor
     Out of the way, that your converse and business
     May be more free.

Cas. I humbly thank you for it. [*Exit Iago.*] I never knew   40
     A Florentine more kind and honest.

                    Enter EMILIA.

Emil. Good morrow, good lieutenant; I am sorry
     For your displeasure, but all will soon be well,
     The general and his wife are talking of it,
     And she speaks for you stoutly: the Moor replies,   45
     That he you hurt is of great fame in Cyprus,
     And great affinity, and that in wholesome wisdom
     He might not but refuse you; but he protests he loves
          you,
     And needs no other suitor but his likings
     To take the safest occasion by the front,   50
     To bring you in again.

Cas.   Yet I beseech you,

31, 33. ha'] *Qq;* haue *F.*   33-5. Iago, / . . . wife, . . . her / . . . Desdemona /]
Iago, . . . her. / . . . Desdemona / *Qq;* Iago . . . wife: / My suit . . . Desdemona /
F.   40. for it] *Q1;* for't *F, Q2.*   43. soon] *Qq;* sure *F.*   48. refuse you] *Q1,*
F; refuse *Q2.*   50. To . . . front] *Qq; not in F.*

v. i. 6); *happy* in Elizabethan retained
more than it does with us of the sense
of "hap" = luck, cf. "by the happy
hollow of a tree Escap'd the hunt"
(*Lr.,* ii. iii. 2), and see note on iii. 242
below.

32.] This line puts beyond doubt the
continuity of action.

41. *Florentine*] i.e. *even* a Florentine
(Cassio being from Florence).

43. *your displeasure*] your being out of
favour; "your displeasure with the
king" (*H 8,* iii. ii. 393, where the king

is displeased with Wolsey, not Wolsey
with the king).

47. *great affinity*] kinsmen of high
rank.

50. *front*] forelock; from a classical
proverb, not used elsewhere by
Shakespeare though common in contemporaries. *Occasio* (opportunity)
was full-haired in front, bald behind;
cf. Peele, *Battle of Alcazar,* ii. iii. 54, "I
doubt not but will watch occasion,
And take her foretop by the slenderest
hair." (Hart.)

If you think fit, or that it may be done,
Give me advantage of some brief discourse
With Desdemona alone.
Emil.   Pray you, come in,
I will bestow you where you shall have time   55
To speak your bosom freely.
Cas.   I am much bound to you.
                                        [*Exeunt.*

SCENE II.—[*The same.*]

Enter OTHELLO, IAGO, *and other Gentlemen.*

Oth. These letters give, Iago, to the pilot,
And by him do my duties to the State:
That done, I will be walking on the works,
Repair there to me.
Iago.   Well, my good lord, I'll do 't.
Oth. This fortification, gentlemen, shall we see 't?   5
Gent. We wait upon your lordship.   [*Exeunt.*

SCENE III.—[*The same.*]

Enter DESDEMONA, CASSIO, *and* EMILIA.

Des. Be thou assur'd, good Cassio, I will do
All my abilities in thy behalf.
Emil. Good madam, do, I know it grieves my husband,
As if the case were his.

54. Desdemona] *Qq;* Desdemon *F.*   56. *Cas.* I . . . you.] *F, Q2; not in Q1*
S.D.] *Qq; not in F.*

Scene II

S.D.] *Qq; Enter Othello, Iago, and Gentlemen F.*   1. pilot] Pilate *Qq;* Pylot *F.*
2. State] *Qq;* Senate *F.*   6. We] *Qq;* Well *F.*

Scene III

3. know] *Qq;* warrant *F.*   4. case] *Qq;* cause *F.*

Scene II
This short scene serves the same purpose as II. ii. above (on which see note). But it also suggests that Iago's method of "drawing the Moor apart" has been to prompt the inspection of the "works". And see Introduction, p. lviii.

Des. O, that's an honest fellow: ... do not doubt, Cassio,   5
        But I will have my lord and you again
        As friendly as you were.
Cas.   Bounteous madame,
        Whatever shall become of Michael Cassio,
        He's never anything but your true servant.
Des. O sir, I thank you; you do love my lord,   10
        You have known him long, and be you well assur'd,
        He shall in strangest stand no farther off
        Than in a politic distance.
Cas.   Ay, but, lady,
        The policy may either last so long,
        Or feed upon such nice and wat'rish diet,   15
        Or breed itself so out of circumstance,
        That I being absent, and my place supplied,
        My general will forget my love and service.
Des. Do not doubt that: before Emilia here
        I give thee warrant of thy place; assure thee   20
        If I do vow a friendship, I'll perform it
        To the last article; my lord shall never rest,
        I'll watch him tame, and talk him out of patience;

---

10. O sir,] *Qq;* I know't: *F.*   12. strangest] *Qq;* strangenesse *F.*   14. The]
Q1; That *F, Q2.*   16. circumstance] *Qq;* Circumstances *F.*

---

11. *known him long*] Othello has
grounds for trusting Cassio.
13. *politic*] dictated by policy.
14–16.] "He may either of himself
think it politic to keep me out of office
so long, or he may be satisfied with
such slight reasons, or so many accidents may make him think my re-
admission at that time improper,
that ..." So Johnson, and though I do
not think it is wholly satisfactory, I
cannot do any better. The trouble is
that *feed upon such nice and waterish diet*
means on the face of it "take such inadequate nourishment", and so fade
away, and we have to force "feed
upon" to mean "be *well* fed" (in spite
of the inadequacy of the food).
15. *nice*] trivial; "The letter was not
nice, but full of charge" (*Rom.*, v. ii. 18).

17. *supplied*] filled up (the original
meaning); "I fill up a place, which
may be better supplied when I have
made it empty" (*AYL.*, 1. ii. 206),
"Thy place in council thou hast rudely
lost, Which by thy younger brother is
supplied" (*1 H 4*, III. ii. 32).
19. *doubt*] expect, fear (as in Scots);
"I doubt he be not well, that he
comes not home" (*Wiv.*, 1. iv. 42), "I
doubt some foul play" (*Ham.*, 1. ii.
255).
22. *article*] clause in a contract.
23. *watch him tame*] a metaphor from
the training of hawks; "you must be
watch'd ere you be made tame, must
you?" (*Troil.*, III. ii. 43). Hart well
adduces, to show the applicability of
the treatment to other animals,
Middleton, *Anything for a Quiet Life*,
I. i. 161, "she railed upon me when I

His bed shall seem a school, his board a shrift,
I'll intermingle every thing he does   25
With Cassio's suit; therefore be merry, Cassio,
For thy solicitor shall rather die
Than give thy cause away.

Enter OTHELLO *and* IAGO.

Emil. Madam, here comes my lord.
Cas. Madam, I'll take my leave.   30
Des. Why, stay and hear me speak.
Cas. Madam, not now, I am very ill at ease,
        Unfit for mine own purpose.
Des. Well, do your discretion.   [*Exit Cassio.*
Iago. Ha, I like not that.   35
Oth. What dost thou say?
Iago. Nothing, my lord, or if—I know not what.
Oth. Was not that Cassio parted from my wife?
Iago. Cassio, my lord? . . . no, sure, I cannot think it,
        That he would sneak away so guilty-like,   40
        Seeing you coming.
Oth.   I do believe 'twas he.
Des. How now, my lord?
        I have been talking with a suitor here,
        A man that languishes in your displeasure.
Oth. Who is't you mean?   45
Des. Why, your lieutenant, Cassio, good my lord,
        If I have any grace or power to move you,

27. solicitor] Solicitor *F;* soiliciter *Q1;* soliciter *Q2.*   28. thy cause away] *F,*
Q2; thee cause: away *Q1.*   S.D. Iago] *F;* Iago, *and Gentlemen Qq.*   31. Why]
Q1, F; Nay *Q2.*   33. purpose] *Qq;* purposes *F.*   40. sneak] *Q1;* steale *F,*
Q2.   41. you] *Qq;* your *F.*

should sleep, And that's you know,
intolerable, for indeed 'Twill tame an
elephant". And see the brilliant
account of the training of a hawk by
T. H. White in *The Goshawk.*
    24. *shrift*] confessional (properly
with penance and absolution added);
"Riddling confession finds but riddling shrift" (*Rom.,* II. iii. 56). If we
are to press the metaphor, Desdemona implies that Othello's penance

will be his reinstatement of Cassio.
    27. *thy solicitor*] the one who solicits
for you; "we single you As our
best-moving fair solicitor" (*LLL.,*
II. i. 28).
    28. *give . . . away*] abandon.
    34. *your discretion*] and his "discre-
tion" is the first disastrous move.
    43.] Iago's first ranging shot mis-
fires altogether because of Desdemona's directness.

His present reconciliation take:
For if he be not one that truly loves you,
That errs in ignorance, and not in cunning,   50
I have no judgement in an honest face,
I prithee call him back.

Oth.   Went he hence now?

Des. Yes, faith, so humbled,
That he has left part of his griefs with me,
I suffer with him; good love, call him back.   55

Oth. Not now, sweet Desdemona, some other time.

Des. But shall 't be shortly?

Oth.   The sooner, sweet, for you.

Des. Shall 't be to-night at supper?

Oth.   No, not to-night.

Des. To-morrow dinner then?

Oth.   I shall not dine at home,
I meet the captains, at the citadel.   60

Des. Why then to-morrow night, or Tuesday morn,
On Tuesday noon, or night, or Wednesday morn:
I prithee name the time, but let it not
Exceed three days: i' faith, he's penitent,
And yet his trespass, in our common reason,   65
(Save that, they say, the wars must make examples
Out of their best) is not almost a fault
To incur a private check: when shall he come?

---

53. Yes, faith] *Qq;* I sooth *F.*   54. has] *Qq;* hath *F.*   griefs] *Qq;* greefe *F.*
55. I suffer] *Q1;* To suffer *F, Q2.*   56. Desdemona] *Q1;* Desdemon *F, Q2.*
61. or] *Qq;* on *F.*   62. noon] *F* (noone); morne *Qq.*   night, or] *Qq;* night;
on *F.*   64. i'faith] *Qq* (Ifaith); Infaith *F.*   66. examples] *Qq;* example *F.*
67. their] *Rowe;* her *Qq, F.*   68. To incur] *Qq;* T'encurre *F.*

48. *reconciliation*] repentance with a
view to reconcilement; cf. "that penitent, as thou callest him, and reconciled king, my brother" (*Wint.*, IV. i.
24).

50. *in cunning*] wittingly, with knowledge—the old sense of *cunning*;
"cunning schoolmasters" (*Shr.*, I. i.
191), "this young scholar, that has
been long studying at Rheims; as cunning in Greek, Latin, and other lan-
guages, as the other in music and
mathematics" (ib. II. i. 56, 79).

59. *dinner*] the mid-day meal, not
evening.

61–2.] This childlike iteration
would try a patience considerably
more placid than Othello's. See Introduction, p. lxv.

67. *not almost*] hardly; "I have not
breath'd almost, since I did see it"
(*Err.*, v. i. 181), "You cannot reason
almost with a man That looks not
heavily" (*R 3*, II. iii. 39).

68. *check*] rebuke; see note on IV.
iii. 20 below.

Tell me, Othello: I wonder in my soul,
What you could ask me, that I should deny?   70
Or stand so mammering on? What? Michael
    Cassio,
That came a-wooing with you, and so many a time
When I have spoke of you dispraisingly,
Hath ta'en your part, to have so much to do
To bring him in? Byrlady, I could do much—   75
Oth. Prithee no more, let him come when he will,
I will deny thee nothing.
Des.   Why, this is not a boon,
'Tis as I should entreat you wear your gloves;
Or feed on nourishing dishes, or keep you warm,
Or sue to you, to do a peculiar profit   80
To your own person: nay, when I have a suit
Wherein I mean to touch your love indeed,
It shall be full of poise and difficulty,
And fearful to be granted.
Oth.   I will deny thee nothing,
Whereon I do beseech thee grant me this,   85
To leave me but a little to myself.
Des. Shall I deny you? no, farewell, my lord.
Oth. Farewell, my Desdemona, I'll come to thee straight.
Des. Emilia, come; be it as your fancies teach you,
Whate'er you be, I am obedient.   90
               [*Exeunt Desdemona and Emilia.*

---

70. could] *Qq;* would *F.*   71. mammering] mam'ring *F*, *Q2;* muttering *Q1.*
72. with] *Qq;* wirh *F.*   75. Byrlady] *Q1;* Trust me *F*, *Q2.*   79. dishes] *Qq.*
F; meats *Pope.*   83. difficulty] *Q1;* difficult weight *F*, *Q2* (waight *F*).   89,
be it] *Qq;* be *F.*   90. S.D.] *Exit* Desd. *and* Em. *Q1; Exit F; Exeunt* Des. *and*
Em. *Q2.*

71. *mammering*] Here it undoubtedly looks as though it had been Q1 which substituted the familiar for the unusual word—and it is an unhappy substitution, since Othello is not muttering, though he is *mammering* in the sense of "hesitating", "shilly-shallying" (see *O.E.D. s.v.*).

80. *peculiar*] special to the individual—sometimes almost "preserved"; "Groping for trouts in a peculiar

river" (*Meas.*, I. ii. 96), "my peculiar end" (I. i. 60 above), and cf. IV. i. 69 below.

83. *poise*] weight, with a suggestion of the judgement needed for right estimation which is implied in the second half of the line; "Occasions, noble Gloucester, of some poise" (*Lr.*, II. i. 122 (Q1 reading)).

89. *as your fancies teach you*] and they lead to his jealousy and her death.

Oth. Excellent wretch, perdition catch my soul,
     But I do love thee, and when I love thee not,
     Chaos is come again.
Iago. My noble lord,—
Oth.   What dost thou say, Iago?
Iago. Did Michael Cassio, when you woo'd my lady,   95
     Know of your love?
Oth. He did, from first to last: ... why dost thou ask?
Iago. But for a satisfaction of my thought.
     No further harm.
Oth.   Why of thy thought, Iago?
Iago. I did not think he had been acquainted with her.   100
Oth. O yes, and went between us very often.
Iago. Indeed?
Oth. Indeed? Indeed: discern'st thou aught in that?
     Is he not honest?
Iago. Honest, my lord?   105
Oth. Honest? ay, honest.
Iago. My lord, for aught I know.
Oth. What dost thou think?
Iago. Think, my lord?
Oth. Think, my lord? By heaven, he echoes me,   110
     As if there were some monster in his thought,
     Too hideous to be shown: thou didst mean something;
     I heard thee say but now, thou lik'st not that,
     When Cassio left my wife: what didst not like?
     And when I told thee he was of my counsel,   115

91. wretch] *Qq, F;* wench *Theobald.*   95. you] *Qq;* he *F.*   98. thought] *F,*
Q2; thoughts *Q1.*   101. often *Q1;* oft *F, Q2.*   103. Indeed? Indeed] *Q1;*
Indeed? I indeed *F, Q2.*   105–6. *Iago . . . honest] as F; one line Qq.*   110.
By . . . echoes] *Q1;* Alas, thou ecchos't *F;* why dost thou ecchoe *Q2.*   111. his]
Q1; thy *F, Q2.*   112. didst] *Q1;* dost *F, Q2.*   113. but] *Qq;* euen *F.*

91. *wretch*] often affectionate, as
here; "The pretty wretch left crying"
(*Rom.*, I. iii. 44).

92–3. *when . . . again*] This would not
seem worth comment but that I have
seen it misunderstood, as though Othello was making a statement of present
fact. The verb in both clauses is, in
effect, future, like '*Tis* at I. i. 63 above.

93.] Here begins the great tempta-

tion scene. Iago's skill is obvious, but
I am not sure that the *variety* of his tactics is always sufficiently observed, and
I hope an occasional pointer will not
seem impertinent. He begins by a few
questions and an apparent reluctance
to make explicit the implications of
them.

99. *No further harm*] with the implication that there is *some* harm.

In my whole course of wooing, thou criedst "Indeed?"
And didst contract and purse thy brow together,
As if thou then hadst shut up in thy brain
Some horrible conceit: if thou dost love me,
Show me thy thought.   120
Iago. My lord, you know I love you.
Oth.   I think thou dost,
And for I know thou art full of love and honesty
And weighest thy words, before thou give 'em breath,
Therefore these stops of thine fright me the more:
For such things in a false disloyal knave   125
Are tricks of custom; but in a man that's just,
They are close denotements, working from the heart,

116. In] *Qq;* Of *F.*   119. conceit] *F, Q2;* counsell *Q1.*   122. thou art] *Qq;*
thou'rt *F.*   123. weighest] *Qq;* weigh'st *F.*   123. give 'em] *Q1;* giu'st them
F; giu'st 'em *Q2.*   124. fright] *F, Q2;* affright *Q1.*   127. They are] *Qq;*
They're *F.*   denotements] *Q1, Capell;* dilations *F, Q2, Rowe, Theobald;* dela-
tions *Steevens 1773.*

117. *purse*] close up, and so
"knit".

119. *conceit*] idea, conception; "You
have a noble and a true conceit Of
god-like amity" (*Mer.V.*, III. iv. 2),
"There's some conceit or other likes
him well, When that he bids good
morrow with such spirit" (*R 3*, III. iv.
49).

121. *you know I love you*] a horrible
reminiscence of Peter's "thou knowest
that I love thee" (St John, xxi. 15–17).

124. *stops*] breakings off; "*York.*
Where did I leave? [i.e. break off my
tale]. *Duch.* At that sad stop, my lord,
Where rude misgovern'd hands . . ."
(*R 2*, v. ii. 4).

127. *close denotements*] I think that
this means "indications of something
shut up and secret"; for this use of
close cf. "secret close intent" (*R 3*, I. i.
157), "and for secrecy, No lady
closer" (*1 H 4*, II. iii. 114); and they
are the outcome of (*working from*) a
heart not governed by passion, which
therefore *weighs its words before it gives
them breath*, whereas the passion-ruled
heart would blurt things out before
giving them due consideration. War-

burton gives roughly this explanation,
though he oddly applies it to F's reading, "dilations". Nobody has made
anything satisfactory of "dilations".
Shakespeare does not elsewhere use
the noun; where he uses the verb it is
in the sense of "extend" or "expand";
"dilate at full What hath befall'n'"
(*Err.*, I. i. 122), "a more dilated farewell" (*All's W.*, II. i. 59), "all my pilgrimage dilate" (I. iii. 153 above),
which is not helpful, and even if he
were using the noun in the Latin sense
of "postponement" or "delay" he becomes intelligible at the cost of being
redundant, since Othello then says no
more than that Iago's *stops* are "close
stops". Many editors are content to
accept Johnson's emendation, "dela-
tions", meaning "occult and secret
accusations"; the objection to this
(apart from Steevens' point that there
is no evidence of the use of the word in
this, its Latin, sense) is that a *stop* can
only very forcedly be described as an
"accusation", however secret. A *dela-
tio*, after all, was the laying of an information, not the making of an insinu-
ation by silence. However, there

That passion cannot rule.

Iago.   For Michael Cassio,
I dare presume, I think that he is honest.

Oth. I think so too.

Iago.   Men should be that they seem,   130
Or those that be not, would they might seem none!

Oth. Certain, men should be what they seem.

Iago. Why then I think Cassio's an honest man.

Oth. Nay, yet there's more in this:
I prithee, speak to me as to thy thinkings,   135
As thou dost ruminate, and give the worst of thought
The worst of word.

Iago.   Good my lord, pardon me;
Though I am bound to every act of duty,
I am not bound to that all slaves are free to;
Utter my thoughts? Why, say they are vile and
   false: 140
As where's that palace, whereinto foul things

129. presume] *Q1;* be sworne *F, Q2.*   130. that] *Q1;* what *F, Q2.*   135. as
to] *F, Q2;* to *Q1.*   136-7. the ... thought ... word] *Q1;* thy ... thoughts ...
words *F, Q2.*   139. that all ... to;] *Qq;* that: All ... free: *F.*   140. vile]
Qq; vild *F.*

'dilations" is, in F; it can hardly have been due to a mere blunder, and the man who put it there, whether Shakespeare or someone else, meant something by it. I have to confess that I have very little idea what that was. But there is, I think, a possible interpretation, though it does not seem to have commended itself to commentators. If we suppose that Shakespeare was using the noun in a sense near to that in which he uses the verb, and exactly our modern sense, we get a picture of a heart "dilating", swelling, with some thought the expression of which is forbidden by self-control (i.e. with what Othello has just described as some horrible conceit shut up in the brain). It is to be noticed that several commentators, including, surprisingly, Johnson and Malone, though not Warburton, take *passion* as object, not subject, of *rule.* The inversion is awkward, and the sense produced

surely untenable, in view of Othello's *weighest thy words before thou give 'em breath,* and of Hamlet's exactly parallel, "the man that is not passion's slave".

129. *presume*] assume (with a suggestion of "as a preliminary hypothesis"); "O! that I thought it could be in a woman—As if it can I will presume in you" (*Troil.,* III. ii. 165), "Presume not that I am the thing I was" (*2 H 4,* v. v. 61).

130-1.] One of Iago's cryptic remarks (see note on I. i. 57 above) which is not, I think, after the first six words, meant to mean much.

139. *free to*] free with regard to (and so, effectively, "free from"): "to" was often used as a loose "preposition of reference". F's punctuation is an oddity, caused probably by the omission of *to.*

140. *say they are*] a new approach, by hypothesis.

Sometimes intrude not? who has a breast so pure,
But some uncleanly apprehensions
Keep leets and law-days, and in session sit
With meditations lawful?   145
Oth. Thou dost conspire against thy friend, Iago,
If thou but thinkest him wrong'd, and makest his ear
A stranger to thy thoughts.
Iago.   I do beseech you,
Though I perchance am vicious in my guess,

142. a breast] *Qq;* that breast *F.*   143. But some] *Qq;* Wherein *F.*   144.
session] *Qq;* Sessions *F.*   sit] *F;* fit *Qq.*   147. thinkest . . . makest] *Qq;*
think'st . . . mak'st *F.*

143. *apprehensions*] conceptions, ways
of taking (L. *apprehendere*) a thing;
"That's a lascivious apprehension—
So thou apprehendest it" (*Tim.*, I. i.
212); sometimes almost "mis-concep-
tion", as in "in his brainish apprehension" (*Ham.*, IV. i. 11).

To "apprehend" is, in Shakespeare,
"to grasp", whether (*a*) physically or
(*b*) by mental faculties, and particularly by something beyond reason;
(*a*) "apprehend thee for a felon here"
(*Rom.*, v. iii. 69), "Whom we have
apprehended in the fact" (*2 H 6*, II. i.
171); (*b*) "you apprehend passing
shrewdly" (*Ado.*, II. i. 85, to Beatrice,
after her analysis of "wooing, wedding,
and repenting"), "a stubborn soul,
That apprehends no further than this
world" (*Meas.*, v. i. 481). The relation
between apprehending and compre-
hending (the latter a business of the
reason only) is worked out in *MND.*,
v. i. 4–20, "Lovers and madmen have
such seething brains, Such shaping
fantasies, that apprehend More than
cool reason ever comprehends", followed by an exposition of this text.
The meanings of the noun precisely
follow those of the verb; (*a*) "go we,
brothers, to the man that took him, To
question of his apprehension (*3 H 6*,
III. ii. 121); (*b*) "The apprehension of
his present portance" (*Cor.*, II. iii. 232),
"a foolish extravagant spirit, full of
forms, figures, shapes, objects, ideas,

apprehensions" (*LLL.*, IV. ii. 68). In
Shakespeare, with one possible exception (*Meas.*, III. i. 76), neither verb nor
noun has any implication of fear; in
"apprehends death no more dread-
fully but as a drunken sleep" (*Meas.*,
IV. ii. 148) the meaning is not that
Barnardine's *fear* of death is no more
frightening than . . . , but that his *idea* of
death is no more frightening, and in
"If the English had any apprehension
they would run away" (*H 5*, III. vii.
150) the Constable does not mean "if
the English were scared", but "if they
had any grasp of realities".

144. *leets*] local courts of justice;
"And rail upon the hostess of the
house, And say you would present her
at the leet" (*Shr.*, Ind. ii. 88).

in session] "on the bench".

146. *conspire*] practise; several times
in Shakespeare with no suggestion of a
joint plot; "but to be Menelaus! I
would conspire against destiny"
(*Troil.*, v. i. 69, where it means little
more than "rebel"), "That 'gainst
thyself thou stick'st not to conspire"
(*Sonn.*, x. 6).

149. *Though*] Though "as" can
sometimes, via the meaning "while",
come very near in sense to "though"
(as I think certainly in *Ant.*, II. ii. 57,
where the reading is disputed), the
evidence seems very flimsy that
"though" could ever mean "as". The
trouble arises from accepting F's

(As I confess it is my nature's plague   150
To spy into abuses, and oft my jealousy
Shapes faults that are not) I entreat you then,
From one that so imperfectly conjects,
You'ld take no notice, nor build yourself a trouble
Out of my scattering and unsure observance;   155
It were not for your quiet, nor your good,
Nor for my manhood, honesty, or wisdom,
To let you know my thoughts.

Oth.   Zounds!

Iago. Good name in man and woman 's dear, my lord;
Is the immediate jewel of our souls: 160
Who steals my purse, steals trash, 'tis something, nothing,

---

151. oft] *Qq;* of *F.*   152. I entreat you then] *Q1;* that your wisedome *F;* that your wisedome yet *Q2.*   153. conjects] *Q1* (coniects); conceits *F, Q2.*
154. You'ld] *Q1;* Would *F, Q2.*   155. my] *Qq;* his *F.*   157. or] *Qq;* and *F.*
158. Zounds] *Q1;* What dost thou meane? *F, Q2.*   159–60. woman's dear, my lord; / Is . . . our souls:] woman's deere my Lord; / Is . . . our soules: *Q1;* woman (deere my Lord) / Is . . . their Soules; *F;* woman (deere my Lord) / Is . . . our soules: *Q2.*

---

reading lower, and assuming that Iago, who is pretending to think aloud, is likely to do so with exact regard to syntax and logic. *Though . . . guess* is simply, I think, a false start, which has the advantage of planting the word *vicious,* and the *then* of l. 152 picks up not from it but from *as . . . are not.*

151. *jealousy*] here, as not infrequently, "an aptitude for critical scrutiny" with no implication of a sense of personal injury; "jealousy what might befall your travel, Being skilless in these parts" (*Tw.N.,* III. iii. 8), "Let not my jealousies be your dishonours, But mine own safeties" (*Mac.,* IV. iii. 29, where Malcolm means "do not regard my careful tests as imputations against your honour"). But Iago, having quietly introduced the *word,* unmasks his full battery twenty lines later.

153. *conjects*] The word occurs elsewhere (see *O.E.D.*) though not in Shakespeare, and it fits better than "conceits" with *imperfectly.* But *coniects* and *conceits* are readily confusable,

though the change from the ordinary to the less common word is more unlikely than vice versa.

155. *scattering*] haphazard, fluttering here and there; "bees That want their leader, scatter up and down, And care not who they sting" (*2 H 6,* III. ii. 125).

156–8. *It were not . . . thoughts*] exasperating Othello by the refusal to disclose the thoughts (cf. note on II. iii. 196 above), with the added implication that if disclosed they would be disquieting.

158. *Zounds!*] In Q1 the control characteristically breaks; F, avoiding oaths, falls flat. *Zounds,* according to A. Walker, "vulgarizes" Othello. See note on III. iv. 95 below.

159–65. *Good name . . . indeed*] Hunter appositely quotes from Wilson's *Rhetorique*: "a slanderer is worse than any thief, because a good name is better than all the goods in the world . . . and a thief may restore that again which he hath taken away, but a slanderer cannot give a man his good name which he hath taken from him."

'Twas mine, 'tis his, and has been slave to thousands:
But he that filches from me my good name
Robs me of that which not enriches him,
And makes me poor indeed.   165
Oth. By heaven I'll know thy thought.
Iago. You cannot, if my heart were in your hand,
   Nor shall not, whilst 'tis in my custody:
   O, beware jealousy;
   It is the green-ey'd monster, which doth mock   170
   That meat it feeds on. That cuckold lives in bliss,
   Who, certain of his fate, loves not his wronger:
   But O, what damned minutes tells he o'er
   Who dotes, yet doubts, suspects, yet strongly loves!
Oth. O misery!   175
Iago. Poor and content is rich, and rich enough,
   But riches, fineless, is as poor as winter
   To him that ever fears he shall be poor:
   Good God, the souls of all my tribe defend
   From jealousy!

166. By heaven I'll . . . thought] *Q1;* Ile . . . thoughts *F, Q2* (Thoughts *F*).
169.] *Q1; Oth.* Ha? / *Iago.* Oh, beware my Lord, of iealousie, *F; Oth.* Ha? *Iag.*
O beware (my Lord) of iealousie; *Q2.*   170. the] *Q1, F;* a *Q2.*   171. That
meat] *Q1;* The meat *F, Q2.*   173. he] *F, Q2;* be *Q1.*   174. strongly] *Qq;*
soundly *F.*   177. fineless] *Qq, F;* endless *Pope.*   179. God] *Q1;* heauen *F,*
Q2 (Heauen *F*).

167. *if*] i.e. "*even* if". Iago here ventures further, from uneasy avoidance to direct refusal.
168.] F's "*Oth.* Ha?", though it may be the interpolation of an actor who felt that some verbal reaction from Othello was needed, is undeniably effective. Without it Iago anticipates any reaction by going straight into further generalities, but generalities which are getting very near to the bone.
170-1. *green-ey'd . . . feeds on*] The wilderness of comment (there are five pages of it in the Furness Variorum alone) seems to be almost wholly beside the point and caused by a failure to understand the picture. We more naturally think of jealousy as something residing in the jealous

man's heart, and issuing from its lair to spread havoc without. Here it is conceived of as a malignant monster, advancing from without to ravage the victim's heart (like Prometheus' eagle) and mocking its victim as it feeds.
177. *fineless*] boundless; not elsewhere in Shakespeare, nor does he use the noun in the general sense of "limit", though he uses it not infrequently in the sense of the specific limit, the end; "All's well that end's well: still the fine's the crown" (*All's W.*, IV. iv. 35—"finis coronat opus"), "is this the fine of his fines?" (*Ham.*, v. i. 113).
179. *tribe*] usually (as several times in *Mer.V.*, and in v. ii. 349 below) more specific than here, but cf. "a whole tribe of fops" (*Lr.*, I. ii. 14).

Oth.   Why, why is this?   180
Think'st thou I'ld make a life of jealousy?
To follow still the changes of the moon
With fresh suspicions? No, to be once in doubt,
Is once to be resolv'd: exchange me for a goat,
When I shall turn the business of my soul   185
To such exsufflicate and blown surmises,
Matching thy inference: 'tis not to make me jealous,
To say my wife is fair, feeds well, loves company,
Is free of speech, sings, plays, and dances well;
Where virtue is, these are more virtuous: 190
Nor from mine own weak merits will I draw
The smallest fear, or doubt of her revolt,
For she had eyes, and chose me. No, Iago,
I'll see before I doubt, when I doubt, prove,
And on the proof, there is no more but this: 195
Away at once with love or jealousy!

184. Is once] *Qq;* Is *F.*   186. exsufflicate] *Capell, and most edd.;* exufflicate *Qq,*
F.   blown] *Qq;* blow'd *F.*   189. well] *Qq; not in F.*   193. chose] *Q1, F;*
chosen *Q2.*

182–3. *follow . . . suspicions*] wax and
wane (in suspicion) like the moon.

186. *exsufflicate] O.E.D.* records no
other example; it is clearly a term of
contempt, and if "blown" means, as
it probably does, "fly-blown", then
exsufflicate presumably means something the same. But see next note on
"blown".

blown] (*a*) "the sun looking with a
southward eye upon him, where he is
to behold him with flies blown to
death" (*Wint.*, IV. iii. 823), "as summer flies, are in the shambles, That
quicken even with blowing" (IV. ii. 67
below); (*b*) possibly "blown up", like a
bubble, but it is hard to adduce a
parallel from Shakespeare, though
"look how imagination blows him"
(*Tw.N.*, II. v. 48) perhaps comes near
it, if it does not mean "carries him
this way and that".

187. *inference*] It looks as though the
unhappy confusion of "infer" and
"imply" was as old as the Elizabethans; "That need must needs infer

this principle" (*John*, III. i. 213, where
it seems to mean "lead to the inference
that . . ."), "this doth infer the zeal I
had to see him" (*2 H 4*, v. v. 15, rather
more than "imply"—"from this can
be inferred . . ."), "Withal I did infer
your lineaments" (*R 3*, III. vii. 12—
"bring in as proof"), "'tis inferr'd to us
His days are foul and his drink dangerous" (*Tim.*, III. v. 74)—where it is
little more than "reported"), "Infer
the bastardy of Edward's children"
(*R 3*, III. v. 74, stronger than "imply"
—"deliberately suggest"). The noun
occurs nowhere else in Shakespeare.

191. *weak merits*] assumption that my
merits are slight.

192. *revolt*] often in Shakespeare in a
more general sense than ours, namely
any "falling off" from allegiance or
obedience; and once in a sense which
may be relevant here, almost =
"revulsion", "Alas! their love may be
called appetite . . . That suffer surfeit,
cloyment, and revolt" (*Tw.N.*, II. iv.
99).

Iago. I am glad of it, for now I shall have reason
To show the love and duty that I bear you
With franker spirit: therefore as I am bound
Receive it from me: I speak not yet of proof;   200
Look to your wife, observe her well with Cassio;
Wear your eye thus, not jealous, nor secure.
I would not have your free and noble nature
Out of self-bounty be abused, look to 't:
I know our country disposition well;   205
In Venice they do let God see the pranks
They dare not show their husbands: their best
      conscience
Is not to leave undone, but keep unknown.
Oth. Dost thou say so?
Iago. She did deceive her father, marrying you;   210
And when she seem'd to shake and fear your looks,
She lov'd them most.
Oth.   And so she did.
Iago.   Why, go to then,

197. it] *Qq;* this *F.*   202. eye] *Qq;* eyes *F.*   206. God] *Q1;* Heauen *F, Q2.*
207. not] *F, Q2; not in Q1.*   208. leave . . . keep] *Q1;* leaue't . . . kept *F;*
leaue't . . . keepe't *Q2.*

197.] Iago is encouraged to a more open advance, and after the outspoken coupling of Cassio with Desdemona, which is the end of generalizations, he plays, in l. 205, what I think is his most devilishly effective card, using Othello's sense of social inexperience. This not only increases Othello's doubts, but also—and this from Iago's point of view is of vital importance—makes it much less likely that he will challenge Desdemona direct, since he will now be afraid of an answer, the possibility of which he cannot face, on the lines of "It is not so, but what an if it were?" or, in other words, "My dear innocent, why are you so upset about what would be only a matter of common form?"

202. *secure*] free from care, and, specifically, "unsuspicious", as in "Though Page be a secure fool" (*Wiv.,* II. i. 240).

204. *self-bounty*] innate generosity; "bounty" and "bounteous" are several times in Shakespeare coupled with "free"—"you yourself Have of your audience been most free and bounteous" (*Ham.,* I. iii. 92), "free and bounteous to her mind" (I. iii. 265 above), and—close in thought to this passage—"that thought is bounty's foe; Being free itself, it thinks all others so" (*Tim.,* II. ii. 242).

206. *pranks*] See note on II. i. 142 above.

207–8. *best conscience . . . unknown*] "the cardinal sin is being found out", or "the eleventh commandment is much more important than the sixth".

212. *go to*] a very common colloquialism, in a variety of senses, sometimes equivalent to our "come off it!", sometimes to "come, come!" and here to "what more do you want?".

She that so young could give out such a seeming,
To seal her father's eyes up, close as oak,
He thought 'twas witchcraft: but I am much to
    blame,   215
I humbly do beseech you of your pardon,
For too much loving you.

Oth.   I am bound to thee for ever.

Iago. I see this hath a little dash'd your spirits.

Oth. Not a jot, not a jot.

Iago.   I' faith I fear it has.
I hope you will consider what is spoke   220
Comes from my love: but I do see you are mov'd,
I am to pray you, not to strain my speech
To grosser issues, nor to larger reach,
Than to suspicion.

Oth. I will not.

Iago.   Should you do so, my lord,   225
My speech should fall into such vile success
As my thoughts aim not at: Cassio's my trusty friend:
My lord, I see you are mov'd.

Oth.   No, not much mov'd,

---

214. seal] *Qq* (seale); seele *F.*   219. I' faith] Ifaith *Q1;* Trust me *F, Q2.*
221. my] *Qq;* your *F.*   you are] *Qq;* y'are *F.*   226. vile] *Qq;* vilde *F.*
227. As] *Qq;* Which *F.*   aim not at] *Qq;* aym'd not *F.*   trusty] *Q1;* worthy
F, Q2.

214. *seal . . . oak*] The difference between Q1 and F is a real difference in sense, and not a mere matter of different spellings, since (see note to Arden *Ant.*, v. ii. 145) in the nearly 100 instances in which Shakespeare uses *seal* in the sense of sealing a letter or in a metaphorical sense derived from it the spelling is invariably *seale* and never *seele.* Here "seel" (the falconry metaphor from sewing up a hawk's eyes) suits well with *eyes*, rather less well with *oak*, though the shift of figure is thoroughly Shakespearean; *oak* is usually explained by reference to the close grain of oak, but one wonders how far back one can trace "oak"= "close fitting door" (as in "sporting one's oak").

223. *grosser . . . reach*] *grosser* can mean "obvious" (as in I. ii. 72 above), and *larger* can mean simply "wider"; but there is a suggestive undertone of our sense of "gross" and of the Elizabethan sense of "large"="licentious", as in "some large jests he will make" (*Ado*, II. iii. 217), "I never tempted her with word too large" (*Ado*, IV. i. 52). And cf. the modern "broad joke".

226. *vile success*] I think that Iago is so elated that he almost gives himself away; but would be saved, even if Othello were in any condition to notice the slip, by the ambiguity of *success*; for external consumption Iago means by the phrase "lamentable result"; "fear of bad success in a bad cause" (*Troil.*, II. ii. 117).

I do not think but Desdemona's honest.

Iago. Long live she so, and long live you to think so!   230

Oth. And yet how nature erring from itself—

Iago. Ay, there's the point: as, to be bold with you,
Not to affect many proposed matches,
Of her own clime, complexion, and degree,
Whereto we see in all things nature tends;   235
Fie, we may smell in such a will most rank,
Foul disproportion; thoughts unnatural.
But pardon me: I do not in position
Distinctly speak of her, though I may fear
Her will, recoiling to her better judgement,   240
May fall to match you with her country forms,
And happily repent.

Oth.   Farewell, if more

236. Fie, we] Fie we *Q1;* Foh, one *F;* Pie we *Q2.*   236–7. such a will most rank, Foul] *Q2;* such a will, most rank Foul *Q1;* such, a will most ranke, Foul *F.* 237. disproportion] *Qq;* disproportions *F.*   242. happily] *Qq, F;* haply so *Pope.*   242–4.] Farewell, if more / . . . set on / . . . Iago.] *Qq;* Farewell, farewell: / If more . . . more: / . . . obserue. / . . . *Iago. F.*

231.] Just when Iago seems to have come to the end of his first phase of operations, Othello himself offers him a new point of departure.

233. *affect*] look with favour on; "Maria once told me she did affect me" (*Tw.N.,* II. v. 27), "I thought the king had more affected the Duke of Albany than Cornwall" (*Lr.,* I. i. 1).

234. *clime . . . degree*] country, colour, and rank.

236.] It is possible to retain Q1's punctuation, *we may smell in such a will, most rank Foul disproportion,* perhaps making the sense plainer by inserting a comma after *smell,* so taking *rank* with *disproportion,* but F's punctuation, as in the present text, is supported not only by better balance but by the common meaning of *will* as something near to "lust", so that *rank* well suits it. For *rank* see note on II. i. 301 above, and for *will,* "he fleshes his will in the spoil of her honour" (*All's W.,* IV. iii. 19), "When the compulsive ardour gives the charge, And reason panders will"

(*Ham.,* III. iv. 86), "the cloy'd will,— That satiate yet unsatisfied desire" (*Cym.,* I. vi. 47).

238. *position*] deliberate thesis or exposition; "I do not strain at the position, It is familiar, but at the author's drift; Who in his circumstance expressly proves That . . ." (*Troil.,* III. iii. 112, Ulysses commenting on "Achilles on beauty"), and (slightly less formal, "hypothesis") "a most pregnant and unforc'd position" (II. i. 235 above).

240. *recoiling . . . judgement*] going back on itself so as to coincide with her no longer disproportioned judgement.

242. *happily*] haply, perhaps; "old Gremio is hearkening still, And happily we might be interrupted" (*Shr.,* IV. iv. 53), "Thy fortune, York, hadst thou been regent there, Might happily have prov'd far worse than his" (*2 H 6,* III. i. 305), "Happily you may find her in the sea" (*Tit.,* IV. iii. 8); in all three instances the "hap" is far from "happy".

Thou dost perceive, let me know more, set on
Thy wife to observe; leave me, Iago.
Iago. [*Going*] My lord, I take my leave.   245
Oth. Why did I marry? This honest creature doubtless
Sees and knows more, much more, than he unfolds.
Iago. [*Returning*] My lord, I would I might entreat your
      honour
To scan this thing no further, leave it to time:
Though it be fit that Cassio have his place,   250
For sure he fills it up with great ability,
Yet if you please to hold him off awhile,
You shall by that perceive him and his means;
Note if your lady strain her entertainment
With any strong or vehement importunity,   255
Much will be seen in that; in the mean time,
Let me be thought too busy in my fears
(As worthy cause I have to fear I am);
And hold her free, I do beseech your honour.
Oth. Fear not my government.   260

---

245. *Going*] *Rowe.*   247–9. unfolds. / *Iago.* (*Returning*) My lord ... / To scan]
Capell (*Returns*); vnfolds. / *Iago.* My Lord ... / To scan *F*, *Q 2*; vnfolds. / My Lord
... / *Iag.* To scan *Q 1*.   250. Though it be fit] *Q 1*; Although 'tis fit *F*; And
though tis fit *Q 2*.   252. please ... awhile,] *Qq* (a while, *Q 2*); please, to him
off a-while: *F*; please, to put him off a-while: *F 2*.   254. her] *Qq*; his *F*.

243–4. *set on ... observe*] almost
Othello's nadir.
  249. *leave it to time*] the one thing that
Othello, as Iago knows, is least likely
to do, and the last thing that Iago in
fact wants him to do.
  253. *means*] methods; "they have
devis'd a mean How he her chamber
window will ascend" (*Gent.*, III. i. 38),
"I'll devise a mean to draw the Moor
Out of the way" (III. i. 37 above); or,
just possibly, "meanings", "intentions", though I cannot find a parallel
to this use in Shakespeare.
  254. *entertainment*] welcome; "with
entertainment Of each new-hatch'd,
unfledg'd comrade" (*Ham.*, I. iii. 64),
"use some gentle entertainment to
Laertes" (ib. v. ii. 215). Hart, reading
F's *his*, interprets as "urge his appointment", but the passages he adduces

from *All's W.* are not cogent, and one
from *Ant.* tells rather the other way—
Enobarbus, commenting on the welcome that those who have deserted
have received from Caesar, says
"Canidius and the rest That fell away
have entertainment, but No honourable trust" (IV. vi. 16).
  257. *busy*] busybody-ing; "Thou
wretched, rash, intruding fool. . .
Thou find'st to be too busy is some
danger" (*Ham.*, III. iv. 31), and cf.
IV. ii. 133 below.
  259. *free*] innocent; see note on II.
iii. 328 above.
  260. *government*] discreet conduct, as
in "Thy meekness saint-like, wife-like
government" (*H 8*, II. iv. 136), or possibly "self-control", but for this, as for
Hart's "conduct of the scheme" it is
not easy to find parallels.

Iago. I once more take my leave.   [*Exit.*
Oth. This fellow's of exceeding honesty,
        And knows all qualities, with a learned spirit,
        Of human dealing: if I do prove her haggard,
        Though that her jesses were my dear heart-strings,   265
        I 'ld whistle her off, and let her down the wind,
        To prey at fortune. Haply, for I am black,
        And have not those soft parts of conversation
        That chamberers have, or for I am declin'd
        Into the vale of years,—yet that's not much—   270
        She's gone, I am abus'd, and my relief
        Must be to loathe her: O curse of marriage,
        That we can call these delicate creatures ours,
        And not their appetites! I had rather be a toad,
        And live upon the vapour in a dungeon,   275
        Than keep a corner in a thing I love,
        For others' uses: yet 'tis the plague of great ones,
        Prerogativ'd are they less than the base,

263. qualities] *Q1;* quantities *F, Q2* (Quantities *F*).   learned] *Qq;* learn'd *F*.
264. dealing] *Q1;* dealings *F, Q2*.   267. Haply] *F;* Happily *Qq*.   270. vale]
F, Q2; valt *Q1*.   275. in] *Qq;* of *F*.   276. a thing] *Qq;* the thing *F*.
277. of] *Qq;* to *F*.

264. *haggard*] wild, not properly
trained, hawk; "like the haggard,
check at every feather That comes
before his eye" (*Tw.N.*, III. i. 72).
    265. *jesses*] short straps on the hawk's
legs, by which it was fastened to the
leash. Only here in Shakespeare.
    267. *at fortune*] at random, "at
every feather", as above.
    268. *soft parts of conversation*] facile
graces of social intercourse. As late as
at least Johnson's time *conversation*
covered much more than speech.
    269. *chamberers*] drawing-room gal-
lants, carpet-knights; but "chamber"
can mean specifically "bedroom";
"I hope the days are near at hand
That chambers will be safe" (*Mac.*, v.
iv. 1).
    271. *abus'd*] deceived; "dear son
Edgar, The food of thy abused
father's wrath" (*Lr.*, IV. i. 21).
    273. *delicate*] dainty, exquisite; sel-
dom with any implication of weak-

ness, but sometimes, as I think here,
with one of "choosiness"; cf. "When
the mind's free The body's delicate"
(*Lr.*, III. iv. 11).
    274. *toad*] a recognized symbol for
anything despicable and detested;
"That bottled spider, that foul bunch-
back'd toad" (*R 3*, IV. iv. 81), "Here is
the babe, as loathsome as a toad"
(*Tit.*, IV. ii. 68).
    278. *Prerogativ'd . . . base*] Hart says
"The great are less free from this
curse than those of low degree"; *pre-
rogativ'd* can no doubt mean "with
prior claim to exemption", but neither
the text nor the gloss seems to me to
make, in this context, any sense.
There is no question of the great being
either less or more liable to be cuckolded than the base; every one is equal,
according to Othello, because "It is
destiny", as inevitable as conception,
birth, and death for every man. The
sentiments are Touchstone's, though

'Tis destiny, unshunnable, like death:
Even then this forked plague is fated to us,   280
When we do quicken: Desdemona comes,
If she be false, O, then heaven mocks itself,
I'll not believe it.

Enter DESDEMONA *and* EMILIA.

Des.   How now, my dear Othello?
Your dinner, and the generous islanders
By you invited, do attend your presence.   285
Oth. I am to blame.
Des. Why is your speech so faint? are you not well?
Oth. I have a pain upon my forehead, here.
Des. Faith, that's with watching, 'twill away again;
Let me but bind your head, within this hour   290
It will be well again.

---

281. Desdemona] *Qq;* Look where she *F.*   282. O, then heaven mocks] *Qq;*
Heauen mock'd *F.*   283. believe it] *Qq* (ir *Q2*); beleeue't *F.*   S.D.] *Qq;*
after comes, *l. 281, F.*   284. islanders] Islanders *F;* Ilander *Qq.*   287.
Why . . . well?] *Qq;* Why do you speake so faintly? / Are you not well? *F.*
289. Faith] *Q1;* Why *F, Q2.*   290. your head] *Q1;* it hard *F, Q2.*   291. well
again] *Q1;* well *F, Q2.*

---

he starts from the lower end of the scale: "Poor men alone? No, no; the noblest deer hath them [the horns] as huge as the rascal" (*AYL.*, III. iii. 59). One feels therefore that Othello ought to be saying that great ones are *no more* exempt from this plague than the base; but I cannot see how to arrive at that meaning without emendation.

280. *forked*] i.e. of the cuckold's horns.

281. *quicken*] sc. in the womb; or perhaps just "are born".

282. *If she . . . itself*] one of those Shakespearean phrases the meaning of which too close a grammatical analysis, like Antony's "rack", "dislimns and makes indistinct". Othello "means" "If she is false, Heaven's own truth is a lie". Malone has two interpretations: "That is, renders its own labours fruitless, by forming so beautiful a creature as Desdemona, and suffering the ele-

gance of her person to be disgraced and sullied by the impurity of her mind—such, I think, is the meaning—the construction, however, may be different. If she be false, Oh, then, even *Heaven itself* cheats us with 'unreal mockery', with false and specious appearances, intended only to deceive". F's "mock'd" makes things a trifle plainer: "The Creator, when he made Desdemona, was laughing at himself, creating a thing so fair without and so false within".

284. *generous*] noble; "The generous and gravest citizens" (*Meas.*, IV. vi. 13).

285. *attend*] await; "The dinner attends you, sir" (*Wiv.*, I. i. 281).

288. *forehead*] thinking of the *fork'd plague*; cf. Leontes' "that is entertainment My bosom likes not, nor my brows, Mamillius" (*Wint.*, I. ii. 119). Desdemona's innocence is unaware of the implication.

Oth.   Your napkin is too little:
                          [*She drops her handkerchief.*
     Let it alone, come, I'll go in with you.
Des. I am very sorry that you are not well.
                          [*Exeunt Othello and Desdemona.*
Emil. I am glad I have found this napkin;
     This was her first remembrance from the Moor,   295
     My wayward husband hath a hundred times
     Woo'd me to steal it, but she so loves the token,
     For he conjur'd her she should ever keep it,
     That she reserves it evermore about her,
     To kiss, and talk to; I'll ha' the work ta'en out,   300
     And give't Iago: what he'll do with it
     Heaven knows, not I,
     I nothing know, but for his fantasy.

                          Enter IAGO.

Iago. How now, what do you here alone?
Emil. Do not you chide, I have a thing for you.   305
Iago. A thing for me? it is a common thing—
Emil. Ha?

291. S.D.] *Rowe.*   293. S.D.] *Qq (after l. 294); Exit F (after l. 292).*   300. ha']
Qq; haue *F.*   301. he'll] *Qq;* he will *F.*   303. nothing know, but for] *Q1;*
nothing, but to please *F, Q2.*   S.D.] *F; after* not I, *l. 302, Qq.*   306. A thing]
Qq; You have a thing *F.*

291. *napkin*] in general, any piece of
"napery", but in Shakespeare always
specifically a handkerchief; even when
in *Hamlet* the Queen offers Hamlet
her "napkin" to rub his brows, she
is not carrying a towel about with
her.

296. *wayward*] unaccountable;
Shakespeare normally uses the word
in our sense of "capricious", "not con-
tinuing in one stay", but that will not
serve here, since Iago has been un-
accountably persistent.

a hundred times] "long time".

300. *ta'en out*] evidently means
"copied" but the only parallels in
Shakespeare are in this play, at III. iv.
178 and IV. i. 148–53, and it is rare
elsewhere.

303. *fantasy*] usually in Shakespeare
means either "love" (as in *AYL.*, II. iv.
28–36, where the equation is stressed
by repetition) or "fanciful imagination" (as in *Ham.*, "Horatio says 'tis
but our fantasy" and "Is not this something more than fantasy?", I. i. 23,
54); here it seems to mean "whim", a
sense in which it is not, I think, elsewhere used in Shakespeare, since a
passage in Hamlet which has been
adduced as parallel seems irrelevant—
"to my shame I see The imminent
death of twenty thousand men, That
for a fantasy and trick of fame, Go to
their graves like beds", where Hamlet
surely does not mean "whim" but an
"idea", even if an illusory idea, of
fame.

112   OTHELLO   [ACT III

Iago. To have a foolish wife.
Emil. O, is that all? What will you give me now,
   For that same handkerchief?
Iago.   What handkerchief?   310
Emil. What handkerchief?
   Why, that the Moor first gave to Desdemona,
   That which so often you did bid me steal.
Iago. Hast stole it from her?
Emil. No, faith, she let it drop by negligence,   315
   And, to the advantage, I being here took 't up:
   Look, here it is.
Iago.   A good wench, give it me.
Emil. What will you do with it, that you have been
   So earnest to have me filch it?
Iago. [*Snatching it*] Why, what's that to you?   320
Emil. If it be not for some purpose of import,
   Give me 't again, poor lady, she'll run mad,
   When she shall lack it.
Iago. Be not you known on 't, I have use for it: ...
   Go, leave me: [*Exit Emilia.*   325
   I will in Cassio's lodging lose this napkin,
   And let him find it: trifles light as air
   Are to the jealous, confirmations strong

308. wife] *F, Q2;* thing *Q1.*   310, 311. handkerchief] *F, Q2;* handkercher *Q1.*
314. stole] *Qq;* stolne *F.*   315. No, faith] *Qq;* No: but *F.*   316. the advan-
tage] *Qq;* th'advantage *F.*   317. it is] *Qq;* 'tis *F.*   318–19. What . . . it?]
Qq; prose F.   320. S.D.] *Rowe.*   what's] *Qq;* what is *F.*   321. If it] *Q1, F;*
If't *Q2.*   322. Give me 't] *Qq;* Giu't me *F.*   324–5. Be not . . . me] *one line
Qq; divided after* on't *F.*   324. not you known on't] *Q1;* not acknowne on't *F;*
not you acknowne on't *Q2.*

316. *to the advantage*] luck being with me.

320. Snatching it] The S.D. is Rowe's, and is now so traditional a piece of stage business that I have let it stand; but it is needless, since Emilia's "What will you do with it?" is natural enough even if she *gives* the napkin to Iago (which is her expressed intention). She is still, as yet, too much under his thumb to dare make an answer to her question a condition of surrendering it.

324. *Be not you known on't*] With either this or F's reading the meaning seems to be "known to be responsible", almost "admitting responsibility"; Steevens quotes from Puttenham, "so would I not have a translator to be ashamed to be acknown of his translation", and Porson from Harington, "Some say, he was married to her privately, but durst not be acknown of it." But I suspect that Iago really means "The less you know about it, the better for you."

As proofs of holy writ; this may do something.
The Moor already changes with my poison: 330
Dangerous conceits are in their natures poisons,
Which at the first are scarce found to distaste,
But with a little act upon the blood
Burn like the mines of sulphur: I did say so:

Enter OTHELLO.

Look where he comes, not poppy, nor mandragora,   335
Nor all the drowsy syrups of the world,
Shall ever medicine thee to that sweet sleep
Which thou owedst yesterday.
Oth. Ha, ha, false to me, to me?
Iago. Why, how now, general? no more of that.   340
Oth. Avaunt, be gone, thou hast set me on the rack,
I swear, 'tis better to be much abus'd
Than but to know't a little.
Iago.   How now, my lord?

330. The . . . poison:] *F*, *Q2*; *not in Q1*.   333. act upon] *F*, *Q2* (acte *F*); art,
upon *Q1*.   334. mines] *F*, *Q2*; mindes *Q1*.   S.D.] *F*; *after l. 333*, *Qq*.
338. owedst] *Qq*; owd'st *F*.   339. to me, to me?] *Qq*; to mee? *F*.   343.
know't] *F*, *Q2*; know'r *Q1*.

331. *conceits*] conceptions, imagin-
ings; see note on l. 119 above.
    334. *mines of sulphur*] Hart quotes
Holland's Pliny, "Sulphur . . . is
engendered within the Islands Aeolia,
which lie between Italy and Sicily . . .
which do always burn by reason thereof", and from Greene "Naught can
serve to quench the aspiring flames
That burn as do the fires of Sicily".
    335–8.] This "incantation of the
high-priest of evil" presents the actor
with a problem somewhat like that of
Mercutio's Queen Mab speech. Is he
to try to keep it in character by deliver-
ing it with a malignant and almost
snarling triumph or is he to give it as a
piece of superb and rounded poetry,
which Shakespeare has put incongru-
ously into Iago's mouth?
    335. *poppy*] opium; not elsewhere in
Shakespeare. Hart compares Jonson,
Sejanus (III. 596), "may they [my

charms] lay that hold upon thy senses,
As thou hadst snuff'd up hemlock, or
ta'en down The juice of poppy and
of mandrakes. Sleep, Voluptuous
Caesar." And cf. Keats' "drows'd
with the fume of poppies" and "the
poppied warmth of sleep".
    mandragora] a soporific; "Give me to
drink mandragora, That I might
sleep out this great gap of time" (*Ant.*,
I. v. 4).
    338. *owedst*] enjoyedst; "owe" is
very common Elizabethan for "own";
"What art thou that keep'st me out
from the house I owe" (*Err.*, III. i. 42).
    339. *to me, to me*] "The second 'to
me' may well be an actor's interpolation; there are, seemingly, a number
of them in the play. Even so, it is some
slight evidence—any being needed—
that the line is meant to be throttled
down in the speaking, not rung out
clear." (Granville Barker).

Oth. What sense had I of her stol'n hours of lust?
    I saw't not, thought it not, it harm'd not me,   345
    I slept the next night well, was free and merry;
    I found not Cassio's kisses on her lips;
    He that is robb'd, not wanting what is stol'n,
    Let him not know't, and he's not robb'd at all.
Iago. I am sorry to hear this.   350
Oth. I had been happy if the general camp,
    Pioners, and all, had tasted her sweet body,
    So I had nothing known: O now for ever
    Farewell the tranquil mind, farewell content:
    Farewell the plumed troop, and the big wars,   355
    That makes ambition virtue: O farewell,
    Farewell the neighing steed, and the shrill trump,
    The spirit-stirring drum, the ear-piercing fife;
    The royal banner, and all quality,
    Pride, pomp, and circumstance of glorious war!   360
    And, O ye mortal engines, whose wide throats

344. sense] *Qq, F;* sent *F2, F3;* scent *F4, Rowe.*   of her] *Qq;* in her *F.*   lust?]
Lust? *F;* lust: *Qq.*   345. not, it] *Qq;* not: it *F.*   me,] *Qq;* me: *F.*   346.
well] *Qq;* well, fed well *F.*   merry;] *Qq;* merrie. *F.*   347. lips;] *Q2;* lips,
Q1; Lippes: *F.*   355. troop] *Qq;* Troopes *F.*   358. the ear-piercing] *Qq;*
th' Eare-piercing *F.*   361. ye] *Qq;* you *F.*   wide] *Qq;* rude *F.*

344.] Othello is by now reduced to unquestioning acceptance of the slander.

sense] perception, awareness; "the public body, . . . feeling in itself A lack of Timon's aid, hath sense withal Of its own fall" (*Tim.*, v. i. 150), "As my great power thereof may give thee sense" (*Ham.*, iv. iii. 62).

352. *Pioners*] sappers, regarded as the lowest type of soldier, so that to be reduced to a "pioner" was a disciplinary degradation, or, sometimes, a mitigation of the death penalty. Hart quotes illustrations from Davies' *Art of War*, 1619 (a man who loses his arms is to be "dismissed with punishment or to be made some abject pioner") and Sir J. Harington's report on Essex's operations in Ireland, in which he speaks of a general capital sentence by court-martial, the sentence being then "miti-

gated by his Lordship's mercy, by which every 10th man was sentenced only to die; the rest appointed to serve in the army for pioneers". The reason for their low repute was that they were merely manual labourers, diggers, with none of the expertise of the engineers; "How now, Captain Macmorris! have you quit the mines? have the pioners given o'er?" (*H 5*, iii. ii. 95); "Well said, old mole, canst work i' the earth so fast? A worthy pioner!" (*Ham.*, i. v. 162).

360. *circumstance*] the word sometimes = "ceremony", as in "his approach So out of circumstance" (= unceremonious; *Wint.*, v. i. 89); here almost "pageantry".

361. *mortal*] lethal; "This news is mortal to the queen:—look down, And see what death is doing" (*Wint.*, iii. ii. 149), "an unction . . . So mortal that,

The immortal Jove's great clamour counterfeit;
Farewell, Othello's occupation's gone!
Iago. Is 't possible, my lord?
Oth. Villain, be sure thou prove my love a whore,   365
Be sure of it, give me the ocular proof,
Or by the worth of man's eternal soul,
Thou hadst been better have been born a dog,
Than answer my wak'd wrath.
Iago.   Is 't come to this?
Oth. Make me to see 't, or at the least so prove it,   370
That the probation bear no hinge, nor loop,
To hang a doubt on: or woe upon thy life!
Iago. My noble lord,—
Oth. If thou dost slander her, and torture me,

362. The] *Qq;* Th' *F.*   great] *Qq;* dread *F.*   clamour] *Q1;* Clamours *F, Q2*
(clamors *Q2*).   367. man's] *Q1;* mine *F;* my *Q2*.   368. better] *Qq;* better *F.*

but dip a knife in it, Where it draws blood no cataplasm so rare ... can save the thing from death That is but scratch'd withal" (*Ham.*, IV. vii. 141).

365. *prove ... whore*] the emphasis, of course, on *prove.*

368. *born a dog*] why a dog in particular? Othello apparently means "the most contemptible of creatures" or else "the creature that meets with the most savage punishments". Cinthio, in the parallel passage, says "mutolo", "dumb", of which there is perhaps an echo in Iago's "I had rather have my tongue cut [out] from my mouth".

371. *hinge, nor loop*] *hinge* is not used by Shakespeare elsewhere in any comparable sense (but of knees or joints in general), and *loop(ed)* is used only twice, both times = window or loophole "all sight-holes, every loop" (*1 H 4*, IV. i. 71); we have therefore to start from scratch, and it is not easy to see what the force of the figure is. Shakespeare often uses startling metaphors, and often combines one highly concrete image with one much less so, when the detail of the picture is given by the first (as, e.g. with one of the examples of *looped*, "loop'd and window'd raggedness", in *Lr.*, III. iv. 31, or

"grunt and sweat under a weary life" (*Ham.*, III. i. 77), but it is not like him to combine in one picture incongruous specific concrete details. The difficulty is *hinge* (since a *loop*, in one sense, is something from which something else can be hung). I take it that Shakespeare is thinking of the original connection of *hinge* with *hang*, but also of the crude form of hinge which consists of a hook and eye, and in which the hook is convenient for hanging things on. This may all seem to be making a fuss about nothing, since the "general sense" is clear; but with an artist of Shakespeare's vivid pictorial imagination we should never, I think, be easily satisfied with "general sense" and a consequent woolly apprehension, when he himself is being concretely specific.

374.] It is natural to suppose that either here (Booth's view), or possibly at *wak'd wrath* (l. 369, Kean's view), Othello takes Iago by the throat. It is at this point, I think, that Iago realizes that he has miscalculated. He counted on being able to put Othello into a jealousy so strong that judgement could not cure; but he did not reckon on part of its strength being directed

Never pray more, abandon all remorse.   375
On horror's head horrors accumulate:
Do deeds to make heaven weep, all earth amaz'd,
For nothing canst thou to damnation add
Greater than that.

Iago.   O grace, O heaven defend me!
Are you a man, have you a soul or sense?   380
God buy you, take mine office,—O wretched fool,
That livest to make thine honesty a vice!
O monstrous world, take note, take note, O world,
To be direct and honest, is not safe,
I thank you for this profit, and from hence   385
I'll love no friend, since love breeds such offence.

---

376. accumulate] *F, Q2;* accumilate *Q1.*   379. defend] *Qq;* forgiue *F.*
381. mine] *Q1, F;* my *Q2.*   382. livest] *Qq;* lou'st *F.*   386. since] *Qq;* sith *F.*

---

so dangerously against himself. Further, Othello still has enough "judgement" left to demand, with violence,
what Iago knows he cannot produce,
ocular proof. From this moment Iago
sees that, for his own safety, both
Cassio and Desdemona must be killed,
and as soon as possible, though neither
death was part of the original plot.

375. *remorse*] Neither here nor in
l. 475 below is the meaning of the
word at all clear, but this is the easier
passage of the two. I think here it is
near to "place of repentance", perhaps
with a reminiscence of another be-
trayer who sought such a place with
tears and did not find it (Hebrews,
xii. 17).

377. *heaven weep*] Cf. "Plays such
fantastic tricks before high heaven As
make the angels weep" (*Meas.,* II. ii.
121).

381. *take mine office*] The natural interpretation is that Iago is sulkily
resigning his position as ancient. Hart,
though admitting this as possible,
glosses *office* as "good will or service";
this makes *take* very awkward; it is
natural enough to say "take (back)
what you have conferred", but you
cannot take back service offered—you
can reject it, which *take* cannot mean,

or accept it, which is not what Iago
means. The only objection to the
natural interpretation is that Shakespeare more often uses *office* of civil
than of military position, e.g., "no
better office than to be beadle" (*Per.,*
II. i. 100), "The insolence of office"
(*Ham.,* III. i. 73); but see "Were I the
general, thou shouldst have my
office" (*Troil.,* v. vi. 4), and "The
trust, the office, I do hold of you" (I.
iii. 118 above).

382. *vice*] Iago clearly does not mean
that he has lived to make his honesty
a sin, but rather a dangerous weakness; Shakespeare normally uses the
word in the sense of "sin" but there are
two or three passages in which it seems
to at least approximate to the meaning
here needed, and to mean "flaw" or
"failing"; "on that vice in him will
my revenge find notable cause to
work" (*Tw.N.,* II. iii. 167, the "vice"
being Malvolio's vanity), "Brother,
you have a vice of mercy in you, Which
better fits a lion than a man" (*Troil.,*
v. iii. 37), "She holds it a vice in her
goodness not to do more than she is
requested" (II. iii. 312 above).

386. *offence*] danger to the lover, I
think, rather than resentment in the
object of the love.

Oth. Nay, stay, thou shouldst be honest.

Iago. I should be wise, for honesty's a fool,
        And loses that it works for.

Oth.   By the world,
        I think my wife be honest, and think she is not,   390
        I think that thou art just, and think thou art not;
        I'll have some proof: my name, that was as fresh
        As Dian's visage, is now begrim'd, and black
        As mine own face: if there be cords, or knives,
        Poison, or fire, or suffocating streams,   395
        I'll not endure it: would I were satisfied!

Iago. I see, sir, you are eaten up with passion,
        I do repent me that I put it to you;
        You would be satisfied.

Oth.   Would, nay, I will.

Iago. And may, but, how, how satisfied, my lord?   400

389–97. *Oth.* By . . . satisfied! *Iago.*] *F, Q2; not in Q1.*   392. my] *F;* her *Q2.*
397. see, sir,] see sir, *Qq;* see *F.*   399. satisfied.] *Qq;* satisfied? *F.*   Would,
nay, I] *Qq;* Would? Nay, and I *F.*

388.] This surly sulkiness is perfectly adjusted to the part of the honest man whose candid speech has landed him in trouble.

389–96.] The absence of these lines from Q1 is very odd. The first six and a half of them, though effective, are not absolutely essential, but l. 396, or at least its last four words, is essential, to lead up to Iago's *You would be satisfied?* three lines below, and the whole passage is, if not essential, desirable, since even the whole of l. 396 is a thin lead-in for Iago's *eaten up with passion.* But an omission by accident is hard to account for, since there is nothing to induce a wrong "take-off", and further it involves the omission of two speech-headings. The best I can suggest is that the cut was intended to start with *By the world* (leaving the speech-heading standing) and end with *endure it.*

392. *my name*] I see little justification for accepting Q2's "*her* name" as most edd. have done. Othello is maddened by the befoulment of his own

honour; it is that which he will not endure, and which only revenge will clear. But Q2's reading is quite tolerable, and it is true that later Othello does show himself moved by the stain on Desdemona's name as well as on his own.

393. *Dian*] the goddess of chastity (and the moon); "The noble sister of Publicola, The moon of Rome; chaste as the icicle That's curdied by the frost from purest snow, and hangs on Dian's temple" (*Cor.,* v. iii. 64).

395. *suffocating streams*] The phrase has elicited almost no comment, but is it very clear? What kind of *stream* can be described as *suffocating?* It is too elaborate a phrase to describe plain "drowning". One might be reminded of Portia's suicide (*Cæs.,* IV. iii. 155) who "swallow'd fire" (? inhaled charcoal fumes), if it were not that fire has just been mentioned. Is the idea perhaps that of a stream of lava?

400.] Iago now moves on to much more brutal and maddening directness.

Would you, the supervisor, grossly gape on,
Behold her topp'd?

Oth.   Death and damnation ... O!

Iago. It were a tedious difficulty, I think,
To bring 'em to that prospect, damn 'em then,
If ever mortal eyes did see them bolster   405
More than their own; what then, how then?
What shall I say? where's satisfaction?
It is impossible you should see this,
Were they as prime as goats, as hot as monkeys,
As salt as wolves, in pride; and fools as gross   410
As ignorance made drunk: but yet I say,
If imputation and strong circumstances,
Which lead directly to the door of truth,
Will give you satisfaction, you may ha't.

Oth. Give me a living reason, that she's disloyal.   415

Iago. I do not like the office,
But sith I am enter'd into this cause so far,

401. you, the supervisor,] you, the superuisor *Q1*; you the super-vision *F*; you, the superuision *Q2*; you be supervisor, *Pope.*   402. topp'd] topt *Qq*; top'd *F*; tupp'd *Theobald and others.*   404. 'em . . . 'em] *Qq*; them . . . them *F*. 405. did] *Qq*; do *F*.   414. may ha't] *Qq*; might haue' *F*.   417. into] *Qq*; in *F*.

401. *supervisor*] I think F's "super-vision" merits consideration, since F clearly took it as the object of *gape on*, as though it meant "the spectacle of Desdemona being *topp'd*", but it is hard to find any parallel for any such sense.

405. *bolster*] I suppose just "share the same pillow", but is there a hint of the picture of "the beast with two backs"?

409-10. *prime . . . hot . . . salt . . . in pride*] all synonyms for lecherous, "on heat"; there is no parallel in Shakespeare for this use of *prime*, and only one for *in pride* (*Lucr.*, 438, "smoking with pride" and perhaps 705, "While lust is in his pride"), but Hart quotes two passages for "proud" in the required sense, in each connected with *salt*, and the other two are common; "She is not hot, but temperate as the morn" (*Shr.*, II. i. 288), "that breeds

hot blood, and hot blood begets hot thoughts, and hot thoughts beget hot deeds, and hot deeds is love" (*Troil.*, III. i. 143), "He spake of her as Dian had hot dreams" (*Cym.*, v. v. 181), "Whose salt imagination yet hath wrong'd Your well-defended honour" (*Meas.*, v. i. 402), "Be a whore still; ... Make use of thy salt hours" (*Tim.*, IV. iii. 83).

412. *imputation . . . circumstances*] "opinion founded on strong circumstantial evidence" (Schmidt).

413. *door of truth*] I think the slightest of pauses after *door*; Othello is led in imagination to stand outside the closed bedroom door.

415. *living*] we should say "sound"; not elsewhere in Shakespeare in this sense, but cf. "lively" in "A reason mighty. . . A pattern, precedent, and lively warrant, For me . . . to perform the like" (*Tit.*, v. iii. 43).

Prick'd to 't by foolish honesty and love,
I will go on: I lay with Cassio lately,
And being troubled with a raging tooth,   420
I could not sleep.
There are a kind of men so loose of soul,
That in their sleeps will mutter their affairs,
One of this kind is Cassio:
In sleep I heard him say "Sweet Desdemona,   425
Let us be wary, let us hide our loves;"
And then, sir, would he gripe and wring my hand,
Cry out, "Sweet creature!" and then kiss me hard,
As if he pluck'd up kisses by the roots,
That grew upon my lips, then laid his leg   430
Over my thigh, and sigh'd, and kiss'd, and then
Cried "Cursed fate, that gave thee to the Moor!"
Oth. O monstrous, monstrous!
Iago.   Nay, this was but his dream.
Oth. But this denoted a foregone conclusion.
Iago. 'Tis a shrewd doubt, though it be but a dream,   435

426. wary] *F, Q2;* merry *Q1.*   428. Cry out,] *Qq;* Cry, oh *F.*   "Sweet
creature!" and then] sweet creature, and then *Qq;* sweet creature: then *F.*
430–2. That grew . . . fate] *as Qq; F lines end* Thigh, / Fate, / .   430. then laid]
Qq; laid *F.*   431. Over] *Qq;* ore *F.*   431–2. sigh'd . . . kiss'd . . . Cried]
Qq; sigh . . . kisse . . . cry *F.*   434. denoted] *F, Q2;* deuoted *Q1.*   435. *Iago.*
'Tis] *Q1;* 'Tis *F, Q2.*

419.] "long time".

426. *wary*] F is probably right, and
certainly more logical, and *wary* misread as *mery* might well lead to
"merry"; but it is often just where F is
the more logical that one becomes
suspicious, and the sudden transition
from enjoyment to the need for caution is not unnatural for a man talking
incoherently in his sleep.

434–5.] Q1's attribution of speeches
is, I think, much the more effective.
In answer to Othello's *monstrous!* Iago,
pursuing his usual tactics of exasperating caution, reminds him that it was
after all only a dream. Othello, "hot
for certainty", is determined to take
inference for fact. Iago then says in
effect "Well, I must admit that the
suspicion seems pretty well based, and,

taken with other things . . .". If it came
from Othello, *'Tis a shrewd doubt* would
be an anticlimax.

434. *foregone conclusion*] previous con-
summation; "By our remembrances of
days foregone" (*All's W.,* I. iii. 142)—
Shakespeare being more logical in his
use of the word than we are.

435. *shrewd*] The word has an odd
variety of meanings: (*a*) ill-tempered,
like our "shrewish", "as curst and
shrewd As Socrates' Xanthippe or a
worse" (*Shr.,* I. ii. 70); (*b*) bitter,
piercing, "shrewd contents" (*Mer.V.,*
III. ii. 244), "shrewd news" (*John,* v. v.
14), "shrewd days and nights" (*AYL.,*
v. iv. 180); (*c*) penetrating (with no
hint of malevolence), "He has a
shrewd wit" (*Troil.,* I. ii. 203), "A
parlous boy; go to, you are too

And this may help to thicken other proofs,
That do demonstrate thinly.

Oth. I'll tear her all to pieces.

Iago. Nay, but be wise, yet we see nothing done,
She may be honest yet; tell me but this,   440
Have you not sometimes seen a handkerchief,
Spotted with strawberries, in your wife's hand?

Oth. I gave her such a one, 'twas my first gift.

Iago. I know not that, but such a handkerchief—
I am sure it was your wife's—did I to-day   445
See Cassio wipe his beard with.

Oth.   If 't be that,—

Iago. If it be that, or any that was hers,
It speaks against her, with the other proofs.

Oth. O that the slave had forty thousand lives!
One is too poor, too weak for my revenge: 450
Now do I see 'tis true; look here, Iago,
All my fond love thus do I blow to heaven, . . .
'Tis gone.
Arise, black vengeance, from thy hollow cell,

436. And this] *Q1; Iag.* And this *F, Q2.*   439. but] *Qq;* yet *F.*   446. If 't]
Qq; If it *F.*   447. any that was hers] *Malone;* any it was hers, *Qq;* any, it was
hers. *F.*   451. do I] *Q1, F;* I doe *Q2.*   true] *F, Q2;* time *Q1.*   454. thy
hollow cell] *Qq, Johnson, Malone;* the hollow hell *F, Steevens (1793).*

shrewd" (*R 3,* II. iv. 35, where the
speaker is commenting on the boy's
precocity); and, lastly, simply "telling", "effective", in a good sense;
"This young maid might do her A
shrewd turn if she pleas'd" (*All's W.,*
III. v. 67); the meaning here is somewhere between (*c*) and (*d*).

437. *thinly*] Cf. I. iii. 108 above,
where also the application is to evidence.

439. *see*] For the last forty lines Iago
has been pitilessly inflaming Othello's
visual imagination. And now he is going to make the nearest approach in
his power to the demanded "ocular
proof".

445.] progress by parenthesis.

447. *any that*] Though Q1 and F concur in *it,* Malone's emendation seems
necessary; *y* is easily misread as *yt.*

454. *thy hollow cell*] Hart quotes from
Armin's *Two Maids of More-clacke*
(1609) "Rouse thee black Mischief
from thy ebon cell", which looks like a
reminiscence. As to F's reading, the
contrast (stressed by supporters of F)
between the *heaven* of two lines above
and "hell" here is hardly valid, since
the real contrast is between vengeance
emerging from its lair and love en-
throned and crowned; and in the passages from Milton which are adduced
in support there is a point in hell being
hollow which seems absent here. But in
the present context there does not seem
much more point in the *cell* being
hollow, and I think the word is suspect
("ebben", which is Armin's spelling, is
not graphically quite impossible); cf.
"hollow mine" at IV. ii. 81 below,
where again hollow seems redundant.

Yield up, O love, thy crown, and hearted throne,   455
To tyrannous hate, swell, bosom, with thy fraught,
For 'tis of aspics' tongues!   [*he kneels.*
Iago. Pray be content.
Oth.   O, blood, Iago, blood!
Iago. Patience I say, your mind perhaps may change.
Oth. Never, Iago. Like to the Pontic sea,   460
Whose icy current, and compulsive course,
Ne'er feels retiring ebb, but keeps due on
To the Propontic, and the Hellespont:
Even so my bloody thoughts, with violent pace
Shall ne'er look back, ne'er ebb to humble love,   465
Till that a capable and wide revenge
Swallow them up. Now by yond marble heaven,

---

455. S.D.] *Qq* (*after* content, *l. 458, Q1*); *not in F.*   458. Pray] *Qq*; Yet *F.*
blood, Iago, blood] *Qq*; blood, blood, blood *F.*   459. perhaps] *Qq*; *not in F.*
460. Never, Iago.] Neuer Iago. *F*; Neuer Iago; *Q2*; Neuer: *Q1.*   460-7. Like
... heaven,] *F, Q2; not in Q1.*   462. feels] *Q2*; keepes *F.*

---

455. *hearted throne*] presumably
"throne in my heart" or perhaps "in
men's hearts".

456. *fraught*] freight.

457. *aspics*'] asps' (the only form in
Shakespeare).

460-7. *Iago . . . heaven*] The absence
of these lines in Q1 must, I think, be
the result of a cut (see Appendix A,
p. 200), though perhaps the cut in fact
ran from *Like* to *Now*, thus leaving
a complete line. Opinions have varied about the lines themselves. Swin-
burne called them "one of the most
precious jewels that ever the prodigal
afterthought of a great poet bestowed
upon the rapture of his readers" and
later, answering the charge of inappro-
priateness, "In other lips, indeed, than
Othello's, at the crowning minute of
culminant agony, the rush of imaginative reminiscence which brings back
upon his eyes and ears the lightning
foam and tideless thunder of the
Pontic sea might seem a thing less
natural than sublime. But Othello has
the passion of a poet closed in, as it
were. and shut up behind the passion

of a hero." Pope, more coolly, commented, "This simile is omitted in the
first edition; I think it should be so, as
an unnatural excursion in this place",
and Steevens emphatically supported
Pope's verdict.

461. *compulsive*] The ordinary meaning, "compelling", will no doubt
serve, as in "the compulsive ardour"
(*Ham.*, III. iv. 86), but is there perhaps
a touch of the passive sense—the head
of water is so high that it *cannot* feel retiring ebb, but must drive always on?

466. *capable*] comprehensive; no
precise parallel in Shakespeare, but
cf. "Being capable of all ill" (*Tp.*, I. ii.
353); it is as though Shakespeare were
using the word as the adjective corresponding to "capacity"—he nowhere uses "capacious"; and cf. "My
great revenge had stomach for 'em
all" (v. ii. 76 below).

467. *marble*] Why marble? Furness
quotes three other passages from
Shakespeare, "monsters . . . whom thy
[the earth's] upward face Hath to the
marbled mansion all above Never
presented" (*Tim.*, IV. iii. 191), "Peep

In the due reverence of a sacred vow,
I here engage my words.

Iago.   Do not rise yet.   [*Iago kneels.*

Witness, you ever-burning lights above,   470
You elements that clip us round about,
Witness that here Iago doth give up
The excellency of his wit, hand, heart,
To wrong'd Othello's service: let him command,
And to obey shall be in me remorse,   475

---

469. S.D.] *Qq* (*after* about, *l. 471, Q1*); *not in* F.   470. you] *Q1, F;* the *Q2.*
473. excellency] *Q1;* execution *F, Q2.*   hand] *Qq;* hands *F.*   475. be in me
remorse] *F, Q2* (remorce *Q2*); be remorce *Q1.*

through thy marble mansion" (*Cym.*,
v. iv. 87, the appeal to Jupiter), "The
marble pavement closes" (*Cym.*, v. iv.
120, after Jupiter has withdrawn); he
then says that in these " 'marbled' is
suggestive of all the imposing pomp of
masonry with cloud-capped towers
and glistening domes". This is very
doubtful. Both the Cymbeline passages seem to suggest a gap or inter-
stice through which Jupiter first
"peeps" and which then "closes"—
not a characteristic feature of a
"pomp of masonry". And the use of
the word in *Tim.* must, I think, be
taken closely with "crisp heaven"
eight lines before. For this "crisp" the
best that Onions can do is to invent a
tentative second meaning "(?) shining, clear" beside the usual "curled,
rippled". But I think that in all three
places "marble(d)" is referring to the
floor of heaven with its "curled" and
shifting clouds (Shelley's "fleecy
floor"). It is the sense the word bears
in "marbled paper", some kinds of
which are much like a lightly clouded
sky. But this hardly helps the problem
here. Perhaps it means no more than
"shining". Dr Brooks suggests that
marble is appropriate as being "no
less unrelenting in its hardness and
purity (and demand for purity) than
Othello and his vow themselves".

471. *elements*] See note on II. iii. 333
above; the word here seems to mean
something like "powers of nature", or,

more narrowly, "heavenly powers".

clip] enclose; "No grave upon the
earth shall clip in it A pair so famous"
(*Ant.*, v. ii. 360), "clipp'd in with the
sea That chides the banks of England,
Scotland, Wales" (*1 H 4*, III. i. 44).

473. *excellency*] In our modern sense
this is a colourless word as against F's
"execution", but see note on II. i. 64
above.

475. *remorse*] Schmidt's "compunc-
tion of conscience", unsatisfactory at
l. 375 above, seems plain impossible
here, since it is not obedience, but *non*-
obedience, that will cause pricks of
conscience. Some edd. have, in despair,
inserted a negative. Though Shakespeare, I think, never uses the word
quite in the modern sense of "repen-
tant regret" he almost always uses it to
mean "pity resulting from a change of
heart" or "pity" simply; "Hence both
are gone with conscience and remorse" (*R 3*, IV. iii. 20, of the murderers), "My sisterly remorse con-
futes mine honour" (*Meas.*, v. i. 101),
where it is clearly just "pity" since
Isabella had nothing to be remorseful
about), "with as little remorse as they
would have drowned a blind bitch's
puppies" (*Wiv.*, III. v. 10). So far as I
can see, Shakespeare nowhere uses the
word with any connotation of "conscience", except perhaps in the passage in *1 H 4*, I. ii. 105–29, with its
"What says Monsieur Remorse?",
and (again perhaps) in the two pass-

What bloody work so ever. [*They rise.*

Oth. I greet thy love;
Not with vain thanks, but with acceptance bounteous,
And will upon the instant put thee to 't,
Within these three days, let me hear thee say
That Cassio's not alive.

Iago. My friend is dead: 480
'Tis done as you request, but let her live.

Oth. Damn her, lewd minx: O, damn her!
Come, go with me apart, I will withdraw
To furnish me with some swift means of death,
For the fair devil: now art thou my lieutenant. 485

Iago. I am your own for ever. [*Exeunt.*

476. work so ever] *Qq;* businesse euer *F.* S.D.] *Capell (Rising).* 481. as you request] *Qq;* at your Request *F.* 482. minx . . . her!] *Qq* (minks); Minx: / O damne her, damne her. *F.*

ages in this play. In these two passages we can, I suppose, stay uneasily content with "pity", but it is weak in the first passage, where the required sense seems to be "abandon all hope of repentance"; nor is it very satisfactory here, in the sense of "pity for Othello". Here the meaning required is precisely Hamlet's "perfect conscience" (v. ii. 67) where also the work which conscience will approve is a bloody one, but how to educe that meaning from the text I do not see. The imperfect line in Q1 rather suggests some confusion in the MS. Hart, quite happy with "conscience simply", complains that "some of the commentators have laboured this passage into a wonderful mash". But even making a mash is sometimes more useful than slurring over.

477. *bounteous*] The word is normally used of the giver rather than the receiver (see l. 204 above) but from the sense of "unrestrained" we can get the "whole-hearted" which seems needed here; better than empty thanks is an acceptance which makes immediate use of the gift.

478. *put thee to't*] put you to the proof; cf. Lavache in *All's W.*, II. ii.

14–68, proving that "O Lord, sir!" is an answer which will "serve fit to all questions", and saying "Nay, put me to't".

480. *is dead*] Theobald gives two interesting parallels: "In like manner Jonson in his *Cataline* (*sic*) expresses the impetuosity of Cethegus for the death of Cicero, 'He shall die. *Shall* was too slowly said; he's dying, that Is yet too slow; he's dead'. But this is a copy from Seneca's *Hercules Furens*: 'Si novi Herculem Lycus Creonti debitas poenas dabit. Lentum est, dabit; dat; hoc quoque lentum est; dedit.' "

481. *but let her live*] Iago knows the surest way to secure that she shall not live is to suggest that she shall.

485. *now . . . lieutenant*] Both aims of Iago's original "double knavery" are now achieved.

486. *I am your own for ever*] Another of Booth's admirable notes (expanding what he has said before): "To portray Iago properly you must seem to be what all the characters think, and say, you are, not what the spectators know you to be; try to win even them by your sincerity. Don't *act* the villain, don't *look* it or *speak* it (by scowling and growling, I mean), but *think* it all the

SCENE IV.—[*The Same.*]

Enter DESDEMONA, EMILIA, *and the Clown.*

Des. Do you know, sirrah, where the Lieutenant Cassio lies?

Clo. I dare not say he lies any where.

Des. Why, man?

Clo. He is a soldier, and for one to say a soldier lies, is
stabbing.   5

Des. Go to, where lodges he?

Clo. To tell you where he lodges, is to tell you where I lie.

Des. Can any thing be made of this?

Clo. I know not where he lodges, and for me to devise a
lodging, and say he lies here, or he lies there, were   10
to lie in mine own throat.

Des. Can you inquire him out, and be edified by report?

Clo. I will catechize the world for him, that is, make
questions and by them answer.

Des. Seek him, bid him come hither, tell him I have   15
moved my lord in his behalf, and hope all will be well.

Clo. To do this is within the compass of a man, and therefore I'll attempt the doing of it.   [*Exit.*

Scene IV

S.D. Desdemona] *F*, *Q2*; Desdemonia *Q1*.   Emilia] *F* (Æmilia); Emilla *Qq*.
and the Clown] *Qq* (*Clowne*); *and Clown F*.   1. the Lieutenant] *Qq*; Lieutenant *F*.
4. *Clo.*] *F*, *Q2*; *not in Q1*.   He is] *Qq*; He's *F*.   one] *Qq*; mee *F*.   is] *Qq*;
'tis *F*.   7–8. *Clo.* To tell . . . this?] *F*, *Q2*; *not in Q1*.   10. here . . . there] *F*;
there *Qq*.   11. mine own] *F*, *Q2*; my *Q1*.   16. in] *Qq*; on *F*.   17. a man]
Q1; mans Wit *F*; mans witte *Q2*.   18. I'll] *Qq*; I will *F*.   of it] *Qq*; it *F*.

time. Be genial, sometimes jovial,
always gentlemanly. [I should query
the last word.] Quick in motion as in
thought; lithe and sinuous as a snake.
A certain bluffness (which my temperament does not afford) should be
added to preserve the military flavour
of the character; in this particular I
fail utterly, my Iago lacks the soldierly
quality. My consolation is that we
know him more as a courtier than as a
soldier."

Scene IV

10.] F is very probably right, Q1

having taken off from the second *lies.*

11. *in mine own throat*] Cf. "I do nothing in the world but lie, and lie in my
throat" (*LLL.*, IV. iii. 12), "In thy foul
throat thou liest" (*R 3*, I. ii. 93),
"Through the false passage of thy
throat, thou liest" (*R 2*, I. i. 125),
"thou liest in thy throat" (*Tw.N.*, III.
iv. 173), "gives me the lie i' the
throat" (*Ham.*, II. ii. 609).

17. *compass*] range; "It strains me
past the compass of my wits" (*Rom.*,
IV. i. 47), a passage which may be
thought to tell for (or against) the F
reading here.

Des. Where should I lose that handkerchief, Emilia?
Emil. I know not, madam.   20
Des. Believe me, I had rather lose my purse
         Full of crusadoes: and but my noble Moor
         Is true of mind, and made of no such baseness
         As jealous creatures are, it were enough
         To put him to ill thinking.
Emil.   Is he not jealous?   25
Des. Who, he? I think the sun where he was born
         Drew all such humours from him.

                    Enter OTHELLO.

Emil.   Look, where he comes.
Des. I will not leave him now; let Cassio
         Be call'd to him. How is it with you, my lord?
Oth. Well, my good lady: [*Aside*] O, hardness to dissemble!
         How do you do, Desdemona?
Des.   Well, my good lord.   31
Oth. Give me your hand; this hand is moist, my lady.
Des. It yet has felt no age, nor known no sorrow.
Oth. This argues fruitfulness, and liberal heart;
         Hot, hot, and moist, this hand of yours requires   35

19. that] *Qq*; the *F*.   21. lose] *Qq* (loose); haue lost *F*.   27. S.D.] *Qq*; *after comes F*.   28-9. now; let Cassio / . . . lord?] now, / Let Cassio . . . Lord? *Q1*; now, till Cassio be / Call'd . . . Lord? *F*; now, / Till Cassio . . . Lord? *Q2*.   29. is it] *Qq*; is't *F*.   30. *Aside*] *Hanmer*; *not in Qq, F*.   33. yet has] *Qq*; hath *F*.   35. Hot, hot] *F, Q2*; Not hot *Q1*.

22. *crusadoes*] Portuguese coins stamped with a cross, current in England at the time, at a value of three shillings.

28. *let Cassio . . .*] The Q1 and F texts have different implications; in Q1 Desdemona gives orders for Cassio to be summoned, while she will detain Othello till she can put them face to face, in F she expresses her determination to go on with her suit till (with slight awkwardness of expression) Othello himself summons him. And see l. 46 below.

30. *my good lady*] He has never yet addressed her so formally.

32. *moist*] The palm, if hot and moist, was taken to be an indication of "hot" desires, if dry and cold, the reverse; "his sweating palm, The precedent of pith and livelihood" (*Ven.*, 25), "There's a palm presages chastity" (*Ant.*, I. ii. 49).

34. *liberal*] free, and so "too free" and so "loose"; "Why, here's a girl! I think she knows not well, There were so many, whom she may accuse. —It's sign that she hath been liberal and free" (*1 H 6*, v. iv. 80). Fruitfulness takes its colour from *liberal*, and cf. "Nay, if an oily palm be not a fruitful prognostication . . ." (*Ant.*, I. ii. 55); and cf. II. i. 163 above, and note.

A sequester from liberty; fasting and praying,
Much castigation, exercise devout;
For here's a young and sweating devil here,
That commonly rebels: 'tis a good hand,
A frank one.

Des.   You may indeed say so,   40
For 'twas that hand that gave away my heart.

Oth. A liberal hand; tne hearts of old gave hands,
But our new heraldry is hands, not hearts.

Des. I cannot speak of this; come, come, your promise.

Oth. What promise, chuck?   45

Des. I have sent to bid Cassio come speak with you.

Oth. I have a salt and sullen rheum offends me,
Lend me thy handkerchief.

Des. Here, my lord.

---

36. praying] *Qq*; Prayer *F*.   40. frank one] *Qq, F;* very frank one *Hanmer;* frank one too *Capell*.   42. hearts . . . hands] *Qq, F;* hands . . . hearts *Hanmer*.   44. come, come,] *Q1;* Come, now *F;* come now *Q2*.   47. sullen] *Qq;* sorry *F*.

36. *sequester*] in Shakespeare's usual sense of "sequestration"; see note on I. iii. 346 above.

37. *exercise*] i.e. religious "exercises". "And in no worldly suit would he be mov'd, To draw him from his holy exercise" (*R 3*, III. vii. 62).

40. *frank*] in the sense of "liberal" above; but does he mean also one that gives away its secrets?

43. *our new heraldry . . .*] It is difficult, I think, to escape from seeing here an allusion to the new order of baronetage instituted by King James in 1612, of which the badge was the addition of a hand gules to the coat of arms. Many commentators have revolted against admitting that Shakespeare could have made so inartistic a topical interpolation eight years after the play was written. It is just possible that Othello means no more than that in the bad modern fashion it is only hands that are given, while hearts remain fancy-free, and owe no loyalty. Malone gives this interpretation, but even so, with characteristic honesty, he boggles at the neglect of the specific "heraldry",

and says "I do not, however, undertake to maintain that the poet, when he used the word 'heraldry', had not the new order of baronets in his thoughts". And a topical allusion was to Shakespeare almost as fatal a Cleopatra as a "clench", though such allusions are usually in lighter contexts.

44. *I cannot . . . this*] in effect "I don't know what you are talking about, and so cannot take you up on it".

45. *chuck*] a common "term of endearment", and not necessarily at all patronizing or contemptuous; Macbeth uses it to Lady Macbeth (III. ii. 45) and Antony to Cleopatra (IV. iv. 2); but IV. ii. 24 below shows that it could be used contemptuously.

46. *I have sent*] This seems decisive in favour of Q1 at l. 28.

47. *salt . . . rheum*] running cold in the nose; "Where France?—In her forehead . . . Where England?—I guess it stood in her chin, by the salt rheum that ran between France and it" (*Err.*, III. ii. 126–33); *sullen*, in the sense of "obstinate" is more pointed than F's "sorry".

Oth. That which I gave you.   50
Des. I have it not about me.
Oth. Not?
Des. No, faith, my lord.
Oth.   That's a fault: that handkerchief
    Did an Egyptian to my mother give,
    She was a charmer, and could almost read   55
    The thoughts of people; she told her, while she kept it
    'Twould make her amiable, and subdue my father
    Entirely to her love: but if she lost it,
    Or made a gift of it, my father's eye
    Should hold her loathly, and his spirits should hunt   60
    After new fancies: she dying, gave it me,
    And bid me, when my fate would have me wive,
    To give it her; I did so, and take heed on 't,
    Make it a darling, like your precious eye,
    To lose, or give 't away, were such perdition   65
    As nothing else could match.
Des.   Is 't possible?
Oth. 'Tis true, there's magic in the web of it;
    A sibyl, that had number'd in the world
    The sun to make two hundred compasses,
    In her prophetic fury sew'd the work;   70
    The worms were hallow'd that did breed the silk,
    And it was dyed in mummy, which the skilful
    Conserve of maidens' hearts.

52. Not?] *F;* Not. *Qq.*   53. faith] *Q1;* indeed *F, Q2.*   57.] *ends one page and is repeated at top of next in Q1.*   60. loathly] *Q1* (lothely); loathed *F, Q2.* 63. wive] *Qq;* Wiu'd *F.*   65. lose] *Qq* (loose); loose't *F.*   69. make] *Q1;* course *F, Q2.*   72–3. which . . . Conserve] *Q2* (Concerue); which . . . Conseru'd *F;* with . . . Conserues *Q1.*

57. *amiable*] desirable; stronger than our rather placid sense; "amiable lovely death" (*John*, III. iv. 25).

68. *sibyl*] prophetess; "The spirit of deep prophecy she hath, Exceeding the nine sibyls of old Rome" (*1 H 6*, I. ii. 55).

70. *fury*] afflatus; the word not infrequently has no connotation of anger, but rather of inspiration, possibly of incoherence—"wild and whirling words"; "What zeal, what

fury, hath inspir'd thee now?" (*LLL.*, IV. iii. 229, the King on Berowne's rhodomontade), "a tale Told by an idiot, full of sound and fury, Signifying nothing" (*Mac.*, v. v. 26).

72. *mummy*] liquor supposed to be derived from embalmed bodies and used for medicine or magic; cf. Sir Thomas Browne "Mummy is become merchandize . . . and Pharaoh is sold for balsams".

73. *Conserve*] *Q1's Conserues* (neglect-

Des.   I' faith, is 't true?
Oth. Most veritable, therefore look to 't well.
Des. Then would to God that I had never seen it!   75
Oth. Ha, wherefore?
Des. Why do you speak so startingly and rash?
Oth. Is 't lost? is 't gone? speak, is it out o' the way?
Des. Heaven bless us!
Oth. Say you?   80
Des. It is not lost, but what an if it were?
Oth. Ha!
Des. I say it is not lost.
Oth.   Fetch 't, let me see it.
Des. Why, so I can sir, but I will not now,
This is a trick, to put me from my suit,   85
I pray let Cassio be receiv'd again.
Oth. Fetch me that handkerchief, my mind misgives.
Des. Come, come,
You'll never meet a more sufficient man.
Oth. The handkerchief!
Des.   I pray, talk me of Cassio.   90
Oth. The handkerchief!
Des.   A man that all his time
Hath founded his good fortunes on your love,
Shar'd dangers with you,—
Oth. The handkerchief!

73. I' faith] *Q1;* Indeed? *F;* Indeed, *Q2.*   75. God] *Qq;* Heauen *F.*   seen
it] *Qq;* seene't *F.*   77. rash?] *F, Q2;* rashly. *Q1.*   78. is it] *Qq;* is't *F.*
79. Heaven] *Q1; not in F, Q2.*   82. Ha!] Ha. *Qq;* How? *F.*   83. see it] *Qq;*
see 't *F.*   84. sir,] *Qq; not in F.*   86. I pray] *Qq;* Pray you, *F.*   87. that]
Qq; the *F.*   90-1. *Des.* I pray ... handkerchief!] *Q1; not in F, Q2.*

ing for the moment its *with*) would be
a not unusual singular verb with a
plural subject, and the generalizing
present is likelier than the particu-
larizing past, but I fancy that F preserved the original reading, but with
the common *d : e* error, and that Q2
therefore is right. But Q1 makes *conserves* a noun. There is just this to be
said for it, that the verb, meaning "to
make a preserve of", is not the most
appropriate word to describe the dis-
tillation of a liquor, and so "conserves

of maidens' hearts" may be taken as
an addition to, not a description of,
mummy.
77. *startingly*] ? disconnectedly; "she
did speak in starts distractedly"
(*Tw.N.,* II. ii. 22).
rash] ? urgently; cf. "My lord, I
scarce have leisure to salute you,
My matter is so rash" (*Troil.,* IV. ii.
62).
90-1.] F's omission is as clear a case
as such things can be of a wrong take-
off.

Des.   I' faith, you are to blame.
Oth. Zounds!   [*Exit.*   95
Emil. Is not this man jealous?
Des. I ne'er saw this before:
    Sure there's some wonder in this handkerchief,
    I am most unhappy in the loss of it.
Emil. 'Tis not a year or two shows us a man: 100
    They are all but stomachs, and we all but food;
    They eat us hungerly, and when they are full,
    They belch us.

Enter IAGO *and* CASSIO.

    Look you, Cassio and my husband.
Iago. There is no other way, 'tis she must do it,
    And lo, the happiness! go, and importune her.   105
Des. How now, good Cassio, what's the news with you?
Cas. Madam, my former suit: I do beseech you,
    That by your virtuous means I may again
    Exist, and be a member of his love,
    Whom I, with all the duty of my heart,   110
    Entirely honour; I would not be delay'd:
    If my offence be of such mortal kind,
    That neither service past, nor present sorrows,
    Nor purpos'd merit in futurity,
    Can ransom me into his love again,   115

94. I' faith] *Q1*; Insooth *F, Q2*.   95. Zounds! *Exit*] *Q1* (Zouns.); Away. *Exit Othello F*; Away. *Exit Q2*.   98. handkerchief] handkercher *Qq* (*and so regularly elsewhere*); Handkerchikfe *F*.   99. loss of it] *F, Q2* (losse); losse *Q1*.   104. do it] *Qq*; doo't *F*.   110. duty] *Q1*; Office *F, Q2* (office *Q2*).   113. neither] *Q1*; nor my *F*; not my *Q2*.

95. *Zounds!*] Dr Alice Walker calls this "as objectionable as his oath at III. iii. 158" (another "Zounds"). This is a very remarkable comment. A man of strong feeling who believes himself to have been cuckolded is not likely to be very temperate in his language. And why, when the "glass of fashion", under less provocation, says " 'Swounds . . . I am pigeon-liver'd", is it permissible? In any case, if the susceptibilities of delicate taste are to be the criterion of the authenticity of a reading, where are we? Might I not as justifiably, and as uselessly, say that I find F's "Away!" impossibly feeble?

101. *but*] only (not "they are almost"); cf. II. i. 222 above.
105. *happiness*] good luck; see note on III. iii. 242 above.
109. *Exist*] I suppose with the implication "My present existence is no better than a life in death".
112. *mortal*] fatal; see note on III. iii. 361 above.

But to know so must be my benefit;
So shall I clothe me in a forc'd content,
And shut myself up in some other course
To fortune's alms.

Des.   Alas, thrice-gentle Cassio,
My advocation is not now in tune;   120
My lord is not my lord, nor should I know him,
Were he in favour as in humour alter'd.
So help me every spirit sanctified,
As I have spoken for you, all my best,
And stood within the blank of his displeasure   125
For my free speech: you must awhile be patient;
What I can do I will, and more I will
Than for myself I dare, let that suffice you.

Iago. Is my lord angry?

Emil.   He went hence but now,
And certainly in strange unquietness.   130

Iago. Can he be angry? I have seen the cannon,
When it hath blown his ranks into the air;

---

118. shut] *F, Q2;* shoote *Q1.*   119. alms] *Qq, F;* arms *Pope.*

116. *But . . . benefit*] To be sure even of that will be better than uncertainty.

118. *shut . . . up*] Neither this nor Q1's *shoote* is very easily interpretable; the passage can mean "confine myself to some other way of life that may lead to Fortune's benefits" but *shut* is an oddly strong word for that, and the passage which Steevens quotes to support it from *Mac.,* II. i. 16 seems irrelevant, since "shut up In measureless content" is a picture of enclosure in a state of mind, not in a course of action. I have taken F's reading only because it can be made to mean something, whereas Q1's, even with "on" for *in,* and in spite of Mason's defence, hardly can. But I suspect that *shoote* is an error for "suit" (the error occurs elsewhere, e.g. *LLL.,* IV. i. 111, where Q reads "shooter" for "suitor", thereby emphasizing the pun) and that the word, suggested perhaps by *clothe,* means "to equip and adjust myself to".

122. *favour*] external appearance

and expression (more than just "face"; it is "everything by which, at first glance, one recognizes a person"); "I do remember in this shepherd boy Some lively touches of my daughter's favour" (*AYL.,* v. iv. 26), "to sit and draw His arched brows, his hawking eye, his curls . . . every line and trick of his sweet favour" (*All's W.,* i. i. 105), "look up clear; To alter favour ever is to fear" (*Mac.,* i. v. 72).

humour] mood (as in our "good humour", "bad humour"); "see what humour he is in" (*Wiv.,* II. iii. 79), "when you do cross his humour" (*1 H 4,* III. i. 171).

125. *within the blank of*] as the target for; "As level as the cannon to his blank" (*Ham.,* IV. i. 42), "See better, Lear; and let me still remain The true blank of thine eye" (*Lr.,* i. i. 160). In the present passage the *within* implies, I suppose, as the strict meaning "within the limits of 'scatter' of his (grape) shot".

And (like the devil) from his very arm
Puff'd his own brother, and can he be angry?
Something of moment then: I will go meet him,   135
There's matter in 't indeed, if he be angry.   [*Exit.*

Des. I prithee do so: something sure of state,
Either from Venice, or some unhatch'd practice,
Made demonstrable here in Cyprus to him,
Hath puddled his clear spirit, and in such cases   140
Men's natures wrangle with inferior things,
Though great ones are the object.
'Tis even so; for let our finger ache,
And it indues our other healthful members
Even to that sense of pain; nay, we must think   145
Men are not gods;
Nor of them look for such observances
As fits the bridal: beshrew me much, Emilia,
I was (unhandsome warrior as I am)

---

134. can he be] *Qq;* is he *F.*   136. S.D.] *F; not in Qq.*   139. demonstrable
here] *Qq, F;* here demonstrable *Pope.*   142. the] *Qq;* their *F.*   142–6.] *as
Qq;* . . . so. / . . . endues / . . . sense / . . . Gods, /*F.*   145. that] *Qq;* a *F.*
147. observances] *Qq;* obseruancie *F.*

133.] There is an ellipse here, and one so awkward that at least one actor thought it necessary to fill it in with "yet he stood unmoved". Since Iago is speaking quite collectedly, and moreover working out a logical train of thought, it would be natural for him to complete the picture. The ellipse would be much easier if it were not for the repeated *can he be angry?* It should be noticed that F, though it produces an unmetrical line, and has been followed by very few edd., gives a strained, but possible, meaning, if we take "is" to be a vivid historic present, so that the phrase = "and was he (on that occasion) angry?" All that is then suppressed is the negative answer to the rhetorical question. Dr Brooks makes the ingenious conjecture that the preparer of the copy for F intended to get rid of the subjunctive in l. 136 and read *he is*, but that the alteration found its way into two lines earlier.

138. *unhatch'd practice* . . .] plot which

has hitherto come to nothing and only now been uncovered.

140. *puddled*] muddied (as in "the people muddied, Thick and unwholesome in their thoughts and whispers" (*Ham.*, IV. v. 81)), and cf. for the literal sense the "pails of puddled mire" thrown on Antipholus to quench his burning beard in *Err.*, v. i. 173.

142. *object*] real target, point at issue.

144–5. *indues . . . to*] *indue* can no doubt be taken as a variant spelling of "endue = endow", but *to* then becomes impossible and should be "with"; the word is here clearly used in some such sense as the literal meaning of "induces", i.e., "leads into", and so "imbues with" or "infects with".

147. *observances*] tender attentions; "It [love] is . . . All adoration, duty, and observance" (*AYL.*, v. ii. 101)

149. *unhandsome*] not living up to my character as; "handsome" has often

　　　　Arraigning his unkindness with my soul;   150
　　　　But now I find I had suborn'd the witness,
　　　　And he's indicted falsely.
Emil. Pray heaven it be state-matters, as you think,
　　　　And no conception, nor no jealous toy
　　　　Concerning you.   155
Des. Alas the day, I never gave him cause!
Emil. But jealous souls will not be answer'd so;
　　　　They are not ever jealous for the cause,
　　　　But jealous for they are jealous: 'tis a monster,
　　　　Begot upon itself, born on itself.   160
Des. Heaven keep that monster from Othello's mind!
Emil. Lady, amen.
Des. I will go seek him, Cassio, walk hereabout,
　　　　If I do find him fit, I'll move your suit,
　　　　And seek to effect it to my uttermost.   165
Cas. I humbly thank your ladyship.
　　　　　　　　　　　　[*Exeunt Desdemona and Emilia.*

　　　　　　　　　　Enter BIANCA.

Bian. Save you, friend Cassio!
Cas.　　　　　　　　　　What make you from home?
　　　　How is it with you, my most fair Bianca?
　　　　I' faith, sweet love, I was coming to your house.
Bian. And I was going to your lodging, Cassio;   170
　　　　What, keep a week away? seven days and nights?
　　　　Eight score eight hours, and lovers' absent hours,
　　　　More tedious than the dial, eight score times?
　　　　O weary reckoning!
Cas.　　　　　　　　　Pardon me, Bianca,
　　　　I have this while with leaden thoughts been press'd, 175

153–5.] *as Qq;* bee / ... Conception, / ... you. / *F* (Iealious).　　159. they are]
Qq; they're *F.*　　'tis] *Qq;* It is *F.*　　161. that] *Qq;* the *F.*　　166. S.D.] *Qq;*
Exit F.　　168. is it] *Qq;* is't *F.*　　169. I' faith] *Q1;* Indeed *F, Q2.*　　174. O]
F, Q2 (Oh); No *Q1.*　　175. leaden] *F, Q2;* laden *Q1.*

the sense of "proper", "fitting"; cf.
2 H 6, III. ii. 13 (Q version) where all is
"handsome" about the bed and the
corpse because it is according to
orders.

154. *conception*] supposition.
171.] "long time".
172. *Eight score eight*] Bianca does her
sum right—eight score plus eight, not
eight score times eight.

But I shall in a more convenient time
Strike off this score of absence: sweet Bianca,
> [*Giving her Desdemona's handkerchief.*

Take me this work out.
Bian.   O Cassio, whence came this?
This is some token from a newer friend;
To the felt absence, now I feel a cause,   180
Is 't come to this?
Cas.   Go to, woman,
Throw your vile guesses in the devil's teeth,
From whence you have them; you are jealous now
That this is from some mistress, some remembrance.
No, by my faith, Bianca.
Bian.   Why, whose is it?   185
Cas. I know not, sweet, I found it in my chamber;
I like the work well; ere it be demanded,
As like enough it will, I'ld have it copied;
Take it, and do 't, and leave me for this time.
Bian. Leave you, wherefore?   190
Cas. I do attend here on the general,
And think it no addition, nor my wish,

---

176. convenient] *Q1;* continuate *F, Q2.*   181. this?] *Q1;* this? Well, well *F,*
Q2 (well, well. *Q2*).   185. by my faith] *Q1;* in good troth *F, Q2.*   186.
sweet] *Qq;* neither *F.*   188. I'ld] *Qq;* I would *F.*

176. *convenient*] not just "when it suits me", but "fitting", i.e. "when I am in key for it"; "all convenient speed" (*Mer.V.*, III. iv. 56), "It were convenient you had such a devil" (*Tit.*, v. ii. 90), "more convenient is he for my hand Than for your lady's" (*Lr.*, IV. v. 31).

177. *Strike . . . absence*] pay your account rendered, so that the entry can be struck out; "score" is common for "reckoning"; "That thou didst love her, strikes some scores away From the great compt" (*All's W.*, v. iii. 56), "he parted well, and paid his score" (*Mac.*, v. vii. 81).

178. *Take . . . out*] copy, cf. l. 188 and IV. i. 148–53 below.

186. *in my chamber*] cf. III. iii. 326 above.

191. *attend . . . on*] wait for; more commonly in this sense without *on*, but cf. "Tarry I here, I but attend on death" (*Gent.*, III. i. 186).

192. *addition*] Usually in Shakespeare (apart from its simple meaning) the word means "title", and in particular "additional title" or nickname; "devils' additions, the names of fiends" (*Wiv.*, II. ii. 316), "How do you now, lieutenant?—The worser that you give me the addition Whose want even kills me" (IV. i. 104 below), "for thy vigour, Bull-bearing Milo his addition yield To sinewy Ajax" (*Troil.*, II. iii. 260), "from this time, For what he did before Corioli, call him, With all the applause and clamour of the host, Caius Marcius Coriolanus! Bear The addition nobly ever" (*Cor.*, I. ix. 62);

   To have him see me woman'd.

Bian.   Why, I pray you?

Cas. Not that I love you not.

Bian.   But that you do not love me:
   I pray you bring me on the way a little,   195
   And say, if I shall see you soon at night.

Cas. 'Tis but a little way that I can bring you,
   For I attend here, but I'll see you soon.

Bian. 'Tis very good, I must be circumstanc'd.   [*Exeunt.*

193-4. *Bian.* Why . . . not] *F, Q2; not in Q1.*   193. pray] *Qq;* ptay *F.*
199. S.D.] *Qq; Exeunt omnes F.*

indeed the only parallel to its meaning here, which seems to be "credit", is in Hamlet's "They clepe us drunkards, and with swinish phrase Soil our addition" (*Ham.*, I. iv. 19).

199. *be circumstanc'd*] yield to circumstances; not elsewhere in Shakespeare as verb.

ACT IV

SCENE I.—[*The same.*]

Enter IAGO *and* OTHELLO.

Iago. Will you think so?
Oth.   Think so, Iago?
Iago.   What,
    To kiss in private?
Oth.   An unauthoriz'd kiss.
Iago. Or to be naked with her friend abed,
    An hour, or more, not meaning any harm?
Oth. Naked abed, Iago, and not mean harm?   5
    It is hypocrisy against the devil:
    They that mean virtuously, and yet do so,
    The devil their virtue tempts, and they tempt heaven.
Iago. So they do nothing, 'tis a venial slip;
    But if I give my wife a handkerchief—   10

ACT IV

Scene 1

S.D.] *Qq; Enter Othello, and Iago F.*   5. abed] *Qq;* in bed *F.*   9. So they] *Qq;*
if they *F.*

6. *hypocrisy . . . devil*] "This means,
hypocrisy to cheat the devil. As common hypocrites cheat men by seeming
good, and yet living wickedly, these
men would cheat the devil, by giving
him flattering hopes, and at last
avoiding the crime which he thinks
them ready to commit" (Johnson).

8. *they tempt heaven*] I suppose this
means that they wilfully put themselves in a situation where the fall from
virtue is so easy that even heaven will
be hard put to it to save them; cf. "we
are devils to ourselves When we will
tempt the frailty of our powers"
(*Troil.*, IV. iv. 95).

10. *handkerchief*] I have never understood why Shakespeare makes Iago—
and that rather clumsily—recall
Othello to the handkerchief, which he
seems (l. 20) to have forgotten. The
handkerchief was earlier useful as a
piece of (potentially) ocular proof
which Othello was demanding. But it
is highly dangerous for Iago, since it
may at any moment provoke a challenge from Othello to Cassio, if they
meet, on a point of refutable detail, not
on general guilt. And Iago's courage,
though undoubted, is not the kind that
takes *needless* risks. And he has reduced
Othello to such a condition of unthink-

135

Oth. What then?

Iago. Why then 'tis hers, my lord, and being hers,
    She may, I think, bestow 't on any man.

Oth. She is protectress of her honour too,
    May she give that?   15

Iago. Her honour is an essence that's not seen,
    They have it very oft that have it not:
    But for the handkerchief—

Oth. By heaven, I would most gladly have forgot it:
    Thou said'st (O, it comes o'er my memory,   20
    As doth the raven o'er the infected house,
    Boding to all) he had my handkerchief.

Iago. Ay, what of that?

Oth.   That's not so good now.

Iago. What if I had said I had seen him do you wrong?
    Or heard him say—as knaves be such abroad,   25
    Who having, by their own importunate suit,
    Or voluntary dotage of some mistress,
    Convinced or supplied them, cannot choose
    But they must blab—

Oth.   Hath he said anything?

Iago. He hath, my lord, but be you well assur'd,   30
    No more than he'll unswear.

Oth.   What hath he said?

---

14. protectress] *Qq, F;* proprietor *Warburton.*   21. infected] *Qq;* infectious *F.*
27. Or] *F, Q2;* Or by the *Q1.*   28. Convinced] Conuinced *Q1 (Dev. and Chip.),*
F; Concured *Q1 (Capell);* Coniured *Q2.*

ing rage that the risk is now needless.

16. *essence*] entity.

17. *They have . . . not*] one of Iago's cryptic remarks, meaning, I take it, that many people are erroneously credited with the possession of this invisible essence.

21. *raven*] The raven was supposed to be not only a bird of ill-omen and the harbinger of death but also a carrier of infection; "like the sad presaging raven, that tolls The sick man's passport in her hollow beak, And in the shadow of the silent night Doth shake contagion from her sable wings" (Marlowe, *Jew of Malta,* II. i.

i), "I would croak like a raven; I would bode, I would bode" (*Troil.,* v. ii. 188), "As wicked dew as e'er my mother brush'd With raven's feather from unwholesome fen" (*Tp.,* I. ii. 321).

28. *Convinced or supplied*] overcome their reluctance (by importunate suit) or satisfied their desires (in their voluntary dotage); "his two chamberlains Will I with wine and wassail so convince" (*Mac.,* I. vii. 63), "this is the body That took away the match from Isabel And did supply thee at thy garden-house In her imagin'd person" (*Meas.,* v. i. 204).

Iago. Faith, that he did . . . I know not what he did.
Oth. But what?
Iago. Lie.
Oth.   With her?
Iago.   With her, on her, what you will.
Oth. Lie with her, lie on her?—We say lie on her, when   35
    they belie her,—lie with her, zounds, that's fulsome!
    Handkerchief—confessions—handkerchief! To con-
    fess, and be hanged for his labour. First, to be hanged,
    and then to confess; I tremble at it. Nature would
    not invest herself in such shadowing passion without   40
    some instruction. It is not words that shake me thus.
    Pish! Noses, ears and lips. Is 't possible?—Confess?
    —Handkerchief?—O devil!   [*He falls down.*
Iago. Work on,
    My medicine, work: thus credulous fools are caught,   45
    And many worthy and chaste dames, even thus

32. Faith] *Q1;* Why *F, Q2.*   33. But what?] *Q1;* What? What? *F;* What? *Q2.*   36. zounds] *Q1; not in F, Q2.*   37–43. To confess . . . devil] *F, Q2; not in Q1.*   41. that] *Q2;* that *F.*   43. S.D.] *Q1; Falls in a Traunce F; Falles in a trance Q2.*   44–8. Work on . . . Cassio?] *as in F; as prose Qq.*   45. medicine, work:] *Qq;* Medicine workes. *F.*

32.] the old technique of hesitancy.

34. *on her*] the last turn of the screw, and Othello breaks.

36. *fulsome*] usually surfeiting, nauseating (exactly Scots "stawsome"); "It is as fat and fulsome to mine ear As howling after music" (*Tw.N.,* v. i. 113), but cf. "the ewes, being rank, In end of autumn turned to the rams . . . And, in the doing of the deed of kind, He stuck them [the peeled wands] up before the fulsome ewes" (*Mer.V.,* I. iii. 81, where *fulsome* practically = the preceding *rank*).

37–43.] I am not clear that F's lines add much, but it may have been thought, and perhaps rightly, that Othello's raving passion needed for verisimilitude longer to develop before he "falls in a trance", and they may therefore be addition rather than cut.

40. *shadowing*] Hart says "overspreading and intensifying itself with gloom", but why "itself"? Does not Othello mean, so far as he means anything, that his mind is becoming darkened, and that that could not happen without some influence more potent than words. Of the other occurrences of the word as verb or participle in Shakespeare, in one it means "conceal", in one "shelter", and in one "darkened"; "thereby shall we shadow The numbers of our host" (*Mac.,* v. iv. 6), "Shadowing their right under your wings of war" (*John,* II. i. 14), "The shadow'd livery of the burnish'd sun" (*Mer. V.,* II. i. 2).

45. *work*] Judging by the standard of effectiveness no one, I imagine, would hesitate between *work* and F's "works"; but equally no one can say that F's reading is impossible, and Rowe, Pope, and Hanmer all retained it, though later edd. have mostly gone over to Qq.

All guiltless, meet reproach. What ho, my lord,
My lord, I say! Othello! . . .

Enter CASSIO.

How now, Cassio?

Cas. What's the matter?
Iago. My lord is fall'n into an epilepsy,   50
This is his second fit, he had one yesterday.
Cas. Rub him about the temples.
Iago.   No, forbear,
The lethargy must have his quiet course,
If not, he foams at mouth, and by and by
Breaks out to savage madness: look, he stirs: 55
Do you withdraw yourself a little while,
He will recover straight; when he is gone,
I would on great occasion speak with you.   [*Exit Cassio.*
How is it, general? have you not hurt your head?
Oth. Dost thou mock me?
Iago.   I mock you? no, by heaven.   60
Would you would bear your fortunes like a man!
Oth. A horned man's a monster, and a beast.
Iago. There's many a beast then in a populous city,
And many a civil monster.
Oth. Did he confess?
Iago.   Good sir, be a man,   65
Think every bearded fellow that's but yok'd

---

48. Cassio] *Qq; Cvssio F.*   52. No, forbear] *Qq; not in F.*   58. S.D.] *Rowe;*
after mock me? *Q2; not in Q1, F.*   60. you? no, by] *Qq* (no by); you not, by *F.*
61. fortunes] *Qq;* Fortune *F.*   65. confess] *Qq;* confesse it *F.*   Good] *F, Q2;*
God *Q1 (Capell).*

47. *reproach*] shame; almost always
in Shakespeare stronger than our
sense, e.g. "black scandal or foul-fac'd
reproach" (*R 3*, III. vii. 229).

51. *yesterday*] when? on the high
seas, or between retiring with Desdemona and being roused by the brawl?
Another touch of "long time".

53. *lethargy*] coma; "Peace is a very
apoplexy, lethargy; mulled, deaf,
sleepy, insensible" (*Cor.*, IV. v. 240).

54–5.] "long time".

56–8.] Iago is quick both to avoid

the danger of Othello confronting
Cassio when he comes to his senses,
and to secure Cassio's return when he
is ready for him.

64. *civil*] among the citizens; "civil
blood makes civil hands unclean"
(*Rom.*, Prol. 4).

66. *yok'd*] sc. in the marriage bond;
the usual, and possible, interpretation,
but I fancy that here, in view of the
following *draw*, the picture is not of
being yoked to the marriage partner,
but simply of being under a burden-

May draw with you; there's millions now alive
That nightly lies in those unproper beds
Which they dare swear peculiar: your case is better:
O, 'tis the spite of hell, the fiend's arch-mock,   70
To lip a wanton in a secure couch,
And to suppose her chaste. No, let me know,
And knowing what I am, I know what she shall be.
Oth. O, thou art wise, 'tis certain.
Iago.   Stand you awhile apart,
Confine yourself but in a patient list: 75
Whilst you were here erewhile, mad with your grief—
A passion most unsuiting such a man—
Cassio came hither; I shifted him away,
And laid good 'scuse upon your ecstasy,

68. lies] *Q1* (lyes); lye *F, Q2*.   71. couch,] *Q2;* Cowch; *F;* Coach, *Q1*.
76. erewhile, mad] *Q1;* o're-whelmed *F;* orewhelmed *Q2*.   77. unsuiting]
unsuting *Q1 (Dev.);* unfitting *Q1 (Capell), Q2;* resulting *F*.   79. 'scuse] *Qq*
(scuse); scuses *F*.

some restriction, as in "the yoke of
inauspicious stars" (*Rom.*, v. iii. 111)
and "groaning underneath this age's
yoke" (*Cæs.*, i. ii. 61); the bearded fellow's partner under the yoke is then
the next bearded fellow, whose sorrows
he shares.

68. *unproper*] not (solely) his own;
"proper" often means little more than
"own"—"these my proper hands"
(*Wint.*, ii. iii. 139), though sometimes
the exclusiveness is stressed, as in
"Thyself and thy belongings Are not
thine own so proper . . ." (*Meas.*, i. i.
29); and cf. i. iii. 69 above.

69. *peculiar*] See note on iii. iii. 80
above.

71. *secure*] free from care (sometimes
with the suggestion of foolishly so);
"Page is an ass, a secure ass: he will
trust his wife" (*Wiv.*, ii. ii. 318),
"Open the door, secure, fool-hardy
king" (*R 2*, v. iii. 43).

72–3. *No . . . shall be*] another of
Iago's cryptic remarks; I suppose he
implies "knowing my own temper I
know what her fate would be".

75. *patient list*] bounds defined by
patience; "you have restrained your-

self within the list of too cold an
adieu" (*All's W.*, ii. i. 52)—unless
possibly list here = "listening".

79. *ecstasy*] being beside oneself (the
original Greek meaning), the degree
of derangement varying from actual
madness to hysterical excitement; in
Ham., iii. iv. 105–44, the equation with
madness is explicit, since the Queen
first says "Alas! he's *mad*" and later
picks this up with "This bodiless creation *ecstasy* Is very cunning in", to
which Hamlet replies "*Ecstasy!* My
pulse, as yours, doth temperately keep
time, And makes as healthful music. It
is not *madness* That I have utter'd:
bring me to the test, And I the matter
will reword, which *madness* Would
gambol from", whereas in *Ado*, ii. iii.
156–69 the *ecstasy* which has over-
borne Beatrice so that she weeps, sobs,
and tears her hair is not much more
than what we should call "being in a
taking", while in *Mer.V.*, iii. ii. 111,
"O love! be moderate; allay thy ecstasy" Portia is experiencing no more
than a transport of delight as Bassanio
chooses the leaden casket. This is the
only sense in which Shakespeare uses

Bid him anon return, and here speak with me,   80
The which he promis'd: but encave yourself,
And mark the jeers, the gibes, and notable scorns,
That dwell in every region of his face;
For I will make him tell the tale anew,
Where, how, how oft, how long ago, and when,   85
He has, and is again to cope your wife:
I say, but mark his gesture; marry, patience,
Or I shall say you are all in all in spleen,
And nothing of a man.

Oth.   Dost thou hear, Iago?
I will be found most cunning in my patience;   90
But—dost thou hear?—most bloody.

Iago.   That's not amiss:
But yet keep time in all; will you withdraw?
                                    [*Othello withdraws.*
Now will I question Cassio of Bianca;

80. Bid] *Q1*; Bad *F*, *Q2*.   return] *F*; retire *Qq*.   81. but] *Qq* (But *Q2*); Do
but *F*.   82. jeers] Ieeres *Q1*; Fleeres *F*; geeres *Q2*.   86. has] *Qq*; hath *F*.
88. you are] *Qq*; y'are *F*.   92. S.D.] *Rowe.*

the word elsewhere, and I see no
reason—particularly if one accepts the
Q1 reading—for trying to find another, though it is true that Cotgrave
defines *Extase* as "extasie, or trance".
   82. *notable*] (not "outstanding" but
simply) observable.
   85–6.] "long time".
   86. *cope*] encounter, close with; "he
yesterday coped Hector in the battle"
(*Troil.*, I. ii. 34).
   88. *spleen*] Hart quotes an enlighten-
ing note by Gifford: "The spleen
seems to have been considered as the
source of any sudden or violent ebullition, whether of mirth or anger." This
explains the apparent contradictori-
ness of some passages in Shakespeare;
"my presence May well abate the over
merry spleen Which otherwise would
grow into extremes" (*Shr.*, Ind. i. 136),
"If you desire the spleen, and will
laugh yourselves into stitches, follow
me" (*Tw.N.*, III. ii. 75), "Out, you
mad-headed ape! A weasel hath not
such a deal of spleen As you are toss'd

with" (*1 H 4*, II. iii. 83, where Lady
Percy is commenting on neither mirth
nor anger, but on Hotspur's wild excitement at the prospect of action),
"I will fight Against my canker'd
country with the spleen Of all the
under fiends" (*Cor.*, IV. v. 96), "It is a
cause worthy my spleen and fury"
(*Tim.*, III. v. 115).
   92. *keep time*] maintain control; elsewhere in Shakespeare only in the
literal musical sense.
   93–155. Granville Barker has some
interesting observations. Here, he
says, "Othello is brought to the very
depth of indignity. Collapsed at Iago's
feet, there was still at least a touch of
the tragic in him, much of the pitiful.
But to recover from that only to turn
eavesdropper, to be craning his neck,
straining his ears, dodging his black
face back and forth like a figure in a
farce—was ever tragic hero treated
thus? [A touch of the Rymer manner
here]. . . Most actors of Othello, I
think, have shirked this scene and

A housewife that by selling her desires
Buys herself bread and clothes: it is a creature   95
That dotes on Cassio: as 'tis the strumpet's plague
To beguile many, and be beguil'd by one.

Enter CASSIO.

He, when he hears of her, cannot refrain
From the excess of laughter: here he comes:
As he shall smile, Othello shall go mad,   100
And his unbookish jealousy must conster
Poor Cassio's smiles, gestures, and light behaviour,
Quite in the wrong. How do you now, lieutenant?
Cas. The worser, that you give me the addition,
Whose want even kills me.   105
Iago. Ply Desdemona well, and you are sure on 't.
Now if this suit lay in Bianca's power,
How quickly should you speed!

95. clothes] *Qq* (cloathes); Cloath *F.*   97. S.D.] *Qq; after* comes, *l. 99, F.*
98. refrain] *Qq;* restraine *F.*   101. conster] *Qq;* conserue *F.*   102. behaviour]
Qq; behauiours *F.*   103. now] *Qq; not in F.*   107. power] *Qq;* dowre *F.*

Salvini . . . justified its omission on the
ground that it belittled a man of such
'haughty and violent temper', was not
in other words—we may fairly
gather—in accord with Salvini's own
dignity either. But that is, of course,
the very point of it. From the dignity
of the play's beginning Othello sinks to
this, to rise again to the tragic dignity
of its end. The dodging in and out of
hiding and the rest of the painfully
grotesque pantomime is, of course, the
most striking feature of the scene."

94. *housewife*] The word has not usually in Shakespeare the 'pejorative'
sense of "courtesan" or "hussy" except
as applied to Fortune, and in *2 H 4,*
III. ii. 344, "the over-scutched hus-
wives"; but there can be no doubt that
that is what Iago here means and that
it represents the fact. But there is also
little doubt that Bianca is also a housewife in the normal sense, a citizen of
Cyprus, with her own house, and not a
mere camp-follower.

her desires] can no doubt mean "her
desirability", but Iago may be being
more subtle and seeing in Bianca a
good example of "voluntary dotage".

101. *unbookish*] ill-educated, unpractised; Othello, when he starts to construe (*conster*) Cassio's behaviour, will,
like an ignorant schoolboy, make howl-
ers in his translation.

conster] F's "conserue", though an
easy error for a written *construe*, is
not at all an easy one for a printed
conster.

104. *addition*] See note on III. iv. 192
above.

107–8.] one of Iago's few pieces of
clumsiness; even if Bianca were in any
position to help—which she is not—
even she could not be more assiduous
in Cassio's suit than both Cassio and
Iago know that Desdemona has been.
But it serves for the transition to Bianca
that Iago needs. F's "dowre" is possible, but probably no more than a
turned letter.

Cas.   Alas, poor caitiff!

Oth. Look how he laughs already!

Iago. I never knew a woman love man so.   110

Cas. Alas, poor rogue, I think i' faith she loves me.

Oth. Now he denies it faintly, and laughs it out.

Iago. Do you hear, Cassio?

Oth.   Now he importunes him
    To tell it on; go to, well said, well said.

Iago. She gives it out that you shall marry her,   115
    Do you intend it?

Cas. Ha, ha, ha!

Oth. Do you triumph, Roman, do you triumph?

Cas. I marry her? what? a customer;
    I prithee, bear some charity to my wit,   120
    Do not think it so unwholesome. Ha, ha, ha!

Oth. So, so, so, so; laugh that wins.

Iago. Faith, the cry goes, you shall marry her.

Cas. Prithee say true.

Iago. I am a very villain else.   125

Oth. Ha' you scor'd me? Well.

109–55.] *All Othello's speeches marked "Aside" by Theobald and other edd.*   110. a
woman] *Qq;* woman *F.*   111. i' faith] *Q1;* indeed *F, Q2.*   114. on] *Qq;* o're
F.   well said] *Qq;* well said, well said *F.*   118. you . . . you] *Qq;* ye . . . you *F.*
Roman] *Qq, F* (Romaine *F*)*;* rogue *Warburton.*   119–21.] *Q2;* I marry her?
I prithee . . . wit, / . . . ha. / *Q1;* I marry. What? A customer; prythee beare /
some . . . it / So . . . ha. / *F.*   122. laugh] *Q1;* they laugh *F, Q2* (laugh, *F*).
123. Faith] *Q1;* Why *F, Q2.*   you shall] *Q1;* that you *F;* that you shall *Q2.*
126. Ha'] *Qq;* Haue *F.*   scor'd me? Well.] *F, Q2* (scoar'd)*;* stor'd me
well. *Q1.*

---

108. *caitiff*] here used in contemptuous pity, "poor wretch"; usually
with less pity and more contempt.

112. *faintly*] not really meaning it;
"He prays but faintly and would be
denied" (*R 2*, v. iii. 103).

114. *well said*] See note on II. i. 167
above.

118. *Roman*] I have no explanation
to offer for this word. Elsewhere in
Shakespeare it is used either in a
neutral (historical), or in a com-
plimentary, sense, like Horatio's
"antique Roman"; and even Macbeth's "like a Roman fool" is ascribing
folly not to Romans in general, but to a

particular Roman practice. Is it used
simply from association with *triumph*?

119. *customer*] courtesan; "I think
thee now some common customer"
(*All's W.*, v. iii. 291, the King to Diana
after the cross-examination about the
ring). Hart well compares Rowlands,
Letting of Humour's Blood, etc., "a punk,
or else one of the dealing trade".

120. *wit*] judgement; see note on II.
i. 129 above.

122. *laugh that wins*] Cf. Whetstone,
2 Promos and Cassandra, "let them laugh
that winneth in the end".

126. *scor'd me*] This can mean simply
"wounded" as in "score their backs"

Cas. This is the monkey's own giving out; she is persuaded
   I will marry her, out of her own love and flattery, not
   out of my promise.

Oth. Iago beckons me, now he begins the story.   130

Cas. She was here even now, she haunts me in every place.
   I was t' other day talking on the sea-bank, with certain Venetians, and thither comes this bauble; by
   this hand, she falls thus about my neck:—

Oth. Crying "O dear Cassio!" as it were: his gesture   135
   imports it.

Cas. So hangs, and lolls, and weeps upon me; so hales,
   and pulls me, ha, ha, ha!

Oth. Now he tells how she pluck'd him to my chamber.
   I see that nose of yours, but not that dog I shall   140
   throw 't to.

Cas. Well, I must leave her company.

Enter BIANCA.

130. beckons] *Qq;* becomes *F;* becons *F2.*   132. t'other] *Qq* (tother) ; the
other *F.*   133. this] *Qq;* the *F.*   133–4. by this hand, she falls] *Q1* (fals) ; and
falls me *F;* fals me *Q2.*   137. hales] *Qq;* shakes *F.*   140. I see] *Qq;* oh, I
see *F.*   142. S.D.] *Qq; after* comes, *l. 143, F.*

(*Ant.,* IV. vii. 12) but one feels that it
should mean "scored off me" for
which no Elizabethan parallel is to be
found in *O.E.D.*

128. *flattery*] in the sense of "she
flatters herself that"; the noun is not
elsewhere used by Shakespeare in this
sense, except perhaps in *Sonn.,* xlii. 14,
but for the verb cf. "Unless I flatter
with myself too much" (*Gent.,* IV. iv.
195), "joy . . . flatters her it is Adonis'
voice" (*Ven.,* 978).

130. *beckons*] makes a sign to (not
"summons").

132. *t'other day*] another indication of
"long time" unless we assume the very
awkward interval (see Introduction,
p. lxix) between Acts III and IV.

sea-bank] sea-shore; "Stood Dido
with a willow in her hand Upon the
wild sea-banks" (*Mer.V.,* v. i. 10) but
I think that in the present passage, and
perhaps in both, there is a suggestion

of something raised above sea-level,
dunes, or even an esplanade; cf.
"brow of the sea" (II. i. 53 above).

133. *bauble*] bit of frippery; "it is a
paltry cap, A custard-coffin, a bauble,
a silken pie" (*Shr.,* IV. iii. 81), specifically the jester's stick with its ass-
capped head.

139.] "long time".

140–1. *nose . . . throw't to*] Slitting or
cutting off the nose was a recognized
form of punishment or revenge; but I
do not see the point of Othello's not
seeing the dog. Perhaps Othello's
rising fury is already beyond logical
thinking. Dr Brooks comments, "Othello does not see the dog because the
dog is not here yet; nor is the moment
for cutting off Cassio's nose. When Othello sees both the nose and the dog, the
vengeance will no longer be merely foreseen. Othello will be in the
act of taking it. How ferociously

Iago. Before me! look where she comes.

Cas. 'Tis such another fitchew; marry, a perfum'd one.
What do you mean by this haunting of me?   145

Bian. Let the devil and his dam haunt you, what did you
mean by that same handkerchief you gave me even
now? I was a fine fool to take it; I must take out the
whole work, a likely piece of work, that you should
find it in your chamber, and not know who left it   150
there! This is some minx's token, and I must take out
the work; there, give it the hobby-horse, whereso-
ever you had it, I'll take out no work on 't.

Cas. How now, my sweet Bianca, how now, how now?

Oth. By heaven, that should be my handkerchief!   155

Bian. An you'll come to supper to-night, you may, an
you will not, come when you are next prepar'd for.

[*Exit.*

Iago. After her, after her.

Cas. Faith, I must, she'll rail i' the street else.

Iago. Will you sup there?   160

Cas. Faith, I intend so.

---

143. Iago.] *Q1, F; not in Q2.*   144. Cas.] *F; not in Qq.*   fitchew] *F, Q2* (Fitchew); *ficho Q1.*   one.] one, *Q1*; one: *Q2*; one? *F.*   149. whole work,] *Q1*; worke, *Q2*; worke? *F.*   150. not know] *Qq*; know not *F.*   152. it the] *Qq*; it your *F.*   156. An . . . an] *Qq*; If . . . if *F.*   159. Faith] *Q1*; *not in F, Q2.* i'the street] *Qq*; in the streets *F.*   160. Will . . . there?] *Q1, F*; You sup there. *Q2.*   161. Faith] *Q1*; Yes *F, Q2.*

---

vivid this makes his imagination of the vengeance he foresees himself taking!"

143. *Before me!*] presumably a comfit-maker's euphemism for " 'Fore God!"; cf. *Tw.N.*, II. iii. 197, and *Cor.*, I. i. 126.

144. *fitchew*] polecat, noted for strong smell and lechery; "The fitchew nor the soiled horse goes to 't With a more riotous appetite (*Lr.*, IV. vi. 125). *such another* means, I suppose, "like all the rest of them". The imagined (or real) odour of polecat is overlaid by Bianca's strong perfume.

148–53. *take out*] See note on III. iii. 300 above.

151. *minx*] both here, and in Othello's "Damn her, lewd minx",

more strongly abusive than in our use; the only other occurrence in Shakespeare, where Malvolio addresses Maria as "minx" (*Tw.N.*, III. iv. 135), is indecisive.

152. *hobby-horse*] a loose woman (? because anyone can "mount" her); "My wife's a hobby-horse; deserves a name As rank as any flax-wench that puts to Before her troth-plight" (*Wint.*, I. ii. 276). Qq's *the* is at least as effective as F's *your*; Bianca means "the minx I'm talking about". (Perhaps confusion of y^e and y^r.)

157. Exit] Bianca's exit is a piece of pure luck for Iago which he immediately uses to get rid of Cassio.

160.] Cf. Macbeth's questions to Banquo before he goes riding.

Iago. Well, I may chance to see you, for I would very fain
    speak with you.
Cas. Prithee come, will you?
Iago. Go to, say no more.   [*Exit Cassio.* 165
Oth. [*Advancing*] How shall I murder him, Iago?
Iago. Did you perceive, how he laughed at his vice?
Oth. O Iago!
Iago. And did you see the handkerchief?
Oth. Was that mine?   170
Iago. Yours, by this hand: and to see how he prizes the
    foolish woman your wife! she gave it him, and he
    hath given it his whore.
Oth. I would have him nine years a-killing; a fine woman,
    a fair woman, a sweet woman!   175
Iago. Nay, you must forget.
Oth. And let her rot, and perish, and be damned to-night,
    for she shall not live; no, my heart is turn'd to stone;
    I strike it, and it hurts my hand: O, the world has not
    a sweeter creature, she might lie by an emperor's   180
    side, and command him tasks.
Iago. Nay, that's not your way.
Oth. Hang her, I do but say what she is: so delicate with
    her needle, an admirable musician, O, she will sing
    the savageness out of a bear; of so high and plenteous 185
    wit and invention!
Iago. She's the worse for all this.
Oth. A thousand thousand times: and then of so gentle a
    condition!

---

165. S.D.] *Qq; not in F.*   166. *Advancing*] *Collier.*   171–3. *Iago.* Yours . . .
whore] *F; not in Qq (but Iag. as catch-word after l. 170 in Q1).*   174. *Oth.*] *Q1, F;
not in Q2.*   176. forget] *Q1;* forget that *F, Q2.*   177. And] *Qq;* I, *F.*
178. stone] *Q1, F;* a stone *Q2.*   179. has] *Qq;* hath *F.*   183. but] *Q1, F;* not
Q2.   188. A thousand] *Qq;* Oh, a thousand, a *F.*

171. *prizes*] rates; "these movers
that do prize their hours At a crack'd
drachma" (*Cor.,* I. v. 4).
    174. *him*] This gives some support to
the view that at III. iii. 449 above
Othello is talking about Cassio.
    180–1.] Cf. "to stand by Caesar
And give direction" (II. iii. 115
above); this parallel perhaps suggests

a different interpretation of that passage.
    185–6. *of so . . . invention*] a side of
Desdemona of which we do not see
much in the play.
    188–9. *gentle a condition*] "so much
the high-born lady"; "mean and
gentle all" (*H 5,* IV Prol. 45), "Most
gentle and most valiant Hector"

Iago. Ay, too gentle.   190

Oth. Ay, that's certain, but yet the pity of it, Iago:
O Iago, the pity of it, Iago!

Iago. If you be so fond over her iniquity, give her patent
to offend, for if it touches not you, it comes near
nobody.   195

Oth. I will chop her into messes... Cuckold me!

Iago. O, 'tis foul in her.

Oth. With mine officer!

Iago. That's fouler.

Oth. Get me some poison, Iago, this night; I'll not expos- 200
tulate with her, lest her body and beauty unprovide
my mind again, this night, Iago.

Iago. Do it not with poison, strangle her in her bed, even
the bed she hath contaminated.

Oth. Good, good, the justice of it pleases, very good.   205

Iago. And for Cassio, let me be his undertaker: you shall
hear more by midnight.

Oth. Excellent good. [*A trumpet within.*] What trumpet is
that same?

Enter LODOVICO, DESDEMONA, *and Attendants.*

191. Ay,] *Q1* (I); Nay *F, Q2.*   191–2. Iago: O Iago, the pity of it, Iago] *F;*
Iago, the pitty *Q1;* Iago, oh the pitty *Q2.*   193. be] *Qq;* are *F.*   194.
touches] *Qq;* touch *F.*   200. night; I'll] night. Ile *F;* night Ile *Qq* (I'le *Q1*).
208 S.D.] *A Trumpet Qq* (*after* midnight, *l. 207*); *not in F.*   209. S.D.] *Qq, F*
(*after l. 207*).

(*Troil.*, IV. v. 226). Iago takes *gentle* in
the sense of "yielding".

191.] F may represent the original
reading; or perhaps Burbage found
that he needed more time, and so more
words, to display Othello's torment.

193. *patent*] carte blanche; "by his
[my dead husband's] authority he
remains here, which he thinks is a
patent for his sauciness" (*All's W.*, IV.
v. 69).

196. *messes*] dishes of food.

200–1. *expostulate*] argue at length;
"The time now serves not to expostulate" (*Gent.*, III. i. 252), "stay not to
expostulate; make speed" (*3 H 6*, II. v.
135), "to expostulate What majesty
should be..." (*Ham.*, II. ii. 86).

201. *unprovide*] undo my readiness,
slacken my resolution which is now
'bent up'; for "provide" in the sense of
make ready, cf. "You, niece, provide
yourself [sc. for exile]" (*AYL.*, I. iii.
90), "Prepare you . . . We will ourselves provide" (*Ham.*, III. iii. 2, 7).

203.] The purchase of poison might
be dangerous for Iago.

206. *undertaker*] to "undertake" is
just to "take on", but here, and perhaps elsewhere, there may be a pun on
our sense of "undertaker"; "It is not
fit your lordship should undertake
every companion that you give offence
to" (*Cym.*, II. i. 29), "give my charge up
to Sir Nicholas Vaux, Who under-
takes you to your end" (*H 8*, II. i. 96).

Iago. Something from Venice, sure; 'tis Lodovico,   210
    Come from the duke, and see, your wife is with him.
Lod. God save the worthy general!
Oth.   With all my heart, sir.
Lod. The duke and senators of Venice greet you.
                                    [*Gives him a letter.*
Oth. I kiss the instrument of their pleasures.
                                [*Opens the letter, and reads.*
Des. And what's the news, good cousin Lodovico?   215
Iago. I am very glad to see you, signior: . . .
    Welcome to Cyprus.
Lod. I thank you; how does Lieutenant Cassio?
Iago. Lives, sir.
Des. Cousin, there's fall'n between him and my lord   220
    An unkind breach, but you shall make all well.
Oth. Are you sure of that?
Des. My lord?
Oth. [*Reads*]. "This fail you not to do, as you will..."
Lod. He did not call, he's busy in the paper: 225
    Is there division between thy lord and Cassio?
Des. A most unhappy one; I would do much
    To atone them, for the love I bear to Cassio.
Oth. Fire and brimstone!
Des.   My lord?
Oth.   Are you wise?
Des. What, is he angry?
Lod.   May be the letter mov'd him;   230
    For, as I think, they do command him home,
    Deputing Cassio in his government.
Des. By my troth, I am glad on 't.

210–11. Something . . . him] *Qq* (sure, *Q1*); I warrant something from
Venice, / 'Tis Lodovico, this, comes from the Duke. / See, your wife's with
him *F*.   212. God save the] *Q1;* Save you *F, Q2*.   213. and] *Qq;* and
the *F*.   S.D.] *Rowe.*   214. S.D.] *Capell (subst.); not in Qq, F*.   223, 233.
lord?] *F* (Lord); Lord. *Qq*.   224. S.D.] *Theobald.*   226. between thy] *Q1;*
'twixt my *F, Q2*.   228. To atone] *Qq* (attone); T'attone *F*.   233. By my
troth] *Q1,* Trust me *F, Q2*.

228. *atone*] reconcile, make at one;
"I was glad I did atone my country-
man and you" (*Cym.,* I. iv. 44).
231–2. Lodovico seems to accept the
possibility that his recall to Venice

may anger Othello. But why should
it? He is only being recalled from a
post which has now, with the destruction of the Turkish fleet, become a
sinecure.

Oth.   Indeed!
Des.   My lord?
Oth. I am glad to see you mad.
Des.   How, sweet Othello?
Oth. Devil!   [*Striking her.* 235
Des. I have not deserv'd this.
Lod. My lord, this would not be believ'd in Venice,
          Though I should swear I saw 't: 'tis very much,
          Make her amends, she weeps.
Oth.   O devil, devil!
          If that the earth could teem with women's tears,   240
          Each drop she falls would prove a crocodile:
          Out of my sight!

234. How] *Qq;* Why *F.*   235. S.D.] *Theobald.*   240. women's] *Qq*
(womens); womans *F.*

234. *glad to see you mad*] This is an
obscure remark, and suspicious because it comes at a point where clarity
is, for dramatic effect, essential. There
may have been some corruption, but
Cowden Clarke's transposition of *glad*
and *mad*, though it has some plausi-
bility in view of (possibly) the same
type of error at II. iii. 158 and 207
above is not very helpful, and before
one attempts to tinker it is important
to notice the carefully repetitive structure of the whole passage. While, from
l. 215, Desdemona is talking to Lodovico, Othello is occupied with the
letter, but has an ear for the conversation, and makes his ironic or savage
comments half aside, so that Desdemona three times, with "My lord?",
shows her puzzlement. To her first
question he makes no reply, to her
other two he does, and therefore *I am
glad . . .* ought to be in some way
parallel to *Are you wise?* And I think
that if we interpret *Are you wise?* as
meaning "are you in your right wits?"
(i.e. thus openly to speak of love for
Cassio) we can wrest some meaning
out of *I am glad . . .*, namely "I am glad
to see that you have so manifestly
taken leave of your senses, and betrayed yourself publicly." I do not pretend

that this is satisfactory, but I have no
emendation to suggest.

235. S.D.] Theobald's insertion is
more than justified by l. 268 below.

240–1. *earth . . . crocodile*] I think that
teem with = "bring forth", as in *Tim.*,
IV. iii. 191, where Timon, addressing
the earth, says "Teem with new monsters", and, if that is so, then *she* will be
the earth, and *falls* also mean "bring
forth", as in *Mer.V.*,I. iii. 88, where the
fulsome ewes "did in eaning time Fall
parti-colour'd lambs". But Onions
takes *teem with* as a nonce-use for "conceive by", when *she* is Desdemona, and
falls the common, and less specific,
"lets fall". This perhaps gives a more
coherent picture, and has the merit
that it gives more force to *prove* =
"turn into".

Crocodile's tears were (and are)
proverbial for "false tears", usually in
early accounts wept by the crocodile
over its victim; but Hart well adduces
a passage from Hakluyt (Sparke's nar-
rative of Hawkins' second voyage)
where the crocodile's tears are a decoy
to allure the victim, and so are applied
particularly to women's tears; cf.
"the mournful crocodile With sorrow
snares relenting passengers" (*2 H 6*,
III. i. 226).

Des.   I will not stay to offend you.   [*Going.*
Lod. Truly, an obedient lady:
       I do beseech your lordship, call her back.
Oth. Mistress!   245
Des. My lord?
Oth. What would you with her, sir?
Lod.   Who, I, my lord?
Oth. Ay, you did wish that I would make her turn:
       Sir, she can turn, and turn, and yet go on,
       And turn again, and she can weep, sir, weep;   250
       And she's obedient, as you say, obedient;
       Very obedient. Proceed you in your tears.
       Concerning this, sir,—O well-painted passion!—
       I am commanded here: . . . get you away,
       I'll send for you anon. . . Sir, I obey the mandate,   255
       And will return to Venice: . . . Hence, avaunt!
                                        [*Exit Desdemona.*
       Cassio shall have my place; and, sir, to-night,
       I do entreat that we may sup together,
       You are welcome, sir, to Cyprus. . . Goats and monkeys!
                                                        [*Exit.*

Lod. Is this the noble Moor, whom our full senate   260
       Call all in all sufficient? This the noble nature,
       Whom passion could not shake? whose solid virtue
       The shot of accident, nor dart of chance,
       Could neither graze, nor pierce?
Iago.   He is much chang'd.
Lod. Are his wits safe? is he not light of brain?   265
Iago. He's that he is; I may not breathe my censure,

---

242. S.D.] *Rowe.*   243. an] *Qq; not in F.*   254. here: . . .] *Q1;* home: *F;*
home: . . . *Q2.*   256. S.D.] *Rowe.*   261. This the noble nature] *Qq;* Is this
the Nature *F.*   266-7. is; . . . if, as] is, . . . censure, . . . be, if as *Q1;* is: . . .
censure. . . . be: if what *F;* is, . . . censure, . . . be if what *Q2*

257.] With Desdemona's exit
Othello recovers himself, and for a
moment becomes the servant of the
state and the courteous host, though
the control is brief, and breaks again
on his own exit.

261. *noble nature*] The repeated
noble is not, I think, impossible, but it

looks as though F objected to it as both
repetitive and unmetrical. But why
did F insert a quite needless "Is",
leaving the line still hypermetrical,
when the obvious cure was simply the
deletion of *noble*?

266. *censure*] See note on II. iii. 184
above.

What he might be; if, as he might, he is not,
I would to heaven he were!

Lod.   What, strike his wife?

Iago. Faith, that was not so well; yet would I knew
That stroke would prove the worst!

Lod.   Is it his use?   270
Or did the letters work upon his blood,
And new create this fault?

Iago.   Alas, alas!
It is not honesty in me to speak
What I have seen and known; you shall observe him,
And his own courses will denote him so,   275
That I may save my speech: do but go after,
And mark how he continues.

Lod. I am sorry that I am deceiv'd in him.   [*Exeunt*

SCENE II.—[*A Room in the Castle.*]

Enter OTHELLO *and* EMILIA.

Oth. You have seen nothing, then?
Emil. Nor ever heard, nor ever did suspect.
Oth. Yes, and you have seen Cassio and she together.
Emil. But then I saw no harm, and then I heard
Each syllable that breath made up between 'em.   5
Oth. What, did they never whisper?
Emil.   Never, my lord.
Oth. Nor send you out o' the way?
Emil. Never.

272. this] *Qq;* his *F.*   274. him] *Q1, F; not in Q2.*   275. denote] *Qq:* deonte
F.   276. after] *Q1, F;* after him *Q2.*

Scene II

3. Yes, and] *Qq;* Yes, *F.*   she] *Qq, F;* her *Pope.*   5. 'em] *Qq;* them *F.*

267–8.] perhaps the most cryptic of
all Iago's similar remarks.

270. *use*] custom; "his use was to put
a ducat in her clack-dish" (*Meas.*,
III. ii. 138).

274. *What . . . known*] "long time".

275. *denote*] reveal.

Scene II

3. *she*] The "ungrammatical" nominative for accusative is not uncommon in Shakespeare.

Oth. To fetch her fan, her mask, her gloves, nor nothing?
Emil. Never, my lord. 10
Oth. That's strange.
Emil. I durst, my lord, to wager she is honest,
  Lay down my soul at stake: if you think other,
  Remove your thought, it doth abuse your bosom;
  If any wretch ha' put this in your head, 15
  Let heaven requite it with the serpent's curse,
  For if she be not honest, chaste, and true,
  There's no man happy, the purest of her sex
  Is foul as slander.
Oth.   Bid her come hither, go. [*Exit Emilia.*
  She says enough, yet she's a simple bawd 20
  That cannot say as much: this is a subtle whore,
  A closet, lock and key, of villainous secrets,
  And yet she'll kneel and pray, I ha' seen her do 't.

Enter DESDEMONA *and* EMILIA.

Des. My lord, what is your will?
Oth.   Pray, chuck, come hither.
Des. What is your pleasure?
Oth.   Let me see your eyes, ... 25
  Look in my face.
Des.   What horrible fancy 's this?
Oth. [*To Emilia*] Some of your function, mistress,

9. her mask, her gloves] *Qq;* her Gloves, her Mask *F.* 15. ha'] *Qq;* haue *F.*
16. heaven] *F, Q2* (Heauen *F*); heauens *Q1.* requite] *Q1;* requit *F;* require
Q2. 18. her sex] *Q1* (Sex); their wiues *F, Q2.* 23. ha'] *Qq;* haue *F.*
24. Pray] *Qq;* Pray you *F.*

16. *serpent's curse*] I suppose the implication is that the crime is worthy of Satan himself; see Genesis, iii. 14.
18. *her sex*] I do not understand why A. Walker thinks that this "loses the point"; on the contrary, the more general statement is the more emphatic—"even the purest *maiden* is ..."
20. *simple*] naïve, uninventive; "What simple thief brags of his own attaint?" (*Err.*, III. ii. 16).
22. *closet*] elsewhere in Shakespeare almost always of a room, though here

it seems to mean a cupboard or safe (as in modern American); "Get me a taper in my study, Lucius... The taper burneth in your closet, sir" (*Cæs.*, II. i. 7, 35), "Nurse, will you go with me into my closet?" (*Rom.*, IV. ii. 34), "She desires to speak with you in her closet" (*Ham.*, III. ii. 350); but see *Mac.*, v. i. 5, "I have seen her rise from her bed, ... unlock her closet, take forth paper ..."
24. *chuck*] See note on III. iv. 45 above.

> Leave procreants alone, and shut the door,
> Cough, or cry hem, if anybody come;
> Your mystery, your mystery: nay, dispatch.   30
>
> [*Exit Emilia.*

Des. Upon my knees, what does your speech import?
     I understand a fury in your words,
     But not the words.
Oth. Why, what art thou?
Des. Your wife, my lord, your true and loyal wife.   35
Oth. Come, swear it, damn thyself,
     Lest, being like one of heaven, the devils themselves
     Should fear to seize thee, therefore be double-damn'd,
     Swear thou art honest.
Des.   Heaven doth truly know it.
Oth. Heaven truly knows, that thou art false as hell.   40
Des. To whom, my lord? with whom? how am I false?
Oth. O Desdemona, away! away! away!
Des. Alas the heavy day, why do you weep?
     Am I the occasion of those tears, my lord?
     If haply you my father do suspect   45
     An instrument of this your calling back,
     Lay not your blame on me; if you have lost him,
     Why, I have lost him too.
Oth.   Had it pleas'd heaven
     To try me with affliction, had he rain'd

---

30. nay] *Qq;* May *F.*   31. knees] *Qq;* knee *F.*   does] *Qq;* doth *F.*   33.
But . . . words] *Qq; not in F.*   42. O Desdemona] *Qq;* Ah Desdemon *F.*
44. occasion] *Qq;* motiue *F.*   those] *Qq;* these *F.*   47, 48. lost . . . lost] *F,*
Q2; left . . . left *Q1.*   48. Why] *Qq; not in F.*   49. he] *Qq;* they *F.*   rain'd]
F, Q2; ram'd *Q1.*

28. *procreants*] would-be copulators.
29. *cry hem*] several times in Shake-speare for "clearing the throat"; "these burrs are in my heart—Hem them away" (*AYL.*, I. iii. 17), "Now play me Nestor; hem, and stroke thy beard, As he being dress'd to some oration" (*Troil.*, I. iii. 165).
30. *mystery*] trade, métier; "A bawd, sir? Fie upon him! He will discredit our mystery.—Do you call your occu-pation a mystery?—Ay, sir; a mys-tery" (*Meas.* IV. ii. 29, 37, Abhorson's

"mystery" being hangmanship), "In-struction, manners, mysteries and trades" (*Tim.*, IV. i. 18).
47. *lost*] One wonders at first in what sense Othello can be said to have "lost" Brabantio? Desdemona is thinking back to the days when her father "loved" Othello and "oft invited him", and the sense is that in which one "loses" a friend.
49. *try me with affliction*] The mention of *sores* suggests that there is here a reminiscence of the afflictions of Job.

All kinds of sores and shames on my bare head,　　　50
Steep'd me in poverty, to the very lips,
Given to captivity me and my hopes,
I should have found in some part of my soul
A drop of patience; but, alas, to make me
A fixed figure, for the time of scorn　　　　　　55
To point his slow unmoving fingers at . . . oh, oh.
Yet could I bear that too, well, very well:
But there, where I have garner'd up my heart,
Where either I must live, or bear no life,
The fountain, from the which my current runs,　　　60
Or else dries up, to be discarded thence,
Or keep it as a cistern, for foul toads
To knot and gender in! Turn thy complexion there;

50. kinds] *Qq;* kind *F.*　　52. hopes] *Qq;* utmost hopes *F.*　　53. part] *Qq;* place *F.*　　55. A fixed] *Qq;* The fixed *F.*　　56. slow unmoving] *Qq;* slow, and mouing *F.*　　fingers] *Q1;* finger *F, Q2.*　　oh, oh] *Qq; not in F.*　　63. complexion] *Qq;* complexion *F.*

55–6. *A fixed . . . fingers at*] This seems to me the clearest possible example of F simplifying, and so weakening, from a pedestrian dislike of illogicality. No doubt *slow unmoving* is a contradiction; but is it any more than a compression of the image in *Sonn.*, civ. 9, "yet doth beauty, like a dial-hand, Steal from his figure, and no pace perceiv'd". The hand of the clock points at a figure on the dial and its motion is so slow that it seems motionless. "Slow and moving" is surely un-Shakespeareanly pedestrian—if it is slow it must be moving; in other instances where he uses a first adjective plus "and" as equivalent to an adverb, the second adjective is a vivid one.

60. *fountain*] spring; we keep the sense in "fountain-head". "The spring, the head, the fountain of your blood is stopp'd" (*Mac.*, II. iii. 105).

62. *cistern*] Cf. "So half my Egypt were submerg'd and made A cistern for scal'd snakes" (*Ant.*, II. v. 94).

63. *knot . . . gender*] Neither occurs elsewhere in Shakespeare, but we have "as I hate the engendering of toads" (*Troil.*, II. iii. 170).

63–5. *Turn . . . hell*] This is a most tiresome crux, coming at a moment when any clog on apprehension is particularly vexatious. The reading of the text is that of Q1, except for semicolon for comma after *there* and F's inserted comma after *Patience.* F's *thou* for *thy* may well be right, but since I fancy that the trouble goes deeper than to be curable by the alteration of one word I have let Q1 stand. (*a*) *Turn thy complexion*, ought, on the evidence of other uses of *complexion* in Shakespeare, to mean "change colour", and not either "change expression" or "turn your head", but it could, I suppose, mean something near the latter, "turn your fair-skinned beauty this way"; (*b*) I feel that *Patience* is probably an exhortation to Desdemona, and not an address to a personified virtue, and that the *cherubin* is almost certainly Desdemona, and not Patience; (*c*) *I* is a common printing for "Ay", but the absence of any comma after it, or even after *here*, suggests that it is the pronoun; (*d*) the real trouble is the word *Patience*, since even if it is addressed to Desdemona why

> Patience, thy young and rose-lipp'd cherubin,
> I here look grim as hell!   65

Des. I hope my noble lord esteems me honest.

Oth. O, ay, as summer's flies, are in the shambles,
> That quicken even with blowing:
> O thou black weed, why art so lovely fair?
> Thou smell'st so sweet, that the sense aches at thee,   70
> Would thou hadst ne'er been born!

Des. Alas, what ignorant sin have I committed?

Oth. Was this fair paper, this most goodly book,
> Made to write "whore" on? . . . What, committed?
> Committed! O thou public commoner!   75
> I should make very forges of my cheeks,
> That would to cinders burn up modesty,
> Did I but speak thy deeds. What committed!
> Heaven stops the nose at it, and the moon winks,
> The bawdy wind, that kisses all it meets,   80

---

64. Patience, thy] Patience thy *Qq*; Patience, thou *F*.   67. summer's] *Qq*
(summers); Sommer *F*.   flies, are] *Q1*; Flyes are *F*; flies are *Q2*.   68–70.
blowing: . . . thee] *Qq*; blowing. Oh thou weed: / Who art . . . faire, and . . .
sweete, / That . . . thee / *F*.   71. ne'er] *Qq* (ne're); neuer *F*.   74. on] *Q1*;
upon *F, Q2*.   75–8. Committed! . . . committed!] *F, Q2; not in Q1*.

---

should Othello demand her patience? I have sometimes wondered whether at *Turn* Othello puts his hand under her chin—as I think he clearly does at l. 25—and turns her head towards a mirror, in which both see their faces and he comments on the contrast. But that, though it would serve well enough as a piece of business on a modern set, seems improbable on the Elizabethan stage. It would account for the rather awkward *there*, and would make *Patience* a parenthetic ejaculation as she shrinks from his hand.

69. *black weed*] F's omission of *black* enables it to complete an incomplete line, but leaves it with two incomplete lines to end the speech with. A. Walker describes *black* as "ruinous exaggeration" and finds the use of the word by the black Othello "singularly *mal à propos*". Opinions will differ. (See p. 220.)

72–82. . . . *committed*] Othello's furi-

ous iteration of Desdemona's unhappily chosen word depends on its Elizabethan use absolutely as = "commit adultery"; "commit not with man's sworn spouse" (*Lr.*, III. iv. 80).

75. *commoner*] whore; "a commoner o' the camp" (*All's W.*, v. iii. 196), and cf. "This Doll Tearsheet should be some road.—I warrant you, as common as the way between St Albans and London" (*2 H 4*, II. ii. 182).

79. *winks*] shuts the eyes (not, as in our use, only momentarily); "good boy, wink at me, and say thou sawest me not" (*Tim.*, III. i. 48), "winking Mary-buds begin To ope their golden eyes" (*Cym.*, II. iii. 26, where it means "with eyes tight shut"), "her andirons . . . were two winking Cupids Of silver" (*Cym.*, II. iv. 88, where the blind Love-gods' eyes were permanently shut (not mischievously winking, as the modern reader is apt to suppose).

Is hush'd within the hollow mine of earth,
And will not hear 't: ... what committed,—
Impudent strumpet!
Des.   By heaven, you do me wrong.
Oth. Are not you a strumpet?
Des.   No, as I am a Christian:
If to preserve this vessel for my lord   85
From any hated foul unlawful touch,
Be not to be a strumpet, I am none.
Oth. What, not a whore?
Des.   No, as I shall be sav'd.

Enter EMILIA.

Oth. Is 't possible?
Des. O heaven, forgiveness.
Oth.   I cry you mercy,   90
I took you for that cunning whore of Venice,
That married with Othello: you, mistress,
That have the office opposite to Saint Peter,
And keeps the gates in hell, ay, you, you, you!   94
We ha' done our course; there's money for your pains,
I pray you turn the key, and keep our counsel.   [*Exit.*
Emil. Alas, what does this gentleman conceive?
How do you, madam? how do you, my good lady?
Des. Faith, half asleep.
Emil. Good madam, what's the matter with my lord?   100
Des. With who?
Emil. Why, with my lord, madam.

81. hollow] *F, Q2;* hallow *Q1.*   82 what committed,—] *Qq;* What committed? *F.*   83. Impudent strumpet!] *Capell; at end of previous line Qq; not in F.*   86. hated] *Q1;* other *F, Q2.*   88. S.D.] *Q1; after* you, mistress, *l. 92, F; after* Venice, *l. 91, Q2.*   90. O heaven, forgiveness] O heauen forgiuenesse *Q1;* Oh Heauen forgiue us *F, Q2* (O heauen *Q2*).   mercy] *Q1;* mercy then *F, Q2.*   94. gates in hell] *Qq;* gate of hell *F.*   ay, you, you, you] *Q1* (I); You, you: I you *F;* you, you, I, you *Q2.*   95. ha'] *Qq;* haue *F.*

81. *hollow mine*] Cf. III. iii. 454 above.

85. *vessel*] Cf. "to possess his vessel in sanctification and honour" (1 Thess., iv. 4).

86. *hated*] There seems no reason why F should have preferred "other";

throughout the scene Desdemona is expressing her own revulsion at the thought of unfaithfulness, not merely an ethical condemnation. A. Walker thinks that *hated* "loses the point" (see Appendix D, p. 219).

97. *conceive*] imagine.

Des. Who is thy lord?

Emil.   He that is yours, sweet lady.

Des. I ha' none, do not talk to me, Emilia,
      I cannot weep, nor answer have I none,   105
      But what should go by water: prithee, to-night
      Lay on my bed our wedding sheets; remember,
      And call thy husband hither.

Emil.   Here is a change indeed!
                                        [*Exit.*

Des. 'Tis meet I should be us'd so, very well;
      How have I been behav'd, that he might stick   110
      The smallest opinion, on my greatest abuse?

                Enter IAGO *and* EMILIA.

Iago. What is your pleasure, madam? How is't with you?

Des. I cannot tell: those that do teach young babes
      Do it with gentle means, and easy tasks;
      He might ha' chid me so, for, in good faith,   115
      I am a child at chiding.

Iago.   What is the matter, lady?

Emil. Alas, Iago, my lord hath so bewhor'd her,
      Thrown such despite, and heavy terms upon her,

103. *Des.* Who . . . lady.] *F, Q2; not in Q1.*   104. ha'] *Qq;* haue *F.*   105.
answer] *Qq* (answere *Q2*)*; answeres *F.*   107. our] *Q1;* my *F, Q2.*   108.
Here is] *Qq;* Heere's *F.*   109. very well] *Q1;* very meet *F, Q2* (meete *F*).
111. smallest opinion, on my greatest abuse] *Q1;* small'st opinion on my least
misuse *F, Q2.*   115. ha'] *Qq;* haue *F.*   116. at] *Q1;* to *F, Q2.*

106. *go by water*] be conveyed by
tears (and so, as she cannot weep, she
cannot give *any* answer); *water* is very
common for "tears", e.g. "a world of
water shed Upon the parting of your
wives and you" (*1 H 4*, III. i. 95).

109. *meet . . . well*] One would readily
accept F's second "meet" if it were not
that a compositor's natural blunder is
to create a repetition when none is
there rather than to miss one when it
is. Desdemona is using both *meet* and
well ironically.

110–11. *stick . . . opinion*] Cf. "Opinion, that so sticks on Marcius" (*Cor.*,
I. i. 277); *opinion* must here, unusually,
mean unfavourable opinion.

111. *greatest abuse*] "least" is a typical
F "improvement" which looks neat
and convincing till one thinks, when it
becomes apparent that it misses the
point, which is that even her *greatest*
fault is so small that it does not merit
censure. The alteration is thorough,
since *abuse* is a strong word, inconveniently so to be coupled with
"least"; "give him chastisement for
this abuse" (*1 H 6*, IV. i. 69).

116. *at chiding*] when chidden (not
"I am an unpractised chider").

117–18.] Emilia has been listening
at the door.

118. *despite*] abuse; it is not easy to
find a parallel in Shakespeare for this

As true hearts cannot bear.

Des. Am I that name, Iago?

Iago.   What name, fair lady?   120

Des. Such as she says my lord did say I was?

Emil. He call'd her whore: a beggar in his drink
Could not have laid such terms upon his callat.

Iago. Why did he so?

Des. I do not know, I am sure I am none such.   125

Iago. Do not weep, do not weep: alas the day!

Emil. Has she forsook so many noble matches,
Her father, and her country, all her friends,
To be call'd whore? would it not make one weep?

Des. It is my wretched fortune.

Iago.   Beshrew him for it!   130
How comes this trick upon him?

Des.   Nay, heaven doth know.

Emil. I will be hang'd, if some eternal villain,
Some busy and insinuating rogue,
Some cogging, cozening slave, to get some office,

119. As ... bear] *Qq;* That ... beare it *F.*   121. says] *Qq;* said *F.*   127. Has]
Qq; Hath *F.*   128. Her ... friends,] Her Father, and her Countrey, all her
friends, *Q1;* Her Father? And her Country? And her Friends? *F;* Her Father,
and her Countrey, and her Friends, *Q2.*   130. for it] *Qq;* for't *F.*

use of the word, but "Go, see him out
at gates, and follow him, As he hath
follow'd you, with all despite" (*Cor.,*
III. iii. 136) seems to come nearest.

123. *callat*] slut; "Contemptuous
base-born callot as she is" (*2 H 6,* I. iii.
86).

132. *eternal*] "The word", says Hart,
"is commonly used as here in Ireland
without any further sense than an
intensive, and might be replaced
by 'unmitigated' "; or, in fact, by
"bloody". Furness appositely compares the colloquial use of "everlasting", and the American " 'tarnal".

133. *busy*] busybody-ing; "On
meddling monkey, or on busy ape"
(*MND.,* II. i. 181), "the busy meddling
fiend" (*2 H 6,* III. iii. 21), "Thou
find'st to be too busy is some danger"
(*Ham.,* III. iv. 33).

insinuating] This has in Shakespeare

much less of our sense of "hinting" and
much more of its original meaning of
"working oneself into favour"; "I cannot insinuate with you in the behalf of
a good play" (*AYL.,* Epil. 9), "without
all colour Of base insinuating flattery" (*1 H 6,* II. iv. 34).

134. *cogging*] cheating; "Since you
can cog, I'll play no more with you"
(*LLL.,* v. ii. 236), "Smile in men's
faces, smooth, deceive, and cog" (*R 3,*
I. iii. 48, and five lines lower occurs
insinuating). *Cozening* is much the
same.

to get some office] For the sake, one
imagines, of dramatic irony, Shakespeare makes Emilia get unnaturally
near the truth; slandering a woman is
not, in general, a step towards office,
and it may be noticed that Othello has
made no mention to Desdemona of
any specific "partner in guilt" but

Have not devis'd this slander, I'll be hang'd else.   135
Iago. Fie, there is no such man, it is impossible.
Des. If any such there be, heaven pardon him!
Emil. A halter pardon him, and hell gnaw his bones!
Why should he call her whore? who keeps her company?
What place, what time, what form, what likelihood?
The Moor's abus'd by some outrageous knave,   141
Some base notorious knave, some scurvy fellow;
O heaven, that such companions thou 'ldst unfold,
And put in every honest hand a whip,
To lash the rascal naked through the world,   145
Even from the east to the west!
Iago.   Speak within doors.
Emil. O, fie upon him! Some such squire he was,

140. What . . . likelihood?] *Qq* (for me *Q1*, place what *Q2*); What Place? What Time? / What Forme? What liklyhood? / *F.*   141. outrageous] *Q1;* most villanous *F, Q2.*   143. heaven] *Qq;* Heauens *F.*   145. rascal] *Qq;* Rascalls *F.*   146. to the] *Q1;* to th' *F;* to'th *Q2.*   doors] *Qq* (dores); doore *F.*   147. him] *Qq;* them *F.*

treated her as a common promiscuous prostitute. Had he mentioned Cassio, Emilia's guess would have had firmer grounds. It is true, however, that he has mentioned Cassio specifically to *Emilia,* at the opening of the scene, and, if one concentrates on that, the unnaturalness becomes of a different kind, namely Emilia's obtuseness in not at once equating her husband with the cogging slave who wants Cassio's office; and that she does not so equate him is plain from her astonishment in the final scene. If one wonders why Othello makes no mention of Cassio to Desdemona, the answer, I think, is that Shakespeare dared not allow him to. The specific accusation would have provoked from Desdemona such a flaming denial—the denial that she makes, too late, just before her death—that even Othello's confidence must have been shaken, and he might "send for the man, and ask him".

140. *form*] I suppose like our loose use of "shape", as "what kind of concrete shape can you give this supposition?"

likelihood] perhaps our sense, but see note on I. iii. 108 above.

141–2. *outrageous . . . notorious*] going beyond all bounds . . . infamously well known; but I doubt whether either is here much more than an "intensive", like Emilia's earlier "eternal", and (I think) Malvolio's "notorious wrong" and "most notorious geck and gull" (*Tw.N.,* v. i. 341, 355).

143. *companions*] fellows, in a derogatory sense, perhaps from the idea of "hangers-on"; "Has the porter his eyes in his head, that he gives entrance to such companions?" (*Cor.,* IV. v. 12), "this same scall, scurvy, cogging companion" (*Wiv.,* III. i. 123).

146. *Speak within doors*] speak lower; "you don't want the whole street to hear"; Onions notes that "in Warwickshire the phrase 'Speak within the house' was current till recently in the same sense".

147. *squire*] clearly contemptuous, but not at all clear why. A squire was, in one sense, a knight's attendant, and often an aspirant to knighthood; "Of

That turn'd your wit, the seamy side without,
And made you to suspect me with the Moor.
Iago. You are a fool, go to.
Des.   O good Iago,   150
What shall I do to win my lord again?
Good friend, go to him, for, by this light of heaven,
I know not how I lost him. Here I kneel:
If e'er my will did trespass 'gainst his love
Either in discourse of thought or actual deed,   155
Or that mine eyes, mine ears, or any sense,
Delighted them in any other form,
Or that I do not yet, and ever did,
And ever will (though he do shake me off

---

150. O good] *Q2*; O Good *Q1*; Alas *F*.   153–66. Here . . . make me.] *F*, *Q2*;
not in *Q1*.   155. discourse of] *F*; discourse, or *Q2*.   157. them in] *Q2*; them:
or *F*.

---

other lords and barons, knights and
squires, Full fifteen hundred, besides
common men", "The rest are princes,
barons, lords, knights, squires, And
gentlemen of blood and quality" (*H 5*,
IV. viii. 83, 94); in another sense he
was a respectable landed proprietor,
like Robert Faulconbridge—"A land-
less knight makes thee a landed
squire" (*John*, I. i. 177). There are two
passages in *Lr.*, which indicate that
squires (and knights) were sometimes
in low water financially; "No squire in
debt and no poor knight" are among
the Fool's improbabilities in III. ii. 86,
and Lear repudiates the idea that he
should "squire-like, pension beg, To
keep base life afoot" at the court of
France (II. iv. 217); and Don John
describes Claudio ironically as "A
proper squire!", but means no more
than "a typical young gallant" (like
Chaucer's Squire). The only downright derogatory use of the word in
Shakespeare comes from Cloten, who
sneers at Posthumus as "a base slave,
A hilding for a livery, a squire's cloth,
A pantler" (*Cym.*, II. iii. 127).

148. *the seamy side without*] Cf.
"Whom love hath turn'd almost the
wrong side outward" (II. iii. 48 above).

149. *suspect me*] This disposes of any
idea that Iago's suspicions of Othello
(I. iii. 385, II. i. 290) were figments,
invented during momentary "motive-
hunting" and dismissed. They have
been real, and lasting, enough for him
to challenge Emilia.

155. *discourse of thought*] process of
thinking (with no idea of speech), as
several times in Shakespeare's later
plays—in the earlier it is commonly
used in our sense of "connected
speech"; "is your blood So madly hot
that no discourse of reason, Nor fear of
bad success in a bad cause, Can qualify
the same" (*Troil.*, II. ii. 115), "a beast,
that wants discourse of reason" (*Ham.*,
I. ii. 150); and once or twice it is
used absolutely (without "reason",
"thought" or other particularization)
in somewhat different though cognate
senses—"imagin'd worth Holds in
his blood such swoln and hot discourse" (*Troil.*, II. iii. 184)—where the
image is, I think, of a stream "cours-
ing" in spate), "He that made us with
such large discourse, Looking before
and after" (*Ham.*, IV. iv. 36, where the
sense of "range" is immediately further defined by "capability" and
"reason").

To beggarly divorcement) love him dearly,   160
Comfort forswear me! Unkindness may do much;
And his unkindness may defeat my life,
But never taint my love. I cannot say "whore":
It does abhor me now I speak the word;
To do the act that might the addition earn   165
Not the world's mass of vanity could make me.

Iago. I pray you, be content, 'tis but his humour,
The business of the state does him offence,
And he does chide with you.

Des. If 'twere no other,—

Iago.   'Tis but so, I warrant you;   170

[*Trumpets.*

Hark, how these instruments summon you to supper,
And the great messengers of Venice stay:
Go in, and weep not, all things shall be well.

[*Exeunt Desdemona and Emilia.*

Enter RODERIGO.

How now, Roderigo?

Rod. I do not find that thou deal'st justly with me.   175

Iago. What in the contrary?

Rod. Every day thou doffest me with some device, Iago,

163. cannot] *F, Q2;* can't *Pope.*   164. does] *F* (do's); doth *Q2.*   168–9.
offence, And . . . you] *Qq;* offence *F.*   170. 'Tis] *Qq;* It is *F.*   warrant you]
Qq; warrant *F.*   *Trumpets*] *Rowe.*   171. summon you] *Qq;* summon *F.*
172. And the great messengers of Venice stay] *Q1;* The Messengers of Venice
staies the meate *F;* The meate, great Messengers of Venice stay *Q2.*   173. S.D.]
F; Exit women Qq.   177–82.] *as prose F, Q2;* Iago; / And . . . / All . . . / Advantage . . . / Nor . . . already / I . . . sufferd. / *Q1.*   177. doffest] *Qq;* dafts *F.*

164. *abhor*] fill with abhorrence.
165. *addition*] See III. iv. 192 above,
and note.
167. *humour*] mood (sometimes
settled, in the Jonsonian sense, sometimes passing, as here); "I hope my
holy humour will change; it was wont
to hold me but while one tells
twenty" (*R 3*, I. iv. 120).
171–2.] Did the hypothetical corrector of Q1, or the compositor of
F, needlessly change *stay* to "staies"?
Or was "staies" the original, gram-
maticized by Q1? Q2 is interesting, as

an example of how errors arise. The
editor, I take it, wanting to arrive at
F, deleted *And* and *great*, and wrote *the
meate* in the right hand margin for
insertion at the end of the line; the
compositor took it to be for substitution, and assumed that the intended
deletion was of *And the*.
177. *doffest*] *doff* and *daff* are alternative spellings, but Shakespeare
seems normally to use *doff* for the
literal meaning (as in "made us doff
our easy robes of peace" (*1 H 4*, v. i.
12)), and *daff* for the metaphorical, as

and rather, as it seems to me, thou keepest from me
all conveniency than suppliest me with the least advantage of hope: I will indeed no longer endure it,   180
nor am I yet persuaded to put up in peace what
already I have foolishly suffered.

Iago. Will you hear me, Roderigo?

Rod. Faith, I have heard too much, for your words and
performance are no kin together.   185

Iago. You charge me most unjustly.

Rod. With nought but truth. I have wasted myself out of
means: the jewels you have had from me, to deliver
to Desdemona, would half have corrupted a votarist:
you have told me she has receiv'd 'em, and return'd 190
me expectation, and comforts, of sudden respect, and
acquittance, but I find none.

178. me, thou] *Q1*; me now, *F, Q2*.   184–5.] *as prose F*; Faith ... words, / And
... together. *Q1*; Sir ... much. / For ... performance. / Are ... together. *Q2*.
184. Faith, I] Faith I *Q1*; Sir, I *Q2*; I *F*.   for] *Qq*; and *F*.   185. perfor-
mance] *Qq*; Performances *F*.   187. With nought but truth.] With naught but
truth; *F*; With nought but trueth: *Q2*; *not in Q1*.   188. means] *Qq*; my
meanes *F*.   188–9. deliver to] *Qq*; deliuer *F*.   190. has] *Qq*; hath *F*.   191. expectation,] *Qq*; expectations *F*.   192. acquittance] *Q1*; acquaintance *F, Q2*.

here ("put me off"), but cf. "He that
unbuckles this, till we do please To
daff't for our repose" (*Ant.*, IV. iv. 12).

179. *conveniency*] a vague word;
properly "what is fitting", "what suits
a person's wishes"; here roughly
"everything that makes life worth
living".

181. *put up*] our "put up with", but
the original metaphor is more apparent: compare "Why so earnestly seek
you to put up that letter? ... What
needed then that terrible despatch of
it into your pocket?" (*Lr.*, I. ii. 28, 33)
with "I must pocket up these wrongs"
(*John*, III. i. 200), and for the use here,
cf. "be dishonour'd openly, And
basely put it up without revenge"
(*Tit.*, I. i. 432).

189. *votarist*] one who has taken
vows, and so a nun; "the sisterhood,
the votarists of Saint Clare" (*Meas.*,
I. iv. 5).

191. *respect*] another Protean word,
for which "consideration" in its many

senses is perhaps the nearest modern
equivalent; "the gain propos'd Chok'd
the respect of likely peril fear'd" (*2 H4*,
I. i. 183), "many of the best respect in
Rome" (*Cæs.*, I. ii. 59), "There's the
respect That makes calamity of so long
life" (*Ham.*, III. i. 68), "I have a
widow aunt ... And she respects me as
her only son" (*MND.*, I. i. 157).
Roderigo does not expect, or even
desire, that Desdemona should, any
more than the widow aunt, regard him
as a person to be "respected" for
moral worth; he wants her to give him
some consideration.

192. *acquittance*] discharge of a debt;
properly the written acknowledge-
ment of such discharge; "you can produce acquittances For such a sum"
(*LLL.*, II. i. 160). As to F's reading, the
implication of I. i. 96 seems to be that
Roderigo is already "acquainted"
with Desdemona and the variant looks
like the substitution of the ordinary
word for the rare.

Iago. Well, go to, very well.

Rod. Very well, go to, I cannot go to, man, it is not very
     well, by this hand, I say 'tis very scurvy, and begin   195
     to find myself fopp'd in it.

Iago. Very well.

Rod. I say it is not very well: I will make myself known to
     Desdemona; if she will return me my jewels, I will
     give over my suit, and repent my unlawful solicita-   200
     tion, if not, assure yourself I'll seek satisfaction of you.

Iago. You have said now.

Rod. Ay, and I have said nothing but what I protest in-
     tendment of doing.

Iago. Why, now I see there's mettle in thee, and even   205
     from this time do build on thee a better opinion than
     ever before, give me thy hand, Roderigo: thou hast
     taken against me a most just exception, but yet I
     protest, I have dealt most directly in thy affairs.

Rod. It hath not appear'd.   210

Iago. I grant indeed it hath not appeared, and your
     suspicion is not without wit and judgement: but,

193. very well] *F, Q2;* very good *Q1.*   194. it is] *Q1;* nor 'tis *F, Q2* (tis *F,* t'is
Q2).   195. by . . . scurvy] *Q1;* Nay I think it is scuruy *F;* I say t'is very
scuruy *Q2.*   196. fopp'd] *Qq, F* (fopt) *;* fobb'd *some edd.*   198. I say it is] *Qq;*
I tell you, 'tis *F.*   201. I'll] *Qq* (I'le *Q1,* Ile *Q2*); I will *F.*   203. and I have]
Q1; and *F, Q2.*   206. time] *Q1;* instant *F, Q2.*   208. exception] *F;* concep-
tion *Qq.*   209. affairs] *Q1;* affaire *F, Q2* (Affaire *F*).

196. *fopp'd*] fooled; the verb is rare
and not elsewhere in Shakespeare, but
"foppery" seems to mean "fooling",
"deception" both in "the guiltiness of
my mind . . . drove the grossness of the
foppery into a received belief" (*Wiv.,*
v. v. 132, where Falstaff comments on
the trick of the fairies) and in "This is
the excellent foppery of the world"
(*Lr.,* I. ii. 132).

202. *You have said*] "Now you're
talking"; Onions includes this passage
along with others (e.g. *Tw.N.,* III. i. 12,
Ant., II. vi. 110) in which the phrase
clearly means "You say true", but that
meaning will hardly serve here. Iago is
flattering Roderigo by pretending
to admire his spirit, and he therefore
admits that he has seeming grounds

for his charge, but he does not admit
the truth of it.

208. *exception*] "take exception(s) to
(or with)" is common in our sense,
though usually with the thing, not the
person, objected to, and F's reading is
very probably right, and certainly the
easier. But if right, why was it replaced
by the more awkward? "Conception"
in itself is well enough, in the sense in
which it is used in III. iv. 154 above,
"erroneous idea", but "conception
against" rather than "about" is not
easy. Q2, however, was content to
retain it.

209. *directly*] straightforwardly; "indirectly and directly too Thou hast
contriv'd" (*Mer.V.,* IV. i. 360).

212. *wit*] See note on II. i. 129 above.

Roderigo, if thou hast that within thee indeed, which
I have greater reason to believe now than ever, I
mean purpose, courage, and valour, this night show   215
it; if thou the next night following enjoyest not
Desdemona, take me from this world with treachery,
and devise engines for my life.

Rod. Well, is it within reason and compass?

Iago. Sir, there is especial command come from Venice,   220
to depute Cassio in Othello's place.

Rod. Is that true? why then Othello and Desdemona return again to Venice.

Iago. O no, he goes into Mauritania, and takes away with
him the fair Desdemona, unless his abode be linger'd   225
here by some accident, wherein none can be so determinate as the removing of Cassio.

Rod. How do you mean, removing of him?

Iago. Why, by making him uncapable of Othello's place,
knocking out his brains.   230

Rod. And that you would have me to do.

Iago. Ay, and if you dare do yourself a profit and right, he
sups to-night with a harlot, and thither will I go to
him; ... he knows not yet of his honourable fortune:

213. within] *Qq;* in *F.*   216. the next] *Qq;* rhe next *F.*   enjoyest] *Qq;* enioy
F.   219. Well, is] *Qq;* Well: what is it? Is *F.*   within reason] *Qq;* within,
reason *F.*   220. command] *Q1;* commission *F,* *Q2* (Commission *F*).
224. takes] *Qq;* taketh *F.*   228. of him] *Qq;* him *F.*   232. and if] *Qq;* if *F.*
right] *Qq;* a right *F.*   233. harlot] *Q1;* harlotry *F,* *Q2.*

218. *engines for*] devices against (i.e.
machinations rather than machines);
" 'Tis policy and stratagem must do
That you affect; ... our empress, with
her sacred wit, ... shall file our engines
with advice" (i.e. put the finishing
touches to our plot, *Tit.,* II. ii. 104,
120–3).

219. *compass*] See note on III. iv. 17
above.

224. *Mauritania*] Iago very seldom
tells a direct lie on a matter of fact
which can be readily checked, but he
has to take some risk in his haste to
stampede Roderigo.

226. *determinate*] finally effective.

230. *knocking out his brains*] Iago's

impatient descent to plain brass tacks
reminds one of Richard's retort (in
Q1) to Buckingham's tentative question: "*Buck.* Now, my lord, what shall
we do if we perceive / Lord Hastings
will not yield to our complots? *Glo.*
Chop off his head, man." (*R 3,* III. i.
191).

233. *harlot*] F's "harlotry" is, in
Shakespeare, a much weaker word,
not much more than "baggage";
Glendower and Capulet speak of their
daughters in identical terms, "a peevish self-will'd harlotry" (*1 H 4,* III. i.
197, *Rom.,* IV. ii. 14). Is it perhaps this
time F that is guilty of "memorial
contamination"?

if you will watch his going thence, which I will 235
fashion to fall out between twelve and one, you may
take him at your pleasure: I will be near to second
your attempt, and he shall fall between us: come,
stand not amaz'd at it, but go along with me, I will
show you such a necessity in his death, that you shall 240
think yourself bound to put it on him. It is now high
supper-time, and the night grows to waste: about it.

Rod. I will hear further reason for this.

Iago. And you shall be satisfied.   [*Exeunt.*

SCENE III.—[*Another Room in the Castle.*]

Enter OTHELLO, LODOVICO, DESDEMONA, EMILIA,
and Attendants.

Lod. I do beseech you, sir, trouble yourself no further.
Oth. O, pardon me, it shall do me good to walk.
Lod. Madame, good night. I humbly thank your ladyship.
Des. Your honour is most welcome.
Oth.   Will you walk, sir? . . .
O Desdemona,—   5
Des. My lord?
Oth. Get you to bed, o' the instant I will be return'd,

244. S.D.] *F, Q2; Ex.* Iag. *and* Rod. *Q1.*

Scene III

S.D.] . . . *Lodovico, Desdemona . . . F;* . . . Desdemona, Lodovico . . . *Qq (after l. 242
of preceding scene Q1).*   2. it shall] *Qq;* 'twill *F.*   3. Madame] *Q1;* Madam *F,
Q2.*   6. lord?] *Capell;* Lord. *Qq, F.*   7. bed, o' the instant] *Q1;* bed on th'
instant, *F;* bed o' the instant, *Q2.*   7–8. return'd, forthwith, dispatch] *Qq*
(forthwith dispatch *Q2); return'd forthwith: dismisse F.*

239. *amaz'd*] often in Shakespeare
much weaker than our sense; here not
much more than "taken aback";
sometimes "bemused" as in "I am
amaz'd with matter" (*Cym.,* IV. iii. 28).

241. *high*] fully; "'tis high time that
I were hence" (*Err.,* III. ii. 163).

Scene III

3. *Madame*] I have retained Q1's

spelling, since it is at least possible that
it represents a more formal expression
of respect than "Madam". In *Rom.,* II.
ii. 167, where in Q2F Romeo surprisingly addresses Juliet as "my
neece", and so has to be emended, in
Q1 he says "Madame", which one
may, I think, take as the lover's half-
humorous formality of address (like
"Madonna").

forthwith, dispatch your attendant there: . . . look it
be done.

Des. I will, my lord.   [*Exeunt Othello, Lodovico, and Attendants.*

Emil. How goes it now? he looks gentler than he did.   11

Des. He says he will return incontinent:
He hath commanded me to go to bed,
And bade me to dismiss you.

Emil.   Dismiss me?

Des. It was his bidding, therefore, good Emilia,   15
Give me my nightly wearing, and adieu,
We must not now displease him.

Emil. I would you had never seen him!

Des. So would not I, my love doth so approve him,
That even his stubbornness, his checks and frowns,—   20
Prithee unpin me,—have grace and favour in them.

Emil. I have laid those sheets you bade me on the bed.

Des. All's one, good faith: how foolish are our minds!
If I do die before thee, prithee shroud me
In one of those same sheets.

Emil.   Come, come, you talk.   25

Des. My mother had a maid call'd Barbary,
She was in love, and he she lov'd prov'd mad,
And did forsake her; she had a song of "willow",
An old thing 'twas, but it express'd her fortune,
And she died singing it; that song to-night   30
Will not go from my mind . . . I have much to do,

8. look it] *Qq;* look't *F.*   10. S.D.] *Exeunt Qq; Exit F.*   12–13. incontinent:
He hath] *Qq;* incontinent, And hath *F.*   14. bade] *Q2;* bad *Q1;* bid *F.*   18. I
would] *Q1;* I, would *F;* Would *Q2.*   20. checks and] *Qq;* checks, his *F.*
21. in them] *Qq; not in F.*   22. those] *Qq;* these *F.*   25. those] *F, Q2;* these
Q1.   26. Barbary] *Qq;* Barbarie *F.*   28. had] *F, Q2;* has *Q1.*   31–52. I
have . . . next.] *F, Q2; not in Q1.*

8. *dispatch*] dismiss.

12. *incontinent*] at once; see note on
I. iii. 305 above.

20. *stubbornness*] See note on I. iii. 228
above.

checks] rebukes; "rebuke and check"
(*2 H 4,* IV. iii. 34), "Rebukeable And
worthy shameful check" (*Ant.,* IV. iv.
30); and see III. iii. 68 above.

21. *grace and favour*] attractiveness
and charm; "hell itself She turns

to favour and to prettiness" (*Ham.,*
IV. v. 188).

22, 25. *those . . . those*] so *Q2;* the distinction in *Q1* and *F,* between *these* and
those, looks deliberate, but *these* is
awkward in either place.

25. *talk*] sc. idly; "how you do run
on!"; "Poor prattler, how thou
talk'st!" (*Mac.,* IV. ii. 62).

31–2. *I have . . . But*] it is all I can do
not to.

But to go hang my head all at one side
And sing it like poor Barbary: prithee dispatch.
Emil. Shall I go fetch your night-gown?
Des.   No, unpin me here;
This Lodovico is a proper man.   35
Emil. A very handsome man.
Des. He speaks well.
Emil. I know a lady in Venice would have walk'd bare-
foot to Palestine for a touch of his nether lip.
Des. [*Singing*]
   The poor soul sat sighing, by a sycamore tree,   40
    Sing all a green willow:
   Her hand on her bosom her head on her knee,
    Sing willow, willow, willow.
   The fresh streams ran by her, and murmur'd her moans,
    Sing willow, willow, willow.   45
   Her salt tears fell from her, which soften'd the stones;—
Lay by these:—
    Sing willow, willow, willow.
Prithee hie thee: he'll come anon:—
   Sing all a green willow must be my garland.   50
   Let nobody blame him, his scorn I approve,—
Nay, that's not next. Hark! who's that knocks?
Emil. It is the wind.
Des. I call'd my love false love; but what said he then?
   Sing willow, willow, willow: 55
   If I court moe women, you'll couch with moe men.
Now get thee gone; good night: mine eyes do itch,
Does that bode weeping?

---

33. Barbary] *Q2*; Brabarie *F*.   38–9. barefoot] *F*; barefooted *Q2*.   39.
nether] *F*; neither *Q2*.   40. *Des. (Singing)*] *Rowe*; Desdemona *sings. Q2; Des.
F.   sighing*] *Q2*; *singing F*.   41. *willow*] *Q2*; *Willough F* (*and so throughout
the song*).   46. *which*] *Q2; and F*.   49. hie] *Q2*; high *F*.   52. who's that]
Qq; who is't that *F*.   53. It is] *Q1*; It's*F*; T'is *Q2*.   54–6. *I . . . men*] *F, Q2*;
not in *Q1*.   54. *false love*] *F*; *false Q2*.   then] *Q2; theu F*.   57. Now] *Q1*;
So *F, Q2*.   58. Does] *Qq*; Doth *F*.

35.] What did Shakespeare intend
by this sudden transition to Lodovico?
Is Desdemona for a moment "matching Othello with her country forms"?
One is tempted to wonder whether

there has not been a misattribution of
speeches, so that this line as well as the
next should be Emilia's. See Introduction, p. lxvii, note 1.

56. moe] more (of number).

Emil.   'Tis neither here nor there.

Des. I have heard it said so. O, these men, these men!
Dost thou in conscience think,—tell me, Emilia,—   60
That there be women do abuse their husbands
In such gross kind?

Emil.   There be some such, no question.

Des. Wouldst thou do such a deed, for all the world?

Emil. Why, would not you?

Des.   No, by this heavenly light!

Emil. Nor I neither, by this heavenly light,   65
I might do it as well in the dark.

Des. Wouldst thou do such a thing for all the world?

Emil. The world is a huge thing, it is a great price,
For a small vice.

Des.   Good troth, I think thou wouldst not.

Emil. By my troth, I think I should, and undo 't when I   70
had done it; marry, I would not do such a thing for
a joint-ring; or for measures of lawn, nor for gowns,
or petticoats, nor caps, nor any such exhibition; but,
for the whole world? ud's pity, who would not make
her husband a cuckold, to make him a monarch? I   75
should venture purgatory for it.

Des. Beshrew me, if I would do such a wrong,
For the whole world.

Emil. Why, the wrong is but a wrong i' the world; and

59–62. *Des.* I have . . . question] *F, Q2; not in Q1.*   62. kind] *F;* kindes *Q2.*
63. deed] *Q1, F;* thing *Q2.*   66. do it as well in the] *Q1;* doo't as well i' th' *F;*
as well doe it in the *Q2.*   67. Wouldst] *F, Q2;* Would *Q1.*   thing] *Q1;* deed
F, Q2.   68. world is] *Qq;* world's *F.*   69. Good troth] *Q1;* Introth *F, Q2* (In
troth *Q2*).   70. By my troth] *Q1;* Introth *F, Q2* (In troth *Q2*).   71. done it]
Qq; done *F.*   72. or] *Qq;* nor *F.*   73. or] *Q1; not in F, Q2.*   nor caps] *Q1, F*
(Caps); or Caps *Q2.*   such] *Q1;* petty *F, Q2.*   74. the whole world?] *Q1;* all
the whole world: *F;* the whole world: *Q2.*   ud's pity] *Q1;* why *F, Q2.*
75. husband a] *Qq;* husbanda *F.*   cuckold] *F, Q2* (Cuckold); Cuckole *Q1.*
76. for it] *Qq;* for't *F.*   77. such a wrong] *Q1, F;* such wrong *Q2.*

60. *in conscience*] with real conviction,
"cross your heart and hope to die";
"I will speak my conscience of the
king" (i.e. my reading of him, which
I am sure is right) (*H 5*, IV. i. 124),
"Now, Warwick, tell me even upon
thy conscience, Is Edward your true
king?" (*3 H 6*, III. iii. 113).

72. *joint-ring*] ring made in separable
halves.
lawn] fine linen; "Lawn as white as
driven snow" (*Wint.*, IV. iii. 220).
73. *exhibition*] This usually means
"maintenance" (see note on I. iii. 236
above), but here it looks as though it
must mean "offer".

    having the world for your labour, 'tis a wrong in   80
    your own world, and you might quickly make it
    right.

Des. I do not think there is any such woman.

Emil. Yes, a dozen, and as many to the vantage, as would
    store the world they played for.   85
    But I do think it is their husbands' faults
    If wives do fall: say, that they slack their duties,
    And pour our treasures into foreign laps;
    Or else break out in peevish jealousies,
    Throwing restraint upon us: or say they strike us,   90
    Or scant our former having in despite,
    Why, we have galls: and though we have some grace,
    Yet have we some revenge. Let husbands know,
    Their wives have sense like them: they see, and smell,
    And have their palates both for sweet, and sour,   95
    As husbands have. What is it that they do,
    When they change us for others? Is it sport?
    I think it is: and doth affection breed it?

84. to the] *Qq;* to'th' *F.*   86–103. But . . . so] *F, Q2; not in Q 1.*

84. *to the vantage*] over and above; cf. "My fortunes every way as fairly rank'd, If not with vantage" (*MND.,* I. i. 101).

88. *pour . . . laps*] possibly with a rather crudely physical double entendre; *lap* is a somewhat slippery word, since sometimes it seems to take the sense of the verb and mean "embrace", but sometimes to be used in a more restricted sense than ours; "Shall I lie in your lap?—No, my lord. —I mean, my head upon your lap?— Ay, my lord.—Do you think I meant country matters?" (*Ham.,* III. ii. 120). *our* = that should be ours, and *foreign* = alien.

91. *scant . . . despite*] reduce our allowances to spite us; or possibly, as Hart suggests, speak scornfully of our inferior estate before marriage. The use of *scant* elsewhere in Shakespeare points to the former; "scant her duty", "scant my sizes" (*Lr.,* II. iv. 142, 178), "Scant not my cups" (*Ant.,* IV. ii. 21);

but "Spoke scantly of me" (*Ant.,* III. iv. 6) perhaps supports the other, since it probably means "spoke slightingly" rather than "spoke little"; and cf. also "The gentleman is of no having" (*Wiv.,* III. ii. 75).

92. *galls*] tempers; the word does not always imply *bad* temper, and sometimes comes near to "spirit"; "But when they would seem soldiers, they have galls, Good arms, strong joints, true swords" (*Troil.,* I. iii. 237), "it cannot be But I am pigeon-liver'd, and lack gall To make oppression bitter" (*Ham.,* II. ii. 612).

94. *sense*] the use of the five senses; "Things hid and barr'd, you mean, from common sense?" (*LLL.,* I. i. 57).

97, 101. *sport*] See note on II. i. 226 above.

98. *affection*] often "what affects one strongly", and so nearer to passion than our rather placid sense; cf. *affects* at I. iii. 263 above.

    I think it doth. Is 't frailty that thus errs?
    It is so too. And have not we affections?　　　　　100
    Desires for sport? and frailty, as men have?
    Then let them use us well: else let them know,
    The ills we do, their ills instruct us so.
Des. Good night, good night: God me such usage send,   104
    Not to pick bad from bad, but by bad mend!   [*Exeunt.*

102. them . . . them] *F;* em . . . em *Q2.*　　104.] *Qq;* Good . . . night: / Heauen
. . . send. / *F.*　　　　God] *Q1;* Heauen *F, Q2.*　　　　usage] *Q1;* uses *F, Q2.*

104. *usage*] Neither this nor F's "uses" is very clear; either means, I suppose, "habit of thought and conduct". Nor is the next line very perspicuous, though one may take Desdemona to mean "not to follow an ill example to ill-doing (as Emilia suggests) but to learn by it and go the better way". Dr Brooks suggests that we should adhere to the more ordinary sense of *usage* = "treatment", and take *to* = "with the result that", i.e. "so that I do not learn evil from evil but learn the better way of suffering."

ACT V

SCENE I.—[*A Street.*]

Enter IAGO *and* RODERIGO.

Iago. Here stand behind this bulk, straight will he come,
  Wear thy good rapier bare, and put it home,
  Quick, quick, fear nothing, I'll be at thy elbow;
  It makes us or it mars us, think of that,
  And fix most firm thy resolution.
Rod. Be near at hand, I may miscarry in 't.
Iago. Here at thy hand, be bold, and take thy sword. [*Retires.*
Rod. I have no great devotion to the deed;
  And yet he has given me satisfying reasons,
  'Tis but a man gone: forth, my sword, he dies.   10
Iago. I have rubb'd this young quat almost to the sense,
  And he grows angry now: whether he kill Cassio,
  Or Cassio him, or each do kill the other,
  Every way makes my game; live Roderigo,

ACT V

Scene 1

1. bulk] *Qq;* Barke *F.*   4. of] *Qq;* on *F.*   5. most] *Q1,F ;* more *Q2.*
7. sword] *Q1;* stand *F, Q2.*   S.D.] *Capell.*   8. deed] *F, Q2;* dead *Q1.*
9. has] *Qq;* hath *F.*   11. quat] *F, Q2;* gnat *Q1;* knot *Theobald;* quab *Hanmer;*
quail *Upton.*   12. angry now:] *Q1;* angry. Now, *F;* angry, now, *Q2.*
14. game] *Qq;* gaine *F.*

1. *bulk*] stall of a shop; "stalls, bulks, windows Are smother'd up" (by the crowd, *Cor.*, II. i. 229)

11. *quat*] small boil, which rubbing irritates; *to the sense* must mean "to the quick".

14. *makes my game*] I think probably the true reading, in the sense "gives me the game" (cf. "You are a merry gamester. . . Yes, if I make my play" (*H 8,* I. iv. 45)); graphically there is nothing to choose between *game* and

"gaine", (cf. the *againe—a game* crux at II. i. 227), since a minim confusion would lead to either being read as the other, but "makes my gain" is a colourless phrase from Iago in high excitement at this crisis of his fortunes. The eclectic Q2 has no qualms about retaining *game*, and Granville Barker, also adopting it, comments "The Folio may in general be the better text, but the suggestion of gambling certainly fits the mood of the scene."

He calls me to a restitution large,   15
For gold and jewels, that I bobb'd from him,
As gifts to Desdemona:
It must not be; if Cassio do remain,
He has a daily beauty in his life,
That makes me ugly: and besides, the Moor   20
May unfold me to him; there stand I in peril:
No, he must die, be 't so, I hear him coming.

Enter CASSIO.

Rod. I know his gait, 'tis he, villain, thou diest!
                    [*Makes a pass at Cassio.*
Cas. That thrust had been my enemy indeed,
But that my coat is better than thou think'st;   25
I will make proof of thine. [*Draws, and wounds Roderigo.*
Rod.   O, I am slain!
    [*Iago from behind wounds Cassio in the leg, and exit.*
Cas. I am maim'd for ever, light, ho, murder, murder! [*Falls.*

Enter OTHELLO.

Oth. The voice of Cassio, Iago keeps his word.
Rod. O villain that I am!
Oth.   Hark, 'tis even so.
Cas. O, help, ho! light! a surgeon!   30
Oth. 'Tis he, O brave Iago, honest and just,
That hast such noble sense of thy friend's wrong,
Thou teachest me; ... minion, your dear lies dead,

16. *For*] *Qq*; Of *F*.   19. *has*] *Qq*; hath *F*.   21. *peril*] *Q1* (perrill); much
perill *F*, *Q2* (perrill *Q2*).   22. be't so] *Qq*; But so *F*.   hear] heare *Qq*; heard
F.   23, 26. S.D.s] *Hart (adapting Rowe and Theobald)*; not in *Qq, F*.   24. *my*]
Qq; mine *F*.   25. think'st] *Q1*; know'st *F*, *Q2*.   27. maim'd] maimd *Q2*;
maind *Q1*; maym'd *F*.   light] *Qq*; Helpe *F*.   murder, murder!] murder,
murder. *Q1*; Murther, murther. *F*; murder, *Q2*.   29. Hark, 'tis] *Qq*; It is *F*.

16. *bobb'd*] swindled; "You shall not
bob us out of our melody" (*Troil.*, III.
i. 76).

25. *my coat . . .*] i.e. he is wearing an
under-coat "of proof"—in a modern
play it would be a bullet-proof waist-
coat. Hart well cites Shirley, *The Poli-
tician*, iv. 5, "were you not wounded?
... I prepared a privy coat".

33. *minion*] darling, usually, but not
always, contemptuous; "His company
must do his minions grace, Whilst I at
home starve for a merry look" (*Err.*,
II. i. 87), "But this your minion, whom
I know you love" (*Tw.N.*, v. i. 129),
"brave Macbeth . . . Like valour's
minion carv'd out his passage" (*Mac.*,
I. ii. 16), "Beauteous and swift, the

And your fate hies apace; strumpet, I come;
Forth of my heart those charms, thine eyes, are
    blotted,   35
Thy bed, lust-stain'd, shall with lust's blood be spotted.

                                              [*Exit.*

Enter LODOVICO *and* GRATIANO.

Cas. What ho, no watch, no passage? murder, murder!
Gra. 'Tis some mischance, the cry is very direful.
Cas. O, help!
Lod. Hark!   40
Rod. O wretched villain.
Lod. Two or three groans; it is a heavy night,
    These may be counterfeits, let's think 't unsafe
    To come into the cry without more help.
Rod. Nobody come; then shall I bleed to death.   45

Enter IAGO *with a light.*

Lod. Hark!
Gra. Here's one comes in his shirt, with lights and weapons.
Iago. Who's there? whose noise is this, that cries on
            murder?
Lod. I do not know.
Iago.   Did not you hear a cry?
Cas. Here, here, for heaven's sake help me!
Iago.   What's the matter?
Gra. This is Othello's ancient, as I take it.   51
Lod. The same indeed, a very valiant fellow.
Iago. What are you here, that cry so grievously?

---

34. fate hies apace] *Q1;* vnblest Fate highes *F, Q2* (hies *Q2*).   35. Forth of]
Qq; For of *F.*   38. cry] *Qq;* voyce *F.*   42. groans] *Qq* (grones); groane *F.*
it is a] *Qq;* 'Tis *F.*   45. S.D. Iago *with a light*] *Qq;* Iago *F.*   47. lights] *Qq;*
Light *F.*   49. I] *Qq;* We *F.*   Did] *Qq;* Do *F.*   50. heaven's] heauens *Qq;*
heauen *F.*

minions of their race" (*Mac.*, II. iv. 15).
    37. *passage*] person passing.
    44. *into the cry*] could mean "into the
hunt", but I think simply "to where
the cries come from".
    48. *cries on*] cries out; not uncommon
before a single word, or a name, which

could be put in inverted commas;
"This quarry cries on havoc" (*Ham.*,
v. ii. 378), "Crying on Hector" (*Troil.*,
v. v. 35, where no doubt it may mean
only "crying for", but when Achilles
enters he bursts out "Hector! where's
Hector").

Cas. Iago! O, I am spoil'd, undone by villains,
    Give me some help.   55
Iago. O, my lieutenant! what villains have done this?
Cas. I think the one of them is hereabout,
    And cannot make away.
Iago.   O treacherous villains!
    What are you there? come in and give some help.
                        [*To Lodovico and Gratiano.*
Rod. O, help me here!   60
Cas. That's one of 'em.
Iago.   O murderous slave, O villain!
                        [*Stabs Roderigo.*
Rod. O damn'd Iago, O inhuman dog, . . . oh, oh, oh.
Iago. Kill him i' the dark? Where be those bloody thieves?
    How silent is this town! Ho, murder, murder!
    What may you be, are you of good or evil?   65
Lod. As you shall prove us, praise us.
Iago. Signior Lodovico?
Lod. He, sir.
Iago. I cry you mercy: here's Cassio hurt by villains.
Gra. Cassio!   70
Iago. How is it, brother?
Cas. My leg is cut in two.
Iago.   Marry, heaven forbid!
    Light, gentlemen, I'll bind it with my shirt.

Enter BIANCA.

Bian. What is the matter, ho? who is 't that cried?
Iago. Who is 't that cried?   75

56. my] *Q1; me, F, Q2.*　57. the one] *Qq,* that one *F.*　59. S.D.] *Theobald.*
60. here!] *Qq* (here.)*; there. F.*　61. 'em] *Qq;* them *F.*　S.D.] *Rowe*
(*subst.*)*; Thrusts him in Q2; not in Q1, F.*　62. dog, . . . oh, oh, oh.] *Qq;*
Dogge! *F.*　63. him i'the] *Q1;* men i'th' *F, Q2.*　those] *Qq;* these *F.*
71. is it] *Qq;* is't *F.*

54. *spoil'd*] usually = despoiled or
ravaged, here "hurt to death", as
with the noun in "here thy hunters
stand, Sign'd in thy spoil, and crim-
son'd in thy lethe" (*Cæs.,* III. i. 205).
66. *praise*] See note on II. iii. 127
above.

75.] Iago's precise echo of Bianca's
question is, I think, unnatural (though
in the dark he would no doubt in some
way challenge the voice) and corruption may be suspected. I was glad to
find this suspicion shared by Granville
Barker: "There may be, I think, a

174   OTHELLO   [ACT V

Bian. O my dear Cassio, O my sweet Cassio!
  Cassio, Cassio!
Iago. O notable strumpet! Cassio, may you suspect
  Who they should be, that thus have mangled you?
Cas. No.   80
Gra. I am sorry to find you thus, I have been to seek you.
Iago. Lend me a garter. So:— O for a chair,
  To bear him easily hence!
Bian. Alas, he faints! O Cassio, Cassio, Cassio!
Iago. Gentlemen all, I do suspect this trash   85
  To bear a part in this: patience awhile, good Cassio:
  Lend me a light; know we this face, or no?
  Alas, my friend, and my dear countryman:
  Roderigo? no,—yes, sure: O heaven, Roderigo.
Gra. What, of Venice?   90
Iago. Even he, sir, did you know him?
Gra.   Know him? ay.
Iago. Signior Gratiano, I cry you gentle pardon:
  These bloody accidents must excuse my manners,
  That so neglected you.
Gra.   I am glad to see you.
Iago. How do you, Cassio? O, a chair, a chair!   95
Gra. Roderigo!
Iago. He, 'tis he.   [*A chair brought in.*

76. O my] *Qq;* My *F.*   77. Cassio, Cassio!] *Qq;* Oh Cassio, Cassio, Cassio. *F.*
79. thus have] *Qq;* haue thus *F.*   82–3. *Iago.* Lend . . . hence] *F, Q2 (as
prose Q2); not in Q1.*   86. bear a part] *Qq;* be a party *F.*   86–7. this:
patience . . . or no?] *Q1;* this Iniurie. / Patience awhile, good Cassio. Come,
come; / Lend . . . or no? / F; this iniurie: patience awhile good Cassio; / Come,
come, lend me a light: / Know . . . no? / Q2.*   89. O heaven,] *Q1;* Yes, 'tis *F,
Q2 (yes, tis Q2).*   97. He] *Qq;* He, he *F.*   S.D.] *Capell (Enter Some with a
Chair).*

textual error here in Iago's repetition
of Bianca's 'Who is't that cried?'. He
can scornfully echo her; I see no other
reading, nor very much dramatic
point in that. It is possible, therefore,
that Iago's original sentence is lost and
that the printer has replaced it with
this".
  79. *mangled*] sometimes, as here, just
"wounded", without our suggestion of
"haggled"; "pluck the mangled Ty-

balt from his shroud" (*Rom.*, IV. iii. 53,
Tybalt having been killed by a clean
sword-thrust).
  86. *To bear* . . .] F offers us two un-
exceptionable lines: they may perhaps
represent the original, but the padding
"Come, come" makes me suspect that
the whole thing is a piece of tinkering.
The laconic *To bear a part in this* seems
to me more appropriate to Iago in the
hurry of the moment.

O, that's well said, a chair:
Some good man bear him carefully from hence,
I'll fetch the general's surgeon: [*To Bianca*] for you,
    mistress,
Save you your labour;—he that lies slain here, Cassio, 100
Was my dear friend, what malice was betwixt you?
Cas. None in the world, nor do I know the man.
Iago. [*To Bianca*] What, look you pale?—O, bear him out
    o' the air.   [*Cassio and Roderigo are borne off.*
Stay you, good gentlewoman; look you pale, mistress?
Do you perceive the gestures of her eye?   105
Nay, an you stir,—we shall have more anon:
Behold her well I pray you, look upon her,
Do you see, gentlemen? nay, guiltiness
Will speak, though tongues were out of use.

Enter EMILIA.

Emil. 'Las, what's the matter? what's the matter, hus-
    band?   110

97. a] *Qq;* the *F.*   99, 103. *To Bianca*] *Johnson.*   101. betwixt] *Qq;* between *F.*   103. out o'th'] *Qq;* o'th' *F.*   104. gentlewoman] *Qq;* gentlemen *F.*   105. gestures] *Qq* (ieastures); gastnesse *F.*   106. an you stir] *Qq* (stirre); if you stare *F.*   have] *Qq;* heare *F.*   109. S.D.] *Qq; not in F.*   110. 'Las, what's ... what's] *Qq;* Alas, what is ... / What is *F.*

97. *well said*] well done; "Well said, Hal! to it, Hal" (*1 H 4*, v. iv. 75, where Hal is not saying anything, but fighting for his life), "*Cer.* Make fire within; Fetch hither all the boxes in my closet. ... *Re-enter Servant, with boxes, napkins, and fire.* Well said, well said; the fire and cloths" (*Per.*, III. ii. 80–7) and cf. II. i. 167 above.

100. *Save you ...*] Bianca is tending Cassio.

101. *malice*] ill-will, cause of quarrel; see note on II. iii. 266 above.

104. *good gentlewoman*] Bianca, I think, as was natural, moves to go off with Cassio, and Iago stops her. If so, his address is savagely ironic. Malone took this view, and thought that Gratiano and Lodovico would naturally stay with Iago. Others, supporting F, argue that they would naturally start to escort Cassio, and are stopped by Iago.

105–6. *gestures ... stir ... have*] Neither Q1 (followed by Q2) nor F makes particularly good sense. *gestures* and *gastnesse* (if written as *gastnes*) would be readily confusable, *stirre–stare* and *haue–hear(e)* rather less readily (Q1's spelling *ieastures* need mean no more than the compositor "heard" in his mind what he took to be the soft *g*). And *gestures* is not impossible in a more general sense than ours (cf. "their gesture sad", in *H 5*, IV, Chor. 25). But why, whether she stirs or stares, they will either have or hear more anon, is far from clear. I fancy that *Nay, an you stir* (if right) is parenthetic, an uncompleted threat (cf. "Nay, an you strive,—" at v. ii. 82 below).

Iago. Cassio has here been set on in the dark,
  By Roderigo, and fellows that are 'scap'd,
  He's almost slain, and Roderigo dead.
Emil. Alas, good gentleman! alas, good Cassio!
Iago. This is the fruit of whoring; pray, Emilia,   115
  Go know of Cassio where he supp'd to-night:
  What, do you shake at that?
Bian. He supp'd at my house, but I therefore shake not.
Iago. O, did he so? I charge you go with me.
Emil. Fie, fie upon thee, strumpet!   120
Bian. I am no strumpet, but of life as honest
  As you, that thus abuse me.
Emil.   As I? faugh, fie upon thee!
Iago. Kind gentlemen, let's go see poor Cassio dress'd;
  Come, mistress, you must tell 's another tale.
  Emilia, run you to the citadel,   125
  And tell my lord and lady what has happ'd:
  Will you go on, I pray? [*Aside*] This is the night
  That either makes me, or fordoes me quite. [*Exeunt.*

---

111. has] *Qq*; hath *F*. 113. dead] *Qq*; quite dead *F*. 115. fruit] *Qq*;
fruits *F*. pray] *Q1*; Prythe *F*; prithee *Q2*. 120. Fie, fie] *Q1*; Fie *Q2*; Oh
fie *F*. 122. faugh, fie] *Q1* (fough); Fie *F*; now fie *Q2*. 126. has] *Qq*; hath
F. 127. on, I pray?] on, I pray, *Q1*; on afore? *F*; on? I pray: *Q2*. 128.
makes] *F*, *Q2*; markes *Q1*.

---

113. *dead*] Even devoted supporters
of F pass over "quite dead" in silence.
But it was not, perhaps, in intention, so
silly and sea-lawyerish as it appears.
I guess that the corrector wrote a
marginal "quite" as a substitute for
dead (picking up the *almost*), and that it
was mis-taken as an insertion, with
comic results. It is even possible that
what the corrector wrote was not
"quite", but "quit", in the sense of
"dismissed" = "dead".

123. *dress'd*] i.e. his wound.

128. *makes me*] just in our sense—
"he's a made man"; "There's enough
to make us all" (*1 H 4*, II. ii. 63),
"You're a made old man" (*Wint.*, III.
iii. 124).

fordoes] ruins; no exact parallel in
Shakespeare, who elsewhere uses the
word either of suicide, as in "To lay the
blame upon her own despair, That she
fordid herself" (*Lr.*, v. iii. 256), or of
tiredness, as in "the heavy ploughman
snores, All with weary task fordone"
(*MND.*, v. ii. 3).

SCENE II.—[*A Bedchamber in the Castle.*]

DESDEMONA *in bed asleep.*

Enter OTHELLO, *with a light.*

Oth. It is the cause, it is the cause, my soul,
  Let me not name it to you, you chaste stars:
  It is the cause, yet I'll not shed her blood,
  Nor scar that whiter skin of hers than snow,
  And smooth, as monumental alabaster;   5
  Yet she must die, else she'll betray more men.
  Put out the light, and then put out the light:

Scene II

S.D.] *Enter* Othello *with a light.* Q1 *; Enter* Othello, *and* Desdemona *in her bed.* F*;
Enter* Othello *with a light, and* Desdemona *in her bed.* Q2. 5. alabaster] alablaster
Qq, F. 7. the . . . the] Qq, F; the . . . thy Hanmer.

S.D.] On the modern stage there is usually a lamp by the bed, as well as the light which Othello brings with him: and there has to be, to enable us to see the scene. On the daylit Elizabethan stage this was not needed, and even the "light" with which Q1 equips Othello was (in spite of the imaginative use which Shakespeare makes of it) no more than one of those "code signs", like "night-gowns", of which Elizabethan plays are full, as helps in indicating night-time.

1. *cause*] That *the cause* is Desdemona's unchastity is clear from the next line, but what precisely Othello means by *It is the cause* is far from clear. And it does not help to suggest that Othello's thoughts, in his distress, are imprecise and disconnected. As the rest of the speech shows, nowhere in the play is he cooler and more coherent. It is noticeable that now, as l. 6 suggests and ll. 17–19 put beyond doubt, he regards what he is about to do as an act of inevitable justice, and no longer an act of revenge I do not think, therefore, that these words are self-justificatory (as though he were

saying with Antony "I have savage cause"), but rather that they express his feeling that "the cause" is so weighty that the doom which Justice demands, and of which he is now the almost unwilling instrument, is inescapable. In other words, and in a feeble paraphrase, "the cause is all that now matters."

7.] Attempts have been made to clarify this line either by italicizing the second *the* (thus making the second *light* the light of life in general), as Rowe (ii) and Pope did, or by emending the second *the* to *thy* (= Desdemona's), as Hanmer did. But I believe that Upton and (for once) Warburton, followed by Johnson, were right in proposing *Put out the light, and then— Put out the light?* Warburton's explanation is characteristically cumbrous, but clear. "The meaning is, I will put out the light, and *then* proceed to the execution of my purpose. But . . . he breaks short, and questions himself . . . as much as to say, But hold, let me first weigh the reflections which this expression so naturally excites." On this interpretation the movement of

If I quench thee, thou flaming minister,
I can again thy former light restore,
Should I repent me; but once put out thine,   10
Thou cunning pattern of excelling nature,
I know not where is that Promethean heat
That can thy light relume: when I have pluck'd the
      rose,
I cannot give it vital growth again,
It must needs wither; I'll smell it on the tree, [*Kisses her.*
A balmy breath, that doth almost persuade   16
Justice herself to break her sword: once more:
Be thus, when thou art dead, and I will kill thee,
And love thee after: once more, and this the last,
So sweet was ne'er so fatal: I must weep,   20

---

10. thine] *Qq*; thy light *F*.   11. cunning] *Q1*; cunning'st *F*, *Q2*.   13. relume]
Malone; re-Lume *F*; returne *Q1*; relumine *Q2*.   the rose] *Qq*; thy Rose *F*.
15. must needs] *Qq*; needs must *F*.   it] *Qq*; thee *F*.   S.D.] *Q2*; *He kisses her*
Q1 (after last, l. 19); not in F.   16. A balmy] *Qq*; Oh Balmy *F*; Ah balmy
Globe.   doth] *Qq*; dost *F*.   17. Justice . . . more:] Iustice her selfe to breake
her sword once more, *Q1*; Iustice to breake her Sword. One more, one more: *F*;
Iustice her selfe to breake her sword: one more; *Q2*.   19. once more, and this
the last,] *Q1*; One more, and that's the last. *F*; one more, and this the
last: *Q2*.

Othello's thought is almost exactly parallel to Hamlet's: "To die, to sleep; To sleep; perchance to dream: ay, there's the rub; For in that sleep of death what dreams may come . . ."

8. *flaming minister*] cf. "and his ministers a flaming fire" (Psalm civ. 4).

11. *cunning . . . nature*] *cunning* = wrought with skill (the old sense of "cunning" as noun); *pattern* = product of particular excellence (as we should say "model"; and *excelling* = excellent, in the Elizabethan sense, more precise and emphatic than ours—"nature at the height of her artistry, surpassing even herself" (cf. II. i. 65 above).

12. *Promethean*] Prometheus, in the Greek tale, brought down fire to men from Heaven; "They sparkle still the right Promethean fire" (*LLL.*, IV. iii. 351).

13. *relume*] *relume* and *returne* would

be easily confused, but it looks as though Q1's reading was the result of the substitution by someone, in the first instance very probably an actor, of the common word for the rare. This is the first occurrence of *relume* recorded by *O.E.D.*, and it is uncommon even later.

the rose] F's *thy* would be an easy error of repetition; but that need not prevent it being the right reading, though I think that it is metrically rougher, and in sense less effective, than Q1's.

17. *Justice . . . sword*] Sword and scales were emblems of Justice; "upon this sword of justice" (*Wint.*, III. ii. 125), "poise the cause in Justice' equal scales" (*2 H 6*, II. i. 202).

The sacrifice of *herself* in favour of the iterative assault on the emotions, or "tear-jerk", at the end of the line, seems to me an enfeebling change.

But they are cruel tears; this sorrow's heavenly,
It strikes when it does love: she wakes.

Des. Who's there? Othello?

Oth.   Ay, Desdemona.

Des. Will you come to bed, my lord?

Oth. Have you pray'd to-night, Desdemona?

Des.   Ay, my lord.   25

Oth. If you bethink yourself of any crime,
Unreconcil'd as yet to heaven and grace,
Solicit for it straight.

Des. Alas, my lord, what may you mean by that?

Oth. Well, do it, and be brief, I will walk by,   30
I would not kill thy unprepared spirit,
No, heaven forfend, I would not kill thy soul.

Des. Talk you of killing?

Oth.   Ay, I do.

Des.   Then heaven
Have mercy on me!

Oth.   Amen, with all my heart!

Des. If you say so, I hope you will not kill me.   35

Oth. Hum!

Des. And yet I fear you, for you are fatal then,
When your eyes roll so: why I should fear, I know not,
Since guiltiness I know not, but yet I feel I fear.

Oth. Think on thy sins.

Des.   They are loves I bear to you.   40

Oth. And for that thou diest.

---

22. when] *Q1; where F, Q2.*   does] *Qq; doth F.*   she wakes.] *Qq, F* (She
F)*; as* S.D. *Anon. conj.* (*apud Cambridge*), *reading* It . . . Othello? *as one line.*
25. Desdemona] *Qq;* Desdemon *F.*   29. Alas] *Qq;* Alacke *F.*   may] *Q1, F;*
doe *Q2.*   32. heaven] *Qq;* Heauens *F.*   33–4. Talk . . . heart!] *arranged as by
Capell; each speech a separate line in Qq, F.*   35. so] *Qq; not in F.*   37. you are]
Q1; you're *F;* y'are *Q2.*   41. And] *Qq;* I, and *F.*   diest] *Qq;* dy'st *F.*

---

21. *cruel tears*] meaning, I think, that
the tears are no sign of faltering
purpose.

22. *strikes . . . love*] "Whom the Lord
loveth he chasteneth"; hence the
heavenly of the preceding line. *when*
and *where*, graphically almost indifferent, produce different senses;
when implies "just *because* it loves",

where "*even* where (i.e. though) it
loves"; and cf. *Ant.,* IV. xiii. 38, where
F's *when* is usually emended to
"where".

28. *Solicit*] pray for pardon; twice
in Shakespeare of prayers to Heaven
though not for pardon—but usually of
petitions to men.

37–8. *fatal . . . so*] "long time".

Des. That death's unnatural, that kills for loving;
　　Alas, why gnaw you so your nether lip?
　　Some bloody passion shakes your very frame,
　　These are portents; but yet I hope, I hope,　　　　45
　　They do not point on me.
Oth.　　　　　　　　　　Peace, and be still!
Des. I will, so, what's the matter?
Oth. That handkerchief which I so lov'd, and gave thee,
　　Thou gavest to Cassio.
Des.　　　　　　　No, by my life and soul,
　　Send for the man and ask him.　　　　　　　　50
Oth. Sweet soul, take heed, take heed of perjury,
　　Thou art on thy death-bed.
Des.　　　　　　　　Ay, but not yet to die.
Oth. Yes, presently:
　　Therefore confess thee freely of thy sin,
　　For to deny each article with oath　　　　　　　55
　　Cannot remove, nor choke the strong conceit,
　　That I do groan withal: thou art to die.
Des. Then Lord have mercy on me!
Oth.　　　　　　　　　　I say, amen.
Des. And have you mercy too! I never did
　　Offend you in my life, ... never lov'd Cassio,　　60
　　But with such general warranty of heaven,
　　As I might love: I never gave him token.
Oth. By heaven, I saw my handkerchief in his hand:

---

45. I hope, I hope] *F*; I hope *Qq*.　　51–4.] *see note below.*　　53. Yes] *Qq*; *not in F.*　　56. conceit] *Q1*; conception *F*, *Q2* (Conception *F*).　　58. Then Lord] *Qq*; O Heauen *F*.　　63. in his] *Qq*; in's *F*.

47. *what's the matter?*] not just "what's wrong with you?" but "what is the real issue?"

52–3. The text is verbally that of *Qq*, but the lineation is a matter of taste. The early printers do not use the modern typographical device whereby a half-line which completes a half-line of the previous speaker is offset to the right, and a new speaker, as with Desdemona here, always starts a fresh line. (See Appendix F, p. 227.) Desdemona's *Ay, but not yet to die* may

therefore be taken either as completing Othello's *Thou art on thy death-bed*, or as being itself completed by his *Yes, presently*. With F, which has no *Yes*, only the first alternative is open.

53. *presently*] See note on II. i. 213 above.

55. *article*] item (in the accusation); see note on I. iii. 11 above.

56. *conceit*] belief (with more of the note of "conviction" and less of "imagination" than usual).

O perjur'd woman, thou dost stone thy heart,
And makest me call what I intend to do   65
A murder, which I thought a sacrifice;
I saw the handkerchief.

Des.   He found it then,
I never gave it him, send for him hither,
And let him confess a truth.

Oth.   He has confess'd.

Des. What, my lord?   70

Oth. That he hath ... us'd thee.

Des.   How? unlawfully?

Oth. Ay.

Des.   He will not say so.

Oth.   No, his mouth is stopp'd,
Honest Iago hath ta'en order for 't.

Des. My fear interprets then, ...
What, is he dead?

Oth.   Had all his hairs been lives,   75

64. thy] *Q1;* my *F, Q2.*   65. makest] *Q1;* makes *F;* makst *Q2.*   69. And
let] *Q1;* Let *F, Q2.*   has] *Qq;* hath *F.*   71. That] *F, Q2;* Thar *Q1.*
... us'd thee] *Q2* (vsde); vs'd thee *F;* ... vds death *Q1.*   74-5. My fear
... dead?] My feare interprets then, ... what is he dead? *Qq (as one line)* ; Oh,
my feare interprets. What is he dead? *F (one line); for lineation see note below.*
75-6. Had all ... all] *Qq;* Had all ... Reuenge / Had ... all *F.*

64. *thy*] F's "my", no doubt the
easier reading, has been accepted by
almost all edd. except Johnson, and
even he did not go further than suspecting that Q1 was right. In fact
there is less difference in sense than
there appears to be; the progress of
Othello's thought, set out in full, is
something like this: (*a*) Desdemona is
perjuring herself, (*b*) this argues a
stony obduracy, (*c*) which hardens my
heart, and (*d*) makes me call ... With
"my" (*b*) is suppressed and (*c*) explicit,
with *thy* (*c*) is suppressed and (*b*)
explicit.

66. *murder ... sacrifice*] Othello
means, I think, that he feels the motive
of personal revenge rising again and
ousting that of impersonal justice.

71. *us'd thee*] Q1's *ud's death*, preceded by a dash, cannot just be dismissed as "undignified" and therefore

"certainly an interpolation" (see
Appendix D, p. 219). Othello's
choked breaking off, and the oath, are
dramatic enough. But, equally, it cannot stand alone, for then we have no
lead-in for Desdemona's question.
Alexander makes the interesting suggestion that we should retain both, so
reading *That he hath—ud's death—us'd
thee.* It should, however, be observed
(much as I should like to retain Q1)
that (*a*) this produces a hypermetrical
line, and (*b*) the corruption of *us'd thee*
to *ud's death* would have been even
easier than it now appears if we assume an original spelling *usde the.*

73. *ta'en order for*] taken steps to
secure; "I will take order for her keeping close" (*R 3,* IV. ii. 52).

74-6. Either Qq's or F's lineation
is possible, but if we accept Q1's
double hyphen as justifying the

My great revenge had stomach for 'em all.

Des. Alas, he is betray'd, and I undone.

Oth. O strumpet, . . . weepest thou for him to my face?

Des. O, banish me, my lord, but kill me not.

Oth. Down, strumpet!   80

Des. Kill me to-morrow, let me live to-night.

Oth. Nay, an you strive,—

Des. But half an hour, but while I say one prayer!

Oth. 'Tis too late.   [*he stifles her.*

Des. O Lord, Lord, Lord!   85

Emil. [*Within*] My lord, my lord! what, ho, my lord, my lord!

Oth. What voice is this? Not dead? not yet quite dead?

I that am cruel, am yet merciful,

I would not have thee linger in thy pain, . . .

So, so.

76. 'em] *Qq;* them *F.*   78. O] *Qq;* Out *F.*   weepest] *Qq;* weep'st *F.*
82. an] *Qq;* if *F.*   83. hour, but] *Q1;* houre. *Oth.* Being done, there is no
pawse. *Des.* But *F,* Q2 (don *and* pause. *Q2*).   84. 'Tis] *Qq;* It is *F.*   S.D.]
Qq; Smothers her *F.*   85. O . . . Lord!] *Q1; not in F,* Q2.   86. *Emil.* (*Within*)]
Steevens, *etc.;* Emillia *calls within Qq;* Æmilia *at the doore. F.*   87. voice] voyce
Qq; noise *F.*

starting of a fresh line with *What,
is he dead?*, the Qq lineation is the
neater, and I think that the single
line for *My great revenge . . . 'em all*
is more effective.

76. *My great . . . all*] Cf. "Till that a
capable and wide revenge Swallow
them up" (III. iii. 466 above).

83–6.] Granville Barker makes what
seem some very just comments on this
passage; "Q1, besides the omission of
'Being done, there is no pause', and
such slight changes as to *he stifles her*
and *Emillia calls within,* has, after *It is
too late,* Des. *O Lord. Lord. Lord.* Since
Dyce reproved Collier for admitting
this to the edited text . . . on the
grounds that the effect involved was,
first, 'not a little comic' and secondly
'disquietingly vulgar', no other editor
appears to have raised the question.
But it is worth consideration at least.
For the effect (saving Dyce's opinion)
would at least be neither comic nor
vulgar, and might prove to be very

poignant indeed. Imagine it: Desdemona's agonized cry to God, and as
the sharp sound of it is slowly stifled,
Emilia's voice at the door rising
through it, using the same words in
another sense. A macabre duet, and
unaccountable enough to call from
Othello a most distraught 'What
voice is this?' " A. Walker, though she
also finds the echo macabre, feels that
it "strikes a jarring note".

90. *So, so*] Some commentators and
some actors have taken the view that
here Othello stabs Desdemona. For
this there is less than no justification in
the text. Both Q1 and F give an S.D.
for the stifling, but no other; further,
though Othello might well, under
stress, forget his intention not to shed
Desdemona's blood or scar her skin
(ll. 3, 4), his later words (l. 203) *Whose
breath indeed these hands have newly
stopp'd* are more naturally taken as a
literal statement of fact than as a peri-
phrasis for "have killed". The notion

Emil. [*Within*] What ho, my lord, my lord!
Oth.   Who's there?   90
Emil. [*Within*] O good my lord, I 'ld speak a word with you!
Oth. Yes, 'tis Emilia, by and by: she's dead:
    'Tis like she comes to speak of Cassio's death;
    The noise was here; ha, no more moving,
    Still as the grave: shall she come in? were 't good?   95
    I think she stirs again; no, what's the best?
    If she come in, she'll sure speak to my wife.
    My wife, my wife, my wife; I ha' no wife;
    O, insupportable! O heavy hour!
    Methinks it should be now a huge eclipse   100
    Of sun and moon, and that the affrighted globe
    Should yawn at alteration.
Emil. [*Within*] I do beseech you I may speak with you, . . .
    Good my lord!

90. (*Within*)] *F; not in Qq.*   91. (*Within*)] *Malone.*   I'ld] *Qq* (I'de); I
would *F.*   94. here] *Qq;* high *F.*   96. the best] *Qq;* best to do *F.*   98. My
wife, my wife, my wife;] *Q1;* My wife, my wife: what wife? *F;* My wife, my
wife, what wife? *Q2.*   ha'] *Qq* (ha); haue *F.*   102. Should] *Qq;* Did *F.*
103–4. I do . . . lord] *one line Qq;* I do beseech you / That I . . . you. Oh good
my Lord / *F.*   104. Good] *Q1;* Oh good *F, Q2* (O *Q2*).

that the stabbing must be admitted,
to account for Desdemona's pallor
(l. 274)—even though new difficulties
then arise over the paleness of her
smock—seems to be disposed of by the
majority verdict of the medical comment interestingly marshalled by Furness (Var. ed., pp. 303–7) which deals
also with Desdemona's ability to
speak at ll. 118–26.

    94.] The obscurity of F's "The noise
was high" is emphasized by the divergence of comment: Booth thought it
referred to the noise of the struggle between Othello and Desdemona—but
why introduce a reason for Emilia's
arrival other than that just stated,
Cassio's death? Irving took the *noise* to
be Emilia's own knocking. Hart, more
reasonably, says "Probably refers to
the attack upon Cassio, where there
was undoubtedly much noise". But
this, though it makes Othello's comment reasonable, makes it also, surely,

cumbrously, and in the context most
undramatically, so. Othello then says
'*Tis like . . . death* "because there was
enough noise to have roused her and
made her inquisitive". Q1's reading
is not easy, but can, I think, be effective. Othello's thoughts "shuttle" between Desdemona on the bed and
Emilia outside the door; and his
movements may naturally correspond.
I think that on l. 93 he turns from the
bed to move to the door, then suddenly
checks, as though listening, and then
turns to the bed again with *The noise
was here.*

    100–2. *eclipse . . . yawn*] For the
connection (to us puzzling) between
eclipses and earthquakes which cause
the earth to *yawn* in chasms, Hart very
appositely quotes Holland's *Pliny,* ii.
80, under heading "Of the Gaping
Chinks of the Earth", "They [earth-
quakes] fortune also to be when the
Sun and Moon are eclipsed".

Oth. I had forgot thee: O, come in, Emilia.   105
    Soft, by and by; let me the curtains draw.
    Where art thou?   [*Unlocks the door.*

            Enter EMILIA.

                What's the matter with thee now?
Emil. O, my good lord, yonder 's foul murders done!
Oth. What, now?
Emil.   But now, my lord.
Oth. It is the very error of the moon,   110
    She comes more near the earth than she was wont,
    And makes men mad.
Emil. Cassio, my lord, has kill'd a young Venetian,
    Call'd Roderigo.
Oth.   Roderigo kill'd,
    And Cassio kill'd?
Emil.   No, Cassio is not kill'd.   115
Oth. Not Cassio kill'd? then murder 's out of tune,
    And sweet revenge grows harsh.
Des. O, falsely, falsely murder'd!
Emil.   O Lord, what cry is that?
Oth. That? what?
Emil. Out and alas! it is my lady's voice;   120
    Help, help, ho, help! O lady, speak again,
    Sweet Desdemona, O sweet mistress, speak!
Des. A guiltless death I die.
Emil. O, who has done this deed?
Des. Nobody, I myself, farewell: 125

---

105. forgot] *Q1, F;* forgotten *Q2.*   O, come] O come *Q1;* oh come *F;* come
Q2.   107. *Unlocks the door*] *Theobald.*   S.D. *Enter* Emilia] *after* draw, *l. 106,*
Qq; after now, *l. 107, F.*   109. What,] *Q1;* What? *F, Q2.*   111. near the]
Qq; neerer *F.*   113. has] *Qq;* hath *F.*   118. O Lord,] *Q1;* Alas! *F;* Ahlas,
Q2.   120. it is] *Q1;* that was *F;* it was *Q2.*   124. has] *Qq;* hath *F.*

---

110. *error*] wandering from her
true course.
112. *makes men mad*] The very word
"lunacy" shows the age and strength
of the belief in the connection between
the moon and madness.
118.] For the supposed absurdity of
Desdemona reviving enough to speak

(even if only three brief speeches),
see the medical comments mentioned
in note on l. 90 above; and cf. also *The
Duchess of Malfi*, IV. ii, where the
Duchess, 150 lines after "the execu-
tioners strangle her", revives enough
to listen to Bosola and to speak, even
though only two words.

Commend me to my kind lord, O, farewell!   [*she dies.*
Oth. Why, how should she be murder'd?
Emil.   Alas, who knows?
Oth. You heard her say, herself, it was not I.
Emil. She said so, I must needs report a truth.
Oth. She's like a liar gone to burning hell,   130
   'Twas I that kill'd her.
Emil.   O, the more angel she,
   And you the blacker devil!
Oth. She turn'd to folly, and she was a whore.
Emil. Thou dost belie her, and thou art a devil.
Oth. She was false as water.
Emil.   Thou as rash as fire,   135
   To say that she was false: O, she was heavenly true!
Oth. Cassio did top her, ask thy husband else;
   O, I were damn'd beneath all depth in hell,
   But that I did proceed, upon just grounds,
   To this extremity; thy husband knew it all.   140
Emil. My husband?
Oth. Thy husband.
Emil. That she was false to wedlock?
Oth. Ay, with Cassio: nay, had she been true,
   If heaven would make me such another world,   145
   Of one entire and perfect chrysolite,
   I 'ld not have sold her for it.
Emil. My husband?
Oth.   Ay, 'twas he that told me first,
   An honest man he is, and hates the slime
   That sticks on filthy deeds.
Emil.   My husband?   150

126. *she dies*] *Qq; not in F.*   128. heard] *Qq;* heare *F.*   129. a truth] *Qq;* the truth *F.*   135. as rash] *Q1;* art rash *F, Q2.*   144. nay] *Qq; not in F.* 148. me first] *Qq;* me on her first *F.*

133. *folly*] wantonness; not often in this sense in Shakespeare (not nearly so often, I think, as Schmidt believes), but one case seems clear—"Sweet honey Greek, tempt me no more to folly" (*Troil.*, v. ii. 18), and others are on the borderline, sometimes with a double sense; and cf. in this play "her

folly helped her to an heir" (II. i. 137) and "hath all those requisites in him that folly and green minds look after" (II. i. 244).
   140. *extremity*] last extreme of justice.
   146. *chrysolite*] topaz; only here in Shakespeare.

Oth. What needs this iteration? woman, I say thy husband.
Emil. O mistress, villainy hath made mocks with love!
    My husband say that she was false!
Oth.   He, woman;
    I say thy husband: dost understand the word?
    My friend, thy husband, honest, honest Iago.   155
Emil. If he say so, may his pernicious soul
    Rot half a grain a day! he lies to the heart,
    She was too fond of her most filthy bargain.
Oth. Ha!
Emil. Do thy worst,   160
    This deed of thine is no more worthy heaven,
    Than thou wast worthy her.
Oth.   Peace, you were best.
Emil. Thou hast not half the power to do me harm
    As I have to be hurt: O gull, O dolt,
    As ignorant as dirt; thou hast done a deed ...   165
    I care not for thy sword, I'll make thee known,
    Though I lost twenty lives: help, help, O help!
    The Moor has kill'd my mistress, murder, murder!

Enter MONTANO, GRATIANO, IAGO, *and others.*

Mon. What is the matter? How now, general?
Emil. O, are you come, Iago? you have done well,   170

151. iteration? woman, I] *Qq;* itterance, Woman? I *F.*   152–5. *Emil.* O . . .
Iago] *F, Q2; not in Q1.*   153. say that] *Q2;* say *F.*   163. the] *Qq;* that *F.*
166. known] *F;* know *Qq.*   167. O] *Qq;* hoa *F.*   168. has] *Qq;* hath *F.*
S.D. Gratiano] *Q1, F;* Gragantio *Q2.*   and others] *Qq; not in F.*

152. *made mocks with*] This must
apparently mean "made a mock of",
but elsewhere in Shakespeare the preposition for this sense is "at", and
where he uses "with" it is instrumen-
tal, e.g. "a time is come to mock at
form" (*2 H 4*, IV. v. 117), and "As we
are mock'd with art" (*Wint.*, v. iii.
68).

163–4. *Thou hast not . . . hurt*] "I have
in this cause more power to endure than
thou hast power to inflict" (Johnson,
quoted with approval by Hart). One
differs from Johnson at one's peril, but
surely this misses the whole point.

Emilia is not saying anything about
her endurance; she is speaking of her
capacity for feeling pain, in her distress for Desdemona, which is far
beyond anything which Othello can
inflict. Also "we need our attention
drawn to the new spirit to which her
love for her mistress nerves her, and
which readers her later as impervious
to Iago's threats as she is to Othello's
here." (Dr Brooks.)

164. *gull*] dupe; "made the most
notorious geck and gull That e'er invention play'd on" (*Tw.N.*, v. i.
355).

That men must lay their murders on your neck.
All. What is the matter?
Emil. Disprove this villain, if thou be'st a man;
    He says thou told'st him that his wife was false,
    I know thou didst not, thou art not such a villain: 175
    Speak, for my heart is full.
Iago. I told him what I thought, and told no more
    Than what he found himself was apt and true.
Emil. But did you ever tell him she was false?
Iago. I did.   180
Emil. You told a lie, an odious damned lie;
    Upon my soul, a lie, a wicked lie!
    She false with Cassio; did you say with Cassio?
Iago. With Cassio, mistress; go to, charm your tongue.
Emil. I will not charm my tongue, I am bound to speak: 185
    My mistress here lies murder'd in her bed.
All. O heavens forfend!
Emil. And your reports have set the murder on.
Oth. Nay, stare not, masters, it is true indeed.
Gra. 'Tis a strange truth.   190
Mon. O monstrous act!
Emil.   Villainy, villainy, villainy!
    I think upon 't: I think I smell 't: O villainy!
    I thought so then: I'll kill myself for grief:
    O villainy, villainy!
Iago. What, are you mad? I charge you get you home.   195
Emil. Good gentlemen, let me have leave to speak,
    'Tis proper I obey him, but not now:
    Perchance, Iago, I will ne'er go home.

---

171. murders] *F* (Murthers)*; murder *Qq*.   172. *All.*] *Q1; Gra. F, Q2*.
175. thou art] *Qq; thou'rt F*.   186–94. My . . . villainy!] *F, Q2; not in Q1*.
188. murder] *F; murderer Q2*.   192. smell't: O villainy] *F; smell a villany
Q2*.   198. Perchance] *Q1, F; Perhaps Q2*.

178. *apt*] The Shakespearean use is
normally near to the modern, either
"fitting" or "well fitted for"; but in
this play, at II. i. 282, "That she loves
him, 'tis apt and of great credit" it
apparently means "plausible", and
here "fitting the facts".

184. *charm your tongue*] sc. into
silence; "To tame a shrew, and charm
her chattering tongue" (*Shr.*, IV. ii.
58), "charm thy riotous tongue" (*2 H 6*,
IV. i. 64), "Peace, wilful boy, or I will
charm your tongue" (*3 H 6*, v. v. 31).

186–94.] The absence of these lines
from Q1 is probably the result of a cut,
but it may have been found that some
more give and take in dialogue was
desirable, and so they were added.

Oth. O! O! O!   [*Falling on the bed.*

Emil.   Nay, lay thee down, and roar,
For thou hast kill'd the sweetest innocent   200
That e'er did lift up eye.

Oth.   [*Rising*] O, she was foul:
I scarce did know you, uncle, there lies your niece,
Whose breath indeed these hands have newly stopp'd;
I know this act shows terrible and grim.

Gra. Poor Desdemona, I am glad thy father's dead;   205
Thy match was mortal to him, and pure grief
Shore his old thread atwain: did he live now,
This sight would make him do a desperate turn,
Yea, curse his better angel from his side,
And fall to reprobation.   210

Oth. 'Tis pitiful, but yet Iago knows
That she with Cassio hath the act of shame
A thousand times committed; Cassio confess'd it,
And she did gratify his amorous works,
With the recognizance and pledge of love,   215
Which I first gave her; I saw it in his hand,
It was a handkerchief; an antique token
My father gave my mother.

Emil. O God, O heavenly God!

Iago.   Zounds, hold your peace.

199. S.D.] Oth. *falls on the bed* Qq (*fals Q1*); *not in* F.   201. *Rising*] *Theobald.*
204. terrible] *Qq;* horrible *F.*   205. Desdemona] *Qq;* Desdemon *F.*   207.
atwain] *Q1* (atwane); in twaine *F, Q2.*   210. reprobation] *Qq;* Reprobance
F.   212. hath] *Q1, F;* had *Q2.*   215. the] *Q1;* that *F, Q2.*   219. O God,
O heavenly God] *Q1;* Oh Heauen! oh heauenly Powres! *F;* O heauon,
O heauenly powers *Q2.*   Zounds] *Q1;* Come *F, Q2.*

203. *Whose . . . stopp'd*] See note on
l. 90 above.

206. *mortal*] See note on III. iii. 361
above.

207. *thread*] sc. of life, which it was
the prerogative of the Fate Atropos to
sever with her shears.

209–10 *curse . . . . reprobation*] curse so
that he would lose the guardianship of
his good angel and fall into damnation
(for which *reprobation* was the technical theological term).

213.] "long time".

219.] Granville Barker, adopting

Q1's reading, comments as follows:
"The difference, at this point, is not a
slight one; Q1 striking the far stronger
note. It is generally admitted that the
text of *Othello* bears many marks of the
1605 'Act against Swearing' (and one
has but to glance at the Concordance,
with its two entries under 'God' and
its long list under 'heaven'). The line
in the Quarto has, therefore, that
much inferential claim to be what
Shakespeare first wrote. But a more
important argument in its favour is
its challenging intent, so closely akin

Emil. 'Twill out, it will: I hold my peace sir, no,   220
    I'll be in speaking, liberal as the air,
    Let heaven, and men, and devils, let 'em all,
    All, all cry shame against me, yet I'll speak.
Iago. Be wise, and get you home.
Emil.   I will not.
                      [*Iago offers to stab Emilia.*
Gra.   Fie,
    Your sword upon a woman?   225
Emil. O thou dull Moor, that handkerchief thou speak'st on,
    I found by fortune, and did give my husband;
    For often with a solemn earnestness,
    More than indeed belong'd to such a trifle,
    He begg'd of me to steal it.
Iago.   Villainous whore!   230
Emil. She gave it Cassio? no, alas, I found it,
    And I did give 't my husband.
Iago.   Filth, thou liest!
Emil. By heaven I do not, I do not, gentlemen;
    O murderous coxcomb! what should such a fool   234
    Do with so good a woman?
Oth.   Are there no stones in heaven

---

220. 'Twill out, it will . . . no] 'Twill out, 'twill: I hold my peace sir, no *Q1*;
'Twill out, 'twill out. I peace? / No *F*; Twill out, twill out: I hold my peace sir,
no *Q2*.   221. I'll be in speaking,] *Qq*; No, I will speake *F*.   air] *Q1* (ayre);
north *F*, *Q2* (North *F*).   222. 'em] *Qq*; them *F*.   224. S.D.] *Rowe*.   226.
on] *Qq*; of *F*.   231. gave] *Qq*; giue *F*.   235. woman] *Qq*; wife *F*.

to Laertes' 'Do you see this, O God?',
to Macduff's 'Did heaven look on and
would not take their part?' (which
should surely read 'God', the whole
scene hereabouts being enfeebled by
repeated 'heavens'); and, of course, to
more than one passage in *King Lear*. . .
This challenging attitude towards
divinely permitted evil is characteristic of the mature tragedies."

221. *air*] No one, presumably,
would have questioned Q1's word, but
for F's "north" and for the fact that
Q2 made the alteration to the latter, a
point of some importance, since it
implies that Q2 not only preferred it
but found it easy to understand, which

is more than we do. Hart, making the
best of a doubtful case, thinks that the
reference is to the north country, and
the freedom of northerners' speech
especially in asseverations, and suggests that the somewhat derogatory
allusion was altered in deference to
King James.

234. *coxcomb*] "Mome, malt-horse,
capon, coxcomb, idiot, patch!" (*Err.*,
III. i. 32), "an ass and a fool and a
prating coxcomb" (*H 5*, IV. i. 79).

235. *stones*] thunderbolts; "Can
heaven not spare one bolt for this
villain? Are all needed for thunder?"
(Hart); cf. "The gods throw stones of
sulphur" (*Cym.*, v. v. 241).

    But what serves for the thunder? Precious villain!
                   [*He runs at Iago. Iago stabs Emilia.*
Gra. The woman falls, sure he has kill'd his wife.
Emil. Ay, ay, O lay me by my mistress' side.   [*Exit Iago.*
Gra. He's gone, but his wife's kill'd.
Mon. 'Tis a notorious villain; take you this weapon,   240
    Which I have here recover'd from the Moor:
    Come, guard the door without, let him not pass,
    But kill him rather; I'll after that same villain,
    For 'tis a damned slave.
                   [*Exeunt Montano and Gratiano.*
Oth.   I am not valiant neither,
    But every puny whipster gets my sword;   245
    But why should honour outlive honesty?
    Let it go all.
Emil.   What did thy song bode, lady?
    Hark, canst thou hear me? I will play the swan,
    And die in music: [*Singing*] Willow, willow, willow.
    Moor, she was chaste, she lov'd thee, cruel Moor,   250
    So come my soul to bliss, as I speak true;

---

236. Precious] *Q1, F*; pernitious *Q2.*   S.D.] *The Moore runnes at* Iago. Iago
kils his wife. Qq (*runs, kills Q2*); *not in F.*   237. has] *Qq;* hath *F.*   238. S.D.]
Qq; not in F.   240. you this] *F;* your *Qq.*   241. here] *Qq; not in F.*
244. S.D.] *Qq* (*Mont.*); *Exit F.*   247-9. What . . . *willow.*] *F, Q2; not in Q1.*
249. *Singing*] Dyce.

236. *Precious*] colloquially intensi-
fies a word of abuse; "you precious
pandar", "Thou precious varlet"
(*Cym.*, III. v. 81, IV. ii. 83).

240. *notorious*] out-and-out (not
necessarily with the connotation of
"well known"); "you have done me
wrong, Notorious wrong" (*Tw.N.*,
v. i. 340). Cf. IV. ii. 142 above.

you this] The difference between Q
and F is important for stage business.
With *your*, an unarmed Othello has to
snatch Gratiano's sword for his attack
on Iago. Montano disarms him and
returns the sword to its owner. With
you this the sword is his own, taken from
him and given to Gratiano for safe
custody. The critical question is "Was
Othello armed when he entered at the
beginning of the scene?" And Emilia's

"I care not for thy sword" at l. 166
seems to make it plain that he was.
Recover'd in Elizabethan English can
as well mean "taken away from" as
"taken back from".

244. *neither*] Cf. "nay, that cannot be
so neither" (*Gent.*, II. iii. 18), "And not
be all day neither" (*All's W.*, II. i. 94).

245. *whipster*] "A vague term of reproach, contempt, or the like"
(*O.E.D.*); but it is not clear why it is a
term of contempt. May it be from a
boy whipping a top?

246. *why . . . honesty*] Why should
any concern for reputation remain
active when honour in the true sense
of an honourable life has been lost?

248-9. *swan . . . music*] an allusion to
the belief that the otherwise tuneless
swan sings just before its death.

So speaking as I think, I die, I die.   [*She dies.*

Oth. I have another weapon in this chamber,
It is a sword of Spain, the ice-brook's temper;
O, here it is; uncle, I must come forth.   255

Gra. [*Within*] If thou attempt it, it will cost thee dear;
Thou hast no weapon, and perforce must suffer.

Oth. Look in upon me then, and speak to me,
Or, naked as I am, I will assault thee.

Enter GRATIANO.

Gra. What is the matter?
Oth.   Behold, I have a weapon,   260
A better never did itself sustain
Upon a soldier's thigh: I have seen the day,

---

252. I die, I die] *Qq*; alas, I dye *F*.   S.D.] *Qq*; *not in F.*   254. It is] *Qq*; It
was *F*.   the ice-brook's] the Ice brookes *F*; the Isebrookes *Qq*; the Ebro's
Pope, Theobald, Capell.   256. (*Within*)] Gra. *within, opposite l.* 255, *Q1*; *not in F,
Q2.*   258. to] *Qq*; with *F*.   259. S.D.] *Theobald* (*Re-enter*).

---

254. *sword of Spain . . . ice-brook's
temper*] Spain, and in Shakespeare's
time especially Bilbao, as well as
Toledo, was famous for swords. It is
the fashion at the moment to point out
that "Isebrooke" (the Qq spelling
here) was one of several contemporary
spellings of Innsbruck, and that Innsbruck produced notably fine steel
which was imported into England
from the early sixteenth century till the
Civil War. As a piece of information
this is interesting; as a comment on
the present passage it seems quite beside the point. Dillon (on "Weapons",
in *Shakespeare's England*, I. 133) airily
says "Othello's expression merely
means a Spanish blade of the best
Innsbruck temper". But that surely is
a very odd description of a sword. It is
as though one should say "Here is a
first-rate Toledo—well, no, I really
mean an Innsbruck", since on this
interpretation there was nothing for
the famous Spanish craftsman to do
but fit a hilt and scabbard to an
Innsbruck-forged blade.
Steevens, not improbably, though

perhaps too particularizingly, was for
identifying the *ice-brook* with the Salo,
the small stream on which Bilbilis
stood, which Martial described as
"armorum temperator" (*Epig.*, IV. lv.
15), and even more significantly as
"qui ferrum gelat" (I. l. 12). It should,
however, be noticed that though
"icicle" appears in such forms as
"isicle" and "ysicle", the plain "ice",
in a number of occurrences where I
have checked it, is uniformly spelt with
a *c*; in *H 5* (Q), however, "Iceland"
appears as "Iseland" (II. i. 44).
255–60.] Othello here "proceeds to
play a grimly comic little practical
joke upon Gratiano. . . A typically
Shakespearean device: to follow the
tragic moment of Emilia's death by
this semi-comic trick, so both separat-
ing it from the tragedy still to come,
and heightening this by contrast."
(Granville Barker.)
259. *naked*] unarmed; " Thrice is he
arm'd that hath his quarrel just, And
he but naked, though lock'd up in
steel, Whose conscience . . ." (*2 H 6,*
III. ii. 233).

That with this little arm, and this good sword,
I have made my way through more impediments
Than twenty times your stop: but O vain boast,   265
Who can control his fate? 'tis not so now.
Be not afraid, though you do see me weapon'd:
Here is my journey's end, here is my butt,
And very sea-mark of my utmost sail.
Do you go back dismay'd? 'tis a lost fear: 270
Man but a rush against Othello's breast,
And he retires. Where should Othello go?
Now: how dost thou look now? O ill-starr'd wench,
Pale as thy smock, when we shall meet at count,
This look of thine will hurl my soul from heaven,   275
And fiends will snatch at it: cold, cold, my girl,
Even like thy chastity; O cursed slave!
Whip me, you devils,
From the possession of this heavenly sight,
Blow me about in winds, roast me in sulphur,   280

---

265. your] *F, Q2;* you *Q1.*   267–73. Be . . . wench,] *F, Q2; not in Q1.*
269. And] *F;* The *Q2.*   273. Now: how] *F;* How *Q2.*   274. count] *Q1;*
compt *F, Q2.*   277. cursed] *Qq;* cursed, cursed *F.*   278. you] *Qq;* ye *F.*

---

264. *impediments*] "cracking ten
thousand curbs Of more strong link
asunder than can ever Appear in your
impediment" (*Cor.*, i. i. 74).

267–73.] The absence of these lines
from Q1 is very surprising. They do
not seem to be at all a probable cut,
since the transition to *Pale as thy smock*
becomes impossibly abrupt. The best
that I can suggest is that in the
original l. 273 ended with the second
now, that the Q1 compositor took off
wrongly from it instead of from the
now in l. 266, and that F in making the
insertion completed the incomplete
line. "Ill-starr'd wench" is not a very
happy address to Desdemona, and in
fact the pause represented by the incomplete line, as he moves again to
the bed, would be effective. Or perhaps the cut was meant to end, and
possibly begin, a line earlier, running
from *Who* to *go?*

268. *butt*] aim, and so "goal"; "as
an aim or butt" (*H 5,* i. ii. 186).

269. *sea-mark*] beacon, or other pro-
minent object that helps a landfall;
"Like a great sea-mark, standing
every flaw, And saving those that eye
thee" (*Cor.*, v. iii. 74).

270. *lost*] idle; "It were lost sorrow to
wail one that's lost" (*R 3,* ii. ii. 11).

273. *wench*] could be used as an
address of affection and even respect,
or very much the reverse; Lucio so
addresses Isabella, whom he regards
as "a thing ensky'd and sainted", and
Titus Andronicus calls his much
loved daughter "sweet wench".

274. *Pale . . . smock*] See note on l. 90
above.

count] clearly "day of judgement",
though not elsewhere in Shakespeare
in this sense; but cf. *John,* iv. ii. 216,
"when the last account 'twixt heaven
and earth Is to be made".

Wash me in steep-down gulfs of liquid fire!
O Desdemona, Desdemona dead,
Oh, oh, oh.

Enter LODOVICO, MONTANO, *Officers with* IAGO, *prisoner,*
and CASSIO *in a chair.*

Lod. Where is this rash and most unfortunate man?
Oth. That's he that was Othello; here I am.　　　285
Lod. Where is this viper? bring the villain forth.
Oth. I look down towards his feet, but that's a fable,
　　　If that thou be'st a devil, I cannot kill thee.
　　　　　　　　　　　　　　[Wounds Iago.
Lod. Wring his sword from him.
Iago.　　　　　　　　I bleed, sir, but not kill'd.
Oth. I am not sorry neither, I 'ld have thee live,　　　290
　　　For in my sense 'tis happiness to die.
Lod. O thou Othello, that wert once so good,
　　　Fall'n in the practice of a damned slave,
　　　What should be said to thee?
Oth.　　　　　　　　Why, anything,
　　　An honourable murderer, if you will:　　　295
　　　For nought did I in hate, but all in honour.
Lod. This wretch hath part confess'd his villainy:
　　　Did you and he consent in Cassio's death?
Oth. Ay.
Cas. Dear general, I did never give you cause.　　　300
Oth. I do believe it, and I ask you pardon;
　　　Will you, I pray, demand that demi-devil

282–3. O . . . dead, Oh, oh, oh.] O . . . dead, O, o, o. *Qq* (dead; *Q2*); Oh
Desdemon! dead Desdemon: dead. Oh, oh! *F.*　283. S.D.] *Enter* Lodouico,
Montano, Iago, *and officers.* Cassio *in a Chaire Qq* (*Q2* omits Iago); *Enter* Lodouico,
Cassio, Montano, and Iago, with Officers *F.*　284. unfortunate] *F*; infortunate *Qq.*
286. this] *Q1*; that *F, Q2.*　288. If that] *F, Q2*; If *Q1.*　S.D.] *Rowe.*
289. Wring] *Q1*; Wrench *F, Q2.*　292. wert] *Qq*; was *F.*　293. damned] *Qq*;
cursed *F.*　294. should] *Qq*; shall *F.*　296. did I] *Qq*; I did *F.*　300. did
never give] *Qq*; never gave *F.*　301. you] *Qq*; your *F.*　302. you, I] *F, Q2*;
you *Q1.*

287. *feet . . . fable*] i.e. that the devil
had cloven hoofs for feet.

291. *in my sense*] not "as I use the
word" but "to one who feels as I
do".

293. *practice*] machinations; "Malicious practices against his state"
(*1 H 6*, IV. i. 7), "thou art suborn'd
against his honour In hateful practice"
(*Meas.*, v. i. 107).

Why he hath thus ensnar'd my soul and body?

Iago. Demand me nothing, what you know, you know,
From this time forth I never will speak word.   305

Lod. What, not to pray?

Gra.   Torments will ope your lips.

Oth. Well, thou dost best.

Lod. Sir, you shall understand what hath befall'n,
Which, as I think, you know not: here is a letter,
Found in the pocket of the slain Roderigo;   310
And here another; the one of them imports
The death of Cassio; to be undertook
By Roderigo.

Oth. O villain!

Cas.   Most heathenish, and most gross!

Lod. Now here's another discontented paper,   315
Found in his pocket too, and this, it seems,
Roderigo meant to have sent this damned villain,
But that, belike, Iago in the nick
Came in, and satisfied him.

Oth.   O the pernicious caitiff!
How came you, Cassio, by a handkerchief,   320
That was my wife's?

Cas.   I found it in my chamber,
And he himself confess'd it even now,
That there he dropp'd it, for a special purpose,
Which wrought to his desire.

Oth.   O fool, fool, fool!

Cas. There is besides in Roderigo's letter   325
How he upbraids Iago, that he made him

---

317. to have] *Qq*; t'have *F*.   318. nick] *Q1*; interim *F, Q2*.   319. O the] *Qq*;
Oh thou *F*.   caitiff] catieffe *Qq*; Caitiffe *F*.   320. a] *Qq*; that *F*.   322. it]
Q1; it but *F, Q2*.

314. *gross*] not, I think, "plain" as at
I. ii. 72 above, but "outrageous",
"monstrous"; "I will acquaint his
majesty Of those gross taunts" (*R 3*,
I. iii. 105), "every hour He flashes
into one gross crime or other" (*Lr.*,
I. iii. 4).
318. *nick*] F's "interim" seems a
clear case of sophistication.

320. *a*] Q1's reading is clearly the
right logic for a cross-examining
counsel, since Cassio has no notion
that the handkerchief is of any importance; to him it is merely something
whose unexpected presence in his room
puzzled him; but it is so important to
Othello that F's "that" is perhaps
more natural.

Brave me upon the watch, whereon it came
That I was cast; and even but now he spake,
After long seeming dead, Iago hurt him,
Iago set him on.　　　　　　　　　　　　　　330
Lod. You must forsake this room, and go with us,
Your power and your command is taken off,
And Cassio rules in Cyprus: for this slave,
If there be any cunning cruelty,
That can torment him much, and hold him long,　335
It shall be his: you shall close prisoner rest,
Till that the nature of your fault be known
To the Venetian state; come, bring him away.
Oth. Soft you, a word or two:
I have done the state some service, and they know 't;　340
No more of that: I pray you in your letters,
When you shall these unlucky deeds relate,
Speak of them as they are; nothing extenuate,
Nor set down aught in malice; then must you speak
Of one that lov'd not wisely, but too well:　　　345
Of one not easily jealous, but being wrought,
Perplex'd in the extreme; of one whose hand,
Like the base Indian, threw a pearl away,

---

338. bring him] *Qq;* bring *F.*　　339. two] *Q1;* two before you goe *F, Q2.*
343. them as they are] *Q1;* me, as I am *F, Q2* (me as I am *Q2*).　　344. then
must you] *Q1, F;* then you must *Q2.*　　348. Indian] *Qq;* Iudean *F.*

327. *Brave*] provoke insolently; "Is't
not enough to break into my garden
... But thou wilt brave me with these
saucy terms?" (*2 H 6,* IV. x. 35, 38);
and cf. I. i. 100 above.
　328. *cast*] See note on I. i. 149 above.
　332. *taken off*] It is not till here that
Othello is in any proper sense
"deposed", and Cassio becomes the
governor, not the governor's deputy.
　339.] F completes the line; probably
more effective dramatically without
the completion.
　343. *extenuate*] tone down—not
necessarily with any sense of "excuse";
"We will extenuate rather than en-
force" (*Ant.,* v. ii. 124).
　346. *easily*] If Othello had said
"naturally" he would have been

speaking the exact truth. See p. lvi.
　347. *Perplex'd*] not so much
"puzzled" as "distracted", pulled this
way and that; "I am perplex'd, and
know not what to say.—What canst
thou say but will perplex thee more,
If thou stand excommunicate and
curs'd?" (*John,* III. i. 221), "In per-
plexity and doubtful dilemma" (*Wiv.,*
IV. v. 86), and, in particular, "What is
in thy mind, That makes thee stare
thus? Wherefore breaks that sigh
From the inward of thee? One, but
painted thus, Would be interpreted a
thing perplex'd" (*Cym.,* III. iv. 4–7).
　348–9. *Indian ... tribe*] F's "Iudean"
has provoked a spate of comment,
attempts being made to identify him
with Herod (who discarded Mari-

Richer than all his tribe: of one whose subdued eyes,
Albeit unused to the melting mood,   350
Drops tears as fast as the Arabian trees
Their medicinal gum; set you down this,
And say besides, that in Aleppo once,
Where a malignant and a turban'd Turk
Beat a Venetian, and traduc'd the state,   355
I took by the throat the circumcised dog,
And smote him thus.   [*Stabs himself.*

Lod. O bloody period!
Gra.   All that's spoke is marr'd.
Oth. I kiss'd thee ere I kill'd thee, no way but this,
Killing myself, to die upon a kiss.   360
                                  [*Falls on the bed, and dies.*

Cas. This did I fear, but thought he had no weapon,
For he was great of heart.
Lod.   [*To Iago*] O Spartan dog,

---

351. Drops] *Q1, F;* Drop *Q2.*   352. medicinal] *Qq;* Medicinable *F.*
354. malignant . . . Turk] *Malignant* and a *Turband Turke Q1;* malignant, and a
Turbond-Turke *F;* Malignant and a Turband *Turke Q2.*   357. S.D.] *Qq; not
in F.*   358. that's] *Qq;* that is *F.*   362. Spartan] Spartane *Q1;* Sparton *F;*
Spartane Q2.

---

amne) or with Judas. But is any more needed, to make Othello's parallel straightforward instead of complicated, than a current traveller's tale of an Indian who, in ignorance of its value, threw away a priceless pearl? No passage giving the episode in those precise terms has, so far as I know, been adduced, but for a number of passages which come very near it the reader may be referred to Furness's Variorum ed., *ad loc.*, and to another passage quoted by Hart from Jonson's *Discoveries.* And cf. Drayton's *Matilda*, l. 287, "The wretched Indian spurns the golden ore", and K. Tillotson's note (Works of M. Drayton, v, 33). Anyone determined to adhere to F may justly point out that the significant letter is not the *u* (easily confusable with *n*) but the *e*, since F nowhere else prints "Indean" but always "Indian", and that the (to

our ears) awkward metre need not detain us, since the dactylic pronunciation would have been normal. It is, by the way, clear that Dryden either accepted "Indian" in this passage, or knew the hypothetical story—perhaps both: "they themselves, like Indians, know not the value of their own commodity" (*Dramatic Poetry of the Last Age*, i. 171 of W. P. Ker ed.).

354. *turban'd*] Why is a matter of head-dress apparently 'pejorative'?

358. *period*] full stop; common in American in this metaphorical sense, though with us *period* = full stop is almost exclusively a printer's term.

362. *Spartan dog*] Why *Spartan*? "Spartan" when applied to a hound normally connotes excellence. Perhaps from the notion of tenacity comes the idea of "relentless", but I feel that we must be missing some allusion, as with "Roman" earlier.

More fell than anguish, hunger, or the sea,
Look on the tragic lodging of this bed:
This is thy work, the object poisons sight,   365
Let it be hid: Gratiano, keep the house,
And seize upon the fortunes of the Moor,
For they succeed to you: to you, lord governor,
Remains the censure of this hellish villain,
The time, the place, the torture: O, enforce it!   370
Myself will straight aboard, and to the state
This heavy act with heavy heart relate.   [*Exeunt.*

---

364. lodging] *Qq;* Loading *F.*   368. succeed to] *Qq;* succeed on *F.*   369.
the censure] *Qq;* the Censure *F.*

---

363. *fell*] grim; "fell and cruel hounds" (*Tw.N.*, i. i. 22), "fell as death" (*Troil.*, iv. v. 268).

364. *lodging*] Shakespeare three times uses *lodge* in the sense of "beat down corn" (by rain or storms); "We'll make foul weather with despised tears; Our sighs and they shall lodge the summer corn" (*R 2*, iii. iii. 161), "Like to the summer's corn by tempest lodg'd" (*2 H 6*, iii. ii. 176), "Though bladed corn be lodg'd and trees blown down" (*Mac.*, iv. i. 55). The word is therefore not in itself suspect, but it is a *countryman's* word, to a townsman almost a dialect word. In *Country Life* for 3 May 1941 appeared an article, "Lodging; an Acute War-Time Problem"; the title suggested an article on billeting of evacuees or the like; but it was, with a vivid photograph, on the disastrous effect of storms on crops. And the picture is surely much more vivid than that of F's "loading". Q2 was evidently not worried by the semi-dialect word, but the change might easily have been made by someone who was so worried, or even by (or for) an actor who found *tragic lodging* awkward to enunciate.

365. *object*] what meets our eyes (not just "a thing"); "The object and the pleasure of mine eye Is only Helena" (*MND.*, iv. i. 176), "The present eye praises the present object" (*Troil.*, iii. iii. 180), "this object [the handless Lavinia] kills me" (*Tit.*, iii. i. 65).

368. *succeed to*] devolve on; "a ring... That downward hath succeeded in his house From son to son" (*All's W.*, iii. vii. 22).

369. *censure*] judgement; "Should censure thus on lovely gentlemen" (*Gent.*, i. ii. 19, where Julia and Lucetta are playing the Portia-Nerissa game over suitors); but once in Shakespeare it comes near to "punishment"—"content To suffer lawful censure for such faults As shall be prov'd upon you" (*Cor.*, iii. iii. 44) and that may be its sense here.

APPENDIX A

(a) I. i. 15. *And in conclusion.* Not essential to sense, but the absence of the *And* is awkward in F.

(b) I. iii. 201. *Into your favour.* Not essential to sense, but very desirable (see note *ad loc.*).

(c) I. iii. 278. Des. *Tonight, my Lord?* Duke. *This night.* Probably an omission by F, the compositor or transcriber having been confused by three *nights*, and taking off for Othello's *With all my heart* from the third of them.

(d) I. iii. 377–80. Four lines of interchange between Iago and Roderigo are represented in F by five words from Roderigo which are not in Q1. It rather looks as though compositor or transcriber had got confused with two *Go to, farewells* and with two *Roderigos*, even though one is in text and one in stage-direction. But this does not account for F's *I'll sell all my land*, and it is possible that F represents a revision, made if the longer interchange was found to drag.

(e) II. i. 82. *And bring all Cyprus comfort.* Some phrase with an opening *and* seems needed to avoid the awkward asyndeton of the two preceding lines in F, followed by *O behold* standing as a line by itself.

(f) III. i. 30. *Do, good my friend.* Convenient, to cover the Clown's exit, but not essential. It makes a complete line with Cassio's greeting to Iago, but since it is not very clear in this passage where verse is meant to replace prose the point may be of no significance.

(g) III. iv. 90–1. Des. *I pray, talk me of Cassio.* Oth. *The handkerchief!* Probably a blunder in F (like that in (c)) caused by confusion with the repeated *handkerchief*, but might be a revision, if the handkerchief was felt to be getting wearisome.

(h) IV. ii. 33. *But not the words.* Not essential, but rounding off the sense; perhaps an F confusion due to the repeated *words*.

(i) IV. ii. 169. *And he does chide with you.* An incomplete line, not essential, but again a convenient rounding off; perhaps omitted by F to secure metrical regularity.

(j) v. ii. 85. Des. *O Lord, Lord, Lord!* This is the only one of the "Q only" passages which is *dramatically* important, since with Q1's reading Othello's *What voice is this?* refers to *Desdemona's* exclamation, and connects with his *Not dead?*, whereas with F's reading it can hardly refer to anything but *Emilia's* voice "within".

Longer "F Only" Passages

(a) i. i. 121–37. An improbable addition and a likely cut, the likelihood being enhanced by the slight awkwardness in sequence of Q1's *I beseech you, If she be . . .*

(b) i. ii. 72–7. I think a certain cut, since one can see the cutter joining the loose ends by reading "Such" instead of "For" at the beginning of l. 78.

(c) i. iii. 24–30. A needless passage from the First Senator, who has said the substance of it already. Probably therefore a cut, but it might, like (possibly) l. 36, be an addition to expand a minor part, or even have been intended for substitution, not addition.

(d) iii. iii. 389–97. An odd cut, since Iago's reply is more effective with it in, but an even odder addition.

(e) iii. iii. 460–7. It is often argued (see note *ad loc.*) that this passage could not possibly have been a cut, on the grounds that no one with so superb a piece of poetic rhetoric in front of him could have been so insensible as to cut it. But this line of argument seems to imply a failure to realize what it is that the cutter has to do. His business is to reduce the length of a play for performance without sacrificing anything *dramatically* essential. It happens that *Othello* is a very difficult play to cut without such sacrifice. Further, the Elizabethan cutter was too familiar with great poetry to feel that every bit of it must be preserved for the theatre. This passage is certainly not dramatically essential; it is even doubtful whether it is, *dramatically*, especially effective. There is a certain power in the blank "Never" followed at once by the vow. But one cannot deny that it may have been an addition.

(f) iv. i. 37–43. If a cut, a not ineffective shortening of Othello's raving. When one hears the speech in full on the stage, one is, I think, aware of a certain awkwardness in the intrusion of the not only coherent but somewhat mannered sentence "Nature ... instruction" into the moving incoherence of the rest. But it may well be argued that Shakespeare felt that Othello needed longer to work up to "*He falls down*" than he had first given him.

(g) IV. ii. 75–8. Quite possibly a mere blunder, the Q1 compositor taking off from the second "What committed?" A possible cut, and not an unadroit one, since *two* somewhat 'conceited' passages, both this and "The bawdy wind ... hear't", are perhaps hardly natural to Othello's present state of mind. And for that very reason I think less probably an addition.

(h) IV. ii. 153–66. A moving passage but hardly an essential one; a probable cut but a possible addition.

(i) IV. iii. 31–52 and 54–6. I think probably a cut, because of the apparently consequential cut at V. ii. 247. But it may be that all the passages were added because at some point in the stage-history of the play a boy actor was available with a greater talent for singing than the one for whom Shakespeare first wrote the part.

(j) IV. iii. 86–103. An undramatic disquisition. Probably a cut.

(k) V. ii. 152–5. A possible cut, but not a very happy one; but also not a very probable addition.

(l) V. ii. 186–94. A possible but awkward cut.

(m) V. ii. 267–73. As it stands, a very clumsy cut; but I suggest that the cut was intended to end, and perhaps also start, a line earlier.

I think then that with only one of these passages (g), is absence from Q1 likely to have been due to a compositor's blunder, and that with the rest it is reasonably attributable to cutting. I should regard all but (e), (f), (h), and (i) as almost certain cuts, and those four as probable cuts but possible additions.

SHORTER "F ONLY" PASSAGES

I. ii. 20. Needed for both metre and sense. Probably omitted by Q from confusion with the two *knows*.

I. ii. 65. Very desirable for sense. Q1 perhaps took the brackets for an indication of deletion. Or it may be that the cutter wanted, unwisely, to get rid of all references to magic and drugs except the general ones in ll. 78–9, which come with awkward abruptness if this line as well as 72–7 is cut.

I. iii. 16. An incomplete line, with a non-significant proper name. Perhaps a cut, but if so one wonders why it was ever there (see note *ad loc.*).

I. iii. 36. An interesting line, possibly an addition, to give a touch of colour to a pasteboard. But if an addition, clumsily made, since the messenger would not naturally carry on his syntax through the interruption, but would resume with something like "Some thirty sail".

I. iii. 63. As at I. ii. 65, brackets probably mistaken by Q1 for indication for deletion.

I. iii. 118. Essential, and its absence from Q1 can hardly have been due to anything but mere carelessness.

I. iii. 194. Perhaps due to the same blunder by Q1 as I. ii. 20, but see note *ad loc.*

I. iii. 311 (*O villainous!*). Quite inessential, but useful, and perhaps an actor's addition or request.

I. iii. 363 (*if I depend on the issue*). A kind of glossing extension.

I. iii. 379 (*I'll sell all my land*). See comment on the passage in the "Q only" list.

II. i. 39–40 (*Even till . . . regard*). About equally odd as cut or as addition. If a cut, perhaps because the phrase was felt to be not only far from lucid in itself, but also too mannered for Montano.

II. i. 157. Clearly, since it is the rhyming line, a careless omission by Q1.

II. i. 239–59. An interesting passage, since it includes a higher proportion of variants than almost any other of the like length in the play, and this is thrown into prominence by the comparatively close coincidence of the two texts on either side of the passage. Apart from several verbal variants, like F's *slipper and subtle* instead of *subtle slippery*, one or two blunders, like F's *mutabilities* instead of *mutualities*, and one (probable) easing of syntax by F, there are the following words and phrases peculiar to F: in 239, *most* and *loose* (making *and most hidden loose affection*); 239–40 (after *Affections*), *Why none, why none*; 242 (before *Besides*), *A devilish knave*; 251 (between *Moor* and *Didst*), *Blest pudding*; 252 (after *his hand?*), *Didst not mark that?*; 253 (between *Yes* and *but*), *that I did*; 254, *obscure* (as epithet to *prologue*); 257 (before *When these*), *Villainous thoughts, Roderigo*; 258 (between *the* and *main*), *Master and*; 259 (after *conclusion*), *Pish.* Since it is difficult to imagine a reason for so many words being omitted in so short a space, these look like the result of a design to enliven the passage, mostly, it will be noticed, by parenthetic words and phrases which do not affect the sense.

II. ii. 9 (*of feasting*). More probably an addition than either a cut or accidental omission.

II. iii. 97 (*and there be souls must not be saved*). Possibly an omission by Q1, due to the two *saved*s, possibly an 'improving' balance added in F.

II. iii. 254. F has a third *reputation* before *I ha'*. It would be easily omitted, but perhaps Burbage was fond of 'triples', as in *Hamlet*.

II. iii. 271–3 (*Drunk ... shadow?*). An improbable omission, and not, I think, a very probable cut, since it is both short and effective. It looks rather like an addition, colouring up Cassio's part with a bit of characteristic self-deprecation.

III. i. 20 (between *vanish* and *away*) *into air*.

III. i. 56. An exit half-line for Cassio, *I am much bound to you*. Not at all essential, but useful as covering the exit, and (more or less) regularizing the metre. Hardly a cut, just possibly a careless omission, but a quite natural addition in rehearsal.

III. iii. 168–9. After *custody* F reads Oth. *Ha!* Iago. *Oh, beware my Lord of jealousy*. Hardly a careless omission by Q1 and probably therefore a regularization of metre by F.

III. iii. 330. A quite probable omission, through confusion of *poison* and *poisons*, but a possible addition, if it was felt that something more specific than l. 331 was needed as a point of reference for Iago's *I did say so* in l. 334.

III. iv. 7–8. Not essential, but useful; if an omission, perhaps due to a confusion of *To tell you where* and *I know not where*.

III. iv. 10 (between *lies* and *there*) *here, or he lies*. Perhaps an omission, due to confusion between *here* and *there*, but possibly an over-elaborating addition. Both this and the last might have been concessions to the Clown, lengthening, even if only by a trifle, his meagre part.

III. iv. 193–4 (*Why ... you not*). Must, I think, be an omission (though an odd one), since Cassio's remark, or something like it, is needed for lead-in to Bianca's *But that you do not love me*.

IV. i. 119 (after *wit*) *what? a customer?* Probably an addition—again, it will be noticed, to Cassio's part.

IV. i. 171–3. A very odd omission, since Iago's speech, or something like it, is essential. But it is clear that the Q1 compositor had a speech for Iago in front of him, and indeed probably set it, since after Othello's *Was that mine?*, which is the last line on the page, there is, as catch-word, a speech-heading "Iag.", and the next page starts with a fresh speech-heading for Othello.

IV. i. 192. Instead of the second *the pity*, F has the expanded *oh, Iago, the pity of it, Iago*. The omission of the *whole* of the phrase, from confusion with the three *Iago*s, might be natural, but the omis-

sion of *oh*, *Iago*, and *of it*, *Iago*, leaving the second *the pity* standing, seems improbable. I fancy an actor's (authorized) addi-
tion.

IV. ii. 52 (between *my* and *hopes*) *utmost*. Perhaps a regularizing addition, since though Q1's line can be made to scan, the stresses
are awkward, and F's, even if overcrowded, runs more naturally, though metrically even smoother would have been *me and
all my*.

IV. ii. 103 (both speeches). A very awkward omission, but it can
hardly have been anything else.

IV. ii. 187 (*With nought but truth*). An improbable omission, but not
a wholly convincing or necessary addition, since Roderigo's
exasperation might well leave out this logical step.

IV. ii. 219 (between *Well* and *is it*) *what is it?* Probably an omission, due to taking off from the second *is it*.

V. i. 77. F has a third *Cassio*, making another 'triplet'.

V. i. 82–3. An improbable omission. Perhaps an addition, to prepare longer in advance for the entry of the chair in l. 97.

V. ii. 83 (between *hour* and *but while*) Oth. *Being done, there is no
pause*. An improbable cut, but as an addition none too lucid.
Perhaps it was felt in rehearsal that some words were needed,
rather than silence, during Desdemona's "striving".

V. ii. 247–9 (*What did ... willow*). Either cut or addition, according
to which view one takes of the passages in IV. iii.

V. ii. 339. F completes the line with *before you go*. Probably a metrically regularizing addition. The commanding abruptness without it is effective.

APPENDIX B

VARIANTS IN STAGE-DIRECTIONS

(I have not listed as variants either the expansion of contractions
(e.g. *Ex.* to *Exit* or *Oth.* to *Othello*), or the consistent variants of
Roderigo and *Emillia* (Q) as against *Rodorigo* and *Æmilia* (F).)

Q1	F
I. i. 1 Enter Iago and Roderigo.	Enter Rodorigo, and Iago.
81 Brabantio at a window.	Aboue (immediately after speech-heading Bra.)
144 (no S.D.)	Exit.

159 Enter Barbantio in his night gowne, and seruants with Torches.	Enter Brabantio, with Seruants and Torches.
ii. 1 Enter Othello, Iago, and attendants with Torches.	Enter Othello, Iago, Attendants, with Torches.
28 Enter Cassio with lights, Officers, and torches.	Enter Cassio, with Torches.
52 Enters Brabantio, Roderigo, and others with lights and weapons.	54 Enter Brabantio, Rodorigo, with Officers, and Torches
iii. 1 Enter Duke and Senators, set at a Table with lights and Attendants.	Enter Duke, Senators, and Officers.
12 Enter a Messenger	Enter Saylor.
32 Enter a 2. Messenger	Enter a Messenger.
46 Enter Brabantio, Othello, Roderigo, Iago, Cassio, Desdemona, and Officers.	Enter Brabantio, Othello, Cassio, Iago, Rodorigo, and Officers.
120 Exit two or three.	(no S.D.)
170 Enter Desdemona, Iago, and the rest.	Enter Desdemona, Iago, Attendants.
293 Exeunt.	Exit.
300 Exit Moore and Desdemona.	Exit.
379 Exit Roderigo.	Exit.
402 Exit.	(no exit for Iago)
ii. i. 1 Enter Montanio, Governor of Cypres, with two other Gentlemen.	Enter Montano, and two Gentlemen.
19 Enter a third Gentleman.	Enter a Gentleman.
51 Enter a Messenger (and "A sail . . ." given to him as he enters)	Within. A Saile, a Saile, a Saile (but no messenger's entry)
57 A shot.	(no S.D.)
65 Enter 2. Gentleman.	Enter Gentleman.
80 Enter Desdemona, Iago, Emillia, and Roderigo.	Enter Desdemona, Iago, Rodorigo, and Aemilia.
91 [within.] A saile, a saile.	(in text, not as S.D.)
178 Trumpets within.	(no trumpets)
198 they kisse.	(no S.D.)
212 Exit.	Exit Othello and Desdemona.

ii. 1	Enter a Gentleman reading a Proclamation.	Enter Othello's, Herald with a Proclamation.
11	(no exit)	Exit.
iii. 1	Enter Othello, Cassio, and Desdemona.	Enter Othello, Desdemona, Cassio, and Attendants.
11	Exit Othello and Desdemona.	Exit.
57	Enter Montanio, Cassio, and others.	Enter Cassio, Montano, and Gentlemen.
130	Exit Rod.	(no exit for Rodorigo)
136	Helpe, helpe, within	(no S.D.)
137	Enter Cassio, driving in Roderigo.	Enter Cassio pursuing Rodorigo.
147	they fight.	(no S.D.)
148	A bell rung.	(no S.D.)
154	Enter Othello, and Gentlemen with weapons.	Enter Othello, and Attendants.
240	Enter Desdemona, with others.	Enter Desdemona attended.
251	Exit Moore, Desdemona, and attendants.	Exit.
326	Exit.	Exit Cassio.
372	(no exit for Roderigo)	Exit Rodorigo
378	Exeunt.	Exit.
III. i. 1	Enter Cassio, with Musitians and the Clowne.	Enter Cassio, Musitians, and Clowne.
20	(no exit for Musicians)	Exit Mu.
29	Enter Iago. (but no exit for Clown)	Exit Clo. Enter Iago.
56	Exeunt	(no S.D.)
ii. 1	Enter Othello, Iago, and other Gentlemen.	Enter Othello, Iago, and Gentlemen.
iii. 28	Enter Othello, Iago, and Gentlemen.	Enter Othello, and Iago.
90	Exit Desd. and Em.	Exit.
293	Ex. Oth. and Desd.	292 Exit
458	he kneeles.	(no S.D.)
471	Iago kneeles.	(no S.D.)
iv. 1	Enter Desdemonia Emilla and the Clowne.	Enter Desdemona, Aemilia, and Clown.
17	Exit.	Exit Clo.
94	Exit.	Exit Othello.
135	(no exit for Iago)	Exit.

164 Exeunt Desd. and Emillia.	Exit.
198 Exeunt.	Exeunt omnes.
IV. i. 1 Enter Iago and Othello.	Enter Othello, and Iago.
37 He fals downe.	43 Falls in a Traunce.
165 Exit Cassio.	(no exit for Cassio)
207 A Trumpet.	(no trumpet)
ii. 173 Exit women. Enter Roderigo.	Exeunt Desdemona and Aemilia. Enter Rodorigo.
243 Exit Iag. and Rod.	Exeunt.
iii. 1 Enter Othello, Desdemona, Lodouico, Emillia, and Attendants. (put earlier, after "about it" in l. 241 of preceding scene)	Enter Othello, Lodouico, Desdemona, Aemilia, and Attendants.
9 Exeunt.	Exit.
v. i. 36 Ex. Enter Lodouico and Gratiano.	Exit Othello. Enter Lodouico and Gratiano.
45 Enter Iago with a light.	Enter Iago.
109 Enter Em.	(no entry for Emilia)
ii. 1 Enter Othello with a light.	Enter Othello, and Desdemona in her bed.
19 He kisses her.	(no S.D.)
84 he stifles her.	Smothers her.
85 Emillia calls within.	Aemilia at the doore.
126 she dies.	(no S.D.)
168 Enter Montano, Gratiano, Iago, and others.	Enter Montano, Gratiano, and Iago.
199 Oth. fals on the bed.	(no S.D.)
235 The Moore runnes at Iago. Iago kils his wife.	(no S.D.)
238 Exit Iago	(no exit for Iago)
244 Exit Mont. and Gratiano.	Exit.
252 she dies.	(no S.D.)
256 Gra. within.	(no S.D.)
283 Enter Lodouico, Montano, Iago, and Officers Cassio in a Chaire.	Enter Lodouico, Cassio, Montano, and Iago, with Officers.
357 He stabs himselfe.	(no S.D.)
360 He dies.	Dyes
372 Exeunt omnes.	Exeunt.

The relation of Q2 to Q1 is interesting. In the first place it is substantially identical with Q1, even in some minor points of spelling

e.g. it retains "Emillia", and even follows Q1 in a misprint
"Emilla" at III. iv. 1, and "Montanio" at II. i. 1 and II. iii. 57, but
"Montano" at v. ii. 168). Typographically it follows Q1 in the use
of roman type for proper names and italic for the rest. It makes a
few corrections, such as "Brabantio" for "Barbantio" at I. i. 159,
"Enter" for "Enters" at I. ii. 52, "Exeunt" for "Exit" at I. iii. 120,
"Cyprus" for "Cypres" at II. i. 1, "Trumpet" for "Trumpets" at
II. i. 178, "Exeunt" for "Exit" at II. i. 212 and III. iii. 90, "Desdemona" for "Desdemonia" at III. iv. 1, inserts the necessary exit for
Cassio at IV. i. 58 (here correcting both Q1 and F). It sometimes
expands an abbreviation, usually where it allots a whole line to
an S.D. which Q1 had compressed into the margin. It makes
one or two blunders, omitting Emilia's exit at IV. ii. 30, reading
"Gragantio" for "Gratiano" at v. ii. 168, and omitting Iago from
the entry at v. ii. 283. But on the whole it is a straightforward reproduction of Q1, retaining—apart from two of the three blunders
last mentioned—all that Q1 had and F had not.

Its significant divergences are as follows:

(i) II. ii. 1. "Enter Othello's Herauld, reading a Proclamation"
(i.e. preferring F, though deleting its intrusive comma).

(ii) II. iii. 155. Substitutes an S.D. "he faints" where F has "He
dies" in the text, and Q1 has neither (see note *ad loc.*).

(iii) III. i. 1–2. Here the 'editor' of Q2 takes a line of his own, thus:

> *Enter* Cassio, *with Musitians.*
> *Cas.* Masters, play here, I will content your paines,
>   Something thats brief, and bid good morrow Generall.
>   *They play, and enter the Clowne.*

(iv) IV. i. 43. "Falles in a trance" (i.e. preferring F).

(v) IV. ii. 88. Puts Emilia's entry four lines later than Q1 and a
line earlier than F.

(vi) v. i. 61. Adds "Thrusts him in", which is in neither Q1 nor F.

(vii) v. ii. 1. Conflates the other two texts into "Enter Othello with
a light, and Desdemona in her bed."

(viii) v. ii. 15. Retains Q1's S.D. for the kiss (which is not in F) but
puts it four lines earlier, after "I'll smell it on the tree" instead of after "and this the last".

APPENDIX C

PUNCTUATION

I have said most of what I want to say about Shakespearean punctuation in general in the Preface to *Antony and Cleopatra* in this edition (pp. xi–xviii), and I may as well repeat the substance of it here. In the last forty years or so a great deal more attention has been paid to the punctuation of the early Quarto and First Folio texts than had been paid by earlier editors, who felt themselves free to play any old Harry they chose with the original punctuation. This increased attention was largely due to Percy Simpson's *Shakespearian Punctuation* (1911). To this book, something of a landmark in Shakespearean scholarship, I will return later, but for the moment it is worth while to ask *why* earlier editors felt justified in allowing themselves such freedom. The assumption that punctuation could be properly treated much more high-handedly than words arose, I think, in part from a misconception which has nothing to do with Simpson's thesis, and which can be examined without reference to it. To editors accustomed to a style of punctuation mainly 'syntactical', a guide to logical comprehension, the punctuation of early Shakespeare texts inevitably seemed very strange, and it was not unnatural that instead of looking for a principle behind it they dismissed it as haphazard and careless, and rectified it according to their own principles.[1] But the idea that punctuation is anyway much more likely to have been carelessly handled than words depends on a misconception of how a compositor works. The compositor is a man who is trying to turn, as accurately as he can, the 'copy' in front of him into something which, when duly dealt with by the printer, will reproduce that copy in a printed page. Before the invention of linotype or monotype machines, the compositor did this by selecting, one by one, from the 'cases' in front of him a series of pieces of type corresponding to the marks on the paper of the copy. Whether these "marks"

---

1. The attitude of almost all these editors, and most of their successors, is well expressed by Johnson, and his statement is significant, since it comes from an editor who, so far as the verbal text was concerned, was extremely conservative, and never emended himself or accepted the emendations of others except where he considered that there was overwhelming cause. "In restoring the authour's works to their integrity, I have considered the punctuation as wholly in my power; for what could be their care of colons and commas, who corrupted words and sentences. Whatever could be done by adjusting points is therefore silently performed. . ." The right answer to Johnson's rhetorical question, "what care . . .", as I have tried to suggest, is "about the same" instead of the one which he implies, "none"

are letters or marks of punctuation (or, for that matter, spaces, which are also pieces of type) is a matter of indifference to him; each must be represented by its appropriate piece of type. He does not say "so long as I get the letters right it does not matter what happens to the punctuation." Give him the following four marks in the manuscript, *end:*, and he is no more likely to set a comma instead of the colon than to set an *e* for the *d* (in an Elizabethan printing-house he was in fact a good deal less likely, since in Elizabethan script *e* and *d* were very easily confused, so that we have *end* for an undoubted *due* in Sonnet LXIX). It is true that there may be with punctuation slightly more danger of 'foul case', and also that punctuation seems to suffer somewhat readily from the malady known as 'transposed pointing' where the compositor's eye registers the right symbol but puts it in the wrong place, or registers the right pair of symbols but transposes their positions. But in general the 'expectation of error' should not be much higher with punctuation than with letters, unless the fault lies with the original copy. If we put it at double we are putting it high.

But editors till quite recently have put it far higher than that, and, using the freedom to which they considered they were entitled, they changed the punctuation, for the most part making it heavier, by substituting semi-colons or colons for commas, and full-stops for semi-colons and colons; but sometimes the changes worked in the opposite direction, when a heavier stop was lightened to a comma. Their operations as a whole, therefore, had two results: they slowed up the general rate of delivery; and they made the tempo more monotonous and often destroyed an effect of which Shakespeare—if for the moment we may assume that the punctuation was his—was clearly fond, that namely of giving three or four rapidly running phrases, separated only by commas, and ending them with the heaviest pause at his command, the full stop. Shakespeare, that is, was writing for dramatic delivery, while his editors re-write him for logical comprehension from the page. Many readers must have noticed that the actor frequently does not deliver his lines in the least as his modern text has carefully prepared them for him, but reverts—often no doubt simply from his actor's just instinct, and not from consultation of Quarto or Folio—to the delivery that Shakespeare intended for him, and indicated as his intention.

But in the last few lines above I have, of course, been begging, or partly begging, a main question. Have we any justification for assuming that the punctuation which the early texts represent, or, occasionally misrepresent, was Shakespeare's? Simpson's main thesis, in the book already mentioned, was this, that "Shakespearian" punctuation was not, like ours, an aid to understanding the syntactical construction of a sentence, but rather a guide to how the sentence should be delivered. It was "dramatic" or "rhetorical" rather than logical, and was, largely for that reason, usually considerably lighter than ours. Further, since it was not confined within the comparatively narrow limits of syntactical exposition, it was an instrument which could be used to indicate considerable, and often subtle, varieties of interpretation. It was a dramatic tool, not a grammatical one.

Of the fundamental soundness of Simpson's general idea there is, I think, little doubt, and of its importance, if sound, no doubt at all. But it is true that in the natural enthusiasm created by the application of a new idea a good deal of nonsense was talked, and attempts were made, for example, to justify every apparently intrusive comma by over-subtle argument which would not stand up to examination. As a result there has been a strong reaction, and some critics, eager to pounce on absurdities of detailed example, have been led—I think misled—into dismissing the whole theory as moonshine.[1]

Two distinct questions arise. Is the punctuation of the early texts an approximation to Shakespeare's own? If not, has it any connection with theatrical performance, or is it the compositor's own, following 'house-style' (if any), or his own temporary whim? Now those critics who hold that, except in a few special instances, it is idle to descry Shakespeare's, or any other playwright's, own intentions in the punctuation of the early texts, can justifiably point to the famous three pages of *Sir Thomas More*, which are most inadequately punctuated, and to some, though not all, of the other extant dramatic manuscripts of the period. But they seem tacitly to assume that if the punctuation is not the author's, then it is the compositor's. This is surely not so, and the view, I think, depends on a failure to imagine what must have happened to an author's manuscript after it was delivered to the players. Sir Edmund Chambers gives a clear account[2] of the operations of the man he calls the "stage-reviser"—the man, that is, who prepared the manuscript for direct use in the theatre, checking entries and exits, amplifying, if necessary, the stage-directions, and so on. But even Chambers does no more than glance by implication at another operation which this man must, so far as I can see, have conducted if it had not already been done. Before a play can go into

1. There is a balanced criticism of the theory in Chambers' *William Shakespeare*, I, pp. 190–6. I think he misses one point.
2. *Op. cit.*, pp. 108–23.

production, each actor must be handed a transcript of his part. But no actor can efficiently study an unpunctuated, or very inadequatly punctuated, part. Hence someone, whether the author himself or the "stage-reviser" (probably identical with the book-keeper), must complete the punctuation before these transcripts are made and handed out. And if the author is in close contact with the players (as, for example, Shakespeare and Heywood were) my guess is that the "someone" is likely to have been the author himself. But at least it seems moderately certain that the printed punctuation is the compositor's attempt to reproduce what was before him, and that that was at least contemporary *theatrical* punctuation.

But can we with any justification suppose that the punctuation of the original manuscript was Shakespeare's own? The probability, now generally accepted, that the manuscript which went to the printer was either Shakespeare's own original, or at worst at only one remove from that, does not much help us, since it can always be argued that, though the words were his, the punctuation was not, but was inserted by someone else. We are reduced therefore to an examination of a few bits of direct evidence and to a consideration of likelihood. The question to which we are trying to find what must be at best a largely conjectural answer is "Was Shakespeare a careless punctuator?"

In the first place it is demonstrable and generally admitted that on occasion he was extremely careful. The passage in *MND*., v. i. 108–15, is punctuated (i.e. mispunctuated, beyond the range of the wildest compositor's nightmare) to indicate the breathless misdelivery of the prologist; and the comments of Theseus and Lysander put this beyond doubt. Chambers also admits as examples of care on Shakespeare's part "Pistol's gabble when he eats the leek or the pace of Margaret's tongue in *Much Ado About Nothing*" (*H5*, v. i. 49, *Ado*, iii. iv. 78 onwards—both passages are unhappily over-punctuated in most modern editions). But I think that he misses the significance of the two passages, especially of Pistol's. The carefulness of the author, which is admitted, is shown not in punctuation, but in *non*-punctuation. To secure a particular effect he deliberately *omits* normal punctuation. But, if the whole manuscript had been very inadequately punctuated, no one, whether compositor or transcriber, would have noticed anything out of the way or suspected any particular intention on Shakespeare's part; as a result, surely, in would have gone some form of punctuation. Either, then, Shakespeare inserted specific directions that these passages were to be left almost unpunctuated, or these passages were at variance with his normal practice. I think the second alternative the more likely.

This is partly because I find it hard to accept the view that Shakespeare was "normally a rapid writer, who did not trouble about punctuation, but occasionally became more careful". Rapid he may have been, and probably was; but why therefore assume that he did not trouble about punctuation? After all, punctuation (of whatever type) is a tool of any writer's trade, and Shakespeare was a skilled workman; more, he was a skilled *dramatic* workman, who knew precisely the effects he wanted produced by the spoken word. I find it hard to believe that through mere carelessness he robbed himself of a device by the use of which he could go some way towards securing what he wanted.[1]

I think therefore that in the punctuation of the early texts we have, pretty certainly, at least 'playhouse' punctuation, and very possibly a great deal of Shakespeare's own. If this is so, it means that no modern editor can neglect the Q and F punctuation. I should go further, and be prepared to say that no editor can desert it without very careful consideration, and if he does so, does so at his peril. An alteration in the original punctuation should be regarded as no less an emendation than a change in a word, and should be felt to need the same kind of justification. The justification may often be much easier to find, but that is no excuse for not looking for it.

With a large number, then, of Shakespeare's plays—all those for which we have no text but F, and those others for which F, it is generally agreed, used Q for copy, with, as I hope to show, an almost precise adherence to its punctuation—the problem is simple. The editor must use his judgement as to his degree of adherence to the only text he has.

F's adherence to Q's punctuation in these plays is worth a moment's consideration, not least because it suggests another weakness in the theory that F of *Othello* was set from a corrected copy of Q1. If one takes three passages, *LLL.*, iv. iii. 327–65, *MND.*, ii. i. 77–113, and *Ado*, v. i. 268–301, one finds this. There is a large number of *spelling* variants (about one to every two lines), mostly of the trivial type of *othes–oathes*, *suckt–suck'd*, *do–doe*, or substitution of upper-case for lower-case letters, but F retains (in the *LLL.* passage) two odd spellings of Q, *sparcle* and *Achademes*; F corrects two mis-

---

1. It is perhaps worth noticing that Keats, who, in his letters, if not a careless is at least a very limited punctuator, often for long stretches contenting himself with little more than full stops and dashes, is yet, even in his letters, when he copies out a *poem*, a very careful punctuator; and I doubt whether Shakespeare was likely to be more careless than Keats.

spellings of Q and makes one error of its own (*Hesporides*). But in *punctuation* F's adherence to Q is remarkably close. It changes one semi-colon to a colon and omits four commas. If one adds to these passages the famous mis-punctuated prologue (*MND.*, v. i. 108) and finds F exactly reproducing Q, it becomes clear that Elizabethan compositors, or at any rate the compositors who set these passages, did not regard punctuation as something to be scanted of attention.

But the situation with Q1 and F of *Othello* is very different. Take two passages, Iago's speech to Roderigo at i. i. 144–59 and the opening of Othello's to the Senate at i. iii. 76–94. Here is the first in the two versions.

(Q) Farewell, for I must leaue you,
     It seemes not meete, nor wholesome to my pate,
     To be produc'd, as if I stay I shall
     Against the Moore, for I doe know the state,
     How euer this may gaule him with some checke,
     Cannot with safety cast him, for hee's imbark'd,
     With such loud reason, to the Cipres warres,
     Which euen now stands in act, that for their soules,
     Another of his fathome, they haue not
     To leade their businesse, in which regard,
     Tho I doe hate him, as I doe hells paines,
     Yet for necessity of present life,
     I must shew out a flag, and signe of loue,
     Which is indeed but signe, that you shall surely
     Finde him: lead to the Sagittar, the raised search,
     And there will I be with him. So farewell.

(F) Farewell: for I must leaue you.
     It seemes not meete, nor wholesome to my place
     To be producted, (as if I stay, I shall,)
     Against the Moore. For I do know the State,
     (How euer this may gall him with some checke)
     Cannot with safetie cast-him. For he's embark'd
     With such loud reason to the Cyprus Warres,
     (Which euen now stands in Act) that for their soules
     Another of his Fadome, they haue none,
     To lead their Businesse. In which regard,
     Though I do hate him as I do hell apines,
     Yet, for necessity of present life,
     I must show out a Flag, and signe of Loue,
     (Which is indeed but signe) that you shall surely find him
     Lead to the Sagitary the raised Search:
     And there will I be with him. So farewell.

Q1 is very lightly punctuated: in 16 lines it has 1 full stop (in all the passages I am neglecting the final periods that close them), and 1 colon; the rest of the 27 marks of punctuation are commas. F greatly slows the movement, by having 5 full stops and 2 colons. It also indicates, by brackets instead of (once in addition to) commas, 4 parentheses, though this does not affect the rate of movement. The difference in *number* of marks of punctuation is slight (only 2); the salient difference is in the *length* of pause indicated.

Here is the second passage.

Most potent, graue, and reuerend Seigniors,
My very noble and approoued good maisters:
That I haue tane away this old man's daughter,
It is most true: true, I haue married her,
The very head and front of my offending,
Hath this extent no more. Rude am I in my speech,
And little blest with the set phrase of peace,
For since these armes of mine had seuen yeares pith,
Till now some nine Moones wasted, they have vs'd
Their dearest action in the tented field,
And little of this great world can I speake,
More than pertains to feate of broyle, and battaile,
And therefore little shall I grace my cause,
In speaking for my selfe: yet by your gracious patience,
I will a round vnuarnish'd tale deliuer,
Of my whole course of loue, what drugs, what charmes,
What coniuration, and what mighty Magicke,
(For such proceedings am I charg'd withall)
I wonne his daughter.

Most Potent, Graue, and Reueren'd Signiors,
My very Noble, and approu'd good Masters;
That I haue tane away this old mans Daughter,
It is most true: true I haue married her;
The very head, and front of my offending,
Hath this extent; no more. Rude am I, in my speech,
And little bless'd with the soft phrase of Peace;
For since these Armes of mind, had seuen yeares pith,
Till now, some nine Moones wasted, they haue vs'd
Their deerest action, in the Tented Field:
And little of this great world can I speak,
More than pertaines to Feats of Broiles, and Battaile,
And therefore little shall I grace my cause,
In speaking for my selfe. Yet, (by your gratious patience)
I will a round vn-varnish'd uTale deliuer.
Of my whole course of Loue.
What Drugges, what Charmes.

> What Coniuration, and what mighty Magicke,
> (For such proceeding I am charg'd withall)
> I won his Daughter

Here the difference is even more strongly marked. Q1 itself punctuates Othello's speech more heavily than Iago's with 1 full stop and 3 colons in the 18½ lines. But F is heavier not only, as before, in quality (3 full stops, 2 colons, and 4 semi-colons), but also in total number of marks (37 to 29). And the same sort of difference is observable elsewhere, e.g. in Iago's speech at IV. i. 74 ("Stand you awhile apart") and Othello's at v. ii. 1 ("It is the cause"). In the first, each text has 2 colons and 1 semi-colon, but Q1 has no full stops, while F has 4. In the second, Q1 has 6 colons, 4 semi-colons, but no full stop, while F, though it has only 3 colons and no semi-colon, has 12 full stops.

Here, then, is clearly a real problem. Granted that we are right in assuming—and in view of the evidence earlier presented I think we are right—that the compositors were particularly careful with punctuation, we are compelled to conclude that the MSS. from which the two texts were set were markedly different in punctuation as in other things. Which then are we to accept as the more closely representing what Shakespeare intended? I admit that I have no very clear guidance about the answer, so long as one simply compares the passages as they stand, with no antecedent suppositions about the nature of the MSS. behind them. I should suggest the following comments: (a) Q1 is never, I think, inadequately punctuated—i.e. never so lightly that the actor would be at a loss as to his delivery; (b) it seems as though in Q1 a markedly more rapid delivery is indicated for Iago than for Othello; (c) F to a considerable extent, but by no means wholly, levels out this difference. Those, I think, are observable *facts*. But my fourth comment is quite probably coloured by a predisposition in favour of Q1; (d) a good deal of F's punctuation looks as though it were intended to help the *reader*, and therefore approaches modern 'syntactical' punctuation more nearly than Q1. My guess therefore is that with Q1 we are, as in other things, moderately near to Shakespeare, and that F exhibits a good deal of elaboration by Heminge and Condell. But it is no more than a guess, though if one is accepting Q1 in the main for the language, one can hardly without inconsistency desert its punctuation. The punctuation of this edition, therefore, adheres to Q1 so far as that can be done without unduly puzzling the modern reader.

But now consider the bearing of this on Dr Walker's theory of the corrected copy of Q1. If there had been an expectation that the compositors were going to be careless about punctuation, then no one needed to trouble much about it ("They'll get it wrong anyway, so let's not confuse them with more than a very few corrections"); but if the expectation was—as we have seen reason to suppose it would be—precisely the opposite, then the copy would have to be prepared with the most exact care if it was to have any chance of producing the desired text of F. In the $71\frac{1}{2}$ lines of the four passages instanced there would have had to be 40 corrections, 17 deletions, and 20 insertions, an average of just over one change per line. Is it really credible that some 3,000 alterations of this kind were made in a printed Q1, to say nothing of additions and verbal alterations, when, ex hypothesi, there was available a MS. already containing them?

APPENDIX D

DR A. WALKER'S THEORY

1. I suggested in the Introduction that the stage-directions are perhaps "traitors ensteep'd" to clog Dr Walker's keel. She sees the danger, and does her best to skirt it, not, I think, convincingly. She says: "That what was envisaged [i.e. in the assumed transcript which served as copy for Q1] was the reader is evident from a number of the quarto's stage directions which would be unnecessary in prompt copy. [Nine examples follow.] These seem literary in intention and expression, and from their omission from the Folio it would appear that they were not found in the more authoritative manuscript with which the quarto was collated to serve as Folio copy." Certainly it would appear that they were not found in the MS. which lay immediately behind F; but "more authoritative" and "was collated" are good examples of the promotion of hypothesis to established fact.

To examine Dr Walker's specific examples: they are *they kisse* (II. i. 198), *they fight* (II. iii. 147), *he kneeles* and Iago *kneeles* (III. iii. 457 and 469), *He kisses her* (v. ii. 15), *she dies* (v. ii. 126), Oth. *fals on the bed* (v. ii. 199), *The Moore runnes at* Iago. Iago *kils his wife* (v. ii. 236) *He stabs himselfe* (v. ii. 357). I do not see that any of these is particularly "literary" in expression, unless any stage-direction which is not imperatival is necessarily "literary". Which of them "would be unnecessary in prompt-copy"? Of course in a sense *any* stage-direction is unnecessary in prompt-copy, since the producer can by word of mouth secure any piece of business when he wants it. But, since for many pieces of business exact timing is essential, it is a great convenience to everyone concerned if this timing is indicated. I suggest that of these nine examples only two (*she dies* and *He stabs himself*) are both clearly indicated and precisely timed by the text; I suppose that for both the kissings there is something like a tacit stage-direction in the text, though I do not find "this, and this", nor "I'll smell it on the tree" very precise. But the business indicated by four of them is not even clearly indicated in the text. Othello's kneeling is indicated only by Iago's "Do not rise yet" two lines later, and Iago's kneeling is not indicated at all. Emilia's "Nay, lay thee down and roar" would be just as apposite if Othello had fallen in agony on the floor. And, though Iago's killing of Emilia is indicated in the following line, Othello's running at Iago can hardly be said to be stage-directed by "Precious villain!".

Dr Walker's argument seems hardly consistent with some earlier comments of her own in the chapter on *Troilus and Cressida*. She thinks that the MS. for the quarto of that play came "from some private source" and she finds "the most cogent evidence" for this in "the character of the quarto itself, which is notably lacking in just those features which for production would matter most—reliable speakers' names and serviceable stage directions." "Serviceable" seems exactly the right description of these stage-directions in Q1 of *Othello* which Dr Walker dismisses as "unnecessary in prompt copy". It becomes clear that slightness of stage-directions may point to a transcript for a reader, or to one for the theatre, at the discretion of the critic. Indeed a comparison of Dr Walker's two chapters, on *Troilus and Cressida* and *Othello*, is a salutary warning of a danger for ever present in this kind of criticism, the danger of falling into a frame of mind in which evidence, like Humpty Dumpty's words, means what the critic, for the moment, chooses that it shall mean—without prejudice to its meaning something else in another context.

But even acceptance of Dr Walker's view of the *Othello* Q1 stage-directions would leave untouched the point which is crucial for her theory. It is a very simple one: why did any sane person, preparing a copy of Q1 to serve as copy for F, deliberately *delete* a number of stage-directions, including almost all those which illuminate business? At worst they did nobody any harm, and at best they would help a reader's imagination. And surely F, even more certainly than Q, "envisaged" readers.

2. Here are some more passages put forward by Dr Walker as illustrating the "vulgarization" which she finds so prevalent in Q1.

(a) "Othello's 'Zouns' (Q) to Desdemona at III. iv. 95, replaced by 'Away' in the Folio, is as objectionable as his oath at III. iii. 158. So too is Emilia's 'O Lord' ('Alas' F) at v. ii. 118 and, worst of all, Othello's undignified 'vds death' at v. ii. 71." On what grounds "objectionable"? Out of character? undramatic? vulgar? A man of strong passions who believes himself to have been cuckolded is quite apt to use strong language. And why, if Hamlet may say "Swounds, I should take it", without losing his princely dignity, may not Othello also swear without losing his as the great general? Or should we invoke memorial contamination and assure ourselves that what Shakespeare meant Hamlet to say was "Sure, I should take it"? (It will be noticed that F's "Away" is just on a par with Woodhouse's "Away" or 1820's "Go, go!" for Keats' "O Christ!")

(b) "Vulgarization comes out very clearly in I. iii. 251. . . . Where Desdemona in the Folio describes her heart as subdued to the 'very quality' of Othello, the quarto substitutes [again the question-begging word] 'vtmost pleasure'. . . The 'rites' of modern editions (interpreted as 'love's rites') is a misunderstanding of Desdemona almost as bad as the quarto's 'vtmost pleasure'." For this passage I may refer to my note *ad loc.*, adding here only the comment that "rights" barely makes sense. Dr Walker says that Desdemona is asking for the privileges of sharing the hazards of war. But her anxiety to share them is the result of, not the reason for, her love.

(c) "More often than not . . . the readings of the quarto . . . lose the point, as in the substitution of 'her Sex' for 'their Wiues' at IV. ii. 18 or 'hated' for 'other' at IV. ii. 86." One feels that Dr Walker's growing exasperation with Q1 has betrayed her into a hastiness of judgement. In neither instance does Q1 lose the point; it makes a different point, even perhaps a stronger one. In the first, Q1, with "the purest of her Sex Is foul as slander" is saying "even the purest *maiden* is . . ." which is a more sweeping statement than F's "the purest of their Wives is . . ." If I were to follow Dr Walker in begging the question I should say that the *Folio* substitution was made by someone who was anxious to tie the phrase closely to the preceding "There's no man happy"; and it is not beyond possibility that the someone was Shakespeare, preferring connection to effectively hyperbolical emphasis. In the second instance, with F's "From any other foul unlawful touch" the touch is foul and unlawful *because* it is "other", i.e. extra-marital; the whole thing is being considered on a semi-legal basis of wifely duty. With Q1's "From any hated foul unlawful touch" an additional element is present, of purely personal feeling, which has nothing to do with legality; the touch, besides being unlawful, would be, to Desdemona's instinctive feeling, revolting.

(d) "The same kind of ruinous exaggeration is exemplified in the quarto's mangling of iv. ii. 69. 'O thou blacke weed, why art so louely fair? Thou smell'st so sweete...' I find it difficult to suppose that the leading actor of the King's Men would have used a 'blacke weed' as a term of reproach to Desdemona and from the black Othello the words are singularly *mal à propos.*" What has Burbage to do with it, except in so far as, if he would have jibbed at "black weed" (which I think unlikely), this reading at least of Q1 cannot be attributed to memorial contamination arising from an actor's error? But this example is much more instructive than appears from Dr Walker's incomplete citation, from which one would think that the only variant is the presence or absence of "black". Q1 reads:

> O I, as summers flies, are in the shambles,
> That quicken euen with blowing:
> O thou blacke weede, why art so louely faire?
> Thou smell'st so sweete, that the sence akes at thee,
> Would thou hadst ne're bin borne.

F reads:

> Oh I, as Sommer Flyes are in the Shambles,
> That quicken euen with blowing. Oh thou weed:
> Who art so louely faire, and smell'st so sweete,
> That the Sense akes at thee,
> Would thou had'st neuer bin borne.

(Modern editions normally print the last two lines as one (with *ne'er* for *never*) probably rightly, since, though the single line is somewhat congested, its splitting in F is readily accounted for by its length, which is too long for the width of the Folio column.)

Now if we start with the assumption that F's text is correct, then Q1's is indeed a "mangling"; but it is surely an oddly wanton kind of mangling. It starts by introducing an unauthorized "black". This upsets the scansion, so it relineates, ends an incomplete line with "blowing", produces two normal lines, substituting "Why" for "Who", with a consequently more staccato movement of thought, and ends with another incomplete line. Now why are we to suppose that Q1 caused itself all this trouble by the introduction of an unauthorized word?

But suppose that we start with the contrary assumption, that Q1 may represent the original, and F not a mangling but a would-be improving regularization of it. I think that the pause after "blowing" is both effective and natural, as also the bitterly puzzled question followed by the statement and by the incomplete line of the wish. The job of the regularizer is a simple one. All he has to do is to cut out "black", complete the second line with the remaining "Oh thou weed", secure greater syntactical continuity by reading "Who" for "why", and relineate, producing four complete lines, even if the compositor will have to set the last line as two.

Just by way of showing how easy Dr Walker's game is to play, I will add some examples of how it can be played in the opposite direction. I will start with the assumption that Q1, not F, is the nearer to the original, and for the "vulgarization" which she finds so frequent in Q1 will substitute "inept regularization" and "enfeeblement" which one may, if one feels so disposed, detect in F.

1. i. 183: officers of night (Q), officers of might (F): F, not understanding a specific technicality, substitutes a word of vaguely general applicability.

1. ii. 21: provulgate (Q), promulgate (F): F, faced with a nonce-word (though *provulgare* is good enough late Latin), prefers the more ordinary one.

1. iii. 82: set phrase (Q), soft phrase (F): F substitutes by memorial error a word more conventionally suitable to "peace".

1. iii. 251: utmost pleasure (Q), very quality (F): F waters down the outspoken directness of Q, which connects with the preceding "to live with him", and with the "rites" of six lines later, and enfeebles it into a connection with "visage in his mind".

II. i. 11: banning (Q), foaming (F): F, with too little imagination to make anything of "banning", substitutes a vapidly conventional word.

III. iii. 40: sneak (Q), steal (F): F feebly "politifies".

IV. ii. 18: her sex (Q), their wives (F): F weakens the point by a restricting particularity (see note *ad loc.*).

IV. ii. 56: slow, unmoving (Q), slow, and moving (F): F, pedantically logical, and so objecting to the contradiction of "slow" and "unmoving", makes a flaccidly enfeebling change.

IV. ii. 86: hated, foul (Q), other foul (F): F misses a point of characterization, while seeking, perhaps, a logical contrast with "for my lord"; or perhaps memorial contamination, the actor's memory having "failed to hold" the strong word, so that he substituted anything, however feeble, that would scan.

V. II. 318: in the nick (Q), in the interim (F): enfeebling sophistication, encouraged by memorial contamination.

v. ii. 364: loading (Q), lodging (F): same comment (see note *ad loc.*).

The list could be largely extended, and I have drawn attention to other examples in the notes. I hope I need hardly say that the comments above are intended only as examples of the kind of unqualified statement which a critic with a sufficiently determined *parti pris* might permit himself (as Dr Walker does in the opposite direction). All of them should, in my view, be stated more tentatively.

APPENDIX E

IS Q1 AN "EDITED" TEXT?

Greg says[1] "There can be little doubt that Q has been to some extent edited, at least metrically." I do not find very convincing the one metrical instance which he adduces. He points out that after the interchange of couplets between the Duke and Brabantio at I. iii. 210–19 the Senate turns to the urgent business of the night, and the Duke opens the proceedings with a speech in prose, and that in F the transition is marked by a brief prose speech from Brabantio, "I humbly beseech you, proceed to th' affairs of state." "The sudden change to prose," says Greg, very justly, "admirably emphasizes his brushing aside of personal considerations." (Even if one thinks that Brabantio is merely so stricken that he seeks the consideration of state affairs to distract his mind from his own sorrows, that does not affect the transition.) "This effect is weakened in Q, in which the line is reduced to verse: 'Beseech you now, to the affairs of the state'." But both "weakened" and "reduced to" imply the undefended assumption that F's version is antecedent to Q's. Why should not F's be a later modification of Q's, perhaps when the transition of Q was found to be too abrupt? The same assumption underlies Greg's handling of his other six instances of supposedly editorial changes other than metrical. It is taken as axiomatic that the changes were made from something that the hypothetical editor had before him into what we find in Q1, so that no more is needed than to suggest *why* he made them. I think in fact that Greg is probably right about four of these six, though not about the other two; but is there anything here that indicates what can properly be called "editing", with its suggestion of a considered

1. *The Shakespeare First Folio*, p. 373, notes F and G.

editorial process? Can they not all be attributed to the casual and
not always conscious operations of the transcriber, about which
Greg is on far firmer ground and of which he gives an admirable
account (p. 365); though even here I should enter a protest against
two of his examples, "put out thine" and "lodging".

Dr Richard Flatter goes a great deal farther than Greg, and pos-
tulates[1] a man whom he calls "the first editor of the play, i.e. the
man who prepared and 'edited' the text for the Quarto of 1622";
when Dr Flatter is more than usually exasperated with him he becomes "that pedant" or "that unknown grammarian". But I cannot see that Dr Flatter produces any evidence for his existence beyond the fact that he (Dr Flatter) frequently prefers the rhythms of
F to those of Q, and the evidence for his prosodical pedantry, even
if he existed at all, seems very dubious.

Hardly anyone can fail to admire much of Dr Flatter's work. He
seems to me to have "established"—so far as such things can be
established—that Shakespeare often indicates an aside by ending
it on a half line which the next speaker (naturally, since he has not
heard it) does not complete, though modern editors often make
him do so; that an entering speaker (again naturally) does not complete an incomplete line which immediately preceded his entrance;
and that an apparently halting line often includes a metrical gap,
like a rest in music, which indicates a break in thought or a piece of
stage business. On such questions Dr Flatter is valuably illuminating. But it will be noticed that such questions make no demand on
the critic's *ear*; the data are observable by the *eye* on the printed
page. When he turns to prosody it seems to me that he is much
less happy, and is too often as sadly at sea as any critic, however
able, is apt to be when he deals with the poetic rhythms of a language other than his own. Even in this field he is variable, since
some of his comments (e.g. on Marlowe's four-stress lines) show a
sensitive ear, but many of his comments on rhythms in *Othello*
shake one's confidence; perhaps his ear was suffering from a merely
temporary obtuseness because of his dislike of his hypothetical prosodical pedant. Here are some examples:

> And your vnblest Fate highes: Strumpet I come

which Dr Flatter proposes to read as follows (– indicates a stressed,
x an unstressed, syllable) x x – x – – / – x x – . Now no Englishman
could take the stress off *blest* and put it on *un* (though it would be
natural to stress both), but, much more important, the stress on
your, which Dr Flatter denies it, is demanded by the sense, since the

1. *Shakespeare's Producing Hand*, London, Heinemann, 1948.

contrast is with "your minion" of the line before. So the ordinary Englishman, not thinking twice about it, and readily accepting the slow movement of the heavily stressed first half of the line, reads it as x – – – – – / – x x – (or possibly x – x – – – / – x x –). And here is an example which is directly connected with the differences between texts. I will give it as Dr Flatter himself presents it.

"Should I repent me. But once put out thy light
– x x – x / x – x – x –

No doubt the line is slightly defective if we look at it not from the actor's but the prosodist's point of view. The editor changed 'thy light' into 'thine', and so the Quarto reads

Should I repent me; but once put out thine
– x x – x / – x – x –

It did not matter to that pedant that, while achieving his 'regularity', he succeeded in making the line stumble rather than run, having to stress 'but' and 'put'." The comment is so remarkable that one can at first hardly believe that one has read it aright. In the first place, in F's line the stress on "thy", which Dr Flatter, as with "your" in the previous example, denies it, is imperatively demanded by the sense. In the second place, in Q1's line, no one with an ear —not even the poor "pedant"—wants to stress the "but" (any more than the "but" of F's line) and the English reader, without stumbling, reads the line quite naturally as

x x x – x / x – – – –

If this is the most cogent kind of evidence that can be adduced either for the superiority of F over Q1, or for the existence of the ghostly pedant, I think one may reasonably remain unconvinced.

APPENDIX F

"- - -" IN Q1

There is one typographical oddity in Q1 which perhaps merits some attention. Some seventy times there occur three (occasionally four or two) successive hyphens (- - -). All but four of these 'triple-hyphens' are repeated in Q2 (though almost invariably by an ordinary 'em rule' (—)), but only two are repeated in F (again as em rules), though in two other places the closing (II. i. 216) or open-

ing (v. ii. 165) bracket of a parenthesis in F coincides with one of
Q1's triple-hyphens. (Incidentally, though this is not relevant to
the immediate discussion, in two places (II. i. 306, III. iii. 75) Q2 has
a dash where neither of the other two texts has it, and in two others
(III. iii. 306, v. i. 82) F and Q2 have a dash where Q1 has not.) It is
noticeable that nowhere, apart from the two half-exceptions mentioned, is there any relation between Q1's triple-hyphens and the
frequent parentheses of F. So far as F represents them at all, it is by
a heavy mark of punctuation (almost always a colon or full-stop).
But it is also noticeable that in a number of places the absence in F
of the triple-hyphens coincides with a difference of lineation.

Now it is observable that the significance of the triple-hyphens—
or of whatever it was in the compositor's copy that they represent—
is not always the same. Frequently they are just ordinary parentheses, as in the passage I. iii. 342–62 where there is a crop of them,
e.g.

> It cannot be, that *Desdemona* should long continue her loue vnto
> the Moore, - - - put money in thy purse, - - nor he to her; it was a
> violent commencement, and thou shalt see an answerable
> sequestration: put but money in thy purse. - - - These Moores are
> changeable in their wills: - - - fill thy purse with money. (342–8)

Sometimes they indicate an interruption of speech, as at I. ii. 53

> Marry to. - - - - Come Captaine, will you goe?

or v. ii. 165,

> thou hast done a deed - - -
> I care not for thy sword,

and other examples are I. iii. 246, II. i. 65, 120, 177, IV. i. 48.
Sometimes they indicate a pause, as at I. iii. 392

> A double knavery - - - how, how, - - - let me see,

or v. ii. 71

> That he hath - - - - vds death.

Other examples of this are at I. iii. 268, III. iii. 39, 97, IV. ii. 25.
And sometimes they indicate a change of subject, as at II. iii. 26,

> Well, happinesse to their sheetes - - - come Lieutenant, I haue a
> stope of Wine,

or IV. i. 259,

> You are welcome sir to Cypres, - - goates and monkies.

other examples of this are II. iii. 47, III. iii. 5.

But there is a number of places where the significance of the triple-hyphen is different, where it seems to be used to indicate the presence of hypermetrical syllables at the end of the line. Examples of this are:

  (i) And such a one doe I professe myself, - - - - for sir,　(I. i. 55)
  (ii) And will as tenderly be led bit'h nose - - - as Asses are:
(I. iii. 399)
 (iii) Be not you knowne on't, I haue vse for it: - - go leaue me;
(III. iii. 324)
 (iv) All my fond loue, thus do I blow to heauen, - - tis gone.
(III. iii. 452)
  (v) To point his slow vnmouing fingers at - - oh, oh.　(IV. ii. 56)
 (vi) O dambd *Iago*, O inhumaine dog, - - o, o, o.　　(v. i. 62)
 (vii) I neuer did offend you in my life, - - neuer lou'd *Cassio*,
(v. ii. 60)
(viii) I would not haue thee linger in thy paine, - - - so, so.
(v. ii. 89)
 (ix) The death of *Cassio*; to be vndertooke - - - by *Roderigo*.
(v. ii. 312)

Now if this class of triple-hyphen stood by itself, it might be argued that it was no more than a compositor's device to save space, i.e. that, when he found himself with a few extra syllables written in his copy as a separate incomplete line, he set them, when he had room, at the end of the previous line, indicating his operation by the hyphens. But (a) it is observable that, even when there was not room, and he therefore either set the extra syllables as a separate line, or (hypermetrically) at the beginning of the following line, he still set the hyphens, as in these two examples:

> This cannot be by no assay of reason - - -
> Tis a Pageant,
> To keepe vs in false gaze: when we consider　(I. iii. 18)

> I thinke this tale would win my daughter to, - - -
> Good *Brabantio*, take vp this mangled matter at the best,
(I. iii. 171)

and (b) this class of triple-hyphen does not stand alone, and the other uses of it, previously examined, are waste, not saving, of space, since the use of ordinary colons or full-stops (as in F), or, on occasion, of ordinary parenthesis brackets, would be more economical. It is therefore, I think, a reasonable inference that these triple-hyphens represent throughout something that the compositor had before him in his copy (i.e. the assumed transcript) and that he followed this with considerable care. I must leave readers to judge for themselves what further inference, if any, may be drawn as to the carefulness or carelessness of the transcriber. I will only suggest that a careless transcriber is not very likely to take the quite needless trouble of inserting in his transcript a number of things which are not before him in his original.

But apart from this I think that the Q1 triple-hyphens sometimes provide a useful pointer to the intended lineation. At this point it is perhaps worth interjecting some general comments on the recurrent problem of lineation, particularly since many readers who are not familiar with the early texts must, I fancy, be surprised at the frequency with which the problem arises. It arises mainly from a purely mechanical cause. The compositors of Quartos and Folio did not use the convenient modern typographical device whereby, when a fresh speaker completes an incomplete line of the preceding speaker, his opening words are offset to the right. With them, each fresh speech, however short, even if only a monosyllable, was set hard up against the speech-heading. To take an example where there can be no doubt of the correct lineation, since there are unmistakably complete lines each side of the break, both Q and F texts of *Othello* print, at v. ii. 67 (modern spelling):

> I saw the handkerchief.
> *Des*. He found it then.

where the modern printer would have

> I saw the handkerchief.
> *Des*.   He found it then.

Such examples are simple of solution. The complications begin when, whatever we do, we are going to be left with an incomplete line somewhere. Then one has nothing to rely on but one's sense of rhythm, aided on occasion by a sense of the comparative dramatic effectiveness of different placings of the incomplete line. (See note on v. ii. 52–3.)

One or two more examples of the lineation problems that confront a modern editor may be perhaps usefully appended.

(a) I. i. 4–8. Q1 reads:

> *Iag*. S'blood, but you will not heare me.
>   If euer I did dreame of such a matter, abhorre me.
> *Rod*. Thou toldst me, thou didst hold him in thy hate.
> *Iag*. Despise me if I doe not: three great ones of the Citty

F reads

> *Ia.*   But you'l not heare me. If euer I did dream
>   Of such a matter, abhorre me.
> *Rodo.*   Thou told'st me,
>   Thou did'st hold him in thy hate.
> *Iago.*   Despise me
>   If I do not. Three Great-ones of the Cittie,

which would be represented in modern typographical practice thus:

> *Iago.*   But you'll not hear me. If ever I did dream
>   Of such a matter, abhor me.
> *Rod.*   Thou told'st me
>   Thou didst hold him in thy hate.
> *Iago.*   Despise me
>   If I do not. Three great ones of the city,

Q1, that is, produces one normal and smooth-running line for Roderigo, but a first line which is incomplete, and second and fourth lines which are overcrowded, though they can, by rapid delivery, be made into some sort of recognizable verse. F, on the other hand, having expurgated the opening oath, produces a tolerable first line, and a smooth fourth, but two other 'lines' which can indeed be chopped up into the necessary number of syllables (eleven, with either a resolved foot or a feminine ending, in the one, and the regulation ten in the other) but can be made to sound like verse only by putting stresses in impossible places. The usual modern solution is to give up F as a clumsy attempt at regularization rendered necessary by expurgation, and to rely on Q, but with a lightening of the second line by the transference of "abhor me" to a line by itself. This is probably making the best of a not very good job, but since Shakespeare's broken lines have usually some discernible appropriateness and purpose, which can hardly be found in the abrupt break after "abhor me", the solution is not very satisfactory. If we are sufficiently dissatisfied we can try the more heroic course of emendation, safeguarding ourselves with the cautious "corruption may be suspected". We can, for example, taking Q as basis, read

> S'blood, but you will not hear me. If I ever
> Did dream of such a matter, then abhor me

(which is too Fletcherian); or, more simply, cure the second line by deleting "a matter", with or without changing "such" to "this" And we can, more fancifully, complete the first line with the proper name "Roderigo", explaining that in a confused MS. this was muddled with the speech-heading of the next line but one and so omitted. This emendation might be supported by pointing out that otherwise, whereas Iago is named at once, Roderigo does not get a name for more than fifty lines.

(b) I. i. 53–4. This is an interesting example, since Q1 and F are identical in lineation, thus:

> Do well thrive by 'em,
> And when they have lin'd their coats
> Do themselves homage,
> Those fellows have some soul

The F lineation is easily explicable, since each of the single lines of a modern edition would have exceeded the measure of the Folio column. But this explanation will not hold for Q, since even the first line would not have exceeded the length which the Q compositor sometimes permits himself, and the second would have been well inside it. Perhaps the MS. split the lines to avoid overcrowding. However, the correct lineation is here obvious.

(c) I. ii. 48–9. Q1 reads:

> Ile spend a word here in the house, and goe with you.
>   *Cas.* Auncient, what makes he here?

F reads:

> I will but spend a word here in the house,
> And goe with you.
>   *Cassio.* Aunciant, what makes he heere?

The metrical impeccability of F may be taken as an indication either that it preserves the original reading or that it has conducted a neat piece of regularization. The "but" sounds to me a trifle too apologetic for Othello, and the metrical irregularity of Q is to some extent covered by the break of Othello's exit; but F may well be right.

To revert now to the possible aid of Q1's triple-hyphens. As a rule there is very little trouble. We can either regard the lines as deliberately hypermetric, and indicated as such by Shakespeare, or we can follow F and most modern editions by setting the hypermetric words in a line by themselves, as with examples (ii), (iii), (iv), (viii), and (ix) above, or omitting them altogether, as with examples (v) and (vi). (It is not, by the way, clear why F and the modern editions allow "for sir" in example (i) to stand as in Q1, though they shift the "so, so" of example (viii).) But occasionally there is a more dubious case. For example, at I. iii. 15, Q1 prints thus:

    So was I bid report here, to the state.
      Du. How say you by this change?
      1 Sena. This cannot be by no assay of reason - - -
    Tis a Pageant,
    To keepe vs in false gaze: when we consider
    The importancy of *Cypresse* to the *Turke*:
But F has
    So was I bid report here to the State,
    By Signior *Angelo.*
      Duke. How say you by this change?
      1 Sen. This cannot be
    By no assay of reason. 'Tis a Pageant
    To keepe vs in false gaze, when we consider
    Th' importancie of Cyprus to the Turke;

That is to say, F, having landed itself in trouble by the inclusion of
"Signior Angelo" who is as awkward metrically as he is otherwise,
either takes him, along with the Duke's question, as making one
possible but awkward line, or, more probably, leaves him as a half-
line and takes the Duke's question and the first senator's first three
words as making a quite regular line. There is little to choose,
though, since the Q1 hyphens must mean something, I should be
inclined to stick to Q1. (For a possible solution of the Signior Angelo
problem, see note *ad loc.*)

    But there is another place (example (vii) above) which is more
important. Q1 prints thus:

    That I doe groane withall: thou art to die.
      Des. Then Lord haue mercy on me.
      Oth. I say Amen.
      Des. And haue you mercy too:
    I neuer did offend you in my life, - - neuer lou'd *Cassio,*
    But with such generall warranty of heauen,

Of the earlier part of this various lineations are possible in a modern
edition, either

      Des. Then Lord have mercy on me!
      Oth.   I say "Amen".
      Des. And have you mercy too!
    I never did offend you in my life,
    Never lov'd Cassio,
    But with . . .
or
      Des. Then Lord have mercy on me!
      Oth. I say "Amen".
      Des.   And have you mercy too!
    I never . . .

or even

> That I do groan withal:
> Thou art to die.
>   *Des.*   Then Lord have mercy on me!
>   *Oth.* I say "Amen".
>   *Des.*   And have you mercy too!
> I never . . .

But the one thing which is clear is that "I neuer did offend you in my life" is intended to stand as a complete line. F, however, tries something quite different:

> That I do grone withall. Thou art to dye.
>   *Des.* O Heauen haue mercy on me.
>   *Oth.* I say, Amen.
>   *Des.* And haue you mercy too. I neuer did
> Offend you in my life: neuer lou'd *Cassio*,
> But with . . .

This no doubt tidies up the whole passage into a series of complete and metrical lines, but at the cost of breaking up Q1's effective single line "I neuer did offend you in my life", a break which is perhaps the more unfortunate in that it slightly takes the edge off the later echo, "Dear general, I did never give you cause". I think, therefore, that we are wiser to notice Q1's indication and lineate accordingly.

APPENDIX G

THE SECOND QUARTO

Q2 is, in its way, one of the most interesting of Shakespearean texts, because it is clearly the result not only of very careful editorial work (F1 may often be that) but of editorial work which we can check, as we cannot with F1, because we have the same material before us as the editor had.

Q2 was set from a (corrected) copy of Q1. This is now so generally agreed that I need not spend time in demonstrating it; but if any reader cares to check the statement, let him look at i. iii. 311–33 in the two texts. Q2 inserts *O villanous*, reads *do* for *doe*, changes a question mark after *Vertue* to a comma, omits a comma after *Lettice*, and substitutes two *is* and one *a* for the corresponding upper-case letters. Otherwise it corresponds with Q1 not only word for word and letter for letter (with at least three noticeable spellings, *Ginny*, *Isop*, and *syen*—for which, by the way, F1 reads *Gynney*, *Hisope*, and *seyen*), but also, and more significantly, line for line, so far as it can—that is from 317 onwards. (The correspondence cannot be maintained in Iago's first speech, owing to the introduction of *O villanous*.) And this close correspondence is observable throughout. Q2 reproduces the stage-directions of Q1 (besides adding one of its own) and also an unusual typographical feature of Q1, the triple-hyphen between phrases (see Appendix F) though it usually represents them by a single em rule.

But the copy of Q1 had been most carefully collated with F1 (or just conceivably, though most improbably, with the MS. from which F1 was set). Q2 includes all the "F only" passages, and follows F1 in its omissions or modifications of oaths. In detail the collation is very minute, including again and again such small points as the change of Q1's *ashore* to F's *on shore*. In some ten places Q2 ventures on emendations on its own account, almost always reasonably and for the better.

In the upshot Q2 is an eclectic text, and for the determination of the 'true' text it has just this amount of importance. It is not in the least authoritative, since the editor cannot be proved, nor I think, even reasonably supposed, to have had access to any MS. But, for what it is worth, its editor clearly did not regard Q1 as an inferior text, since, in spite of the minuteness with which he sometimes corrects it by F, he still adheres to it, against F, nearly twice as often as he deserts it. When, therefore, in the more critical divergences he adheres to Q1, it means at least this, that a careful contemporary, who was ready enough to alter Q1 when he saw fit, did not feel that in these instances any alteration was called for. Good examples are *bear an (all) excellency* at II. i. 65, and *lodging* at v. ii. 364.

APPENDIX H

ERRORS AND PROBABLE ERRORS IN Q1 AND F OF I. iii AND V. i, ii

It is sometimes interesting, and may be useful, to compare two rival texts simply as specimens of typography, so as to estimate the comparative accuracy of the compositors. The procedure is as follows: (1) To take the nearest approach to a cup of Lethe that one can contrive, so as to forget, so far as may be, that one has ever read the play before in a standard edition, that one has ever read either text, and—most important of all—that one has ever compared the two texts; (2) to read each text independently as though one were reading a proof not against copy, but simply on the look-out for 'literals' and other obvious errors or awkwardnesses—a quite useful check in ordinary proof-reading, since, reading moderately fast, one can pay more attention to sense than is possible or even desirable when one is constantly referring to copy, and also is less liable to fall into the same traps which snared the compositor; (3) to correct the obvious literals, and mark, and sometimes suggest corrections for, other unmistakable errors; to query words or punctuation where error is suspected, but, in the absence of copy, cannot, in Johnson's useful meaning of the word, be "ascertained"; (4) to make a list, in three categories, (i) obvious errors, (ii) suspected errors in words, (iii) suspected errors in punctuation. The last, (iii), is a tricky category, since, however familiar we are with Elizabethan punctuation, there will always be examples which seem unnatural to us but may yet well have been in the copy, and also because here, even more than with the other two categories, if one has any predisposition in favour of either text, it is dangerously easy to slide over awkwardnesses in it which one would notice in the other.

The results of the process as applied to I. iii of *Othello* are given below.

I. iii

(i) Q1
line

line		
37	resterine	? *restemme* (minim error)
51	lacke	*lackd* (e : d error)
55	griefes	*griefe*
106	youth	? *vouch* (foul case and c : t error)
119		(omission of some kind; no object for "take away")
140	Antrees	*Antres*
166	heate	?
230	Cooch	*Couch*
238	Which	*With*
251	Fuen	*Euen* (foul case)
377	what	*What*

F

| 1 | There's | (unmetrical) *There is* |

52	didI	insert space
53	hor	*nor* (foul case)
57	snd	*and*
73	veriesorry	insert space
74	yonr	turned letter
90	uTale	delete *u*
99	main'd	*maim'd* (minim error)
106	wtought	*wrought*
107	over	*overt*
117	herreport	insert space
122	tell	*till*
141	Rocks, Hills whose head touch	(unmetrical and concord); ? *Rocks and Hills whose heads touch*
143	others	*other*
144	*Antropophague*	*Anthropophagi*
145	Grew	(unmetrical); ? *Do grow* or *Did grow*
155	instinctiuely	?
188	Imay	insert space
206	presern'd	*preseru'd* (turned letter)
230	Coach	*Couch*
232	Alacartie	*Alacritie*
244	Grcaious	*Gracious* (transposed letters)
248	That I loue	(unmetrical); ? *do loue* or *did loue*
257	for why	*for which*
299	wordly	*worldly*
300	the the	delete one "the"
327	braine	?
383	such Snpe	(unmetrical and letter omitted) *such a Snipe*
386	She has	*He has* or *He's*

(ii) Q1

line

6	they aym'd reports	? *ayme* (e : d error)
13	Galley	? *Galleys*
87	feate	? *feates*
142	hent	possible, but ? *hint*
220	the state	metrically awkward though possible; ? delete *the*
267	good	a weak word in context
397	Moore a	suspicious absence of verb, though not impossible; ? *Moore's a* or *Moore's of*

F

6	the ayme reports	
106		speech-heading apparently omitted before *To vouch*
130	Battaile	? *Battailes*
139	Travellours	? *Travel's* or *Travellous* (travailous)
147	hence	? *thence*
159	kisses	(seems improbably forthcoming on Desdemona's part)
265	to	? *of*
331	or	(the balance of the sentence seems to demand *our*)
352	errors	(not impossible, but ? *error*)
357	supersubtle	natural balance suggests *a super-subtle*)

(iii) Q1
line

51	night,	*night.*
67–8	of Law, You shall your selfe, read	? delete commas
81	extent no more	insert comma or semi-colon after *extent*
100	confesse perfection, so	delete comma, or ? transposed pointing for *confesse, perfection so*
101–2	driuen, To	? delete comma
155	intentiuely,I	? a heavier stop
158–9	done; She	? *done, She*
196	soule. I haue	*soule, I haue,* or delete stop altogether
210	So let the *Turke,* of	delete comma, or perhaps (transposed pointing) *So, let the Turke of*
222	place, is	? delete comma
230–1	warre, My	? delete comma
238	accomodation? and	delete question-mark or replace by comma
260–1	will, Haue	? delete comma
269–70	dulnesse, My	? delete comma
309	prescription, to dye	? *prescription to dye,*

F

29–30	ease, and gaine To wake, and wage	? *gaine, To* or (transposed pointing) *gaine, To wake and wage*
46	us, To him	? delete comma

62	Nature, so	delete comma
83	mine, had	? delete comma
85	action, in	? delete comma
114	soule, to soule	? delete comma
122–3	heauen, I	? delete comma
175	speake?	*speake.*
206–7	Fortune takes: Pat- ience, her Iniury	? *takes, Patience her Iniury*
239	Why at her Fathers?	*Why, at her Fathers.*
269	*Cupid,* seele	? *Cupid seele*
286	needfull, your	? delete comma
367	reuenge, against	? delete comma
402	Birth, to	? delete comma

In this scene therefore the 'score' of errors of the three different kinds is (i) Q 11, F 29; (ii) Q 7, F 10; (iii) Q 15, F 14. Q contains markedly fewer obvious or probable verbal errors than F. (It will be noticed, by the way, that about 80 per cent of the suggested emendations are confirmed by the other text; but diverse inferences may be drawn from this fact.) But before trying to draw any conclusions it seemed wise to examine another block of the two texts, this time at the end of the play.

Since long lists of words and phrases become wearisome, I will content myself with giving the corresponding 'score' for v. i and ii (together a hundred lines more than i. iii). (i) Q 14, F 27; (ii) Q 8, F 6; (iii) Q 16, F 9. That is to say, in the three scenes together F makes more than double the errors of Q in class (i), about the same in class (ii), and a quarter less in class (iii). It seems therefore not unfair to the compositor of F to suggest that the compositor of Q was at worst not his inferior in skill and carefulness. And if that is so, it follows that we should not, even in part, base any notion of an "inferiority" of Q on a supposed inferiority of workmanship in the printing-house.

I have laboured the point at what may seem undue length, but I think it is of importance, since such an examination of the two texts saves one from the conclusion, no doubt uncritical and largely subconscious, but not unnatural, that F is likely to be verbally the more accurate text because it is so much more sightly. Q1 is a singularly ugly piece of work; the faces of the type were often badly worn, the inking was unequal and often excessive, and the leading, though about the same as that of F, is, in prose passages, because of the longer Q line, inadequate for easy reading.

This line of examination becomes obviously of more importance if we extend the meaning of "compositor"—which I have been so far using in its strict and limited sense of the man who sets type in the printing-house—to include transcribers. We are then trying to form a rough estimate of the comparative liability to error in two "mechanical" chains of transmission, using "mechanical" to imply the process merely of *copying* with such degree of accuracy as the copier can command. And I do not think that this extension of meaning is illegitimate if one bears always in mind its dangers. An ideally perfect compositor, working from an incorrect transcript, *may* produce a result more remote from the original than an inferior compositor working from an ideally perfect transcript, and the degree of remoteness will depend entirely on the degree of incorrectness of the transcript. But this is, for our purposes, of little more than academic interest, since we are concerned with the two chains, and not only with the last link in either. And all that I am trying to suggest is that, before we write off Q 1 as an "inferior" text whose "inferiority" depends in part on inferiority of workmanship, we ought to be able to show, *from the available evidence* (i.e. the two texts), that Q indicates more liability to obvious error, at some point in the chain, than does F. And this, I think, is just what we cannot show. Q may none the less be inferior, but to demonstrate its inferiority we are, I think, driven to a different line of attack.

APPENDIX I
CINTHIO'S NARRATIVE

It seems needless to give the whole of Cinthio's original Italian. The English reader needs that only to help him in deciding whether it seems likely that Shakespeare read the story in the original, a decision which will depend on the observation of verbal parallels. A study of Shakespeare's debt to Cinthio's story, where he accepted, where modified, and where added, can be conducted just as precisely by the use of a translation, and a good deal more simply, since seventeenth-century Italian is not very easy reading.

I am therefore giving Cinthio's story, partly in summary, but mainly in an accurate translation, adding the original Italian only where there seems some possibility of verbal debt. The existing English translations[1] are sometimes inaccurate and often, which is

1. Mrs Lenox, in *Shakespeare Illustrated* (1753); Wolstenholme Parr (1795); J. E. Taylor (1855).

more serious, incomplete, and the translation which follows has been kindly made for this edition by Raymond Shaw.

The French translation by Gabriel Chappuys, first mentioned, with derogatory comment, by Farmer, is not easy to come by (in the original edition) in this country, but it was reprinted by F. Victor Hugo in his edition of Shakespeare.[1] I do not think that it merits Farmer's strictures—it is certainly no more inaccurate than the English translations—but I have found no words or phrases in it that seem to point to Shakespeare's use of it rather than (possibly) Cinthio. Nor can I feel that any of the possible verbal parallels in Cinthio are in the least decisive.[2] I think that there must have been some English translation, now lost. It is possible, of course, that Shakespeare had heard the story from a friend who had read Cinthio, but I feel that the often close parallels between his *story* and Cinthio's point to his having had the latter, in some form, *in extenso* before his eyes. But if he had had it in the original, there would, I think, have been almost certainly much closer *verbal* parallels, the kind of parallels that are observable when he was using Holinshed (and other chroniclers) or North's Plutarch.

Cinthio opens with a description of two main characters, a Moor (unnamed), handsome and valiant, and highly thought of by the Signory (*Signoria*)[3] of Venice, and a virtuous lady of wonderful beauty, named Disdemona, who fell in love with the Moor, as he with her, and, in the face of strong opposition from her parents, married him. They lived in Venice in complete harmony and peace.

Some time later the Signory, on making a change in the composition of the Cyprus garrison, appointed the Moor commander of the fresh troops who were being sent (no reason is suggested by Cinthio for the change). The Moor was delighted at the honour paid him, since such a post was given only to a man of high rank, tried courage, and proved loyalty. But his delight was qualified by the reflection that he must either leave Disdemona behind or submit her to the dangers and discomforts of the voyage. Disdemona, finding out the cause of her husband's trouble of mind, first minimizes the dangers, pointing out that the voyage will be made in a safe and well-equipped ship (*in sicura e ben guarnita nave*),[4] and then says "I am only afraid of being so little loved by you that you should

1. Paris, 1868 (vol. v, pp. 443–58).
2. But see a persuasive article by Maugeri in *Anglia*, II (1948), 3, 1–39.
3. Cf. "My services, which I have done the signiory" (I. ii. 18).
4. Cf. perhaps "His bark is stoutly timbered" (II. i. 48).

think of leaving me in Venice, or that you should persuade yourself that I would rather be safe here than share your danger."[1] The Moor, thus encouraged, embraces his wife, with the words "God keep you long in this love, dear wife."[2] He then embarks with her and all his troops, and has a calm passage to Cyprus.

Cinthio now introduces three more of the characters and tells the whole story of the Ensign's plot as follows:

The Moor had in his company an ensign of fine presence, but with the wickedest nature of any man alive. This man was very dear to the Moor, who was unaware of his wickedness. He hid with fine, proud words, and his presence, the wickedness that was in his heart and displayed outwardly the bearing of a Hector or an Achilles. This scoundrel had also taken his wife, a beautiful and honourable young woman, to Cyprus. Being an Italian, she was much loved by the Moor's wife, and they were together most of the day. In the same company there was also a captain, most dear to the Moor, who went very often to the Moor's house and dined with him and his wife. As Disdemona knew him to be so highly esteemed by her husband, she showed him the greatest kindness. This pleased the Moor very much. The wicked ensign, caring nothing for the loyalty due to his wife or the friendship, loyalty, and duty he owed to the Moor, fell passionately in love with Disdemona and turned all his thoughts to seeing whether he might enjoy her. But he was anxious not to reveal himself, fearing that he might meet sudden death if the Moor should find out. He sought by secret devious ways to bring it to the notice of the lady that he loved her; but she had only the Moor in her thoughts, and gave no thought to the ensign or to anyone else. Everything that the ensign did to kindle in her a love for him was useless. So he imagined that the reason was that Disdemona had become enamoured of the captain and so decided to put him out of the way. Furthermore he changed the love that he bore the lady into the bitterest (*acerbissimo*)[3] hatred, and pondered how he might arrange that, once the captain was killed, if he could not enjoy Disdemona himself, the Moor might also be prevented from enjoying her either. He revolved in his mind various dastardly schemes and finally decided to accuse Disdemona of adultery to her husband, making him think that the captain was guilty. But knowing of the extraordinary love which the Moor felt towards Disdemona, and the friendship which he had for the captain, he understood that it would be impossible to destroy either of them

1. Cf. perhaps "If I be left behind, A moth of peace, and he go to the war . . ." (I. iii. 255).
2. Cf. "The heavens forbid But that our loves and comforts should increase, Even as our days do grow" (II. i. 193).
3. Cf. "acerb" (I. iii. 350).

unless he deceived the Moor by a clever fraud. For this reason he decided to wait for the right time and place to set about this wicked scheme. It was not long before the Moor was obliged to degrade the captain for having attacked a soldier on guard with his sword and wounded him. Disdemona took the affair very much to heart, and often tried to make peace[1] between her husband and the captain. Meanwhile the Moor had told the wicked ensign that his wife was worrying him so much about the captain that he feared he would finally be compelled to recall (*ripigliarlo*)[2] him. This put the idea into the wicked man's head to weave his deceitful plot, and he said, "Perhaps Disdemona has reason to look favourably on him." "And why?" asked the Moor. "I do not wish," replied the lieutenant, "to come between man and wife, but if you would open your eyes[3] you would see for yourself." And the ensign would say no more for fear of the Moor's vigilance. But these words had left such a thorn in the soul of the Moor that he gave himself up completely to thinking of what they could mean, and he became quite melancholy.

One day when his wife was trying to soften his anger against the captain, and asking him not to be forgetful of the services and friendship of so many years for such a small fault, and how that the wounded soldier and the captain were completely reconciled, the Moor became angry and said to her, "It is extraordinary, Disdemona, that you should be so concerned over this man, but he is neither a brother nor a relative, that you should have him so much at heart." The lady, courteous and humble, replied, "I would not wish you to be angry with me; nothing disturbs me but to see you deprived of so dear a friend as the captain has been to you: I know this from what you yourself have said, but he has not committed such a serious crime that you should bear him such hatred. But you are a Moor, and so hot-blooded by nature, that the slightest thing moves you to anger and revenge." At these words the Moor replied more wrathfully, "Someone may feel it who does not expect it: I intend to see such a revenge for the injuries done me, that I shall be satisfied." The lady was quite terrified at these words, and, seeing her husband more angry with her than she had ever known him, said humbly, "I did but speak to you of this with good intention, but that you may have nothing to be angry with me for, I shall not speak to you of it again." Seeing that his wife had repeated her petition in the captain's favour, he thought that the ensign's words had meant that Disdemona was in love with him, and he went to that rogue, very sad, and tried to get him to speak more openly. The

1. Cf. perhaps "I would do much to atone them" (IV. i. 227).

2. Cf. "That she repeals him for her body's lust" (II. iii. 348); this seems the most striking of the possible verbal parallels.

3. Cf. perhaps "Wear your eye thus, not jealous, nor secure" (III. iii. 202).

ensign, intent on doing harm to this poor lady, having first pretended that he did not wish to speak lest it should displease him, gave way to the entreaties of the Moor and said, "I cannot deny that it makes me extremely sorry to have to say something which will be worse for you than any other torture, but since you indeed wish it and because of the care I must have for your honour as my master, I am bound to tell you, for I do not want to fail in satisfying your request and my duty. You must know then that it is a serious matter for your lady to see the captain in disfavour with you, because of the pleasure which she gets with him when he comes to your home, for your blackness already displeases her." These words pierced the heart of the Moor to the very roots. However, to know still more (he already believed all that the ensign had said on account of the suspicions which had already been born in his mind), with a fierce look he said, "I know not what restrains me from cutting out your tongue so bold that it has dared to place such infamy upon my lady." The ensign then said, "I expected no other reward for this, my loving service, but since my duty has carried me so far, and because of my desire to maintain your honour, I answer you that that is just how things stand, and if the lady has closed your eyes[1] by a display of love for you so that you have not seen what you should, that is not why I am telling you the truth, but because the captain himself has told me of it, like some to whom happiness seems incomplete, if not shared with another." And, he added, "Had I not feared your wrath, when he told me this, I should have given him the reward of death, which he richly deserved. But since this is the reward I get for telling you something which concerns you more than anyone, I wish I had said nothing; for silent, I should not have lost your favour." Then, furious, the Moor said, "If you do not make me see with my own eyes what you have told me, rest assured that I shall give you reason to know that it would have been better for you to have been born dumb."[2]

"That would have been easy for me," returned the wicked one, "when he used to come to your home, but now that you have rid yourself of him, not for the reason which is of real import, but for some trivial cause, it is bound to be difficult, although I believe that he still enjoys Disdemona whenever you give him the opportunity, but he must be much more cautious[3]

1. Cf. "seal her father's eyes up" (III. iii. 214).

2. Cf. III. iii. 365-9. This is the point, mentioned in the introduction, which seems to me to tell against any *verbal* debt by Shakespeare to Cinthio. Cinthio says *mutolo*, Shakespeare "a dog". If Shakespeare had been following Cinthio at all closely, one would, I think, have expected, at this forcible moment, a closer correspondence—unless indeed it can be shown that dogs were so commonly proverbial a symbol of dumbness that "a dog" is in effect a translation of *mutolo*.

3. Cf. "Let us be wary" (III. iii. 426).

now than he was before, having become odious to you. But yet I do not lose hope of being able to make you see what you are loth to believe." And with these words they parted.

The unhappy Moor went home feeling as if he had been pierced by a sharp arrow, to await the coming of the day when the ensign would make him see what would make him miserable for ever. But the lady's chastity, which, as he was aware, she guarded so carefully, gave the accursed ensign no less worry, for it seemed to him that there was no way to make the Moor believe what he had falsely told him, and after turning the matter over in his mind, the rogue hit upon a new evil device. As I have said, the wife of the Moor often went to the home of the ensign's wife and would stay with her for the best part of the day. On one occasion he saw that she was carrying with her a handkerchief which he knew had been given to her by the Moor and which had been worked in a most subtle Moorish manner. It was most precious to the lady and to the Moor alike and it entered his mind to steal it away from her secretly, wherewith he might deal the final blow. He had a little girl of three years old who was much loved by Disdemona and one day when the poor lady was visiting this villain's house, he took the little girl in his arms and put her on the lady's lap. She took her and pressed her to her breast, while the trickster, who was surpassingly nimble-fingered, took the handkerchief from her girdle so cunningly that she did not notice it at all and then left her, quite happy. Disdemona, unconscious of what had happened, went home and, busy with other thoughts, did not notice the missing handkerchief. But when, a few days later, she looked for it, but could not find it, she was afraid that the Moor might ask her about it as he often did. The scoundrelly ensign, having picked the right moment, went to the captain and with his rogue's cunning left the handkerchief at the head of his bed. The captain did not notice it until the following morning, when he got out of bed, and as it had fallen on the floor, he stepped on it; and he could not imagine how it came to be in his house. Knowing it to belong to Disdemona, he considered how to return it to her. After having waited until the Moor had left the house he went to the back door and knocked. It seems that fortune was in league with the ensign for the death of the poor woman, for at that exact moment the Moor returned home and, hearing a knock at the door, went to the window and said furiously, "Who is knocking?" The captain, hearing the Moor's voice, and afraid that he would come down and do him harm, ran away without answering a word. The Moor went downstairs, opened the door and went out into the street, but after looking about failed to find him. He then re-entered the house full of spite and asked his wife who it was that was knocking down there. The lady answered that she did not know, which was true. But the Moor said, "It looked like the captain." "I do not know whether it was he or another," she replied. The Moor held back his fury, however much his rage may have burned. He did not wish to do anything before speaking to the ensign, to whom he went at once and told him all that had happened, and begged him to find out all he could about it from the captain. He promised to do so, happy at the way events had turned out.

And he spoke one day to the captain when the Moor was so placed as to be able to see them talking together. Then, speaking to him about everything except the lady, he made him laugh a great deal, and putting on a great show of astonishment, he made many gestures with his head and hands, as if he were hearing wonderful things. The Moor, as soon as he saw them leave each other, went up to the ensign to know what the other had said to him. The ensign, after having caused himself to be entreated for a long time, at last said to him, "He has hidden nothing from me, and he told me that he has enjoyed your wife every time that you, by your absence, have given him an opportunity, and that the last time he was with her she gave him that handkerchief which you gave her when you married her."

The Moor thanked the ensign and it seemed to him that if he discovered that the lady did not have the handkerchief, it would be clear that it was as the ensign had told.

For this purpose, one day after dinner, having entered into conversation with the lady, he asked her for the handkerchief. The unhappy lady, who had so much feared such a request, became red in the face, and to hide her blushes, which the Moor had very well observed, she ran to her chest and pretended to look for it. After having searched for it a long while, "I do not know," she said, "how it comes that I cannot find it just now—perhaps you may have had it yourself." "If I had had it," he said, "why should I ask you for it? But you will look for it more thoroughly another time." When he had left her, he began to think how he might kill the lady and the captain with her in such a way that he might not be thought guilty of the killing. And because he was thinking night and day about this, the lady could not fail to notice that he was not the same towards her as he had been formerly, and she said to him frequently, "What is the matter? Why are you so upset? You, who used to be the merriest man in the world, are now the most melancholy alive." The Moor found various ways of answering her, but she was left no happier. And though she knew she had done nothing which should have caused the Moor such trouble of mind, nevertheless she feared that by their seeing too much of each other she had become a burden to him. And sometimes she would say to the wife of the ensign, "I don't know what to think of the Moor, he used to be always affectionate to me, but now for the last few days he has become another man,[1] and I greatly fear to become an example to children not to marry against the wishes of their parents. And what might the ladies of Italy learn from me, not to follow the man whom nature, Heaven, and the custom of life separates from us. But as I know that he is a good friend of your husband and confides his affairs to him, I beg you that if you have heard anything from him of which you could inform me, please do not fail to help me." And while she was saying all this, she was weeping excessively. The wife of the ensign who knew everything (for it was she whom her husband had wished to use as his tool in killing the lady, but she would never consent) dared not tell anything for fear of her husband. She only said, "Be careful not to give your husband any suspicions of you, and try earnestly to let him see your love and loyalty." "That I am doing," she said, "but nothing is any good!"

The Moor meanwhile was trying in every way to confirm in his mind what he did not want to find, and he asked the ensign to arrange that he might see the handkerchief in the possession of the captain. Though it was difficult for the villain, he nevertheless promised to make every effort to confirm it. Now the captain used to have a woman in his house, who did wonderful embroidery on linen cambric, who, seeing the handkerchief and learning that it belonged to the Moor's lady and was to be returned to her, set about making one like it before it was restored. While she was making it, the ensign noticed that she was standing by a window and could be seen by anyone who passed by in the street. He then drew the attention of the Moor to this, who was now firmly convinced that the honest lady was, in fact, an adulteress. He therefore planned with the ensign to kill her and the captain, and they discussed with each other how it should be done. The Moor asked if he would be the one to kill the captain, promising to be forever grateful to him for it. The other, not wishing to undertake a task at once so difficult and very dangerous, for the captain was alert as well as brave, after many entreaties and after being given a large sum of money, was induced to say that he would try his luck. When this resolve had been made, the captain was one evening leaving the house of a strumpet with whom he had been diverting himself, when the ensign, sword in hand, in the darkness of the night, came up to him and directed a blow at his legs to make him fall. By chance the blow cut him across the right thigh, whereat he fell and the ensign was upon him to finish the killing. But the captain, so courageous was he and accustomed to blood and death, drew his

1. Cf. "Nor should I know him, Were he in favour as in humour altered" (III. iv. 121).

sword, and wounded as he was, got up to defend himself, and cried out in a loud voice "I am assassinated!"

As a result of this, the ensign, hearing people and soldiers who were billeted near by running up, took flight so as not to be taken; then turning round, pretended that he too was running to the alarm. Then, mingling amongst the others, he saw the half-severed leg and judged that even if he were not dead, he would die in any case from that blow, and happy though that made him, he grieved aloud for the captain as if he had been a brother. By morning the affair had spread all over the town, and it also reached the ears of Disdemona who, being of a kind nature and not thinking that it could harm her, showed such great sorrow at the affair that the Moor put the worst construction on it. He went off to find the ensign and said to him, "You will know that my stupid wife is in such distress at the affair of the captain that she has almost lost her mind." "And how could you think differently," said the other, "he being her very soul?" "Her soul, eh?" replied the Moor, "I will draw her very soul from her body, call me no man if I do not wipe this wickedness from the world." And after discussing whether the lady should die by poison or the knife, they hit on a plan which involved neither method.

For the rest of Cinthio's story we may revert to summary, since the differences from Shakespeare's become much wider. The ensign devises a plan to secure Disdemona's death without suspicion falling on either himself or the Moor. They will beat her to death with a sand-filled stocking, and then pull down the already rotten timber of the ceiling upon her, so that she will seem to have been killed by a falling rafter. The plan is successfully carried out. But the Moor, distracted with grief for his dead wife, conceives a hatred for the ensign, and not daring to kill him, for fear of "the inviolable justice of the Signory of Venice", cashiers him. The ensign now plots the ruin of the Moor. He persuades the captain to return with him to Venice. Here he tells him that it was the Moor who had cut off his leg, in jealousy, and then murdered his wife. The captain, thus prompted, accuses the Moor to the Signory, and his charges are supported in detail by the ensign. The Moor is arrested, brought to Venice, and tortured to secure a confession. Failing to secure a confession, the Signory condemns him to perpetual banishment, and he is later killed by the kinsfolk of Disdemona. The ensign pursues his career of villainy with other victims, but in the end is arrested and dies under torture.

It will be noticed that in the central section, from the landing in Cyprus down to the plot of Desdemona's death, Shakespeare runs in many points pretty close to Cinthio. But there are very notice-able differences. In Cinthio:

1. Iago, so far, has no hatred for Othello. His sole motives are first lust, and then hatred, for Desdemona. It is *her* ruin, not her husband's, that he aims to compass.

2. It is not Emilia, but Iago himself, who secures the handker-chief, with the unconscious aid of his small daughter, not the con-scious aid of his wife.

3. Emilia is aware of Iago's design from the outset.

4. There is no equivalent to Roderigo.

On the other hand the circumstances of the cashiering of Cassio, Desdemona's pleas for him, the progress of Iago's 'temptation' and Othello's reactions to it, the use of the handkerchief, Desde-mona's bewilderment, her anxiety to enlist Iago's aid, and Emilia's advice to her, all these are so closely parallel that there can, I feel, be little doubt that Shakespeare was not only acquainted with the general drift of Cinthio's story, but had an intimate and detailed knowledge of it, in some form. His changes are almost all those of the practised dramatist, aiming to secure a tauter plot and a more rounded presentation of character.

PR
2829
A2
R5
1984

Shakespeare, William,
1564-1616.

Othello.

$8.95

PR
2829
A2
R5
1984

Shakespeare,
William, 1564-
1616.

Othello.

$8.95

0415 027012

DATE	BORROWER'S NAME	